Innovators

Innovators

DAVID W. GALENSON
University of Chicago
Universidad del CEMA

Oxford University Press is a department of the University of Oxford. It furthers
the University's objective of excellence in research, scholarship, and education
by publishing worldwide. Oxford is a registered trade mark of Oxford University
Press in the UK and certain other countries.

Published in the United States of America by Oxford University Press
198 Madison Avenue, New York, NY 10016, United States of America.

© Oxford University Press 2025

All rights reserved. No part of this publication may be reproduced, stored in
a retrieval system, or transmitted, in any form or by any means, without the
prior permission in writing of Oxford University Press, or as expressly permitted
by law, by license, or under terms agreed with the appropriate reproduction
rights organization. Inquiries concerning reproduction outside the scope of the
above should be sent to the Rights Department, Oxford University Press, at the
address above.

You must not circulate this work in any other form
and you must impose this same condition on any acquirer.

CIP data is on file at the Library of Congress

ISBN 978-0-19-774561-8

DOI: 10.1093/oso/9780197745618.001.0001

Printed by Sheridan Books, Inc., United States of America

Contents

Preface   vii

Introduction   1

1. Experimental and Conceptual Innovators   5
2. Painters   14
3. Poets   54
4. Sculptors   90
5. Novelists   115
6. Architects   146
7. Photographers   171
8. Filmmakers   193
9. Songwriters   220
10. Scientists and Entrepreneurs   254
11. Generality   287
12. Innovators Alone and Together   311

Notes   335
Index   377

Preface

More than two decades ago, I discovered that great painters' careers have varied enormously: some made their most important work late in their lives, but others produced their major contributions very early in theirs. Paul Cézanne, for example, made his greatest work at the very end of his life, at 67, whereas Pablo Picasso made his greatest contribution at just 26. These results were both surprising and puzzling. Why were there these two very different patterns? And how could a great artist be at his very best as early as 26?

Existing scholarship in economics did not offer an explanation. Economists have devoted a vast amount of attention to estimating workers' productivity over the life cycle, normally measured by the relationship between age and earnings. But this analysis has always been done at highly aggregated levels, averaging over large numbers of workers, and it has never focused on creative people. Nor have estimates of aggregate age–earnings profiles ever found peaks early in workers' careers.

The existing literature in psychology similarly did not provide an answer. Psychologists have systematically studied the life cycles of innovators, asking when in their lives they are most creative. But their quantitative analyses have consistently aggregated individuals by discipline, under the assumption that all innovators within a particular activity—painters or novelists or poets—share a common pattern of creativity over the life cycle. Their studies consequently could not help me understand why the life cycles of individual painters could differ so greatly.

I eventually studied the careers of several hundred modern painters, and I found that there were large numbers of both types—many had early peaks, many others had late peaks. When I extended my analysis to practitioners of other arts, I found similarly large differences in the life cycles of individual innovators within every discipline. It became clear to me that the most important puzzle about creative life cycles was why some great innovators reached their peaks so early and others so late. This became the central question underlying my research.

In studying the careers of major innovators in each of eight different arts, I used the judgments of large numbers of experts to create quantitative profiles of each artist's achievement over the life cycle. In each case, these profiles revealed when in their careers the artists had made their most important contributions. For each painter I made a distribution by age of the paintings by that artist reproduced in textbooks of art history; I also tabulated the numbers of each artist's paintings made at different ages that were included in museums' retrospective exhibitions. I similarly used tabulations of illustrations from collections of appropriate textbooks to measure the careers of sculptors, architects, and photographers. For poets, I tabulated the ages at which they wrote the poems selected for anthologies. I measured the relative amount of space devoted to each of a novelist's books in critical biographies of the writers. I used critics' rankings of films and popular songs to analyze the careers of filmmakers and songwriters, respectively. And for every practitioner I considered in each of these eight arts, I complemented these quantitative measures with qualitative study. I read biographies of artists and critical analyses of their works. Whenever possible, I read what the artists themselves wrote about their work, and about art in general. Finally, while I was measuring artists' careers and reading about them, I studied their work directly—looking at paintings, sculptures, buildings, photographs, and movies, reading poems and novels, and listening to songs.

This course of study was an unusual one for an economist. Yet for me it amounted to a systematic education in artistic creativity, and it allowed me to gain an almost unprecedented perspective on innovation in the modern arts. And in the process, I discovered that my new understanding of the sources of creativity was not unique to the arts, but was general to virtually all intellectual activities. I discovered there are strong and systematic patterns that connect the motivations and methods of individual innovators to both the nature of their achievements and the timing of their life cycles of creativity.

I also discovered that there are two very different kinds of rewards that result from studying innovators systematically with these patterns in mind. One of the gains is that of generalization: recognizing the patterns that emerge from the evidence of the many individual innovators yields a new systematic understanding of the nature of creativity, and the strength of the patterns increases with the number of individuals studied. This is the gain I have deliberately pursued, by consistently enlarging my study to determine the generality of the patterns I found—initially by increasing the number of painters I examined, then expanding the study to poets, novelists, filmmakers, and practitioners of other arts, and finally extending my study beyond the arts.

The other gain was even more surprising to me: this was at the level of the individual innovator. As I proceeded, studying artists whose work I hadn't known well, or at all, often in disciplines I hadn't previously studied, I found instances in which I could explain significant practices of many artists that had not been understood even by experts. In some cases, specific practices of great artists that had previously been regarded as anomalous, or idiosyncratic, or irrelevant to their major achievements, could now be seen as instances of patterns that were shared by other artists. In other cases, separate aspects of an artist's work that had previously been considered to be unrelated could now be seen to have been connected, as joint manifestations of a single underlying creative impulse. The general lesson I took from this is that the patterns I had identified were so basic to creativity that they were associated with many different facets of the processes and products of individual innovators.

This book has been designed to impart both of these categories of benefits. The intent is for readers to gain a new systematic understanding of creativity in intellectual disciplines in general, as well as a greater appreciation of the specific achievements of many of the greatest innovators of the modern era. I have previously published two monographs on creativity. This book is based on more than a decade of additional research, and goes beyond my earlier books in several respects.

Much of the time I have spent researching this book has been devoted to broadening the scope of my analysis, by extending it to innovators in a wider range of disciplines. This book not only considers innovators in a large number of arts, but also scientists and entrepreneurs. Innovators in different activities obviously face different challenges, and extending the analysis to new disciplines required me to gain an understanding of the nature of these problems in each case. In some instances I have been able to take advantage of the work of critics and scholars who have adopted my analysis and have applied it to their own areas of expertise, and in some cases even to their own creativity.

This book also presents a deeper analysis of some innovators I have studied in the past. The abundant secondary literature about many of these important innovators has allowed me to gain greater insight into their contributions, and how those have affected the development of their disciplines.

In more than two decades of studying creativity, I have benefited from discussions with many people, and I have acknowledged many of these elsewhere. Here I will mention only a few debts of the longest standing. Among colleagues, Clayne Pope and the late Gary Becker and Robert Lucas provided encouragement for this unorthodox project. Four editors—Kimberly Brooks, Morgan Kousser, Federico Etro, and Olli Raade—consistently supported my work. Carlos Rodriguez established the Center for Creativity Economics at Universidad del CEMA, which gave me the opportunity to learn from important Argentine artists including Luis Felipe Noe and the late Nicolas Garcia Uriburu and Gyula Kosice.

Earlier versions of some material in this book appeared in *Historical Methods*, *Journal of Applied Economics*, *Research in Economics*, the third edition of the *Encyclopedia of Creativity*, and *Journal of Cultural Economics*.

And I am grateful to Dolly Shishodia for her careful preparation of the final manuscript.

Introduction

Many people have considered the question of when in their lives innovators are most creative. Some have done this in reflecting on their own careers. So for example at the age of 60, Bob Dylan told *Rolling Stone*—a magazine whose name honored a song he had recorded more than three decades earlier—that "When you're young, you're probably writing stronger and a lot quicker."[1] Steve Jobs, who revered Dylan, agreed that aging was harmful to creativity, telling *Playboy* that he regretted turning 30 because "It's rare that you see an artist in his 30s or 40s able to really contribute something amazing."[2]

Academic psychologists have taken a broader approach, seeking to understand creative life cycles in general. They have typically done this by analyzing one discipline at a time. So for example Howard Gardner concluded that "lyric poetry is a domain where talent is discovered early, burns brightly, and then peters out an early age."[3] Others have agreed. Mihaly Csikszentmihalyi wrote that "The most creative lyric verse is believed to be that written by the young," and James Kaufman told the *New York Times* that "Poets peak young."[4]

This view of poets' creativity has not been unanimous, however. In 1944, the poet T. S. Eliot—like Dylan, a Nobel laureate in literature—offered a different opinion, in comparing two great sixteenth-century poets:

> We can also observe . . . that the plays of Christopher Marlowe exhibit a greater maturity of mind and of style, than the plays which Shakespeare wrote at the same age: it is interesting to speculate whether, if Marlowe had lived as long as Shakespeare, his development would have continued at the same pace. I doubt it: for we observe some minds maturing earlier than others, and we observe that those which mature very early do not always develop very far.[5]

Another eminent writer later agreed with Eliot, as Joyce Carol Oates remarked that "[Sylvia] Plath's meticulously documented example suggests how precocity is not maturity, and may in fact impede maturity."[6]

2   INNOVATORS

My research has produced a new understanding of creative life cycles, which provides support for the opinions of Eliot and Oates, and rejects those of the psychologists. My analysis also confirms that Dylan and Jobs were correct in the belief that aging was detrimental to their creativity. This book will demonstrate the value of my analysis in understanding the careers of important innovators in a wide range of activities.

Economics and Creativity

Economists have not traditionally studied the careers of individual innovators. I believe this neglect has been a mistake. There has long been widespread agreement that understanding the sources of economic growth is one of the basic problems for the discipline, but economists have ignored a key element of what their own analyses have identified as the most important source of growth. At a major conference in 2012 devoted to the economics of technological change, Richard Nelson declared that "There is no informed arguing now against the proposition that technological advance is the principal source of long-run productivity growth."[7] The editors of the resulting volume, however, noted that "despite the critical nature of innovation, much remains unclear as to how nations, firms, and academic bodies can encourage this activity."[8]

Encouraging an activity generally requires an understanding of how it occurs. And interestingly, in 1962—at the earlier conference "seen by many as having ushered in the modern era of study of the economics of technological change"—the same Richard Nelson complained that economists had treated inventive ability as a "black box."[9] At that 1962 conference, however, two luminaries specifically suggested how to go beyond the black-box approach. Concerning the source of technological change, Kenneth Arrow observed that "There is really no need for the firm to be the fundamental unit of organization in invention; there is plenty of reason to suppose that individual talents count for a good deal more than the firm as an organization."[10] And for this reason, Simon Kuznets called for more study of creative individuals, declaring that "We need far more empirical study than we have had so far of the universe of inventors; any finding concerning inventors, identified in either uniform or diverse fashion, would be of great value."[11]

Although more than six decades have passed since Arrow's observation and Kuznets' appeal, economists have failed to respond to them. Instead, the study of individuals effectively remains a disciplinary taboo. This failure has prevented economists from achieving a systematic understanding of the sources of the contributions of the most productive people in our society. This is now changing. The research presented in this book may improve our understanding of the creativity of these exceptional individuals, and in so doing may help us to increase their creativity, and that of others.

Innovation and Importance

Economists draw a key distinction between *invention* and *innovation*: an invention is any new product or process, but it becomes an innovation only by virtue of diffusion. The importance of an innovation depends directly on the extent of its diffusion. Innovators are consequently those individuals who produce major changes in their industries.

These terms apply to scholarship as well as to commodities. In an academic discipline, innovations are new practices that change the work of other scholars—by changing their methods, their subjects of study, or both. Important innovations change whole fields, or even disciplines. Great scholars are necessarily innovators, who change their disciplines.

And these same terms apply equally to the arts. Artists have enjoyed great freedom in the modern era, and their innovations have taken many forms. But what has remained true is that important artists are innovators whose work changes the practices of other artists. Important works of art are those that embody their innovations.

It must immediately be emphasized that this importance is not the short-run popularity that gives an artist immediate critical or commercial success, but the long-run impact that places the artist's work in major museums and makes it the subject of study by scholars. There is a widespread belief that artistic success can be fabricated by persuasive critics, entrepreneurial dealers, or wealthy patrons. In the short run, prominent critics, dealers, and collectors can clearly gain an artist considerable fame and fortune. But unless this attention leads to influence on other artists, it cannot gain that artist an important place in art history.

The definition of importance given here for scholars and artists would not surprise either group of practitioners, for influence is the dominant criterion used within intellectual disciplines to gauge importance. A detailed statement to this effect was provided in a lecture given in 1989 by Sir Alan

Bowness, the former director of the Tate Gallery, on the subject of artistic success, subtitled, "How the Modern Artist Rises to Fame." Bowness' theme was that artistic success is not arbitrary or due to chance, but is the result of a systematic process. Among large numbers of journeymen, a few masters emerge: "the museum collection aspires to show a chronological sequence of the work of such artists, carrying forward an argument which forms the material of any history of modern art." These masters all pass through four successive stages on their path to fame: "peer recognition, critical recognition, patronage by dealers and collectors, and finally, public acclaim." The crucial stage is the first: "it is always the artists themselves who are first to recognize exceptional talent." Once artists give a peer their respect, the other stages follow: "Artistic fame is predictable."[12]

Nor is Bowness' analysis applicable only to recent times. More than a century ago, the English painter Walter Sickert, in his capacity as a critic, gave a concise definition of artistic importance. Thus in 1910, he told a skeptical English art world that it could no longer deny the importance of the French Impressionists, explaining that they had "added two things to the language of painting," by enlarging the possibilities of both composition and color. The test of importance was straightforward: "Perhaps the importance that we must attach to the achievement of an artist may properly be measured by the answer to the following question: Have they so wrought that it will be impossible henceforth, for those who follow, ever again to act as if they had not existed?" The Impressionists met this test: "To this there can be but one answer. They have changed the language of painting."[13]

Important innovators are those who change the languages of their disciplines. This book analyzes the processes by which great innovators have done this in a wide range of activities.

1
Experimental and Conceptual Innovators

There are two very different types of creativity, each produced by a different kind of innovator. The two kinds of innovators are not distinguished by their importance; both appear prominently among the greatest practitioners of nearly every intellectual activity in the modern era. They differ instead in the methods by which they arrive at their contributions, and in the purposes of those contributions. In each case their method is the result of a particular conception of their goals, and is associated with specific practices in creating their work. The names I have used for the two types of innovators are *experimental* and *conceptual*.

Across all the arts, experimental innovators are concerned above all with perception. Their art is often dedicated to the observation and description of reality. They are art's empiricists, proceeding inductively to develop new methods of expression based on extended observation and experimentation. They are *seekers*, more concerned with process than with products; they hope to make discoveries in the course of working, so that the final form and meaning of their work are revealed to them in the act of making the work. Their ambitious but vague goals leave them perennially dissatisfied with their work, but uncertain about how to improve it. Their dissatisfaction impels them to change, and their uncertainty leads them to do this tentatively and incrementally, by trial and error. Individual works emerge from an open-ended process of countless changes and revisions. Experimental innovations consequently emerge gradually, over an extended period; these are rarely announced in a single work, but appear piecemeal in a body of related works. No matter how great their achievement, experimental innovators rarely consider any of their works a complete success, and consequently they rarely consider their quest complete.

In contrast, conceptual innovators want their work to express ideas or emotions. Their innovations are based on theories, derived deductively from general principles; their works often employ symbols that refer to larger concepts or morals. Conceptual artists determine the purpose of a work before they begin executing it, so they typically plan their works carefully before executing them systematically. They often create connections between earlier ideas that were previously considered to be unrelated. They consider themselves *finders*, because they are more concerned with the meaning of their final products than with the processes or techniques of their production. The clarity of their intent can allow them to feel that they have fully realized their objectives for a particular work. Conceptual innovations typically appear suddenly, as a new idea can yield a novel work of art that fully expresses the idea.

Each art has its own materials and methods, so these general characteristics necessarily manifest themselves somewhat differently in the practice of each art. Yet in most instances the difference between the two models is straightforward. So for example experimental painters are motivated by aesthetic criteria: their goal is to present visual perceptions. Their paintings are in fact often intended to be records of the specific act of perception that produced them. Experimental painters repeat themselves, painting the same subject many times, gradually changing its treatment by a process of trial and error. Each painting follows directly from those that came before, so experimental painters rarely make preparatory sketches or plans for a painting. They carefully examine their paintings in progress, considering how best to continue to work on them, hoping to discover the appearance of a new form or image. They have trouble deciding when a painting is finished, and they often abandon paintings without considering them complete; they are not necessarily troubled by this, for they typically consider that what they learn while working is more important than making finished works. In fact, they often say that they are more interested in developing a method for making paintings than in actually producing paintings.

Conceptual painters want to communicate specific messages, so their goals for a particular canvas can be stated precisely before its production. They therefore make detailed preparatory sketches or other plans for their paintings. Their execution of their work is often systematic, for all major decisions are made before they begin to paint. They consequently often consider the actual execution of a painting to be perfunctory and of little interest, and some conceptual painters in fact have their paintings executed by assistants, since this is effectively merely a reproduction of an image they have already created. Conceptual innovations appear suddenly, as a new idea produces a new result, so conceptual painters often make individual works that they consider definitive embodiments of an innovation. They then feel free to go on to other, often quite different subjects.

In all the arts, the innovations of experimental and conceptual artists bear contrasting relationships to earlier art. Conceptual artists often effectively make their innovations directly from other art, by creating unexpected syntheses of earlier styles or existing works within their discipline, or even drawing on works from other disciplines. These innovations are often intentionally shocking or transgressive, and paradoxically they frequently violate basic conventions of the art from which they are constructed. In contrast, experimental artists typically study and assimilate the practices of earlier artists, then use them as a point of departure for their own experiments, often subsequently spending extended periods gradually modifying or extending these inherited practices. Their own innovations eventually emerge as mixtures of earlier art and their own independent discoveries.

In all the arts, the basis of experimental art in perception is directly related to the persistent uncertainty of experimental innovators. Observation is inherently uncertain and incomplete. This uncertainty of observation is compounded by uncertainty about how to translate an observation into the artist's chosen medium. Together, these typically cause experimental artists to begin works with imprecise intentions and to make frequent changes in the work during its execution, as they proceed by trial and error. In contrast, the basis of conceptual art in ideation accounts for the confidence and certainty of conceptual innovators. Conceptual artists may begin with observation of external phenomena, but they do not execute their art directly from this observation. Instead, they abstract from reality to create a model that embodies the concept of their intended work. Whatever the form of the model—drawing, outline, diagram, blueprint, maquette—its function is to serve as a plan. This plan then becomes the basis for the final work. The model fully represents the artist's conceptualization of the subject in question, so the execution of the final work is simply a translation of the concept from one medium or place to another. Unlike external phenomena, models can be known with certainty: the artist can know his own idea definitely and completely. The difference between the experimental and conceptual artist is effectively that between induction and deduction: the experimental artist innovates by generalizing from experience and observation, while the conceptual artist innovates deductively, by expressing his own idea or emotion. Inductive results are always provisional, and subject to revision, whereas deductive results can be known conclusively, with certainty.

An important point to recognize is that, as is frequently the case in the social sciences and humanities, categorizing individuals involves judgment.

There is no single characteristic that will necessarily be present to identify an innovator as experimental or conceptual, but rather a group of variables involving goals and methods that when considered together will rarely leave this categorization in doubt. The necessary judgment must also take into account that no innovator is necessarily experimental or conceptual throughout an entire career. Many painters, for example, are trained in one approach as students, then reject it in favor of the other in the course of finding their own independent artistic voice. Yet this does not undermine the validity or usefulness of this approach, for the analysis presented here is a theory of innovation. The key question in categorizing individual innovators involves their major contributions: in each case, what is the nature of the innovation, and how was it produced? That the innovator did not begin his career with the relevant approach, or that he changed his approach sometime after producing his innovative work, is of little or no significance to an understanding of creativity. What matters is how an innovation was made—experimentally, by trial and error, or conceptually, as the result of a new idea.

Career Patterns

The careers of experimental and conceptual innovators differ in a number of ways. There are distinct patterns of work over time associated with each, that result from the differences in their attitudes and processes of discovery.

Experimental artists build their skills gradually over the course of their careers, learning and improving their work over long periods. Because they innovate incrementally, the arrival of their major contributions is usually divided among a number of works on a particular theme or subject, no one of which dominates the others. Contrary to the common notion in which the earliest statement of an innovation is the most important, the later works in these sequences are generally the greatest, because they present the richest and most complete statements of the experimentalist's innovation. It is natural for experimentalists to produce series of related works, as they develop and work out solutions to a problem. These series are open-ended, as the artist explores the problem, but rarely feels he has reached a definitive resolution; the series may be continuous over time, as the artist concentrates exclusively on that problem, or they may be interspersed with other works, as the artist returns to an unresolved problem at intervals. Instead of a single landmark work that declares an innovation, a number of different works may each display small component insights that eventually cumulate into a larger whole. Although the change from any individual work to the next may be almost imperceptible, the cumulative effect of these small changes can be great, and comparison of works done early and late in an important experimental innovator's career generally shows radical differences.

In contrast, conceptual innovations do not depend on the gradual development of skills, but on the formulation of new ideas. Because new ideas can be produced suddenly, conceptual innovators typically arrive precipitously at their discoveries. Their careers are often dominated by a single work, that announces and fully states their innovation. This innovative work differs not only from that of other artists, but from the artist's own previous work. Having achieved a breakthrough that definitively solves a particular problem may then allow the artist to go on to work on a very different problem, unrelated to the first. Many conceptual innovators, however, effectively become captives of their own innovation, and repeat it in their later work without making any significant subsequent development.

One difference in career patterns is thus that whereas experimentalists normally produce a continuous series of closely related works that treat a single motif or subject as the artist works progressively toward a single distant goal, the careers of conceptual innovators are often marked by discontinuities, as the artist works on different challenges. Another difference in the profile over time of the work of the two types of innovators is a product of differing attitudes toward style. In the modern era, these attitudes have diverged sharply, as style has come to play very different roles in experimental and conceptual art. For experimental artists, style involves commitment. Many great experimental artists have considered their careers as lifelong quests with a goal of creating a distinct and unique style that will allow them to present their perceptions truly and fully. These artists do not believe in rapid change or sudden discoveries: they believe improvements can only occur slowly, through deliberate and painstaking efforts. To them, style is not merely an identifying trademark, it is a manifestation of the artist's sincerity and integrity.

In contrast, many modern conceptual innovators have come to regard style as simply a convenient means of expression, that they are free to adopt or discard as the situation at hand dictates. These artists in fact often regard stylistic versatility as a form of creativity. Thus in general, stylistic consistency is an imperative for experimental artists, whereas inconsistency of style is a positive value for many conceptual artists. This difference in attitude produces another difference in the career patterns of the two types of innovator, which reinforces that noted above, for the continuity in the form of the work of an experimental artist whose style evolves gradually over time contrasts with the discontinuity in the work of a conceptual artist whose style may change suddenly and frequently over time. Whatever the specific practice in question, the careers of important conceptual innovators often contain revolutions, whereas the term most often used to describe the careers of great experimental innovators is evolution.

An interesting consequence of the differing practices of the two types of innovator is that in many arts the greatest individual landmarks tend to be the products of conceptual innovators. Great experimental artists often produce a series of important works, no one of which clearly rises above the others as a demonstration of the artist's innovation. In contrast, great conceptual artists often produce individual breakthrough works that clearly embody an important innovation. In surveys of an art's greatest individual works, the most conspicuous individual contributions are disproportionately those that announce the arrival of great conceptual innovations.

Age and Innovation

Experimental and conceptual innovators have very different life cycles of creativity. The art of experimental artists develops over time. Their innovations typically depend on extended, gradual improvement in both their knowledge and understanding of their subject and their technical mastery of their craft. Their major contributions consequently emerge after long periods of study and experimentation, normally late in their careers.

Conceptual innovation does not depend on extended development, but on the formulation of new ideas. These are made quickly, and can occur at any age. Yet the most radical, and therefore generally the most important, conceptual innovations depend on the ability to perceive and appreciate extreme departures from existing practices—the ability to see old problems in new ways—and this tends to diminish with experience, as an artist's habits of thought become more firmly entrenched. Radical conceptual innovations frequently depend on extreme simplification, with severe abstraction from reality, and the ability to do this also declines with age, as the artist becomes increasingly aware of the complexity both of his chosen subject and of the techniques of his own discipline. The most important conceptual innovations therefore typically occur early in an artist's career, when he is least constrained by habits of thought and by awareness of the complexity of his discipline.

Age thus affects experimental and conceptual innovators very differently. Great experimental innovators spend their lives studying the subtleties of their subjects and mastering the techniques of their art. The substance and technique of their late work reflect their mastery of their craft and the lessons they have learned from their long years of research. In contrast, great conceptual innovators are brash young geniuses who see the world simply and clearly, and can consequently violate the existing rules of their disciplines with impunity. Aging inevitably brings greater knowledge, making it more difficult for them to simplify complex problems, and creating habits of thought that they are often unable to break. Whereas age adds to the power of experimental innovators by increasing the depth of both their work and their means of expression, it robs conceptual innovators of the clarity and simplicity that give their early work its force and generality, and in the process often undermines the early boundless confidence in their own abilities that plays a key role in their ambitious goals.

A qualification to this discussion concerns the role of age. What is strictly relevant to the timing of innovation is not an individual's chronological age, but rather the duration of the individual's experience within a particular field. Changes over time in the ability to innovate are not a biological function of aging, but are cognitive consequences of the time an individual has devoted to specific problems. The enemy of radical conceptual innovation is not merely the passage of time, but ingrained habits of thought that arise with the accumulation of effort devoted to thinking about a problem. These typically produce a tendency to become tied to a single way of treating that problem, making it progressively more difficult to imagine very different alternative approaches.

For experimentalists, increasing experience within a discipline generally results in both greater knowledge and improvements in the ability to use that knowledge. More evidence allows better generalizations, and growing technical skills help to formulate and apply these generalizations. These skills may include the judgment that allows the innovator to recognize which experiments are successes and which failures, and the wisdom to see what the innovator needs to learn to make further progress.

For most innovators, age and experience in a discipline are highly correlated, so most conceptual innovators are young geniuses, and most experimental innovators are old masters. Yet exceptional cases can occur, most commonly when a conceptual innovator enters a new discipline at an advanced age. In such cases, a radical innovation that occurs soon after this late entry is fully consistent with the analysis presented here, even though the innovator is not young.

Innovators

This book analyzes the careers of more than fifty innovators, in more than a dozen disciplines. All were among the most important practitioners of their respective disciplines. It is useful here to explain how and why these particular innovators were selected.

Nearly all are deceased. One reason for this is that it allows consideration of their entire life cycles of creativity. It also allows more comprehensive assessment of their importance, and the significance of their contributions. As discussed in the Introduction, importance in a discipline is a function of influence. Although the speed with which innovations diffuse depends on many factors, influence is necessarily manifested over time. Studying innovators of the past allows for the time necessary for others in their disciplines to perceive and react to novel practices, and adapt these to their own purposes. It also allows time for critics and scholars to recognize these influences, and place them in perspective.

Selection of the innovators considered here was in nearly every case based on systematic quantitative evidence. Whether counts of illustrations of paintings in textbooks of art history, of poems reprinted in anthologies, of rankings of films by critics, or comparable measures for other disciplines, these quantitative measures allow us to draw on the judgments of large numbers of experts on each discipline as to the most important practitioners, and their most important works. This has been recognized by scholars. So for example the art historian Robert Jensen explained that "the most convenient way to determine what is currently canonical in the visual arts is by consulting a textbook illustration survey."[1] Similarly, the literary scholar Helen Vendler supported her judgment that "The Colossus" was Sylvia Plath's first mature poem by pointing out that it "is still the earliest poem that most anthologists of Plath include."[2] And the poet James Dickey remarked that not only critics, but also poets, pay attention to anthologies, because they are "perhaps the most important harbinger of lastingness that a writer's work may know during his lifetime," so that "poets look for their names and their best or most typical poems."[3] The first footnote in each chapter of this book will cite the studies that provided the basis for selecting the innovators treated in that chapter.

There are several elements included in all these analyses. One is the categorization of the innovator as experimental or conceptual, based on examination of their attitudes toward their disciplines, their goals for their work, the processes they used in reaching their innovations, and the nature of their contributions. Another is explicit consideration of their life cycles of creativity. The key issues here are when they did their greatest work, and why it was their most important: what was the innovation, and how did it influence others in their discipline? For each innovator, there is also a discussion of why the life cycle followed the path it did. This requires consideration of how and why their work changed over time.

The profiles of the individuals treated here are in effect biographies, not of their lives, but of their creativity—how their creativity developed over the course of their lives, why it took the form it did, and what its impact was. I believe that these profiles offer new insights into the careers of many great individual innovators, while at the same time they demonstrate the powerful patterns that underlie the two basic life cycles of creativity.

2
Painters

In 1933, the distinguished art critic Roger Fry was elected Slade Professor of Fine Art at Cambridge University. In his inaugural lecture, he called for a new approach to the study of art history, declaring that "we have such a crying need for systematic study in which scientific methods will be followed wherever possible, where at all events the scientific attitude may be fostered and the sentimental attitude discouraged." In outlining the form such an approach might take, he observed that "The mere length of time that an artist has lived has then inevitably an influence on the work of art," and offered the following analysis:

> When we look at the late works of Titian or Rembrandt we cannot help feeling the pressure of a massive and rich experience which leaks out, as it were, through the ostensible image presented to us, whatever it may be. There are artists, and perhaps Titian and Rembrandt are good examples, who seem to require a very long period of activity before this unconscious element finds its way completely through into the work of art. In other cases, particularly in artists whose gift lies in a lyrical direction, the exaltation and passion of youth transmits itself directly into everything they touch, and then sometimes, when this flame dies down, their work becomes relatively cold and uninspired.

Fry immediately followed this observation by conceding that "I fear a great deal of this must appear to you to be rather wildly speculative and hazardous."[1] The bold hypotheses of an inaugural lecture might be expected to have become the focus of the new professor's research agenda in the following years. Unfortunately, however, Fry was elected to the Slade professorship at the end of his career rather than the beginning, and his death the following year prevented any effort to document his generalization. Nor did any later art historian take up the challenge of pursuing Fry's analysis of the life cycles of artists' creativity. Now, however, Fry's remarkable insight appears to have anticipated the division of painters into the experimental innovators who develop slowly and the conceptual innovators who make dramatic early contributions.[2]

Some key differences between the two types of artists have been noticed by scholars. In 1972, for example, the art historian Sir Alan Bowness remarked that artists could be divided into realists and idealists (or symbolists), then reflected that "this general tendency for art to divide may depend on certain basic temperamental differences among artists—on, for example, the degree to which the painter or sculptor can envisage the finished work of art before he starts to make it." Bowness then wondered, "Does creation reside in the idea or in the action?"[3] Bowness did not pursue this issue, but it is now apparent that the answer to his question is conditional: creation lies in the idea for conceptualists, who plan their work before making it, but in the action for experimentalists, who find forms in the process of making their work.

Paul Cézanne (1839–1906)

> I seek in painting.
>
> Paul Cézanne[4]

Paul Cézanne was the greatest painter in the early history of modern art. So for example textbooks of art history contain more illustrations of his work than of any other painter who worked during the second half of the nineteenth century.[5] In September 1906, just a month before his death, the 67-year-old Cézanne wrote to a younger friend, the painter Emile Bernard:

> Now it seems to me that I see better and that I think more correctly about the direction of my studies. Will I ever attain the end for which I have striven so much and so long? I hope so, but as long as it is not attained a vague state of uneasiness persists which will not disappear until I have reached port, that is until I have realized something which develops better than in the past, and can thereby prove the theories—which in themselves are always easy; it is only giving proof of what one thinks that raises serious obstacles. So I continue to study.
>
> But I have just re-read your letter and I see that I always answer off the mark. Be good enough to forgive me; it is, as I told you, this constant preoccupation with the aim I want to reach, which is the cause of it.

> I am always studying after nature and it seems to me that I make slow progress. I should have liked you near me, for solitude always weighs me down a bit. But I am old, ill, and I have sworn to myself to die painting....
>
> If I have the pleasure of being with you one day, we shall be better able to discuss all this in person. You must forgive me for continually coming back to the same thing; but I believe in the logical development of everything we see and feel through the study of nature and turn my attention to technical questions later; for technical questions are for us only the simple means of making the public feel what we feel ourselves and of making ourselves understood. The great masters whom we admire must have done just that.[6]

This letter expresses nearly all the characteristics of the experimental innovator: the visual objectives, the conception of his activity as research, the need for accumulation of knowledge, with the conviction that technique must emerge from the study of nature, the distrust of theory, the incremental character and slow pace of his progress, the total absorption in the pursuit of a vague and elusive goal, the frustration with his perceived inability to attain that distant goal of "realization," and the fear that he would not live long enough to reach it. The irony of Cézanne's frustration and fears at the end of his life stems from the fact that it was his most recent work that would come to be considered his greatest, and would directly influence every important artistic development of the next generation.

At the age of 22, in 1861, Cézanne had left his native Aix-en-Provence for Paris, in the hope of becoming a successful painter. This hope was disappointed, however, as he failed the entrance exam for the prestigious Ecole des Beaux-Arts, and had a series of submissions rejected by the jury of the official Salon, the annual exhibition that effectively determined which artists would be able to pursue successful professional careers. Throughout his 20s, Cézanne painted using a traditional academic approach, by making preparatory drawings and oil sketches before executing his paintings. His paintings were often of violent and dramatic subjects, drawn from mythology and history, which he portrayed with heavy, thick brushstrokes in dark colors. In the course of his informal studies in Paris, however, he had met Claude Monet, Camille Pissarro, and several other young artists who were pioneering a radical new approach to art. In 1872, at the age of 33, Cézanne moved to Pontoise, near Paris, to join one of these artists, Camille Pissarro, and he lived there and in nearby Auvers for much of the next two years. This became the turning point in Cézanne's career, and life.

In Pontoise, in the words of Roger Fry, "Cézanne became in effect apprentice to Pissarro."[7] Pissarro was fiercely independent and anti-authoritarian, and his rebellious commitment to Impressionist techniques as a challenge to traditional skills, and the study of nature as an alternative to the academic canon of subjects, appealed strongly to Cézanne, who saw himself as a provincial outsider in Paris' rigidly hierarchical art world. Years later, Cézanne recalled that Pissarro "was like a father to me. You could always ask him questions; he was something like the good God"; in an exhibition catalogue in Aix in 1902 he identified himself as "pupil of Pissarro."[8] He explained that it was only when he studied with Pissarro, "who was indefatigable, that I got a taste for work." This lesson became the basis for Cézanne's storied absorption in his quest for a new art, and his conviction that work was "the only refuge where one can be at peace with oneself."[9]

Under Pissarro's guidance Cézanne's art was transformed, as he adopted several of the key innovations of the Impressionists, including the small brushstrokes, the bright colors, and the use of changes of color instead of shading to achieve the appearance of depth. Cézanne became wholeheartedly committed to the subject matter of Impressionism, as the goal of painting nature would dominate his art for the rest of his life: thus three decades after his return to Aix, he continued to insist that "The real and immense study to be undertaken is the manifold picture of nature."[10] He also adopted the Impressionist practice of painting directly, and he would never again make preparatory drawings for his paintings. Cézanne did not become a genuine Impressionist, however, for he was not temperamentally suited to their primary goal of capturing the fleeting and momentary effects of light and atmosphere, and allowing those effects to dissolve the three-dimensionality of the scene. He was more deliberate and reflective than Pissarro and Monet, and he was more concerned than they with finding the solid structure of objects under their surface colors: Fry explained that Cézanne "saw always, however dimly, behind this veil an architecture and a logic which appealed to his most intimate feelings. Reality, no doubt, lay always behind this veil of color."[11] When he left Pissarro's company to return to Provence, Cézanne set out on a quest to use the colors of Impressionism to create an art as timeless and substantial as that of the Old Masters—in his words, "to make of Impressionism something solid and enduring like the art in museums."[12]

This quest occupied Cézanne's final three decades, much of which he spent isolated in Aix, away from his fellow artists. He considered this a time of intense research, as he explained that he "had resolved to work in silence until the day when I should feel myself able to defend theoretically the result of my attempts."[13] In 1903, he wrote to his friend and dealer, Ambroise Vollard:

> I am working doggedly, for I see the promised land before me. Shall I be like the great Hebrew leader or shall I be able to enter?...
>
> I have made some progress. Why so late and with such difficulty? Is art really a priesthood that demands the pure in heart who must belong to it entirely?[14]

Cézanne's seclusion from Paris' art world made him a mysterious figure; in the early 1890s one critic observed that "he might be described as a person at once unknown and famous."[15] Rumors and legends grew up about his artistic quest, and a few young painters made pilgrimages to Aix to meet him. Emile Bernard, who spent a month in Aix with Cézanne in 1904, reported that "His painting progressed very slowly and involved long contemplation," and concluded that "his method of study was a meditation with a brush in his hand." Bernard recalled that Cézanne had agonized over a single still life during the entire month Bernard had spent with him: "The colors and shapes in this painting changed almost every day, and each day when I arrived at his studio, it could have been taken from the easel and considered a finished work of art."[16] The deliberateness of Cézanne's approach could even necessitate a change in a painting's subject. Referring to a snow scene of Auvers that Cézanne painted in the early 1870s, the artist's friend Dr. Paul Gachet recalled that "he came to the motif twice a day, in the morning and in the evening, in gray weather and in clear; it so happened that he often slaved away at a painting from one season to another, from one year to another, so that in the end the spring of 1873 became the effect of snow, 1874."[17]

Cézanne repeatedly returned to a few favorite motifs. Prominent among these was the most dramatic feature of the landscape of his beloved Provence, Mont Sainte-Victorie, which he painted in oils and watercolors a total of more than eighty times over more than three decades. The diversity of these views prevents any single image from serving as a summary representation of his achievement, but it is telling that it is one of the latest, the 1904 canvas in the Philadelphia Museum of Art, that is reproduced most frequently in textbooks, for its illustration of the richness of his mature style.

Cézanne himself often referred to his enterprise in terms of learning, as for example he wrote in 1904 that "painters must devote themselves entirely to the study of nature and try to produce pictures which will be an education."[18] There is considerable evidence, in fact, that in his later years Cézanne came to conceive of art not as a *product* but as a *process*; finished paintings were not his objective, for his paintings were merely a means to the real goal of learning. He may have rarely considered his works finished. Vollard commented that "When Cézanne laid a canvas aside, it was almost always with the intention of taking it up again, in the hope of bringing it to the point of perfection."[19] Roger Fry noted that Cézanne's mature works show "evidence of incessant revision and continual repainting" in their surfaces "heavily loaded with pigment."[20] Painters traditionally indicated that paintings were finished by signing them, but Cézanne signed only 7 percent of all his canvases, and none at all after 1893.[21] Although Cézanne often referred to his goal of "realization," he appears to have recognized that it was not attainable, as for example in a letter of 1904 he confessed that "I progress very slowly, for nature reveals herself to me in very complex ways; and the progress needed is endless."[22] Less than a month before his death, Cézanne wrote poignantly to his son that "I am so slow in expressing myself that it makes me very sad."[23] Fry's study of Cézanne led him to conclude that "For him the synthesis was an asymptote toward which he was forever approaching without ever quite reaching it; it was a reality, incapable of complete realization."[24]

In fact, however, Cézanne seems to have come to recognize that realization was *not* an asymptote—it was not a fixed point he could approach, but rather a moving target that receded from him faster than he could progress toward it. Paradoxically, he understood that his task became more difficult as he became more skillful. Thus a month before his death he wrote to his son that "I am becoming more clear-sighted before nature," then continued, "but ... the realization of my sensations is always painful. I cannot attain the intensity that is unfolded before my senses. I have not the magnificent richness of coloring that animates nature."[25] As he grew older, his constant application made his vision more acute, allowing him to distinguish ever smaller gradations of color and form in nature; he wrote to Bernard in 1904 that he was "quite positive: an optical sensation is produced in our visual organs which allows us to classify the planes represented by color sensations as light, half tone or quarter tone."[26] But his increased sensitivity made it ever more difficult to create the precise colors on his palette, and to make the necessary marks with his brush, that would accurately render his perception of the object he was portraying.

Yet as Cézanne acknowledged, he did make progress, even if painstakingly and slowly. A survey of art history textbooks reveals that more than 80 percent of all the illustrations of his work are of paintings he executed after the age of 40, and more than one-third are of paintings he made after 60; the single year from which his works are most often reproduced is the final year of his life.[27] In his last letter to his son, written just a week before he died, Cézanne expressed in a postscript his belief that what he had accomplished would have an impact: "I think the young painters are much more intelligent than the others, the old ones see in me only a disastrous rival."[28] Rarely has a prediction been more accurate. Cézanne's late work was the single greatest influence on every major artistic development of the generation that followed. So for example in 1914, the English critic Clive Bell declared that "in so far as one man can be said to inspire a whole age, Cézanne inspires the contemporary movement," and even decades later, in 1951, the American critic Clement Greenberg wrote that "Cézanne, as is generally enough recognized, is the most copious source of what we know as modern art."[29] Today, Cézanne still continues to inspire visual painters; thus the English artist Malcolm Morley recently remarked that "My god is really Cézanne, who introduced the idea of seeing as a sensation rather than a sense of knowing," and the American Brice Marden spoke of his fascination with Cézanne's "intense, long, slow process of working, looking, assimilating."[30]

Although Cézanne's reclusive life in Aix prevented him from realizing it, this influence began even before his death. Early in his own career, Henri Matisse pawned one of his wife's favorite pieces of jewelry to buy *Three Bathers*, a small painting by Cézanne. In the summer of 1905, while he was making the first Fauve paintings that would electrify Paris' art world later that same year, Matisse asked a friend to send him the exact language of a quotation from Cézanne that he remembered from an article by Bernard: "Line and color are not distinct.... When color is at its richest, form takes on its fullest expression."[31] Matisse's radical innovation of Fauvism was inspired in part by Cézanne's rejection of the traditional separation of form (line) and color that caused the effective fragmentation of Cézanne's late paintings. The contour of an object is not a line, but rather the edge of a plane that is foreshortened because it is seen by the viewer at an acute angle. To represent this edge by a single outline violates the reality of the existence of the surface, and late in his life Cézanne denounced this convention as "a fault which must be fought at all costs."[32] His repeated parallel marks created surface patterns as they suggested the series of planes that actually formed objects, and in his late works these brushstrokes often remained distinct and unconstrained. Matisse's autonomous use of color in Fauvism extended and exaggerated this practice. The areas of blank canvas that sometimes remained between Cézanne's individual brushstrokes also became a prominent feature of Matisse's Fauve paintings. Matisse never hesitated to acknowledge his debt to Cézanne: in an interview in 1925, he called Cézanne "a sort of god of painting," and in 1936, when he donated to the city of Paris the small painting for which Amélie Matisse had earlier sacrificed her emerald ring, he declared that "it has sustained me morally in the critical moments of my venture as an artist; I have drawn from it my faith and my perseverance." At the age of 84, when he was asked which painter had influenced him the most, Matisse replied simply, "Cézanne."[33]

In 1907, just a year after Cézanne's death, Pablo Picasso and Georges Braque began to develop Cubism, which quickly succeeded Fauvism as the most revolutionary development in advanced art. Cubism owed a great debt to Cézanne. In many late works by Cézanne, a slight shifting of the artist's vantage point in the course of executing the painting caused visible distortions, including the celebrated discontinuous or split tabletops in still-life compositions.[34] This device increased the illusion of solidity and space, for the viewer is effectively enabled to see around objects portrayed from multiple vantage points. (Noting that this procedure mimicked the way people actually see objects, the English painter David Hockney observed that Cézanne "was the first artist to paint using two eyes."[35]) Picasso and Braque extended and exaggerated this device, multiplying Cézanne's two or three vantage points to a dozen or more, and making Cézanne's subtle shifts in viewpoint greater and more conspicuous. The faceting of objects that was one of the most distinctive features of early Cubism was also a conceptualization of the many planes that were effectively created by Cézanne's "constructive" brushstroke—the small, interlocking, rectangular brushstrokes that remained distinct and individually visible in many late works. Picasso and Braque recognized that each of these brushstrokes functioned simultaneously in two ways—one illusionistic, creating planes that placed objects in depth, the other real, as areas of color on the picture's surface. Like Matisse, Picasso freely acknowledged his debt to Cézanne, as for example in 1943 he called Cézanne "my one and only master. . . . He was like the father of us all."[36] In 1908, seeking to discover the "secret" in Cézanne's creation of space, Braque had traveled to L'Estaque, the small Mediterranean port where Cézanne had often worked. There Braque originated the new geometric space that became a foundation of Cubism. He later said that Cézanne's impact on him during this time "was more than an influence, it was an initiation."[37]

A longstanding criticism has been that Cézanne failed to finish his paintings, as not only individual brushstrokes but even areas of bare canvas often remain visible in his works. Yet his unconcern with hiding the traces of his process to produce finished seamless images served to display his techniques, and to provide a guide for later artists. Thus the painter Jack Tworkov considered Cézanne exceptional for the clarity of his use of color, as he achieved effects of volume and depth without the traditional tools of perspective and shading. He would begin his paintings with light, transparent washes of color, which receded from the viewer. He then proceeded to heavier strokes: areas of deeper color, with thicker paint, advanced toward the viewer. Tworkov saw in the late Cézanne "an orderly and proportional recession of color, based on graduated intensities," a visual reading that explains Cézanne's statement months before his death that "I try to render perspective solely by means of color."[38]

The longer Cézanne worked, the more acutely he became aware of the complexity of his task, and his late paintings can be understood as visual representations of the uncertainty of perception. Cézanne told a friend that "Everything we look at disperses and vanishes, doesn't it? Nature is always the same, and yet its appearance is always changing."[39] Even in front of the motif, a painter is always working from memory, for in the moment of applying paint, he looks at the canvas. For a painter as committed as Cézanne to visual accuracy, this gap between perception and execution became a source of acute anxiety. Cézanne's late works effectively acknowledge and display this process of sequential representation, for each of the visible discrete strokes in his paintings represents one distinct act or moment of perception, and the images are cumulative records of successive viewings. Meyer Schapiro observed that in these paintings, "The form is in constant making ... inviting us to an endless exploration."[40] This changed the role of the viewer of a painting from external observer to active participant, no longer looking at a fixed view from a distance, but now immersed in the landscape, looking around at the surroundings. The intricacy of the task was enormous, for Cézanne's goal was nothing less than to have all of the pieces of a composition collectively create "a harmony which parallels that of nature."[41] A friend who sat for his portrait in 1896 reported that twenty minutes might pass between brushstrokes as Cézanne studied his subject.[42] Bernard's conversations with Cézanne in Aix in 1904 convinced him that Cézanne considered the art he had produced up to that time no more than a beginning of the art he wanted to create, but that he nonetheless believed in his quest: "'I progress every day,' he told me. 'And that's all that matters.'"[43]

On October 15, 1906, severely ill with diabetes, Cézanne collapsed when he was caught in a thunderstorm while painting in the hills above his studio. After lying in the rain for several hours, he was driven home in a cart and carried to his bed. The next day he tried to paint in his garden, but his sister wrote to his son that "he came back dying."[44] He died six days later. A year earlier, he had predicted that "My age and health will never allow me to realize my dream of art that I have been pursuing all my life."[45] Yet he had fulfilled his vow to die painting, and as he had confessed to his son two months before his death, "Painting is what means most to me."[46]

Pablo Picasso (1881–1973)

> I don't seek, I find.
>
> Pablo Picasso[47]

Pablo Picasso was by far the greatest artist of the twentieth century. Remarkably, textbooks of art history contain twice as many illustrations of his work as of that of any other modern artist.[48] He was an archetypal conceptual innovator. In a rare interview he gave to a friend and fellow artist in 1923, Picasso took pains to stress that he was a finder rather than a seeker:

> I can hardly understand the importance given to the word *research* in connection with modern painting. In my opinion to search means nothing in painting. To find, is the thing....
>
> Among the several sins that I have been accused of committing, none is more false than the one that I have, as the principal objective in my work, the spirit of research. When I paint my object is to show what I have found and not what I am looking for....
>
> I have never made trials or experiments. Whenever I had something to say, I have said it in the manner in which I have felt it ought to be said.[49]

24 INNOVATORS

Picasso was both extremely ambitious and extremely precocious. He left his native Spain and settled permanently in Paris in 1904, at the age of 23. During the next decade he made a series of radical innovations that revolutionized both the appearance of art and the behavior of artists, and these led to his unquestioned recognition as the dominant figure in the world of advanced art. Among these innovations was Cubism, which Picasso and his friend Georges Braque created together between 1907 and 1914, and which the historian John Golding described as "perhaps the most important and certainly the most complete and radical artistic revolution since the Renaissance."[50] This was the peak of Picasso's career, as more than half of all the textbooks' illustrations of Picasso's work represent the art he made from the ages of 25 to 34.[51]

Picasso was jealous of the controversy that Matisse and his friends had caused when they first exhibited their Fauve paintings at the 1905 Salon d'Automne, and his competitive instincts were further aroused by the critical success of Le Bonheur de vivre, the large painting Matisse presented at the Salon des Indépendants in 1906.[52] During the winter of 1906–1907, Picasso filled one sketchbook after another with preparatory studies for the largest painting he had ever attempted. The curator William Rubin estimated that Picasso made between four and five hundred studies for Les Demoiselles d'Avignon, "a quantity of preparatory work unique not only in Picasso's career, but without parallel, for a single picture, in the entire history of art."[53] Picasso had deliberately set out to produce a masterpiece, and his success was stunning: the Demoiselles is illustrated in more than 90 percent of all art history textbooks, far more than any other painting from the modern era.[54] The year in which Picasso produced the Demoiselles, at age 26, is not only the single year of his career from which art history textbooks contain the most illustrations, but the single greatest year by that measure for any artist for the entire twentieth century.[55]

The scholar George Heard Hamilton described the Demoiselles d'Avignon as the "watershed between the old pictorial world and the new."[56] The privileged position of the Demoiselles stems from its announcement of the beginning of the Cubist revolution. Both its novel composition and the striking forms of its five nude figures were based on a startling synthesis of a number of disparate earlier styles of art. Thus the angular, simplified features of the figures reflect the influence of African masks and sculptures, as well as ancient Cycladic sculptures and Iberian reliefs that Picasso saw at the Louvre. The geometric faceting of the forms was an exaggeration of the fragmentation produced by the individual brushstrokes of Cézanne's late paintings, just as the combination of radically different viewpoints was an exaggeration of Cézanne's subtle use of slightly differing vantage points. (So for example the body of one of the nude figures is seen from the back, while her face—impossibly—is seen from the front. The squatting pose of this figure, located at the extreme right of the *Demoiselles*, mimicked the pose of one of the figures of Cézanne's *Three Bathers*, which Matisse owned.[57] In just this one figure, Picasso thus simultaneously paid homage to Cézanne, taunted his rival Matisse, and emphasized the radically conceptual nature of his own work.) The *Demoiselles* abruptly abandoned the deep space of Renaissance perspective, as its figures created a novel shallow pictorial space that, like the figures, was broken into angular facets. This new Cubist space appears as solid as the figures it surrounds.

The ugliness of the *Demoiselles* was a brutal departure from the lyrical works of Picasso's blue and rose periods that preceded it, and it jolted the advanced art world. Matisse angrily denounced it as an attempt to ridicule modern painting, and even Braque initially reacted by comparing Picasso to a fairground fire-eater who drank kerosene to spit flames.[58] Yet Braque soon realized that he and Picasso were thinking along similar lines, and they joined in a close collaboration—in Braque's words, "like two mountaineers roped together."[59] One of the most distinctive features of their early Cubism was its construction of forms seen from multiple viewpoints, a device that discarded the traditional function of a painting as a record of the appearance of an object, and replaced it with a conceptual expression of the artist's full knowledge of the object, based on views from many different angles—for example, combining both front and profile views in a portrait. The Cubists' practice of lighting adjacent planes from different directions underscored their creation of spaces that could not exist in reality. Picasso stressed this conceptual foundation of Cubism, declaring that "I paint objects as I think them, not as I see them."[60]

Cubism was quickly perceived by young artists as an exciting new style for a new era. Unlike earlier modern artists, Picasso and Braque took their subject matter from daily life in the modern city. Their depiction of café tables, coffee cups, newspapers, wine carafes, and other ordinary objects effectively made their art the first to celebrate the value of manufactured things.[61] And Cubism offered artists a new freedom, for it broke with the traditional relationship of art to reality. The artist's goal was no longer to imitate reality, but rather to represent it symbolically: in place of the metaphor for earlier painting of holding up a mirror to nature, John Berger suggested that the new model for Cubism was the diagram.[62] The severity of the *Demoiselles* forced this recognition on observers, as in one of the earliest published commentaries on the painting the poet André Salmon called its figures "white numbers on a blackboard," and remarked that "Picasso has laid down the principle of picture-as-equation."[63] No longer restricted to a description of actual appearances, the artist could instead create new personal conceptions of form. Picasso in fact described Cubism as a symbolic system that had to be learned, like a language. Thus in 1923 he remarked that "The fact that for a long time Cubism has not been understood and that even today there are people who cannot see anything in it, means nothing. I do not read English, an English book is a blank book to me. This does not mean that the English language does not exist, and why should I blame anybody else but myself if I cannot understand what I know nothing about?"[64]

Picasso made several other far-reaching contributions during this remarkable early period of radical innovation. In 1912, he glued a piece of oil cloth to a small oval painting, *Still Life with Chair Caning*. This became the first *collage*, violating the tradition that had been honored by artists since the Renaissance, that nothing other than paint should be placed on the two-dimensional surface of a painting. The irreverence of Picasso's use of collage was heightened by the stark contrast between the austerity and cerebrality of his earlier Cubist images and the banality of the references embodied in the torn newsprint and other scrap materials he introduced in his collages (the scholar Kirk Varnedoe drily commented that it was as if "having perfected an exquisite, chamber-music harmony, Picasso ... decided that the perfect next step was to add a kazoo counterpoint").[65] The impact of Picasso's innovation was enormous, for not only was collage immediately adopted by many artists to create new visual effects in their paintings, but other artists equally promptly began to emulate Picasso by creating their own new genres of art. Before 1912 was out, Braque had made the first *papier collé*. In 1913, after a visit to Picasso's studio, the Russian artist Vladimir Tatlin made the first *counter-relief*. Also in 1913, Marcel Duchamp made the first *readymade*. And on and on, artist after artist, decade after decade. Before the invention of collage, advanced art was made up almost exclusively of painting and sculpture. After Picasso demonstrated that one of the most fundamental rules of fine art could be violated with impunity, and that the result was a new genre, scores of young conceptual artists created their own new genres, and over the course of the twentieth century advanced art became progressively balkanized into dozens of independent domains.[66] Collage itself also became a metaphor for the radical combinations of unrelated elements that defined many of these new domains. So for example Damien Hirst, the leader of the Young British Artists of the 1990s, declared that collage was the greatest idea of the twentieth century, and considered it the basis for all his extremely varied conceptual artistic activities, from curating group exhibitions to placing sectioned animals in tanks filled with formaldehyde: "I just see it all like collage."[67]

Early in his career, Picasso initiated another new practice that would also have a vast impact on later artists, by transforming the role of style. Traditionally, an artist's distinctive style had been his hallmark, as basic to his artistic identity as the signature that identified a work as his own. During 1914, Picasso began to violate this tradition. Earlier, he had already become known for changing styles abruptly: in 1912, Roger Fry had warned that "It is dangerous and difficult to speak of Picasso, for he is changing with kaleidoscopic rapidity."[68] But now he began deliberately to alternate styles, simultaneously producing Cubist paintings and classical representational images. No artist had ever done this, and many in the art world questioned Picasso's integrity and sincerity. Yet, again invoking the parallel between art and language, Picasso explained that for him style was merely a means of expression, and that he consequently felt free to change styles as the need arose: "Whenever I had something to say, I have said it in the manner in which I have felt it ought to be said. Different motives inevitably require different methods of expression."[69] John Berger observed that Picasso's life's work was made up "not of stages, because that implies a desired destination, evolution, logical purpose, but made up of metamorphoses—sudden inexplicable transformations."[70] Marcel Duchamp considered this "Picasso's main contribution to art. To have been able to start from a new source, and to keep this freshness with regard to whatever new expressions make the different epochs of his career."[71] Duchamp and other young artists were again quick to seize on Picasso's example, and the practice of stylistic versatility became a pattern that was followed by many of the most important conceptual artists of the twentieth century. As these artists extended Picasso's original practice, the late twentieth century became a time when many prominent artists, including Robert Rauschenberg, Bruce Nauman, Gerhard Richter, Sigmar Polke, and Damien Hirst, varied their approaches so frequently that many critics contended that they had no identifiable style at all. Richter, one of the leading painters of his era, explained in 1984 that "It has now become my identifying characteristic that my work is all over the place," and that "historically speaking, changeable artists are a growing phenomenon. Picasso, for instance, or Duchamp and Picabia—and the number is certainly increasing all the time."[72]

Picasso's remarkable collaboration with Braque was brought to an end by World War I, when Braque was mobilized. Picasso later told his dealer, Daniel-Henry Kahnweiler, "On August 2, 1914, I took Braque and Derain to the Gare d'Avignon. I never saw them again."[73] The statement wasn't literally true, for although Braque was seriously wounded in the war, Picasso saw him many times between 1915 and Braque's death in 1963. But their relationship was never the same, and the most inventive phase of Picasso's career was over.

Picasso did subsequently make one more major contribution. In 1937, after the destruction of the Basque town of Guernica by German bombers acting for General Franco, Picasso painted an enormous mural for the Spanish pavilion at the Paris World's Fair as an expression of his outrage. The painting would become the second most important of the modern era, behind only the *Demoiselles* in frequency of reproduction in art history textbooks.[74] Unlike the *Demoiselles*, however, *Guernica* did not create a new language, but rather put the Cubist idiom to a novel use, for it was the first major painting of the modern era that made an explicitly political statement. Prior to the modern era, the importance of a work of art depended in large part on its subject: the greatest paintings treated classical or religious themes, or portrayed great rulers. This changed with the advent of modern art, as the Impressionists and their successors painted scenes from everyday life. By demonstrating that the most advanced forms of modern art could be used not only for private expression, but for public purposes, *Guernica* became an inspiration for later artists who wanted their work to make social and political statements.

It is difficult to exaggerate the impact of Picasso's early innovations. As a style, Cubism directly influenced such later movements as Futurism, Suprematism, Constructivism, and De Stijl; in the process, it was a central influence on two of the pioneers of abstract painting, Piet Mondrian and Kazimir Malevich. For its impact on painting, the critic Douglas Cooper judged Cubism "the most potent generative force in twentieth-century art."[75] And its impact went far beyond painting, to sculpture, architecture, cinema, photography, and even to literature and poetry.[76] The precedent of the invention of collage prompted conceptual artists to create a series of new hybrid genres that changed the very structure of visual art: today painting no longer dominates the art world, as it did a century ago, but is challenged by such newer genres as installation, photography, video, and performance. And the deliberate alternation of styles led to a new model of artistic behavior that changed the very conception of artistic achievement, so that today, many of the most important artists have no recognizable trademark style. These revolutionary contributions, based entirely on new ideas, had all been completed by the time Picasso was in his early 30s. He went on to paint for another six decades, until his death in 1973, at the age of 92. His amazing energy, which persisted to the end of his life, made him one of the most prolific artists in history. Yet his ability to generate new ideas did not last nearly as long. *Guernica* was an isolated achievement of his 50s, and less than 3 percent of the illustrations of his work in the textbooks represent works he made after 60.[77] On the occasion of a retrospective exhibition of Picasso's art presented after his death, John Richardson, a biographer who was also an old friend of the artist, was saddened by the age profile of his creativity: "All the same, a sad end. Of course it would have been more dignified if the great man could have died in the odor of artistic sanctity, like Titian or Rembrandt or Cézanne. But, let us face it, Picasso's vision had reached its apogee in his thirties."[78]

Jackson Pollock (1912–1956)

> Painting is self-discovery.
>
> Jackson Pollock[79]

By the age of 18, in 1930, Jackson Pollock had been dismissed from ROTC for punching an officer, and had been expelled twice from Los Angeles' Manual Arts High School, the second time for punching a gym teacher.[80] These early problems were due to his rebellious personality, and to the beginning of the alcoholism that would dog him for the rest of his life. Giving up on high school, Jackson decided to emulate his older brother Charles by moving to New York to become an artist.

In New York, Jackson followed Charles in enrolling in the Art Students League, and studying with the realist painter Thomas Hart Benton. Pollock was not a facile or precocious art student. Whitney Darrow, a fellow student who later became a successful cartoonist, recalled that "He wanted to be an 'Artist,' but he didn't seem to enjoy his painting much. And he didn't do that much, either. He was ambitious—either that or extremely neurotic—and unsatisfied, frustrated."[81] But Pollock was encouraged by Benton's conviction that the ambition to be a great artist mattered more for artistic success than great talent.[82] Pollock studied mural painting with Benton, and also in 1936 in the New York studio of the Mexican muralist David Siqueiros, who was experimenting with techniques of applying paint without a brush, including spraying and pouring. After three years at the Art Students League, Pollock took a job as a janitor, then later joined the Federal Arts Project of the Works Progress Administration; with several interruptions, he would remain on the WPA from 1935 to 1943. His development as an artist remained unimpressive, and he was hospitalized in 1938 for treatment of his alcoholism and psychiatric problems. In 1939 his brother Sanford, who was also an aspiring artist, wrote to Charles that "Jack is still struggling with the problems of painting and living."[83] Sanford later recalled that a kind adviser looking at Pollock's art of that period would have suggested he take up plumbing instead.[84] Few of Pollock's early paintings have survived, but those that exist show a heavy influence of Benton's nativist art. Gradually, however, as he approached the age of 30, Pollock began to show signs of developing his own style. In 1941, Sanford reported to Charles that "he has thrown off the yoke of Benton completely and is doing work which is creative in the most genuine sense of the word.... We are sure that if he is able to hold himself together his work will become of real significance. His painting is abstract, intense, evocative in quality." Pollock was working toward a non-representational art, using elements derived from the recent art of both Picasso and Surrealism. Ominously, however, Sanford also told Charles that Jackson's psychiatric difficulties persisted: "He is afflicted with a definite neurosis. Whether he comes through to normalcy and self-dependency depends on many... factors."[85]

Pollock's artistic progress was helped by the company of several other young painters, including Robert Motherwell and William Baziotes, who like him would later become prominent Abstract Expressionists. Although these artists were considered as a group—by themselves as well as others—they did not share a common style; what bound them together was their dissatisfaction with existing styles of painting and their desire to draw on the subconscious to create an art that would communicate their emotions directly, without preconceived ideas or fixed conventions. Each of the Abstract Expressionists eventually developed his own distinctive expressive gestures, but all shared the reliance on visual criteria to judge the progress of their art, and the doubts that arose from the novelty of their efforts and the imprecision of their goals.

The members of this group matured slowly as artists, and Pollock was no exception. A survey of art history textbooks shows that less than 10 percent of all the illustrations of his work were of paintings he made before the age of 30.[86] Recognition of Pollock's talent spread within the art world in 1943, when he had his first solo exhibition, at Peggy Guggenheim's New York gallery. Clement Greenberg, who was to become Pollock's most forceful advocate, wrote in *The Nation* that Pollock's works were "among the strongest abstract paintings I have yet seen by an American."[87] Two years later, Pollock's second solo show led Greenberg to declare him "the strongest painter of his generation."[88] Yet Pollock had not yet reached his creative peak: although the work of the first half of his 30s is clearly more important than that of his 20s, it still accounts for less than 20 percent of the textbooks' total illustrations of his work.

Pollock is widely regarded as having gained his artistic maturity in 1947, at 35, when he began to make completely abstract paintings, using the "drip" or "pour" technique that became his trademark. The problem for the ambitious young American artists who had congregated in New York, and worked in poverty and obscurity to develop their art during the Great Depression and World War II, was how to break away from the powerful European tradition in painting, and particularly to escape from the strong residual influence of Cubism. As early as 1944, Pollock had boldly declared that he had no desire to follow the traditional path for young American artists by studying in Europe, claiming that "I don't see why the problems of modern painting can't be solved as well here as elsewhere." He also wanted to work on a larger scale than artists traditionally did, because he believed the easel painting "to be a dying form, and the tendency of modern feeling is towards the wall picture or mural."[89] Yet the question remained of how to create new forms. Three years later, Pollock devised a bold new technique that produced powerful new images.

A critic who watched Pollock work in 1950 gave this description of the drip technique:

> He has found that what he has to say is best accomplished by laying the canvas on the floor, walking around it and applying paint from all sides. The paint—usually enamel, which he finds more pliable—is applied by dipping a small house brush or stick or trowel into the can and then, by rapid movements of the wrist, arm and body, quickly allowing it to fall in weaving rhythms over the surface. The brush seldom touches the canvas,

but is a means to let color drip or run in stringy forms that allow for the complexity of design necessary for the artist.[90]

Pollock's drip method, with the inevitable spattering and puddling of paint that could not be completely controlled, came to symbolize the absence of preconceived outcomes that was a core value of Abstract Expressionism. In 1947, Pollock himself stressed the critical importance of making discoveries in the process of working: "When I am *in* my painting, I'm not aware of what I'm doing. It is only after a sort of 'get acquainted' period that I see what I have been about. I have no fears about making changes, destroying the image, etc., because the painting has a life of its own. I try to let it come through."[91] In 1950, Pollock explained to an interviewer that his painting was "direct. I don't work from drawings, I don't make sketches and drawings and color sketches into a final painting. Painting, I think, today—the more immediate, the more direct—the greater the possibilities of making a direct—of making a statement."[92] The importance of the working process to Pollock and the other Abstract Expressionists prompted the critic Harold Rosenberg to suggest in 1952 that they should properly be called "action painters," on the grounds that their paintings were visual records of the events that created them.[93]

The precise origins of Pollock's drip method are uncertain. He was exposed to Siqueiros' experiments with pouring and dripping paint as early as 1936. In 1942, together with Motherwell and Baziotes, he listened to the young Chilean artist Roberto Matta, recently arrived from Paris, explain how Surrealist painters used the practice of automatism as a means of accessing the imaginative imagery of the unconscious.[94] Pollock's drip method may have derived from these sources and others, but it differed from earlier processes in both form and intent. Unlike the Surrealists, who began their paintings with random markings or doodling as a prelude to discovering images that could be elaborated into real forms and objects, Pollock might begin by drawing simplified figures, then layer paint over these to dissolve them into abstract images. Lee Krasner, Pollock's widow, recalled that he had once told her that "I choose to veil the imagery."[95]

The drip method was not a mechanical process that routinely turned out similar products. The drip paintings varied considerably in a number of ways, including color; size; material (not only canvas supports, but also metal, cardboard, paper, or board); density (the degree to which the support was fully covered, as opposed to open images in which areas of white ground show through the layers of color); and the relationship of image to edges, as some continue to the ends of the canvas, as if cut from a larger work, whereas others stop short of the edges on all four sides, leaving margins of empty canvas as a frame. Kirk Varnedoe called attention to "the rich variety among the poured or drip pictures," noting that "these were always vastly different paintings, and the list of their crucial dissimilarities—palette; ground; dilution and mix of mediums; speed; structure; density—is so imposing that it virtually belies ... the notion of any common strategy that could be called a style or method." This variety was a result of Pollock's continuing experimentation, as he was "constantly reinventing his approach ... throughout the 'classic' years of 1947–50."[96]

Although the novelty of the drip method attracted considerable public attention, the primary achievement of Pollock's art lay in the innovative qualities of the images he produced. One of these was its elimination of the traditional use of drawing. The lines that Pollock created by sweeping his arm above the canvas no longer defined figures, or bounded spaces, but functioned as an autonomous element in the composition. A second characteristic was the all-over composition of Pollock's paintings: they had no specific central focal point, but gave equal emphasis to the entire picture surface. A third lay in the novel connection of the paintings' form to their process. Pollock's paintings appeared to present a visible record of their own creation, and they could consequently be interpreted as studies of that creative process. A fourth feature was a product of the size of Pollock's paintings, which were often considerably larger than earlier abstract paintings. Pollock had been born in Wyoming and raised in California, and his western background led many viewers to associate these large canvases with the open spaces of western prairies. Pollock had remarked early in his career that "I have a definite feeling for the West; the vast horizontality of the land, for instance."[97] This association underscored the distinctively American character of Pollock's challenge to traditional European art. In 1950, Pollock remarked that a reviewer's criticism that his paintings had no beginning or end was in fact "a fine compliment."[98] The edges of the drip paintings no longer necessarily marked a discrete ending of the work, for the viewer could imagine the image extending indefinitely, beyond the bounds of the canvas.

Pollock's continuous compositions on mural-sized canvases effectively created an environment that enveloped viewers, making them participants in the art rather than simply observers. This prompted one younger artist, Allan Kaprow, to invent Happenings, works of art made spontaneously by actions in real space.[99] Ironically, one effect of Pollock's experimental art was thus to stimulate new forms of conceptual art that renounced painting, as performance art gained considerable popularity in the 1960s and beyond.[100] Yet Pollock's drip paintings also inspired many young experimental artists. So for example the sculptor Richard Serra recalled that when he first saw Pollock's paintings, "as a student, this idea of allowing the form to emerge out of the process was incredibly important." In the late 1990s, Serra remarked that "We evaluate artists by how much they are able to rid themselves of convention, to change history. Well, I don't know of anyone since Pollock who has altered the form or the language of painting as much as he did." Serra admired the "organic quality of Pollock's line, with its swirls and rope-laden splatters. It points to a likeness to nature without being descriptive or illustrative of nature." For Serra, Pollock's drip paintings exhibited "an exuberance in the act of making" that was rare, and he reflected that "for me America has never reached the fulfillment of this aspiration."[101]

Pollock used the drip method almost exclusively for four years, during 1947–1950, and it was in this period that he produced the art for which he is famous. Thus half of all the illustrations of his work in the textbooks surveyed represent paintings done in just these four years. Interestingly, however, it is not the paintings from the earliest of these years that most often appear in the textbooks, but those from the last year of the period: the texts contain three times as many illustrations of paintings done in 1950 as in any of the preceding three years.[102] Because Pollock's contribution was not an idea, it is not its earliest appearance that is most important. Instead, because the contribution was aesthetic, it is the latest, most highly developed uses of the drip technique that are most important. Art scholars have observed that Pollock's execution of his paintings evolved over the course of this period, as he became more skilled in using the new technique he had devised: the greater control he achieved over the consistency and thickness of the paint he poured onto his canvases allowed him to obtain more varied surface textures, and to create larger abstract figures that resulted in more highly resolved compositions. As a result, it is the largest paintings of the last year in which he relied entirely on this technique that represent his greatest achievement.[103] Pollock himself stressed his control of his technique. Thus in a 1950 interview he explained that "with experience—it seems to be possible to control the flow of the paint, to a great extent."[104] And when *Time* magazine published an article in the same year that described his paintings as incomprehensible labyrinths, and quoted a critic who characterized them as chaos, Pollock immediately responded with a telegram that declared "NO CHAOS DAMN IT."[105]

Pollock's paintings of 1947–1950 were made using the drip technique throughout the process of their production, but the degree of control he exerted changed during the process. He began the paintings with random or uncomposed pourings, seeking the unconscious imagery and spontaneity of automatism, but then developed and completed the works with more deliberate and controlled applications of paint that responded to what was already on the canvas. The paintings were thus begun without preconception, and were finished when Pollock was satisfied that he had achieved a visual resolution that grew out of imagery he had found in his initial random markings. The method was rooted in Pollock's visual experimental approach. Lee Krasner described how he would frequently stop to study a work in progress. To look at his large canvases in an upright position, "he'd attach the top edge to a long piece of 2×4, and together we'd lift it up—do you know how much one of those big pictures with all that paint weighed? We'd take it to the wall, and lift it up ladders, and just nail the ends of the 2×4—which stuck out—into the studio wall." After Pollock had examined the painting, they would carry it down again so he could continue layering paint on the horizontal canvas. As he worked on uncut lengths of raw canvas, Pollock often did not consider the size or orientation of the finished painting. Krasner recalled how this complicated the process of completing a painting: "Sometimes he'd ask, 'Should I cut it here? Should this be the bottom?' He'd have long sessions of cutting and editing. . . . Those were difficult sessions. His signing the canvases was even worse. I'd think everything was settled—tops, bottoms, margins—and then he'd have last-minute thoughts and doubts. He hated signing. There's something so final about a signature."[106] Pollock's uncertainty about his work often extended to even deeper levels. Krasner recalled that during the early 1950s, even after he had been recognized as an important artist, one day "in front of a very good painting . . . he asked me, 'Is this a painting?' Not is this a good painting, or a bad one, but a *painting*! The degree of doubt was unbelievable at times."[107]

Art historians judge Pollock to be the most important artist in American history: their textbooks contain more illustrations of his work than that of any other American artist.[108] He was recognized, not only by critics, but by his fellow artists, as the inspirational leader of the Abstract Expressionists, whose remarkable achievements of the 1940s and 1950s definitively shifted the center of the advanced art world from Paris to New York.[109] Even Willem de Kooning, Pollock's chief rival for primacy in the group, was widely quoted as having conceded that "Jackson broke the ice," as he explained that Pollock had made the boldest and earliest break with tradition: "Every so often, a painter has to destroy painting. Cézanne did it. Picasso did it with Cubism. Then Pollock did it. He busted our idea of a picture all to hell. Then there could be *new* paintings again."[110] In a cohort of artists who had lived through two world wars and a Great Depression, and were committed to creating new artistic means for making more direct statements about their anxieties and aspirations, Pollock made the most dramatic breakthrough to large and powerful images that expressed the urgency and spontaneity of their own making: as he said, "I paint it, I don't illustrate it."[111]

Pollock achieved national fame in 1949, when *Life* magazine featured him in a story titled "Is He the Greatest Living Painter in the United States?"[112] He enjoyed the recognition, but he was angered by the disrespect for abstract art that persisted in the popular press, including a flippant 1956 *Time* magazine reference to him as "Jack the Dripper."[113] The prices of his paintings rose modestly during these years, but he never gained real economic security; he looked for work, unsuccessfully, in 1948, and again in 1952.[114] After 1950 he continued to make changes in his art, combining the drip method with a partial return to figuration, but he was not satisfied with the results. His problems with alcohol again intensified. In 1956, Pollock crashed his car while speeding on a road near his home in Long Island, and both he and a young woman who was a passenger were killed. Earlier in the year, the Museum of Modern Art had notified Pollock that he had been chosen to inaugurate a series of solo exhibitions of leading mid-career artists. By the time the show opened in December, it had become a memorial exhibition.[115]

Andy Warhol (1928–1987)

> The reason I'm painting this way is that I want to be a machine.
> Andy Warhol[116]

Andrew Warhola majored in Pictorial Design at Carnegie Institute of Technology in his hometown of Pittsburgh, and graduated in 1949. He moved to New York a week after graduation, and almost immediately began to get good jobs making illustrations for fashion magazines and department stores. A printing error in the credits to his first illustrations in

Glamour magazine shortened his name to *Warhol*, and he decided to keep the truncated name; soon thereafter he also shortened *Andrew* to *Andy*.[117] During the next decade Warhol became one of New York's leading commercial artists: his work appeared in major fashion magazines, he designed stationery for Tiffany and Bergdorf Goodman, and he drew advertisements for several national corporations. His specialty came to be drawings of women's shoes, and by 1955 his primary source of income was the I. Miller shoe company, which regularly published his drawings in the fashion pages of the *New York Times*. These earned him a series of awards, including the highest honor of the Art Directors Club in 1957. Warhol was so busy that he began to hire assistants to make preliminary versions of his drawings, and to use simple mechanical printing techniques to save time.

But Warhol had higher aspirations. In a folder he made for *Vanity Fair* in 1955, he wrote that his paintings were exhibited in galleries and museums.[118] The claim was false, but it expressed a goal. In 1960, while continuing his lucrative commercial art practice, Warhol began making paintings based on comic strips and advertisements. Early in 1962, he began to use stencils to make these paintings. In July, he had his first exhibition of paintings, at a Los Angeles gallery, consisting of thirty-two individual stenciled portraits of Campbell's soup cans—one for each flavor the company made. In August, he began to make paintings by silkscreening, a technique he would use for the rest of his life.[119] He had been fascinated by Hollywood since he was a child, and now he began searching through his collection of publicity pictures for images of his favorite stars. Marilyn Monroe committed suicide on August 4, 1962, and Warhol decided to paint a series of portraits of her, based on a publicity photograph. In November, he had his first New York show of paintings. It included both *Marilyn Diptych* and *Green Coca-Cola Bottles*, which by the metric of frequency of illustration in textbooks would prove to be the two most important paintings he ever made.[120] When Warhol's paintings of soup cans were first exhibited in Los Angeles, they were priced at $100 each, which was only one-tenth as much as he was then getting for a commercial drawing. Yet the impact of the Campbell's soup paintings on the art world was enormous, for they were featured in the first mass-media article on Pop art in *Time* magazine before the Los Angeles show even opened, and they effectively made Warhol into the leader of Pop, the most controversial new movement of its time, almost instantly.[121] In 1963, the artist Robert Indiana described Pop as "Instant Art."[122] The experience of Andy Warhol in 1962 demonstrates the truth of this characterization for both the creation and the reception of this new style.

By the measure of illustrations in art history textbooks, the body of work Warhol made in 1962 was the most important ever made by an American artist in a single year: indeed, Warhol's paintings of 1962 rank second, behind only Picasso's of 1907, in importance for the work of a single year among all artists of the twentieth century.[123] During that year, Warhol made three far-reaching formal innovations: he used serial imagery—not only making multiple paintings of a single image, but often using multiples of the same image within individual paintings; he used mechanical techniques to produce his paintings; and he based his paintings entirely on photographs.[124] These would later become common practices, not only for Pop artists, but for countless other artists for the balance of the twentieth century and beyond.

Pop art was a highly conceptual movement, that substituted preconceived images, taken directly from popular culture, for the complex and esoteric abstract forms created by the Abstract Expressionists. Warhol underscored this contrast by producing his paintings with the industrial technique of silk-screening. He would select a photograph from a newspaper or magazine, then send it to a manufacturer with instructions about the sizes and numbers of the screens (one for each color he intended to use). Working alone in his living room, in three months beginning with August of 1962 Warhol made one hundred paintings. The next year, to increase his productivity even further, he began to hire assistants, and established the practice he would follow for the rest of his career. When the printers delivered the screens to Warhol's studio, smaller paintings would be executed by an assistant, while Warhol would help with larger ones. Gerard Malanga, one of Warhol's principal assistants during the 1960s, described the latter process:

> Andy and I would put the screen down on the canvas, trying to line up the registration with the marks we made where the screen would go. Then oil-based paint was poured into a corner of the frame of the screen, and I would push the paint with a squeegee across the screen. Andy would grab the squeegee still in motion and continue the process of putting pressure on pushing the paint through the screen from his end. We'd lift the screen, and I would swing it away from the painting and start cleaning it with paper towels soaked in a substance called Varnolene. If this was not done immediately, the remaining paint would dry and clog the pores.

Malanga reported that making a painting took about four minutes. He explained that Warhol did not equate mechanical means with perfection: "we worked as mechanically as we could, trying to get each image right, but we never got it right.... Andy embraced his mistakes. We never rejected anything. Andy would say, 'It's part of the art.'"[125]

Warhol's influence was not a function exclusively of his paintings, for he innovated not only in the form of art, but also in creating new types of artistic behavior. He quickly understood that the impact of conceptual art could be greatly enhanced by what the artist said and did. The model that underlay Warhol's behavior was that of the artistic trickster, which had been pioneered by Marcel Duchamp in 1913, when he submitted a porcelain urinal as a work of art to the first exhibition of the American Society of Independent Artists. Although the exhibition was not juried, many of the society's directors were outraged by the submission, and their board voted to reject it. In an article about this episode, Louise Norton, a friend of Duchamp's, declared that "there are those who anxiously ask 'Is he serious or is he joking?' Perhaps he is both!" Duchamp remained enigmatically silent about Norton's question, and few observers were able to accept her suggested resolution. As a result, debates over whether the artist was serious or joking raged on for decades, in the process spreading Duchamp's fame, and increasing his influence.[126]

Warhol fully recognized the power of ambiguity in creating controversy over the sincerity of a radical conceptual innovation, and to this end he created a persona that neatly complemented the simple two-dimensional images of his paintings. This persona effectively presented him as the physical and intellectual equivalent of these naive and unsophisticated images. Often wearing a silver fright wig, Warhol proclaimed his own lack of intelligence—"I'm not more intelligent than I appear"—and his superficiality: "If you want to know all about Andy Warhol, just look at the surface: of my paintings and films and me, and there I am. There's nothing behind it."[127] Warhol's success as artistic trickster was remarkable. During the 1960s and far beyond, art world sophisticates continued to debate whether Warhol's paintings were even art: so for example in 1977 the eminent critic Harold Rosenberg, an important early supporter of Abstract Expressionism, contemptuously dismissed Warhol as "the artist changed into media celebrity and manufacturer of art substitutes."[128] And these debates were consistently accompanied by equally impassioned disagreements over Warhol's intellectual abilities. Thus for example while one prominent critic referred to Warhol as an "art huckster," and a leading art scholar termed him an "idiot savant," the philosopher and critic Arthur Danto considered him the "closest to a philosophical genius of any twentieth-century artist."[129] In surveying this debate, Kirk Varnedoe commented that the effectiveness of Warhol's early Pop paintings lay precisely in their ambiguity: "Go one way or the other—make it only a stupid prank or only a trenchant social statement—and one reduces the power of the achievement." Varnedoe reflected that the 1962 Campbell's soup cans proved that "art does not need to be deep to be profound."[130]

Warhol constructed a remarkably thorough and systematic conceptual assault on many of the most basic and cherished attitudes of the advanced art world, which had been embodied vividly in the philosophical and spiritual claims of Abstract Expressionism. Artists were traditionally respected as exalted beings: Warhol asked, "Why do people think artists are special? It's just another job."[131] The artist's studio was regarded as a hallowed place: Warhol named each of his studios The Factory. Art must necessarily be made by hand: Warhol used silk screens, explaining that "hand painting would take much too long.... Mechanical means are today."[132] Art was created by the inspired touch of the artist: Warhol publicized the fact that his works were made by assistants, remarking that "I think somebody should be able to do all my paintings for me."[133] Great art was the product of deep thought and powerful emotion: Warhol told an interviewer, "I've never been touched by a painting. I don't want to think."[134] Paintings were cherished as unique objects, symbolizing a final survival against the homogenization of modern society: Warhol made sequences of identical paintings, and commented that "I think every painting should be the same size and the same color so they're all interchangeable."[135] Artists were defined as the creators of complex, original images: Warhol explained that "Pop artists did images that anybody walking down Broadway could recognize in a split second—comics, picnic tables, men's trousers, celebrities, shower curtains, refrigerators, Coke bottles—all the great modern things that the Abstract Expressionists tried so hard not to notice at all."[136] Creating a unique personal style was traditionally the artist's highest goal: in 1963 Warhol asked rhetorically, "How can you say one style is better than another? You ought to be able to be an Abstract Expressionist next week, or a Pop artist, or a realist, without feeling you've given up something.... [A]n artist ought to be able to change his style without feeling bad."[137] There was a firm belief in an impenetrable boundary between high and low art that could never be breached: asked in what was to be his last interview, in 1987, about his "transformation from being a commercial artist to a real artist," Warhol responded, "I'm still a commercial artist. I was always a commercial artist."[138] Fine art was understood to be intended exclusively for the cognoscenti: Warhol declared that "Pop art is for everyone. I don't think art should be only for the select few, I think it should be for the mass of American people."[139] Paintings were not mere commodities, and were never to be referred to as capital assets: Warhol explained that "paintings are like stocks and a dealer is like a broker. Art is an investment."[140] Artists were ascetics, oblivious to money: Warhol painted images of dollar bills, and recalled that he had asked his friends for suggestions about subjects for his paintings, until "finally one lady friend of mine asked me the right question: 'Well, what do you love most?' That's how I started painting money."[141] Artists were never supposed to pursue wealth: Warhol wrote, "I have a Fantasy about Money: I'm walking down the street and I hear somebody say—in a whisper—'There goes the richest person in the world.'"[142]

Warhol's desire for wealth was sincere. One of his most systematic and lucrative activities was commissioned portraits, which he began in 1963 and continued for the rest of his life. He would begin with a Polaroid photograph of the client, from which he made a silkscreened canvas, and often added details by hand. He altered the photographs to flatter his clients, in the hope they would later return for new portraits. By the early 1970s he charged $25,000 for a portrait of 40 by 40 inches, and offered additional canvases of the same image in different colors for $5,000 each; these prices rose over time, as his fame increased. Warhol often went to three dinner parties in one evening, as well as cocktail parties and art openings, in search of prospective clients. Bob Colacello, who worked for Warhol as the first editor of *Interview* magazine, estimated that in total Warhol painted more than one thousand individuals, most of whom bought multiple canvases.[143]

The force of Warhol's Pop art lay in its combination of subjects and technique. The Cubists had painted generic manufactured objects, but Warhol copied commercial images of specific brands. He embraced popular taste: he always wore Levi's, and wrote that "I wish I could invent something like blue jeans.... Something mass." He celebrated the equality of mass consumption: "What's great about this country is that America started the tradition where the richest consumers buy essentially the same things as the poorest.... A Coke is a Coke and no amount of money can get you a better Coke than the one the bum on the corner is drinking."[144] He loved common tastes, explaining that he painted Marilyn Monroe because

"She fascinated me as she did the rest of America."[145] Pop's simple and preconceived images could be understood instantly: Robert Indiana observed that "Its comprehension can be as immediate as a crucifixion."[146] And Pop could be spread rapidly and widely by the same media that had originally created its images: the artist Larry Bell remarked that "Modern means of communication and Pop art are a romance that must have been made in heaven."[147]

Warhol influenced generations of younger artists, including many of the leading figures of recent times. His impact began almost immediately after his first Pop paintings. Thus in 1962 two students at the Düsseldorf Academy of Art saw reproductions of early Pop paintings in an art magazine, and promptly emulated their technique. These students, Gerhard Richter and Sigmar Polke, went on to become two of the most influential artists of the late twentieth century, and the cornerstone of their careers was the practice of painting from photographs. Over time, Warhol's influence stemmed from his attitudes as well as his art. So for example Jeff Koons has acknowledged his artistic debt to Pop art, and it is difficult not to hear a debt to Warhol in Koons' public avowal of his desire to sell his work for the highest prices possible, with the explanation that "The market is the greatest critic."[148] Both Damien Hirst's art and his public persona similarly owe a debt to Warhol, whom Hirst has praised for his honesty, and there are distinct echoes of Warhol not only in Hirst's open pursuit of financial success, but in his account of his spot paintings: "I want them to look like a person trying to paint like a machine."[149]

The English critic David Sylvester put his finger on the most basic way in which Warhol changed modern art, when he observed that "all of Warhol's mature work is as if inspired by a revelation that a modern painter could and should exploit the photograph as Renaissance painters exploited classical antiquities." Sylvester noted that Warhol's paintings were not only based on photographs, but were actually about photography: "He created an art that would be utterly meaningless to anyone who didn't realize that it was made from photographs and was about photographs."[150] Even today, whether they make photographs, like Cindy Sherman, Richard Prince, and Jeff Wall, or make paintings based on photographs, like Gerhard Richter, Jeff Koons, and Damien Hirst, a large number of the most important visual artists base their work on photographic images. Warhol was the key figure in this transformation.

Warhol's influence on visual art was almost entirely a product of his early Pop work. Fully 40 percent of all the illustrations of his work that appear in art history textbooks are of paintings he did in the single year of 1962, and more than 80 percent represent paintings he produced in the five-year period beginning in that year.[151] He was 34 in 1962, when he made his most innovative works. What is striking, however, is that he had begun making paintings only in 1960, so his radical innovations in Pop art were made when he had only two years of experience in his new career. Although he had worked as a commercial illustrator for a decade, his conceptual masterpieces of 1962 were effectively made by a novice painter.

Interestingly, Warhol decided to retire from painting in 1965. Although he later reconsidered as the market prices of his paintings rose, he recalled that "Art just wasn't fun for me anymore," because he realized his revolution was over: "I didn't want to keep repainting successful themes.... [T]he basic Pop statements had already been made."[152] His friend and biographer David Bourdon recalled that Warhol wanted to be a jack-of-all-arts: "He fantasized about having a hit movie playing at Radio City Music Hall, a Broadway show at the Winter Garden, a television special, a book on the best-seller list, a Top-40 record, and the cover of *Life*. He truly believed he could keep several careers going simultaneously, winning acclaim in all of them." Warhol in fact began to make movies as early as 1963, to manage a rock band called the Velvet Underground in 1965, and to publish *Interview* magazine in 1969. These activities added significantly to his fame and fortune, both of which grew to impressive proportions, but they also reduced the time he devoted to painting.[153]

Warhol's succinct analysis in 1965 was accurate: his basic Pop statements had already been made, and he would never again make any significant innovation in painting. Yet it is difficult to overstate the impact on advanced art of Warhol's Pop innovations. That early work made him such a towering presence in the art world that when she heard the news of his death in 1987, of complications following routine gallbladder surgery, the critic Lisa Liebmann recalled that "I ran to the window expecting to hear seismic noises coming from the city outside, and to witness a transfiguration.... The shock of so enormous an absence would surely register, it seemed, on reality itself."[154] But for many in the art world the city's appearance had already changed, twenty-five years earlier, for as Warhol had observed, "once you thought Pop, you could never see America the same way again."[155]

Jean-Michel Basquiat (1960–1988)

> I like to have information, rather than just have a brushstroke.
> Jean-Michel Basquiat[156]

Jean-Michel Basquiat was born in Brooklyn. His father, an accountant, had emigrated from Haiti, and his mother was Puerto Rican. His parents separated when he was seven; his mother suffered from depression, and his father kept custody of Jean-Michel and his two sisters. His relationship with his father was difficult, and Jean-Michel ran away from home at 15, living for a time in Washington Square Park. He attended City-As-School, an alternative high school that emphasized the city as a learning institution, and among his classes he studied art history at the Museum of Modern Art.[157]

Basquiat loved to draw, and as a child had wanted to be a cartoonist. His first artistic project began when he and a classmate were smoking marijuana in the CAS student lounge, and Jean-Michel made a joke about the same old shit, which became SAMO. In 1978, Basquiat and Al Diaz began to use magic markers to spread SAMO aphorisms all over SoHo and TriBeCa, with special attention to walls near art schools and galleries. By 1980, disagreements with Diaz led Basquiat to end his graffiti career, which he signified by posting the epitaph "SAMO is dead." But through SAMO Basquiat had befriended some prominent graffiti artists who were becoming art world figures.[158]

The stock market boom of the 1980s produced an explosion in the New York art market, as auction houses broke all historical records for modern and contemporary art, and gallery owners competed to see who could get the highest prices from the wealthiest collectors. A new generation of artists who had grown up with Andy Warhol's Pop art and open pursuit of fame and fortune became famous overnight. And Basquiat became the brightest star in New York's art firmament. In 1981 the poet and critic Rene Ricard wrote in *Artforum* that "If Cy Twombly and Jean Dubuffet had a baby and gave it up for adoption, it would be Jean-Michel"; in 1985 Basquiat was pictured on the cover of the *New York Times Magazine*, photographed in his studio with bare feet, crowned by his trademark dreadlocks, wearing a paint-spattered Armani suit. The accompanying article remarked that "the nature and rapidity of his climb is unimaginable in another era."[159]

Basquiat's first solo New York exhibition, at Annina Nosei's gallery in 1982, was an instant success. All the paintings sold on the first night. Reviewers raved: Lisa Liebmann wrote in *Art in America* of "the unmistakable eloquence of his touch," his "compellingly edgy, allusive messages," and "formal sophistication."[160] A friend recalled that at the opening, an elated Basquiat told him, "'Man, I'm set for life!' He knew he was going to be successful."[161]

It was also in 1982 that Basquiat had a brief romantic relationship with the aspiring dancer and singer Madonna. Her strict regimen of health food and exercise clashed with Basquiat's bohemian lifestyle, and she soon ended the relationship because of his drug problem. But she later told an interviewer that "He was one of the few people I was truly envious of" for what she considered his artistic genius, and she wistfully remembered an evening "having dinner with Andy Warhol, Keith Haring and Jean-Michel at Mr. Chow's and feeling like the luckiest girl in the world."[162]

Basquiat broke the color line in American art. There had been black painters earlier, but they had always been relegated to minor status: thus the *New York Times* stated in 1985 that Basquiat was the "first black artist to achieve anything close to blue-chip status in the contemporary art market."[163] Basquiat also brought the subject of race squarely into fine art. Pop, the representational art of the Civil Rights era, had almost entirely avoided race as a subject, but Basquiat made blacks and their culture the focus of his art. He put scores of black heroes into his paintings, including baseball players, boxers, and jazz musicians. He made paintings titled *History of Black People*, *Slave Auction*, *Jim Crow*, and another simply *Black*. He clearly felt a special kinship with a few individuals. So for example he owned a case of copies of *Bird Lives*, Ross Russell's biography of Charlie Parker, and his paintings often referred to Parker, another young genius who was nearly as famous for his tragic life as for his art.[164]

Basquiat idolized Warhol. A friend recalled that "Andy Warhol was the apple of his eye since he was fifteen or sixteen. He wanted Warhol's fame," another that "He always said that he was going to be the next Warhol." Basquiat pursued Warhol, and gained his attention in 1982 by painting *Dos Cabezas*, a dual portrait of Warhol and himself. The two became close friends: the biographer Phoebe Hoban wrote that "By the time he was twenty-three, Basquiat had realized his fantasy: he was not only Warhol's protégé but his collaborator and partner; they hung out together, worked out together, painted and partied together."[165] One of Basquiat's most celebrated portraits was his 1984 *Andy Warhol as a Banana*, an apparent homage to Warhol's 1966 album cover for the Velvet Underground that featured the image of a banana.[166]

The sociologist Nathalie Heinich observed that Basquiat perfectly embodied the type of the conceptual young genius.[167] He was inspired by Warhol's fame, but his art was distinctively his own, as he created a highly personal style that resembled that of no other artist. His goals were conceptual: "I was trying to communicate an idea.... I was trying to make paintings different from the paintings that I saw a lot of at the time, which were mostly Minimal and they were highbrow and alienating, and I wanted to make very direct paintings that most people would feel the emotion behind."[168]

Nearly all of Basquiat's paintings included words, and some were made up almost entirely of language. Since Braque and Picasso had first begun to include letters and words in their paintings, a series of conceptual painters had used language to refer to popular culture, to pose verbal puzzles, to engage with philosophy, and to make political and social commentaries.[169] Basquiat used language in all these ways. Keith Haring called Basquiat "The supreme poet.... His expertise at the assembling and disassembling of language has revealed new meanings to old words. He used words like paint. He cut them, combined them, erased them, and rebuilt them. Every invention a new revelation."[170]

Basquiat's language contained myriad allusions: scholars have devoted hundreds of pages to tracing and analyzing these.[171] Allusion makes art directly from earlier art, inconsistent with the direct expression of perception that characterizes experimental art. In the enormous volume and range of his allusions, Basquiat placed himself in a lineage of modern conceptual innovators that includes T. S. Eliot, Ezra Pound, James Joyce, Jean-Luc Godard, and Bob Dylan. He often painted with a book in one hand and a brush in the other: "I get my background from studying books. I put what I like from them in my paintings."[172]

Basquiat also made liberal use of collage, another device invented by Picasso and adopted by many later conceptual artists.[173] Collage is intrinsically conceptual: it produces abrupt transitions that call attention to the technique of a work of art, and it juxtaposes elements that were previously unrelated. Basquiat often took collage elements from his own work, as he would xerox his drawings, tear them up, glue pieces to a canvas, and paint over them.[174]

The writer Richard Marshall observed of Basquiat's work of 1981 that "Although he was only twenty-one years of age, the paintings reveal that Basquiat had already established a signature style."[175] His canvases were dense and complex, as images and words jostled against each other: the critic Dick Hebdige commented that "Trying to 'read' a Basquiat painting is like trying to listen to a melody on a radio with a faulty tuner—the dominant signal is constantly under attack from static interference, unannounced intrusions from other stations."[176] The gestural brushstrokes of his paintings reflect the speed with which he worked. Basquiat often painted to a steady stream of Charlie Parker recordings, and his most successful paintings have the power, energy, and drive of Parker's bebop solos.

But Basquiat's rapid artistic rise was soon followed by an equally rapid fall. A 1984 review opened with the declaration that "It's quite absurd to speak of the decline of an artist who's barely 25," but the reviewer felt that Basquiat had lost the complexity that had distinguished his earlier work.[177] His dealer agreed: Mary Boone, who presented Basquiat exhibitions in 1984 and 1985, remarked that "I didn't show him at his creative peak, more at his peak of popularity. He did his best paintings when he was showing with Annina [Nosei, his dealer in 1981–1982]."[178] And the decline continued: the painter Rick Prol, who worked as Basquiat's studio assistant in 1988, reflected that the paintings of that year "in relation to his earlier paintings . . . were really like knocked off and not really worked on that much."[179]

In 1986, the critic Barry Schwabsky offered an explanation for the deterioration of Basquiat's work after 1982. He described the strengths and weaknesses of Basquiat's style: "It can accommodate any kind of mark that remains fixed at the level of inscription, that does not inject any ambiguity into its status as an addition to a surface to which it remains flatly parallel, but it is incapable of assimilating anything suggestive of representational space." Schwabsky noted that this technique had allowed Basquiat to become a very good decorative painter, but that his ambition to achieve more had revealed its constraints, so that over time "we see him flailing more and more against the limitations of his technique." At an age when most aspiring painters were still experimenting with existing styles, Basquiat "has created a distinctive one of his own and is also discovering (as he hadn't three years ago) that it is a trap." Schwabsky speculated that escaping would require Basquiat to develop "a more sophisticated concept of space, one that allows for description as well as inscription."[180] Basquiat may in fact have recognized the limitations of his style earlier than Schwabsky believed. Thus a close friend recalled that in 1982 he had confessed to her that "I feel like a fraud because I'm now selling my work and I don't know how to draw."[181]

In 1983, a dealer proposed that Basquiat and Warhol collaborate on a series of paintings. The project began hopefully: Warhol admitted that he agreed because "I'd run out of ideas," and Basquiat exulted that he had prompted Warhol to paint with a brush for the first time in twenty years.[182] But the results were badly received when they were exhibited in 1985. One review in particular struck a nerve, as a *New York Times* critic called the collaboration "one of Warhol's manipulations," and declared that it made Basquiat "an art world mascot."[183] Warhol instantly understood that his friendship with Basquiat would not survive the slur; he later wrote in his diary of how much he missed Basquiat, and reflected that "Jean-Michel hasn't called me in a month, so I guess it's really over."[184] When Warhol died, unexpectedly, less than two years later, Basquiat was devastated. In 1980, Basquiat had written "SAMO is dead" on walls in the East Village. Now, seven years later, he wrote "A. W. lives—SAMO lives." A friend recalled that "When Andy died it was like his life was over," and the next year it was, dead of an overdose at 27.[185]

Basquiat's art was as controversial as Warhol's: after his death a critic wrote in the *Village Voice* that "he was the most financially successful Black visual artist in history and, depending on whether you listened to his admirers or detractors, either a genius, an idiot savant, or an overblown, overpriced fraud."[186] The statement was hardly an exaggeration: eulogies ranged from Rene Ricard's declaration that "Jean-Michel was touched by God. He was a black saint," to Robert Hughes' judgment that Basquiat was a "small, untrained talent caught in the buzz saw of art world promotion, absurdly overrated by dealers, collectors, and no doubt to their future embarrassment, by critics," in a *New Republic* article titled "Requiem for a Featherweight."[187] Basquiat described his own subject matter as "Royalty, heroism, and the streets," and his art was a synthesis of a number of elements that had previously been excluded from advanced art.[188] Diego Cortez, his first agent, explained that his work "was related to graffiti, the street, Pop art, and the music scene."[189] Mary Boone contended that "Jean-Michel paved the way for not only blacks but artists of color to enter the world. He opened a lot of doors for a lot of artists, Felix Gonzalez-Torres, Takashi Murakami, Kara Walker, Ellen Gallagher. It couldn't have happened without him."[190] Peter Schjeldahl agreed: "As a black artist, Basquiat isn't the Jackie Robinson of the American art world—which, until quite recently, was woefully all but lily-white—so much as its Willie Mays, abolishing forever racial identity as remarkable in the field's top rank."[191]

Basquiat died four months shy of his 28th birthday, so it might seem natural to wonder how much greater his achievement might have been if he had lived a normal life span. Yet his place in art history stems from a bold conceptual innovation he made suddenly in his early 20s. Pop brought images from mass commercial culture into fine art; Basquiat made a parallel contribution, by bringing images from the streets into fine art. Both of these innovations were radical new ideas, that could be executed and understood immediately. Andy Warhol made his basic contribution to visual art primarily within the single year of 1962, and Basquiat's contribution of 1982 mirrored that of his idol in this respect. Basquiat's paintings from that year have achieved the highest average prices at auction of any year in his career, and are more frequently illustrated in art history textbooks than those from any other year.[192]

Jean-Michel Basquiat was an art world meteorite. His conceptual innovation arrived suddenly, it was recognized immediately, and his disastrous fall was almost equally precipitous. The highly conceptual nature of his innovation allowed him to join such earlier young geniuses as Arthur Rimbaud, Georges Seurat, Vincent van Gogh, Hart Crane, Sylvia Plath, Eva Hesse, Ana Mendieta, and his beloved Charlie Parker in making a major contribution in spite of dying tragically young.

Truth and Art

For Cézanne, the purpose of making art was to gain the knowledge that would allow him to achieve his avowed goal of *realization*. Patience was necessary, for as he wrote to a younger artist in 1904, "The understanding of the model and its realization is sometimes very slow in coming." The artist needed to develop a technique that would allow him to express his understanding: "what you must strive to achieve is a good method of construction."[193] In 1905, he warned Bernard not to be satisfied with following "the beautiful formulas of our illustrious predecessors," whose work he studied in the Louvre:

> Let us go forth to study beautiful nature, let us try to free our minds from them, let us strive to express ourselves according to our personal temperament. Time and reflection, moreover, modify little by little our vision, and at last comprehension comes to us.[194]

Cézanne's goal was distant but real: "The truth lies in nature."[195] Less than a year before his death, in a letter to Bernard he made a promise, never fulfilled, that has tantalized artists and scholars for more than a century: "at my age I should have more experience and use it for the general good. I owe you the truth about painting and shall tell it to you."[196] His late paintings, with their many discrete, hatched strokes that do not merge but remain distinct, appear to witness Cézanne's understanding of the inevitable incompleteness of his ability to represent nature whole, and his recognition that he could instead produce only a series of partial representations. Meyer Schapiro contended that Cézanne effectively made his search for visual truth his subject, by making "his sensing, probing, doubting, finding activity a visible part of the painting."[197] If he could never achieve realization, he could nonetheless record the progress he had made toward it for the benefit of artists who came after him, at the same time he showed them his research methods.

Picasso emphatically denied that art could attain truth. In 1923 he told a friend that "We all know that Art is not truth. Art is a lie that makes us realize truth, at least the truth that is given to us to understand." The artist's goal was deception: "The artist must know the manner whereby to convince others of the truthfulness of his lies."[198] Picasso furthermore denied that an artist developed or improved his style over time:

> If an artist varies his mode of expression this only means he has changed his manner of thinking, and in changing, it might be for the better or it might be for the worse.
>
> The several manners I have used in my art must not be considered as an evolution, or as steps toward an unknown ideal of painting. . . . If the subjects I have wanted to express have suggested different ways of expression I have never hesitated to adopt them. . . . This does not imply either evolution or progress.[199]

Art thus had no single goal, and no one correct style. Picasso developed the practice of working simultaneously in different styles, and he denied that any one of these had greater validity than any other. Each was a distinct visual language, that represented a particular view of reality. Each was equally arbitrary and artificial, and had as great a claim to truth as the others.[200] As the critic Christopher Butler observed in another context, an artist's practice of stylistic diversity "enshrines an essentially relativist attitude towards the 'truthful' depiction of reality."[201] Because of this, the artist's path to a style—his research—was of no interest to others; only his results mattered.

And so Picasso contended that art should present achievements, not attempts: "Nobody is interested in following a man who, with his eyes fixed on the ground, spends his life looking for the pocketbook that fortune should put in his path.... What one does is what counts and not what one had the intention of doing".[202]

Under the intellectual influence of Existentialism, most of the Abstract Expressionists avoided such absolute terms as *truth* in describing their goals. But they took from the Surrealist poets and painters the idea of drawing on the subconscious to produce new, personal images that would express their own individuality, and that might serve as examples of the ethical being.[203] In 1947, Pollock stressed that his new drip technique minimized the distance— not only physical, but psychological—between him and his art. Breaking with centuries of tradition, he spread unstretched canvas on the floor, where he was "more at ease," and where he could "feel nearer, more a part of the painting, since this way I can walk around it, work from the four sides and literally be *in* the painting." His tools and materials also broke with fine art tradition: "I continue to get further away from the usual painter's tools such as easel, palette, brushes, etc. I prefer sticks, trowels, knives and dripping fluid paint or a heavy impasto with sand, broken glass and other foreign matter."[204]

Pollock's language implies a rejection of traditions of artificiality, in favor of a more elemental, sincere, and direct art. In a 1950 interview, he explained that modern artists had to find "new means of making their statements." Drawing on the unconscious, the modern artist was "working and expressing an inner world—in other words—expressing the energy, the motion, and other inner forces." The famous drip method was merely a means to this end: "the result is the thing—and—it doesn't make much difference how the paint is put on as long as something has been said. Technique is just a means of arriving at a statement."[205]

Pollock's goal of making a *statement* appears to parallel Cézanne's goal of *realization*: both were working toward the creation of a unique personal style that would allow them to achieve a novel visual resolution that neither could anticipate or describe with any precision. After Pollock's death, Lee Krasner recalled that he sometimes "got hung up" on a painting for weeks, complaining that "This won't come through." Yet he rarely abandoned it: "Generally, he wouldn't give up a canvas. He would just stay with it until it was resolved for him."[206]

Warhol's art ostensibly rejected not only personal style, but also originality. Thus he remarked that "I think it would be great if more people took up silk screens so that no one would know whether my picture was mine or somebody else's."[207] Gerard Malanga explained that "Andy wanted to keep the human element out of his art, and to avoid it he had to resort to silkscreens, stencils, and other kinds of automatic reproduction."[208] Warhol once explained that his avoidance of the personal touch extended even beyond silk-screening the images in his paintings to using a rubber stamp to sign them, because "an artist's signature is part of style. I don't want my art to have a style."[209] Warhol's art avoided personal statements, and instead reflected mass culture, using these impersonal methods to produce uninflected images of familiar objects or people. Malanga remarked that "As far as any visual expression he might have tried to convey in his paintings, I don't think he gave it much thought."[210] Warhol himself stated, "There's nothing really to understand in my work."[211]

Warhol went to great lengths to avoid revealing any motivation for his art. The curator Henry Geldzahler pondered Warhol's stance:

> There is a quality to Andy Warhol's public persona that inspires endless discussion, quite unlike that of any other artist. Such discussions inevitably center on the question of his intentions and the artist's control over the meanings in his work.... He has cultivated to perfection a naïve blankness, a bottomless well of innocence when forced to declare himself on an issue.... The truth is that those of us who have been among his close friends for the past twenty years or more have exactly the same questions about Warhol's intent and control as does the informed public.[212]

Warhol himself stated that "I just paint those objects in my paintings because those are the things I know best."[213]

Warhol's art, like his statements about it, avoided the issue of truth altogether. What Henry Geldzahler recognized in Warhol's persona was equally true of his art, for the ambiguity of the images—were his portrayals of Marilyn, or soup cans, satirical or approving?—was the key to indefinite debate, and publicity. Unlike Cézanne and Pollock, each of whom sought a single style that would yield resolved images to express basic perceptions, and unlike Picasso, who used widely divergent styles to express diverse ideas, Warhol created a style, and an art, founded on ambiguity, that could mean different things to different observers. The critic Blake Gopnik interviewed more than 250 associates of Warhol for a 960-page biography, and concluded that his life presented the same ambiguity as his art: "Was his art a put-on, or was the put-on his art? Was he himself a joke or a genius, a radical or a social climber? As Warhol would have answered: Yes."[214]

Like Warhol, Basquiat shrewdly and aggressively pursued fame, and to this end he also followed Warhol in creating a persona that complemented his art. He epitomized celebrity cool. He produced a hip-hop record with the rapper Fab 5 Freddy, appeared in a music video for the Blondie song "Rapture," starred in a film about the underground art scene in which he was kissed by an angel played by Debbie Harry (who bought *Cadillac Moon,* one of Basquiat's first paintings), played in a noise band with the actor Vincent Gallo, and modeled in a runway fashion show for Comme des Garcons. He understood that Warhol had been a pioneer: "maybe because of people like Andy I think that the artist can be viewed more as a 'hero,' an image." And he understood that this had given him a platform: "I can't say I'm the first recognized Black artist.... Maybe I'm the first to get across to a lot of people ... there's more media coverage."[215]

Basquiat's art made personal statements: he told an interviewer he was "trying to paint a very urban landscape"—how a young black man saw the world.[216] His paintings made frequent reference to blacks and their history, with tributes to great athletes and musicians, canonizing Joe Louis as *St. Joe* and bestowing a kingdom on Charlie Parker as *Charles the First.* His painted commentaries on racism ranged from the history of the transatlantic slave trade to the 1983 beating death of a graffiti artist by New York City transit police. He wanted his art to fill a void: "Black people are never portrayed realistically in ... not even portrayed in modern art enough, and I'm glad that I do that. I use the 'Black' as the protagonist because I am Black, and that's why I use it as the main character in all the paintings."[217]

3
Poets

In an essay on how poems are made, the poet Stephen Spender reflected on two very different types of composition:

> [O]ne is immediate and complete, the other is plodding and only completed by stages. Some poets write immediately works which, when they are written, scarcely need revision. Others write their poems by stages, feeling their way from rough draft to rough draft, until finally, after many revisions, they have produced a result which may seem to have very little connection with their early sketches.

Spender noted that the first of these types was "the more brilliant and dazzling," but he stressed that it did not necessarily produce greater poems, for "genius, unlike virtuosity, is judged by greatness of results, not by brilliance of performance." The difference was between two types of genius: "one type ... is able to plunge the greatest depths of his own experience by the tremendous effort of a moment, the other ... must dig deeper and deeper into his consciousness, layer by layer."[1]

Spender did not pursue the implications of his distinction. Other poets, however, have observed that there are two very different types of poetry. In an interview with *Paris Review* in 1961, Robert Lowell surveyed the current state of poetry:

> [I]t seems to me that we've gotten into a sort of Alexandrian age. Poets of my generation and particularly younger ones have gotten terribly proficient at these forms. They write a very musical, difficult poem with tremendous skill, perhaps there's never been such skill. Yet the writing seems divorced from the culture. It's become too much something specialized that can't handle too much experience. It's become a craft, purely a craft, and there must be some breakthrough back into life....
>
> Any number of people are guilty of writing a complicated poem that has a certain amount of symbolism in it and really difficult meaning, a

wonderful poem to teach. Then you unwind it and you feel that the intelligence, the experience, whatever goes into it, is skin-deep. In Elizabeth Bishop's "Man-Moth" a whole new world is gotten out and you don't know what will come after any one line. It's exploring.... She has gotten a world, not just a way of writing. She seldom writes a poem that doesn't have that exploring quality.[2]

In this brief discussion, Lowell provided a concise characterization of the contrast between conceptual and experimental poetry. In his account, conceptual poetry was difficult, skillful, complicated, artificial, symbolic, academic, and often superficial, whereas experimental poetry was experiential, exploratory, and unpredictable. The difference between these two sets of values can be seen clearly in the work, and lives, of great modern poets.

Robert Frost (1874–1963)

We write of things we see and we write in accents we hear.

Robert Frost[3]

When Robert Frost graduated from high school in Lawrence, Massachusetts, he wanted to be a poet. Yet he did not publish his first book of poems until he was 39 years old. He devoted little of the intervening time to formal education (he dropped out of Dartmouth and Harvard in two attempts at college, and later commented that "We go to college to be given one more chance to learn to read in case we haven't learned in High School. Once we have learned to read the rest can be trusted to add itself unto us."[4]) What he considered the most important part of these two decades was seven years he spent running a one-man chicken farm in Derry, New Hampshire. Frost explained that "solitude was what I needed and valued. I had days and days and days to think the least little thought and do the least little thing. That's where I got my sense that I have forever for accomplishment." The farm's isolation allowed him to develop his poetry without pressure: "My infant industries needed the protection of a dead space around them."[5]

In 1912, Frost took his family to live in England. There, the next year, he published his first book, *A Boy's Will*. This comprised poems he had written over more than two decades, including "My Butterfly," which opened with these lines:

> Thine emulous fond flowers are dead, too,
> And the daft sun-assaulter, he
> That frighted thee so oft, is fled or dead....[6]

This poem had been published in a magazine in 1894, and Frost considered it his "first real poem," but its forced internal rhymes, awkward alliteration, and stilted language clearly distinguish it from his mature work.[7] (Frost did later reflect that in "My Butterfly" he "was even guilty of 'theeing' and 'thouing,' a crime I have not committed since."[8]) Frost was encouraged by favorable reviews of his book, and wrote to a friend that "I expect to do something to the present state of literature in America."[9]

Frost's poetry developed considerably during the three years he spent in England, and in letters to friends he outlined the ideas underlying his informal theory of poetry. Poems should be made from the vernacular: "What I would like is to get so I would never use a word or combination of words that I hadn't *heard* used in running speech." The essence of poetry lay in sound, and accordingly he proposed "a new definition of a sentence: A sentence is a sound in itself on which other sounds called words may be strung." The sounds he approved "are gathered by the ear from the vernacular and brought into books.... I think no writer invents them. The most original writer only catches them fresh from talk, where they grow spontaneously." He was confident that he could make a contribution, writing in 1913: "To be perfectly frank with you I am one of the most notable craftsmen of my time. That will transpire presently." He described his goal: "I alone of English writers have consciously set myself to make music out of what I may call the sound of sense."[10] The "sound of sense" was the abstract sound of language that could be heard "from voices behind a door that cuts off the words," and this was the heart of poetry: "One who concerns himself with it more than the subject is an artist."[11]

Frost wanted his poetry to grow from experience: "I was afraid I hadn't imagination enough to be really literary. And I hadn't. I have just barely enough to imitate spoken sentences.... I'm what you would call reproductive."[12] He wanted readers to recognize his perceptions: "In literature it is our business to give people the thing that will make them say, 'Oh yes I know what you mean.'" He wanted to reach a wide audience: "there is a kind of success called 'of esteem' and it butters no parsnips. It means a success with the critical few.... I must get outside that circle to the general reader who buys books in their thousands.... I want to be a poet for all sorts and kinds."[13]

Frost's second book, *North of Boston*, was published in 1914, and it staked out the territory, geographically and artistically, that he would occupy for the rest of his life. Its title was taken from a heading in the real estate advertisements in the *Boston Globe*, and Frost testified that every person in the book "was friend or acquaintance of mine in New Hampshire."[14] The book's language had changed, as Frost warned a friend that "In *North of Boston* you are to see me performing in a language absolutely unliterary."[15] The poet Derek Walcott marveled that "something wonderful, revolutionary within the convention, happened to Frost's ear between *A Boy's Will* and *North of Boston*. He wrote American. . . . Once that confidence sprung to hand and voice, there was no other road for Frost but greatness."[16] Robert Lowell, a Boston native, appreciated Frost's poems for their description of the New England countryside: "I used to wonder whether I knew anything about the country that wasn't in Frost."[17]

Frost and his family returned to the United States in 1915. He would never again live outside New England; he told a friend that his dream was to buy a farm "where I could live cheap and get Yankier and Yankier."[18] At a time when advanced artists were overwhelmingly concerned with the excitement and sophistication of the modern city, Frost set his poems in rustic rural New England. He often wrote of lone travelers, whose thoughts were sparked by nature. He also wrote of men working—in the words of a biographer, "celebrating physical work better than any poet before him."[19] He wanted to treat familiar subjects in unfamiliar ways: "The subject should be common in experience and uncommon in books. . . . It should have happened to everyone but it should have occurred to no one before as material."[20] He wanted to suit his language to his subjects: "The language is appropriate to the virtues I celebrate."[21] The language must be common: "the great fight of any poet is against the people who want him to write in a special language that has gradually separated from spoken language."[22] In everyday speech, Frost heard "emanations of grandeur and dignity and reverence and heroism and terror."[23]

Frost's colloquial style, familiar themes, and pastoral settings led many critics to dismiss his work as a quaint relic of the past, lacking the complexity of thought and technique essential for significant modern poetry. So for example Malcolm Cowley wrote in 1944 that Frost celebrated the "New England of the tourist home and the antique shop in the abandoned gristmill," and W. W. Robson contended in 1966 that Frost's art was "more akin to that of the short story writer than the poet."[24] Frost disagreed. In a

1931 essay, he declared that poetry involved "the profoundest thinking that we have," because it provided "the one permissible way of saying one thing and meaning another."[25] Frost's admirers pointed to many instances in which the true complexity of Frost's poems has been missed. Generations of schoolchildren, for example, have been taught that the closing lines of "The Road Not Taken"—"Two roads diverged in a wood, and I—/I took the one less traveled by,/And that has made all the difference"—are a tribute to the celebrated American virtues of independence and nonconformism. Ignored by this interpretation is the speaker's earlier comment that "as for that the passing there/Had worn them really about the same," followed by the even more explicit observation that "both that morning equally lay/In leaves no step had trodden black." A further hint that the speaker was in fact not a nonconformist appeared in the lines that immediately precede the famous closing: "I shall be telling this with a sigh/Somewhere ages and ages hence." The speaker may thus be imagining that at that distant future time, he will have simplified and glorified his experience, allegorizing his life's journey for an admiring audience even while recognizing that he is posing. The apparent simplicity of the poem's ostensibly conventional message is thus undercut by ambiguity and irony.[26]

In 1922, at the age of 48, Frost wrote "Stopping by Woods on a Snowy Evening."[27] He called the poem "my best bid for remembrance," and his prediction was acute, for it became his single most frequently anthologized poem.[28] Few poems are as familiar to Americans:

> Whose woods these are I think I know.
> His house is in the village, though;
> He will not see me stopping here
> To watch his woods fill up with snow.
>
> My little horse must think it queer
> To stop without a farmhouse near
> Between the woods and frozen lake
> The darkest evening of the year.
>
> He gives his harness bells a shake
> To ask if there is some mistake.
> The only other sound's the sweep
> Of easy wind and downy flake.

> The woods are lovely, dark and deep,
> But I have promises to keep,
> And miles to go before I sleep,
> And miles to go before I sleep.[29]

The poem's simple language and easy, relaxed rhymes lull the reader, just as the gentle wind and soft snow lull the speaker, and the softness of the repeated consonants "s" and "n" reinforces the peaceful atmosphere that tempts the speaker to yield to the lure of the inviting woods.[30] But "the darkest evening of the year" strikes a sinister note, for snowy nights are not in fact dark. The novelist Vladimir Nabokov, who considered this one of the greatest poems in the English language, wrote of its "prodigious and poignant end—two closing lines identical in every syllable, but one personal and physical, and the other metaphysical and universal."[31] Nabokov's reading is a prime example of the suggestive possibilities of Frost's simple poetry. Frost appreciated this power of ambiguity. When asked whether "Stopping by Woods" was about the temptation of death, as critics often claimed, he replied, "I never intended that, but I did have the feeling it was loaded with ulteriority."[32] And when Josephine Jacobsen told him of her uneasiness at having readers tell her of things in her poems that she had not intended, Frost replied, "Well, I always say that a man is entitled to any oil that's found in his backyard."[33] On occasion, Frost went further, suggesting that he not only welcomed variant interpretations, but invited them. And the invitation might be mischievous. Frost once wrote to a friend that he wanted "to trip the reader head foremost into the boundless. Ever since infancy I have had the habit of leaving my blocks carts chairs and such like ordinaries where people would be pretty sure to fall forward over them in the dark."[34]

As Frost aged, he never lost his commitment to the importance of the speaking voice. So for example he declared in 1939 that "The sound is the gold in the ore."[35] But a biographer observed that the terms Frost used to describe his poetry changed over time, from technical to moral: "His early critical ideas were wholly those of the craftsman; later ideas were those of the philosopher."[36] When Frost was 65, he declared that a poem "begins in delight and ends in wisdom. . . . [I]t runs a lucky course of events, and ends in a clarification of life . . . in a momentary stay against confusion."[37] He considered poetry "a way of grappling with life," and defined a poem as "a way *out* of something."[38] The poet Seamus Heaney explained that Frost regarded poetry as a means of combating "a terror of immense, unlimited, and undefined chaos."[39]

"Stopping by Woods on a Snowy Evening" may illustrate Frost's claim that poetry could check confusion.[40] The poem narrates a struggle between the attraction of nature and the speaker's power of resistance. The strict control of the poem's interlocked rhyme scheme, in which the dissonant third line of one stanza provides the rhyme of the next, parallels the speaker's resistance to the pull of nature. The first line of the final stanza spells out the attraction of nature even as it introduces the rhyme that formally unifies all the lines of that stanza, which expresses the speaker's ability to overcome that attraction. The poem's text thus chronicles the speaker's triumph in refusing to yield, and its form embodies the poet's success in creating structure from the chaos of experience.

For the experimental Frost, the essence of a poem was discovery—"It must be a revelation, or a series of revelations, as much for the poet as for the reader." A poem whose ending was planned in advance would have no power: "No surprise for the writer, no surprise for the reader."[41] Comparing himself to a painter, Frost explained that he wanted his palette to hold "pure, separate colors. Then I will do the mixing on the canvas. The canvas is where the work of art is, where we make the conquest."[42] Like an experimental painter, Frost thus believed that works of art must display discoveries that the artist made in the act of producing them: "You've got to be the happy discoverer of your ends."[43] The greatest achievements could not be anticipated: "You say as you go more than you ever hoped you were going to be able to say, and come with surprise to an end that you foreknew only with some sort of emotion. You have believed the thing into existence."[44] In a study of Frost's poetry that Frost praised, Lawrance Thompson argued that Frost worked toward a specific kind of resolution: "Out of the chaotic confusion of daily impressions and thoughts the poet captures a moment with his words and achieves a kind of crystallization which gives to his chaotic raw materials not only shape but weight."[45] But for Frost refuge could only be temporary. "Provide, Provide," written when Frost was 60, warned that no achievement afforded lasting protection: "No memory of having starred/Atones for later disregard/Or keeps the end from being hard."[46] The provisional nature of the accomplishment reflected Frost's experimental belief that poetry was never final—it was not a product, but a process, an activity, a way of thinking. Frost considered poetry not as an escape from life, but rather as the pursuit of life, "a deeper probing into it, and into ourselves, than ordinary everyday living provides."[47] Frost's embrace of both simplicity and ambiguity marked his fundamentally experimental quest: for him art was a search for an uncertain underlying reality. He once explained that poetry "begins with very simple analogies or metaphors ... and it grows and becomes extended into more and more complex metaphors, until it includes the most profound philosophical thought that human nature is capable of reaching."[48]

Frost achieved his goal of being a poet for all, as he became by far the most popular American poet of the twentieth century. His fame spread well beyond the college classrooms and lecture halls where he earned a comfortable living by what he called "barding around," as for example he was featured on the cover of *Time* magazine in 1950. In 1960, John F. Kennedy closed campaign speeches by quoting the lines "But I have promises to keep,/And miles to go before I sleep," and when Kennedy was elected, he had the 86-year-old Frost read a poem at his inauguration.[49] Frost's enormous popularity, and his carefully cultivated folksy persona, contributed to a tendency for critics to slight his poetry as mere entertainment, but he gained influence among younger experimental poets who admired his realism and subtle use of language. The poet Randall Jarrell grouped Frost with T. S. Eliot and Wallace Stevens as the greatest American poets of the century, and praised "the many, many poems in which there are real people with their real speech and real thought and real emotions."[50] Robert Lowell paid tribute to the mature Frost: "Step by step, he had tested his observation of places and people until his best poems had the human and seen richness of great novels."[51] Seamus Heaney recalled that the first poet who ever inspired him was Frost; he acknowledged "a lifetime of pleasure in Frost's poems as events in language," and applauded Frost for believing "that poetry should be beautiful."[52]

Admirers rejected descriptions of Frost's poetry as provincial or regional, contending that its meaning invariably transcended its ostensible subject. Frost himself suggested that if he had to be classified, he might be called a Synechdochist: "always a larger significance. A little thing touches a larger thing." His poems often began with a description of a specific scene or event, then proceeded to a reflection on its larger significance—"from sight to insight," in Frost's words. The observation of the real was the "delight" in which Frost believed a poem should begin, while the abstraction was the "wisdom" in which it should end. "Stopping by Woods," for example, both narrated a specific event and suggested a meditation on such general themes as temptation and duty.[53] Frost once explained that he wrote about New England "just because I have it all around me," but that his meanings were universal: "I talk about the whole world in terms of New England."[54]

Frost wrote his most celebrated poems during his 40s, and he continued to write poems that are frequently anthologized into his 70s.[55] He believed experience helped a poet, for although a poem should begin as a perception, it could succeed only if it coalesced into an idea: "It finds its thought and succeeds, or doesn't find it and comes to nothing. I suppose it finds it lying around with others not so much to its purpose in a more or less full mind. That's why it oftener comes to nothing in youth before experience has filled the mind with thoughts."[56] Frost also believed that a poet's work became deeper as he grew older. At the age of 63, he considered the poet's life cycle:

> I think that young people have insight. They have a flash here and a flash there. It is like the stars coming out in the sky in the early evening. They have flashes of light. They have that sort of thing which belongs to youth. It is later in the dark of life that you see forms, constellations. And it is the constellations that are philosophy....
>
> I suppose that poets die into philosophy as they grow older—if they don't die the other way. They die into wisdom. Maybe it is a good way to die.[57]

T. S. Eliot (1888–1965)

> We can only say that it appears likely that poets in our civilization, as it exists at present, must be *difficult*.
>
> T. S. Eliot[58]

Thomas Stearns Eliot was born in St. Louis, where his grandfather had founded Washington University. Thomas' family spent summers in Massachusetts, which had been the home of many distinguished ancestors. His grandmother Abigail Adams Eliot, who lived next door throughout his youth, could remember her great-uncle John Adams, second president of the United States, after whose wife she was named, and she also knew his son John Quincy Adams, the sixth president. The historian Henry Adams was a cousin of Thomas', and when Thomas almost inevitably enrolled at Harvard, the university's president, Charles William Eliot, was also a relative.[59]

Eliot's interests in college were poetry and philosophy. Reading Baudelaire showed him "the poetical possibilities ... of the more sordid aspects of the modern metropolis, of the possibility of the fusion between the sordidly realistic and the phantasmagoric."[60] Even more important was his discovery of the symbolist poet Jules Laforgue. This produced "a personal enlightenment such as I can hardly communicate," for Laforgue "was the first to teach me how to speak, to teach me the poetic possibilities of my own idiom of speech." Eliot dated his maturation to reading Laforgue in 1909, explaining that "when a young writer is seized with his first passion of this sort he may be changed, metamorphosed almost, within a few weeks even, from a bundle of second-hand sentiments into a person." Finding his voice in this way instilled in Eliot "an unshakeable confidence."[61]

Eliot attended graduate school at Harvard, with the intention of becoming a professor of philosophy. A year at Oxford on a traveling fellowship led to a change in plans, however. The dynamic and charismatic American poet Ezra Pound, who was living in London, was excited by Eliot's poems, and convinced him to remain in England and become a poet.[62] Eliot married an English woman and settled in London, where he would spend the rest of his life.

Pound's backing resulted in the publication of Eliot's early poems, most notably "The Love Song of J. Alfred Prufrock," which Eliot had written in 1911, at the age of 23. It would become not only the most frequently anthologized poem Eliot ever wrote, but one of the most famous poems of the twentieth century.[63] "Prufrock" was radical both in subject, as the internal monologue of an unprepossessing and alienated middle-aged bachelor, and in technique, with complex allusion, free association of ideas, liberal use of irony, and disorienting metaphors. The great experimental poet William Butler Yeats, a generation older than Eliot, later remembered "Prufrock" as the announcement of "the most revolutionary man in poetry during my lifetime," and lamented its impact: "No romantic word or sound ... could be permitted henceforth.... [N]or must there be any special subject-matter."[64] For many younger poets, the irony and elegance of "Prufrock" established Eliot as a role model. So for example the nascent poet Delmore Schwartz insisted on reading the entire text of "Prufrock" aloud to his high school class, over the complaints of his fellow students, prompting the editors of the school's yearbook to declare that "T. S. Eliot is God, and Delmore Schwartz is his prophet."[65] Schwartz later explained that Eliot had shown poets the way forward: comparing modern life to an unknown land, he wrote that "Eliot is the international hero because he has made the journey to the foreign country and described the nature of the new life."[66] Malcolm Cowley, ten years younger than Eliot, recalled that with his early work Eliot demonstrated that "a Middle Western boy [could] become a flawless poet," writing "perfect poems, poems in which we could not find a line that betrayed immaturity, awkwardness, provincialism or platitude."[67]

Not content to lead solely by example, Eliot also undertook an ambitious critical campaign. With a characteristically scholarly approach, he provided rules to improve contemporary poetry. In his most celebrated essay, "Tradition and the Individual Talent" (1919), he contended that what made any work of art important was its relationship to earlier art: "No poet, no artist of any art, has his complete meaning alone. His significance, his appreciation is the appreciation of his relation to the dead poets and artists." A poet's impact was not only on those who came after him, but equally on those who came before: "what happens when a new work of art is created is something that happens simultaneously to all the works of art which preceded it." It followed that, in order to make a contribution, what the poet needed most was a comprehensive knowledge of the history of literature, which could only be obtained "by great labor." He could then write "not merely with his own generation in his bones, but with a feeling that the whole of the literature of Europe from Homer . . . has a simultaneous existence." This sense of the past would allow the poet to ignore his own feelings in favor of expressing a wider tradition: "The progress of an artist is a continual self-sacrifice, a continual extinction of personality. . . . Poetry is not a turning loose of emotion, but an escape from emotion; it is not the expression of personality, but an escape from personality." Art allowed no self-indulgence: "the more perfect the artist, the more completely separate in him will be the man who suffers and the mind which creates." Poetry must be a rigorous intellectual activity: "The poet must become more and more comprehensive, more allusive, more indirect, in order to force, to dislocate if necessary, language into his meaning."[68]

In 1922, at the age of 34, Eliot published *The Waste Land*. It was obviously different from earlier poetry: the critic Edmund Wilson remarked drily that in 433 lines, Eliot "manages to include quotations from, allusions to, or imitations of, at least thirty-five different writers (some of them, such as Shakespeare and Dante, laid under contribution several times)—as well as several popular songs; and to introduce passages in six foreign languages, including Sanskrit."[69] The poet Conrad Aiken, a college friend of Eliot's, couldn't help noting that "Eliot's sense of the literary past has become so overmastering as almost to constitute the motive of the work. It is as if . . . he wanted to make a 'literature of literature'—a poetry actuated not more by life itself than by poetry."[70] The critic Louis Menand recently described the poem as "a collage of allusion, quotation, echo, appropriation, pastiche, imitation, and ventriloquism."[71] Eliot wanted his poetry to be difficult, in order to raise the status of the art, and his training as a philosopher made it natural for him to do this by making poetry more scholarly; as if to underscore the importance of his many literary allusions, he appended footnotes to *The Waste Land*.

In a poll of eminent American poets taken in 2000, *The Waste Land* was voted Eliot's greatest poem.[72] It was revolutionary: not only have many poets agreed with the American poet Karl Shapiro's judgment in 1960 that "*The Waste Land* is the most important poem of the twentieth century," but many also agreed with the English poet C. Day Lewis in 1934 that "for good or ill, *The Waste Land* has had a far greater influence on present-day verse than the rest of Eliot's work and probably a greater one than any other poetry of the century."[73] *The Waste Land* made innovations in a number of domains.[74] One was its setting. Eliot conspicuously broke with the romantic tradition of pastoral poetry, and like Dickens' novels—which he loved—*The Waste Land* treated the ugliness of the modern industrial city. The brutal departure from beautiful and agreeable surroundings made many contemporaries consider the work not simply un-poetic but anti-poetic. In another radical break, *The Waste Land* had no plot. Many were bewildered by its lack of an omniscient narrator, or even a coherent narrative. It presented instead a series of unrelated speakers, who appeared and departed abruptly, without characterization, transition, or explanation. The poem equally made sudden shifts in rhythm and images. Overall, it violated virtually all traditional forms of continuity. *The Waste Land* did have recurring symbols, many drawn from mythology, a product of Eliot's belief in the importance of historical consciousness. The poem's abundant literary allusions connected the intellectual life of modern London to that of ancient Athens, medieval Florence, and nineteenth-century Paris.[75]

The fragmented images and references of *The Waste Land* perplexed many readers, but many young poets embraced this as a verbal adaptation of Picasso's innovation of collage.[76] Just as collage transformed visual elements by changing their context, so Eliot believed that verbal appropriation transformed its sources; he explained that "Immature poets imitate; mature poets steal; bad poets deface what they take, and good poets make it into something better."[77] Stephen Spender argued that *The Waste Land*'s form reinforced its message: "The poem is about a fragmented culture.... Fragmentariness, when projected into many scenes, with shifts of attention and mood ... gives the poem its apocalyptic visionary force."[78] The poem's depiction of decay and desolation increased its appeal to a generation disillusioned by the carnage and destruction of World War I. Spender recalled that Eliot believed that Western civilization was threatened by impending ruin, and had told Spender he expected that there would be "People killing one another in the streets."[79]

The Waste Land was immediately recognized as pivotal. Ezra Pound, who was committed to making modern poetry more highly conceptual, wrote to a friend that it "is I think the justification of the 'movement,' of our modern experiment, since 1900."[80] The poem became a rallying cry for a cohort of poets intent on defying their elders. In a scene based on a real incident, in his novel *Brideshead Revisited* Evelyn Waugh had an Oxford undergraduate stand on his balcony using a megaphone to recite *The Waste Land* to passersby.[81] Eliot's technical innovations made him an unavoidable presence even for the young conceptual poets who rejected his pessimism and despondency. Hart Crane, who advised a friend he would benefit by studying Eliot (adding "I must have read 'Prufrock' twenty-five times"), conceived his own most ambitious poem, *The Bridge*, as a response to *The Waste Land*: "I would apply as much of [Eliot's] erudition and technique as I can absorb and assemble toward a more positive, or ... ecstatic goal."[82] From a perspective very different from that of Pound and Crane, the experimental poet William Carlos Williams recognized *The Waste Land* as a devastating conceptual innovation, reflecting that "It wiped out our world as if an atom bomb had been dropped upon it." The poem's powerful impact on younger writers destroyed Williams' hopes of convincing the next generation to create a more earthy experimental art: "Eliot returned us to the classroom just at the moment when I felt we were on the point of an escape to matters much closer to the essence of a new art form itself—rooted in the locality.... I knew at once that ... I was most defeated."[83]

Eliot's poetry and criticism together made him a central figure in London's literary establishment. In 1919, he wrote to his mother that "a small and select public.... regards me as the best living critic, as well as the best living poet, in England.... I really think that I have far more *influence* on English letters than any other American has ever had, unless it be Henry James."[84] He became an associate of the luminous Bloomsbury Group, although he was more reserved and conservative than its core of liberal free thinkers, who found his formality amusing (Virginia Woolf invited her brother-in-law Clive Bell to lunch, adding "Eliot will be there in a four-piece suit").[85] Eliot's elitism was more deeply troubling to others, as the social scientist Harold Laski denounced "his horror of the common man" and his "fastidious sensitiveness which seemed to regard whatever is democratic as in its nature vulgar and ugly and barbarous," and even Eliot's friend Spender conceded that he was "altogether too willing to condemn the ordinary living of ordinary people as a form of death."[86]

In 1927, Eliot was baptized and confirmed in the Church of England, and in the same year he became a British citizen.[87] His last major works of poetry, completed in 1942 under the collective title *Four Quartets*, contrasted sharply with "Prufrock" and *The Waste Land*, abandoning impersonality for personal reflection, and openly embracing religion and royalism. With them, he told a friend he had "reached the end of something."[88] He wrote no important poetry thereafter: a biographer observed that in his final two decades, it was "as if the Eliot of the great poems was no longer there."[89]

In 1940, the 52-year-old Eliot gave a memorial lecture for William Butler Yeats. He expressed his fascination at the "continual development" that had allowed Yeats to write exciting poetry late in his life, and his amazement at the earlier case of Shakespeare, whose career revealed a "slow continuous development of mastery of his craft." Ultimately, however, Eliot remained baffled by these illustrious predecessors: "That a poet should develop at all, that he should find something new to say, and say it equally well, in middle age, has always something miraculous about it." The conceptual Eliot could understand age only as destructive to creativity: "Most men either cling to the experiences of youth, so that their writing becomes an insincere mimicry of their earlier work, or they leave their passion behind, and write only from the head, with a hollow and wasted virtuosity."[90] Perhaps it is not surprising that Eliot could not fathom the gradual evolution and late mastery of great experimental artists, because his own career was so different, from his extreme precocity onward. Stephen Spender explained that the most striking feature of Eliot's career was its discontinuities: "It is not just that Eliot never repeated himself and that he wrote a new poem only when he had something new to say and a new way of saying it, but that, at successive stages of his development, the poetry seems to proceed from a different consciousness."[91]

Elizabeth Bishop (1911–1979) and Robert Lowell (1917–1977)

> I prize clarity and simplicity.
> Elizabeth Bishop[92]

> I like to put what I see and hear into poems.
> Robert Lowell[93]

When Elizabeth Bishop and Robert Lowell first met, at a dinner party given by the poet Randall Jarrell in 1947, she was 36, and he was 30. Bishop had just published her first book, *North & South*, and Lowell had just published his second, *Lord Weary's Castle*. Bishop was intimidated by the prospect of meeting Lowell, not least because his book, which would soon win the Pulitzer Prize, was already establishing him as the most important young poet in the United States.[94] To her surprise, however, she felt immediately at ease:

> I didn't feel the least bit afraid, my shyness vanished and we started talking at once.... I remember thinking that it was the first time I had ever actually talked with some one about how one writes poetry—and thinking that it was, that it could be, strangely easy "Like exchanging recipes for making a cake."[95]

The two became close friends, and their friendship lasted until Lowell's death 30 years later. It survived not only a series of failed relationships for both, but also her struggles with alcoholism and depression, and his with manic-depressive illness that necessitated periodic hospitalizations. The correspondence that remains as a record of their friendship comprises more than 450 letters that fill 800 printed pages.

In many respects, Bishop and Lowell could hardly have been more different. Bishop's father, a building contractor in Worcester, Massachusetts, had died when she was less than a year old, and her mother disappeared from her life, committed to a mental institution, when Elizabeth was five. Elizabeth subsequently shuttled among relatives, feeling that she was "always a sort of guest," until she was sent to boarding school at 16.[96] In contrast, Robert Traill Spence Lowell IV was born into a distinguished Boston family. Among his ancestors were the nineteenth-century poet James Russell

Lowell, who succeeded Longfellow as a professor of language at Harvard, and the eccentric and flamboyant twentieth-century poet Amy Lowell (Robert commented that this was like having Mae West as a cousin).[97] When Robert almost inevitably enrolled at Harvard, the university's president, A. Lawrence Lowell, was also a relative.

Bishop and Lowell also differed personally—she "politely formal, shy, and undramatic" even late in life, when she had gained considerable success, he "handsome, magnetic, rich, wild with excitement about his powers."[98] Although Lowell was independently wealthy, he taught, gave readings, and wrote reviews not only out of a sense of responsibility to his profession, but because he enjoyed the attention; Bishop performed these activities very reluctantly and with trepidation, and then only when she needed the money to maintain her modest life style. Lowell was drawn to the central places of the literary world, and lived primarily in New York and Boston, while Bishop avoided those centers, and spent much of her adult life in Key West and Brazil.

Yet in spite of their great differences in background and personality, both Bishop and Lowell had a deep respect for the particular talent of the other, and recognized that their relationship could teach them things that would improve their work. The strength of their friendship stemmed from the fact that both were committed to creating poetry that would help them express what they saw and experienced, and—increasingly as they grew older—provide some stability in otherwise frequently chaotic lives.

Early in his career, Lowell was widely considered a brilliant formalist poet: when he was 27, the poet Allen Tate wrote that "T. S. Eliot's recent prediction that we should soon see a return to formal and even intricate metres and stanzas was coming true, before he made it, in the verse of Robert Lowell."[99] Poems like "The Quaker Graveyard in Nantucket," from *Lord Weary's Castle*, were filled with wordplay and literary allusion:

> All you recovered from Poseidon died
> With you, my cousin, and the harrowed brine
> Is fruitless on the blue beard of the god,
> Stretching beyond us to the castles in Spain....[100]

Bishop's poetry was very different. In reviews of *North & South*, Jarrell remarked that "all her poems have written underneath, *I have seen it*," and Lowell praised "the splendor and minuteness of her descriptions."[101] Her fascination with both vision and description was manifest in what became her most anthologized poem, "The Fish" from *North & South*:

> I looked into his eyes
> which were far larger than mine
> but shallower, and yellowed,
> the irises backed and packed
> with tarnished tinfoil
> seen through the lenses
> of old scratched isinglass.[102]

Bishop's work was more visual than that of most poets, and she was delighted when the art scholar Meyer Schapiro commented that "She writes poems with a painter's eye."[103] Her poems were objective: "The settings, or descriptions of my poems are almost invariably just plain facts—or as close to the facts as I can write them."[104] She was a committed empiricist who had little interest in theories, for she commented that "No matter what theories one may have, I doubt very much that they are in one's mind at the moment of writing a poem or that there is even a physical possibility that they could be."[105] Poems were not planned, but discovered: "You don't ask a poem what it means, you have to let it tell you."[106] Late in her life, she declared that "Observation is a great joy. Some critics charge that I'm merely a descriptive poet which I don't think is such a bad thing at all if you've done it well."[107] Bishop's belief in observation was illustrated by her love of Charles Darwin.[108] She explained that "reading Darwin one admires the beautiful solid case being built up out of his endless, heroic observations, almost unconscious or automatic—and then comes a sudden relaxation, a forgetful phrase, and one feels that strangeness of his undertaking, sees the lonely young man, his eyes fixed on facts and minute details, sinking or sliding giddily off into the unknown."[109] Her admiration for Darwin points to Bishop's conviction that close, careful observation was a way of inquiring, probing the unknown in the hope of gaining new understanding. Rebecca Stott explained that what Bishop recognized in Darwin's writing was the *poetics of the commonplace*: "The grinding of facts is where poetry begins.... The sublime is reached through the commonplace, through the slow accretion of facts."[110]

In mid-career, Lowell became dissatisfied with the formalism of contemporary poetry: he later recalled that during the 1950s "most good American poetry was a symbol hanging on a hat rack."[111] He found his own work opaque: "I felt my old poems hid what they were really about, and many times offered a stiff, humorless, and even impenetrable surface."[112] Psychotherapy prompted him to revisit his childhood, and he began to write autobiographical reminiscences. He decided "to see how much of my personal story and memories I could get into poetry," but discovered that he lacked the technique to do this: "I found I had no language or meter that would allow me to approximate what I saw or remembered."[113] Out of frustration, he began writing only in prose: "In prose you have to be interested in *what* is being said."[114] He found a way back to poetry from several new poems by Bishop, particularly "The Armadillo," which he carried in his wallet for several months.[115] Studying her poem left him wondering "why my own style was so armored heavy and old-fashioned."[116] Her conversational voice and understated treatment of details of common life gave him a means of escaping from what he considered his tendency "to beat the big drum too much."[117] Having first read "The Armadillo" in June of 1957, in mid-August Lowell began writing "Skunk Hour," which he finished a month later.[118] He explained that his poem was modeled on hers: "Both 'Skunk Hour' and 'The Armadillo' use short line stanzas, start with drifting description, and end with a single animal."[119] "Skunk Hour," which Lowell dedicated to Bishop, became the breakthrough to the series of poems that Lowell titled *Life Studies*—"poems as pliant as conversation."[120] His new style allowed description of life: "It's about direct observation, and not symbols."[121]

Lowell's breakthrough in turn had a powerful impact on Bishop. When Lowell sent her drafts of "Skunk Hour" and several other new poems, she uncharacteristically did not respond for more than a month. When she did, she not only discussed his work but reconsidered her own: "Oh heavens, when does one begin to write the *real* poems? I certainly feel as if I never had. But of course I don't feel that way about yours—they all seem real as real—and getting more so." In response to Lowell's comment to Bishop that he felt he had now "broken through to where you've always been," she rejected the compliment: "what on earth do you mean by that? I haven't got anywhere at all, I think." Lowell was excited by his new form, but Bishop was more taken with the content, telling him the new poems "all also have that sure feeling, as if you'd been in a stretch . . . when everything and anything suddenly seemed material for poetry—or not material, seemed to *be* poetry." She reflected on how the enormous differences between their family histories affected their art:

I must confess (and I imagine most of our contemporaries would confess the same thing) that I am green with envy of your kind of assurance. I feel that I could write in as much detail about my Uncle Artie, say—but what would be the significance? Nothing at all . . . Whereas all you have to do is put down the names! And the fact that it seems significant, illustrative, American, etc., gives you, I think, the confidence you display about tackling any idea or theme, *seriously*, in both writing and conversation. In some ways you are the luckiest poet I know!—in some ways not so lucky, either, of course.

After that qualification of her assessment of Lowell's advantages, in recognition of his mental illness, Bishop returned to her own situation: "it is hell to realize one has wasted half one's talent through timidity that probably could have been overcome if anyone in one's family had had a few grains of sense or education. . . . Well, maybe it's not too late!"[122]

Life Studies was published in 1959. The title reflected Lowell's belief that its results were provisional and incomplete, and even after it received the National Book Award he remained uncertain of his achievement: "When I finished *Life Studies*, I was left hanging on a question mark. I am still hanging there."[123] Lowell's doubt about his achievement was perhaps not surprising, for *Life Studies* was about uncertainty. Yet many poets recognized that Lowell had developed a technique that did not merely describe his quest for meaning, but embodied it. The scholar Stephen Matterson commented that "Lowell is not completely in control of the poems in *Life Studies*. . . . *Life Studies* is not written in fulfillment of some prior plan. Part of its greatness is in its heuristic improvisational quality, indicative of an individual seeking coherence and significance in a disordered, troubled life." Lowell married form and content: "one of the real triumphs of *Life Studies* is exactly in its creative inscription of doubt and uncertainty."[124]

In spite of Lowell's self-doubt, his new work quickly began to change contemporary poetry. A review of *Life Studies* labeled it "confessional" poetry, and the term soon gained currency to describe a new tendency. T. S. Eliot had decreed that "Poetry . . . is not the expression of personality, but an escape from personality"; confessional poetry reversed this, making poetry an expression of personality, with no subject too personal.[125] Lowell was not the first poet to write in this manner, but as the scholar Robert Phillips observed, confessional or personal poetry "was not prevalent and imitated until the end of the 1950s, when he broke from the Catholic themes and constipated language of his early work to parade forth the adulteries, arrests, divorces, and breakdowns which constitute his *Life Studies*." Thus in 1973 Phillips could declare that "we are living in an Age of Autobiography," with Lowell "the spiritual father."[126] "Skunk Hour" became Lowell's most frequently anthologized poem, and one of the most celebrated poems of the confessional movement.[127] In it, the speaker openly acknowledged his own illness—"My mind's not right"—as a cause of his troubled vision of a small Maine village.[128]

Lowell's transformation was widely remarked; the poet Donald Hall explained that "Lowell was not the first poet to undertake great change in mid-career, but he was the *best* poet to change so *much*."[129] A number of other poets, including Anne Sexton, W. D. Snodgrass, and Sylvia Plath, soon became associated with the confessional movement. Bishop was not among these, however, for her restraint and sense of privacy made her leery of the new approach. Thus in 1972 she wrote to Lowell that "In general, I deplore the 'confessional'—however, when you wrote *Life Studies* perhaps it was a necessary movement, and it helped make poetry more real, fresh and immediate."[130]

In spite of her distaste for what she considered the unseemly self-exposure of many of the confessional poets, Bishop's art was greatly affected by Lowell's innovation. Slowly and cautiously, her poetry grew more autobiographical, and more expressive of her feelings.[131] A major product of this came in 1975, when Bishop faced a personal crisis, as Alice Methfessel, her partner of five years, began a relationship with a man, and considered marrying him. Bishop's despair produced one of her greatest poems, as her fear that she had lost her lover prompted her not only to express her pain at this loss, but to narrate the pain of losses she had suffered throughout her life.

For "One Art," Bishop used the strict form of a villanelle, a sixteenth-century mode in which the first line of the first stanza recurs as a refrain in later stanzas. Opening with the innocuous statement that "The art of losing isn't hard to master," the poem portrayed life as a series of losses, which grew in magnitude as the poem proceeded, from household items to mementos, to houses, to cities, to a continent, and finally to a lover. The irony of the speaker's initial claim grew with each repetition, as the increasing significance of the losses obviously made them more painful. The contrast between the rigid formal requirements of the villanelle and the poem's intensely emotional content heightened the sense of pain, for as the poem progressed the reader became increasingly aware of the effort the author was making to control her emotions. Although Bishop did not explain her losses in detail, those who knew her could immediately recognize the references: so for example "I lost my mother's watch" was obviously more poignant to those who knew that Bishop had lost her mother at the age of five. In the poem's final stanza, Bishop violated the villanelle's strict form, by changing the words of the repeated line:

> —Even losing you (the joking voice, a gesture
> I love) I shan't have lied. It's evident
> the art of losing's not too hard to master
> though it may look like (*Write* it!) like disaster.[132]

The parenthetic instruction to herself that interrupted the final line emphasized Bishop's conviction that it was the process of recording her loss that would make it bearable: overcoming her grief and producing disciplined poetry were both one art, and the reader was a witness to her struggle.

"One Art" was published in 1976, when Bishop was 65. It became her second most frequently anthologized poem.[133] It contrasted sharply with the poem it followed in that respect, "The Fish," published more than three decades earlier. The young Bishop was a gifted experimental poet who used her eloquence and masterful command of language to describe what she saw. The mature Bishop remained a descriptive experimental poet, but now she had learned to use her clear, precise language to explore and record what she felt. Seamus Heaney wrote of "One Art" that "the conquest of a temptation to self-pity is what the poem manages to effect: wit confronts hurt and holds a balance that deserves to be called wisdom."[134]

Thomas Travisano pointed to specific ways in which Bishop's work developed over time. Her idiomatic language and conversational voice grew more assured, and relaxed. Her understated treatment of small details of everyday life grew subtler. The timing of her poems increasingly worked to allow images to emerge gradually, as if the poem were being composed even as the reader examined it. The tone of her writing became progressively more elegiac, so that even her most personal poems were not confessional in the standard sense of that term: her meditations dealt not only with personal loss, but with the universality of loss. She elevated humble and overlooked subjects, finding "[a]mongst the discarded and ignored ... examples of integrity, dignity, courage, humor, and grace."[135] These qualities made Bishop's poetry an inspiration to younger poets who wanted to make their art from careful observation of life. Bishop always had a characteristically experimental distrust of theorizing about poetry. But late in her life she cautiously generalized about why art might grow with the accumulation of knowledge and experience, in a letter to a literary scholar: "Well, it takes an infinite number of things coming together, forgotten, or almost forgotten, books, last night's dream, experiences past and present—to make a poem."[136]

Bishop once wrote that "Writing poetry is an unnatural act. It takes great skill to make it seem natural."[137] A number of younger poets recognized this skill in Bishop's work. So for example James Merrill praised her understatement and unpretentiousness: "her whole oeuvre is on the scale of a human life; there is no oracular amplification."[138] Octavio Paz commented that Bishop's poetry served as a reminder "that poetry is not in what words say but in what is said between them, that which appears fleetingly in pauses and silence"; to him, the great lesson of her poetry was "the enormous power of reticence."[139] And Seamus Heaney stressed that in spite of the technical perfection of Bishop's work, what was most important was its content: "she tempts us to regard technical and formal matters as something of a distraction, since the poem is so candidly *about* something, engaged with its own business of observing the world and discovering meaning."[140] The novelist Colm Toibin described Bishop's poetry as a "search for pure accuracy."[141] The qualities these writers pointed out were intrinsic not only to Bishop's art but to her personality, for what she valued above all were authenticity and sincerity. She stated this belief in the link between art and life in a memoir for a friend, a self-taught Cuban painter she knew in Key West: "There are some people whom we envy not because they are rich or handsome or successful, although they may be any or all of these, but because everything they are and do seems to be all of a piece, so that even if they wanted to they could not be or do otherwise."[142]

Bishop and Lowell shared a deep commitment to an experimental art, that would privilege observation and experience over ideas and imagination. They had some disagreements, for example concerning necessary degrees of accuracy. Bishop explained that "I always *try* to stick as much as possible to what *really* happened when I describe something in a poem," and referred jokingly to "my George Washington handicap—I can't tell a lie even for art, apparently; it takes an awful effort or a sudden jolt to make me alter facts."[143] In contrast, Lowell explained that even his confessional poetry wasn't literally true: "There's a good deal of tinkering with fact.... I've invented facts and changed things.... Yet there's this thing: if a poem is autobiographical... you want the reader to say, This is true.... And so there was always that standard of truth which you wouldn't ordinarily have in poetry—the reader was to believe he was getting the *real* Robert Lowell."[144]

More fundamentally, however, Bishop and Lowell shared a belief that art should not be separated from life. Both wanted their poetry to grow directly from their lives, not merely to record what they learned, but to be the means by which they learned. Thus Bishop told an interviewer that "Writing poetry is a *way of life*, not a matter of testifying but of experiencing. It is not the way in which one goes about interpreting the world, but the very process of sensing it."[145] Lowell agreed: "A poem is an event, not the record of an event."[146] In an amusing but telling observation, when the poet Stanley Kunitz interviewed Lowell, he reported that "Lowell has no secondary skills or hobbies to distract him from his absorption in literature."[147] In an elegy for a friend, the poet John Berryman, Lowell wrote: "We asked to be obsessed with writing,/and we were."[148]

Because poetry was their preferred method of learning, Bishop and Lowell considered themselves seekers, hoping to make discoveries as they worked. When asked what quality she valued most in poetry, Bishop replied, "Surprise. The subject and the language which conveys it should surprise you. You should be surprised at seeing something new and strangely alive."[149] Similarly, Lowell described the reward after the struggle of writing a poem: "Then the great moment comes when there's enough resolution of your technical equipment, your way of constructing things, and what you can make a poem out of, to hit something you really want to say. You may not know you have it to say."[150]

Both Bishop and Lowell relied on poetry not only to make their lives meaningful, but to make them bearable. Late in his life, Lowell reflected that "It seems our insoluble lives sometimes come clearer in writing." This was always his goal in making his art, though he was sorely aware of its limitations: "All my poems are written for catharsis; none can heal melancholia or arthritis."[151] Bishop's deepest hope for poetry was expressed in the letter she wrote to Lowell after reading his breakthrough poems for *Life Studies*. For her, in those poems, "all the past was illuminated in long shafts here and there, like a long-waited-for sunrise. If only one could see everything that way all the time! It seems to me *it's* the whole purpose of art, to the artist (not to the audience)—that rare feeling of control, illumination—life *is* all right, for the time being."[152]

Sylvia Plath (1932–1963)

> How to express anger creatively?
>
> Sylvia Plath[153]

Sylvia Plath began writing poetry as a child, because she "liked nursery rhymes and . . . thought I could do the same thing." She published a poem when she was eight, in the *Boston Herald*, and "from then on, I suppose, I've been a bit of a professional."[154] Also when Sylvia was eight her father, a German immigrant who taught entomology at Boston University, died as a result of diabetes that he left untreated too long. His death left a "huge, sad hole" that would affect Sylvia throughout her life.[155]

Plath was precocious and driven. She graduated first in her Wellesley high school class, and received a scholarship to Smith College. During the summer before she entered college, she had a short story published by *Seventeen* magazine.[156] At Smith she was elected to Phi Beta Kappa as a junior, went on to graduate summa cum laude, and at commencement won no fewer than five prizes.[157] She also won a competition to serve as a guest editor for *Mademoiselle* magazine in New York for a month during the summer after her junior year.[158]

Yet not all of Plath's life was as successful as her academic record. During the summer of 1953, after her work at *Mademoiselle*, she became depressed and attempted suicide, hiding in a crawl space under her family's house and taking an overdose of sleeping pills. She was found after two days, having vomited the pills while in a coma. She was revived and spent several months at a psychiatric clinic.[159] Plath would struggle with depression throughout her life. In 1958, she wrote in her journal that "It is as if my life were magically run by two electric currents: joyous positive and despairing negative—which ever is running at the moment dominates my life."[160] She tried to achieve perfection in everything she did and was frustrated that she could not tolerate anything less: poignantly, she wrote in her journal in 1957 that "I have a good self, that loves skies, hills, ideas, tasty meals, bright colors. My demon would murder this self by demanding it be a paragon." She confessed that "Not being perfect hurts," and observed that she had lived her whole life "under the shadow of fear . . . that I would fall short of some abstract perfection." She vowed to fight to achieve "not perfection, but an acceptance of myself as having a right to live on my own human, fallible terms."[161]

Plath's ambition never abated; a friend from her college years recalled that when Plath had remarked to her "that she 'would rather have a poem published in *The New Yorker* than anything else in the world,' I understood her to mean it fairly literally."[162] Plath began accumulating rejections from *The New Yorker* while she was in college, and recorded in her journal that she had actually dreamed of picking up a copy of the magazine and seeing a story of hers "in the deeply endearing New Yorker–heading type."[163] She would eventually succeed not only in publishing in *The New Yorker*, but in 1961 receiving a contract in which she agreed to give the magazine first reading of all her poems. Yet Plath's desire to be recognized was not her only motivation. In 1962, she responded to an interviewer's question about the satisfaction she gained from poetry by saying "I don't think I could live without it. It's like water or bread, or something absolutely essential to me. I find myself absolutely fulfilled when I have written a poem, when I'm writing one."[164]

After college Plath went to England on a Fulbright Scholarship, to study literature at Cambridge. In February 1956, she met a young poet, Ted Hughes, at a party for a student literary magazine. The mutual attraction was instant. Her first words to him were a quotation from one of his poems, and within minutes "he kissed me bang smash on the mouth and ripped my hairband off... and my favorite silver earrings.... And when he kissed my neck I bit him long and hard on the cheek, and... blood was running down his face.... And I screamed in myself, thinking: oh, to give myself crashing, fighting, to you."[165] In a letter to her mother, Plath described Hughes as "the strongest man in the world... brilliant poet whose work I loved before I met him, a large, hulking... Adam... with a voice like the thunder of God." Interestingly, she wrote that she had "fallen terribly in love, which can only lead to great hurt." But both were passionately in love—she described them "living in the midst of a singing joy which is the best of Hopkins, Thomas, Chaucer, Shakespeare, Blake, Donne, and all the poets we love together"—and they married less than four months after they met.[166]

Plath and Hughes spent two years in the United States. In 1959 she audited Robert Lowell's seminar at Boston University. The contact with Lowell, who had just written *Life Studies*, would have a major impact on Plath's poetry. Plath and Hughes returned to London late in 1959. The next year they had a daughter, and Plath published her first book of poetry, *The Colossus*. In 1961, the family moved to Devon, where they bought an old house in a little village. There Plath gave birth to their second child, a son, in 1962.

A. Alvarez, the poetry critic of the *Observer*, who became a friend of Plath's, reflected that *Colossus* was "beautiful, but also peculiarly careful, held in check.... It is as though she had not yet come to grips with her subject as an artist." This soon changed, however: "The *real* poems began in 1960, after the birth of her daughter."[167] Ted Hughes agreed: "the truly miraculous thing about her will remain the fact that in two years, while she was almost fully occupied with children and house-keeping, she underwent a poetic development that has hardly any equal on record, for suddenness and completeness."[168]

Plath changed not only her poetry, but also the process by which she produced it. Hughes recalled that "She wrote her early poems very slowly, Thesaurus open on her knee.... Every poem grew complete ... in that laborious inching way, as if she were working out a mathematical problem." Early in 1961, however, she began to write "without her usual studies over the Thesaurus, and at top speed, as one might write an urgent letter. From then on, all her poems were written in this way."[169] Hughes marveled that although Plath's late poems controlled "one of the widest and most subtly discriminating vocabularies in the modern poetry of our language ... these are poems written for the most part at great speed, as she might take dictation."[170]

Remarkably, Plath's greatness as a poet rests primarily on the poems she wrote in a single month, under very trying circumstances. These included her two most frequently anthologized poems, "Daddy" and "Lady Lazarus."[171] During the summer of 1962, Plath discovered that Hughes was having an affair, and in September she insisted that he leave their home. In October, taking care of her two young children by herself, she wrote more than two dozen poems, working almost exclusively in the early mornings, "from dawn to when the babes wake, a poem a day."[172] Thus on October 12, she wrote to her mother that "Every morning, when my sleeping pill wears off, I am up about five, in my study with coffee, writing like mad—have managed a poem a day before breakfast.... Terrific stuff, as if domesticity had choked me."[173]

In December 1962, Plath and her children moved back to London. In January, *The Bell Jar*, a novel Plath had based on her 1953 suicide attempt, was published in England. Early on the morning of February 11, Plath left buttered bread and milk in the bedroom of her sleeping children, sealed the door and window of her kitchen, and killed herself by putting her head in the oven with the gas on. In one of her last poems, written ten days before her death, she wrote "The blood jet is poetry,/There is no stopping it."[174]

Widespread recognition of Plath as an important poet began with the posthumous publication of a volume of her late poems, *Ariel*, in 1965. Her poetry was categorized as confessional in a review by M. L. Rosenthal, the critic who had first used the term to describe Lowell's *Life Studies*.[175] Plath had acknowledged her debt to Lowell's innovation, as she told an interviewer in the fall of 1962 that "I've been very excited by what I feel is the new breakthrough that came with . . . Robert Lowell's *Life Studies*, this intense breakthrough into very serious, very personal, emotional experience which I feel has been partly taboo." Yet whereas Lowell wanted readers to believe that a poem's speaker was the poet himself, Plath did not. She admitted that "my poems immediately come out of the sensuous and emotional experiences I have," but explained that they were not direct statements about those experiences: "I believe that one should be able to control and manipulate these experiences with an informed and an intelligent mind." The manipulation would make private images relate to public issues: "personal experience is very important, but certainly it shouldn't be . . . mirror-looking, narcissistic experience. I believe it should be *relevant* . . . to the larger things, the bigger things such as Hiroshima and Dachau."[176]

In the late poems Plath created a distinctive new voice, with short lines and stanzas that presented surrealistic, hallucinatory, and often violent images in direct, colloquial language. Metaphors came in rapid-fire succession, in short, declarative bursts. The nursery-rhyme simplicity and rhythm of these poems contrasted with their furious emotions, heightening their surreality. Alvarez described Plath's creative process: "Her poetry acted as a strange, powerful lens through which her ordinary life was filtered and refigured with extraordinary intensity."[177] Robert Lowell wrote of *Ariel* that "Everything in these poems is personal, confessional, felt, but the manner of feeling is controlled hallucination, the autobiography of a fever."[178] But what was extraordinary about the October poems was the combination of madness and control: the writer Elizabeth Hardwick observed that "The excessive violence of the language, remarkable as it is, seems to come from a mind speeding along madly and yet commanding an uncanny control of language, sound, rhythm, and metaphor that is the very opposite of madness."[179]

"Daddy" transformed Plath's pacifist German father into a Nazi, tormenting the speaker, his Jewish daughter. The poem also included a reference to Hughes as "The vampire who . . ./. . . drank my blood for a year,/ Seven years, if you want to know." The poem closed triumphantly: "Daddy,

daddy, you bastard, I'm through."[180] Plath considered her father effectively to have committed suicide, and Alvarez believed that with Hughes' betrayal, Plath "felt abandoned, injured, enraged and bereaved as purely and defenselessly as she had as a child twenty years before."[181] The poem was a catharsis; the day it was written, Plath wrote to her mother, "It is *over*. My life can begin."[182] "Lady Lazarus" treated another of Plath's life-long preoccupations, that of self-destruction. The speaker gloated over her conquest of death:

> Dying
> Is an art, like everything else.
> I do it exceptionally well.
>
> I do it so it feels like hell.
> I do it so it feels real.
> I guess you could say I've a call.[183]

The fury of the late poems was a shock even to Plath's admirers: Alvarez recalled that when she first read "Daddy" and "Lady Lazarus" to him, "I was appalled; at first hearing, the things seemed to be not so much poetry as assault and battery."[184]

Plath became a major influence on many later poets.[185] The scholar Linda Martin, for example, recently observed that stylistically for American poetry "the results of the impact of Plath's work are as pervasive as the influence of Ernest Hemingway's terse yet open prose."[186] But Plath's significance extended beyond her impact on poetry. She died in the same year that Betty Friedan's book, *The Feminine Mystique*, effectively initiated the women's movement, and over time Plath's growing reputation as a poet combined with the tragic story of her life to make her a feminist icon. The writer Erica Jong explained that "Sylvia Plath's poetry meant an enormous amount to a whole generation of readers and poets, not only because it was the first poetry by a woman to fully explore female rage—but because it did so with exquisite artistry."[187] When *The Bell Jar* was published in the United States in 1971, it spent six months on the *New York Times* bestseller list.[188] In 2003, Plath was portrayed by Gwyneth Paltrow in *Sylvia*, a BBC film about Plath's romance with Hughes.

At the age of 26, Plath wrote in her journal that what she feared most was the failure of her imagination. Accurate description "paradoxically tells the truth, but the worthless truth, about the world. It is that synthesizing spirit, that 'shaping' force, which prolifically sprouts and makes up its own worlds with more inventiveness than God which I desire. . . . [T]he poverty of life without dreams is too horrible to imagine."[189] Plath's vivid imagination made possible the radical conceptual breakthrough that made her a major poet in spite of the brevity of her life. She did not live to see the great extent of her fame, but she had no doubt about what she had accomplished. In October 1962, with the characteristic certainty of a young conceptual innovator, she wrote to her mother: "I am a genius of a writer; I have it in me. I am writing the best poems of my life; they will make my name."[190]

Composing and Revising

Robert Frost believed that poetry should be the product of spontaneity: he wrote that a poem's "most precious quality will remain its having run itself and carried away the poet with it."[191] Poems should not be planned: "All the best things [a poet] ever uses are things he didn't know he was getting when he was getting them. A poet never takes notes. You never take notes in a love affair."[192] Frost claimed that he wrote only when he was inspired: "Sometimes I can sense that feeling coming on for a couple of days, and then I find that I have to versify." Then he wrote quickly: "I usually do a poem in one sitting, and the longest ones in never more than two sittings."[193]

In fact, Frost's practice appears to have been more complicated. Although he contended the essential thing was that a poem "may not be worried into being," he did allow that it "may be worked over once it is in being."[194] A biographer noted that "Frost's manuscripts reveal that he revised extensively and sometimes took a long time to complete his poems. He then kept them for further consideration and did not publish them for many years." Even after he had achieved sufficient recognition to eliminate delays caused by rejections, he still hesitated to publish, explaining to one editor that "I am so accustomed to having things around for years and years that I find them hard to part with under a year old." When he traveled, he always took manuscripts with him, "things of my own I haven't yet published or haven't yet put the last touch to."[195]

The single most celebrated feature of Frost's most frequently anthologized poem was in fact a product of revision. Frost routinely told audiences that "Stopping by Woods on a Snowy Evening" came to him complete, and that he wrote it entirely without revision.[196] In fact, however, in the first full draft of the poem, the first three lines of the incomplete fourth stanza were:

> The woods are lovely, dark and deep,
> But I have promises to keep,
> That bid me give the reins a shake

He later changed the third line to:

> That bid me on, and there were miles

The final phrase still later led to the final form of the third line:

> And miles to go before I sleep

The doubling of this line was then a product of further reflection. In each of the poem's three stanzas, the third line rhymed with the first, second, and fourth lines of the following stanza. What to do in the final stanza? Frost wrote to a friend that a dead line—one without a rhymed ending—in the last stanza alone would have been a flaw. He considered rhyming all four lines in the last stanza but rejected this because it would have made five rhymed lines (including the third of the preceding stanza). He then considered concluding with a three-line stanza before deciding that "The repetend was the only logical way to end such a poem."[197] What became the most famous feature of what many consider Frost's greatest poem was thus the last touch Frost added to the poem, in searching for a satisfactory way to end it.

The story of the revision of *The Waste Land* is among the most celebrated in the history of modern poetry, as Ezra Pound famously helped T. S. Eliot produce the final version of the poem. As Eliot described it, "I placed before him in Paris the manuscript of a sprawling, chaotic poem called *The Waste Land* which left his hands, reduced to about half its size, in the form in which it appears in print."[198] The scholar Helen Gardner, whom Eliot considered the best critic of his work, judged that "There is, I think, no other example in literature of a poet submitting his work to another poet of equal stature and accepting radical criticism."[199] This collaboration appears to have been a consequence of Eliot's and Pound's conceptual attitude toward their art.

The need for radical revision of *The Waste Land* arose from the fact that Eliot composed poetry in fragments.[200] To create long poems, he needed to devise a form "that allowed him to compose in the jets and spurts of inspiration that came naturally to him, and, like a worker in mosaic, to find a place in his pattern for lines and even passages that had been composed at very different times."[201] In making *The Waste Land* from fragments accumulated over more than seven years, Eliot could accept the help of Pound because of his conception of poetry as an impersonal activity.[202] Eliot's early critical writings stressed that the poet should suppress his own personality: "The greater the verse, the less it seems to belong to the man who wrote it."[203] The key role of the poet's historical sense meant that "the best parts of his work may be those in which ... his ancestors ... assert their immortality most vigorously."[204] The great poet was thus already effectively collaborating with the poets of the past. Eliot's extensive use of quotations from, and allusions to, earlier poetry in *The Waste Land* can be seen as a consequence of this attitude. He even advocated a scientific approach to poetry, arguing that it was in "depersonalization that art may be said to approach the condition of science," and that the poet should emulate the scientist in working "not through a desire to express his personality, but by a complete surrender of himself to the work in which he was absorbed."[205]

Eliot's belief that poems should be constructed impersonally thus predisposed him to accept collaboration in the creation of his art. The same was true for Pound, whom Eliot described as "so passionately concerned about the works of art which he expected his protégés to produce that he sometimes tended to regard them almost impersonally, as art or literature machines to be carefully tended and oiled, for the sake of their potential output."[206] Eliot later explained that Pound's assistance had been valuable because "he didn't try to turn you into an imitation of himself. He tried to see what you were trying to do."[207] From the surviving manuscripts of *The Waste Land*, Gardner concluded that Pound had restricted his revisions to technical problems: "He gave his whole mind to the problem of 'Was this good verse?' 'Is this the right word?' 'Does this strike a false note?' 'Is this becoming monotonous?' He makes no comment on the subject matter of the poem, its religious or philosophic views.... It was Eliot's poem he was working on."[208] Pound appears to have done his job confidently and decisively: Hannah Sullivan commented that "the facsimile documents of *The Waste Land* are a visual testament to the confidence of a master exciser at the top of his game; Pound's clean, bold lines drawn through whole verse paragraphs and sections are sculptural and exacting."[209]

In contrast to Eliot, the experimental Frost declined to submit his work to Pound's ministrations. Frost recalled that when he lived in England, Pound had a regular weekly meeting with a small group of poets, "But I never went to one of those meetings. I said to Pound, 'What do you do?' He said, 'Rewrite each other's poems.' And I said, 'Why?' He said, 'To squeeze the water out of them.' 'That sounds like a parlor game to me,' I said, 'and I'm a serious artist'—kidding, you know. And he laughed and he didn't invite me any more."[210] (Frost's biographer Lawrance Thompson reported an incident in which Pound took one of Frost's lyrics and showed Frost how it could be condensed, to which Frost replied, "Yeah, and spoiled."[211]) For Frost, creativity was personal—"I think a person has to be withdrawn into himself to gather inspiration." He believed that the best poetry was a product of isolated rural life, "individuality and seclusion."[212]

When an interviewer asked Robert Lowell if he revised a great deal, he replied: "Endlessly."[213] This was hardly an exaggeration. Lowell once remarked that "Sometimes there are as many as thirty versions of one poem, and I usually make more changes between magazine publication and book publication. And even when it's in a book, I want to change it again."[214] He often did. One sequence began with the publication of *Notebook 1967–68* in 1969. Lowell then revised these poems and again published them, together with some new poems, in *Notebook*, in 1970. He then carried around a copy of *Notebook* for two years, revising all its poems. In 1973 Lowell published two shorter books—*For Lizzie and Harriet* and *History*—that both consisted of revised versions of poems from *Notebook*.[215] The *Times Literary Supplement* review of the new books was accompanied by a cartoon of Lowell smiling as he turned the handle of a meat grinder chewing up books.[216]

Lowell explained in 1961 that he generally began his poems by writing them in blank verse, then putting in the rhymes. Then began the extended process of revision: "The most I could hope for at first was that the rhymed version wouldn't be much inferior to the blank verse. Then the real work would begin, to make it something much better than the original out of the difficulties of the meter." His revisions were comprehensive: "I don't believe I've ever written a poem in meter where I've kept a single one of the original lines."[217]

In a 1964 interview, Lowell told Stanley Kunitz that "In a way a poem is never finished. It simply reaches a point where it isn't worth any more alteration, where any further tampering is liable to do more harm than good.

There are passages in all my books that make me wince, but I can't do anything with them."[218] Late in his life, Lowell confessed to Bishop that he had spent many "futile hours trying to perfect something satisfactory," always seeking "the unimagined perfect lines or ending," but had often given up. As he approached the age of 60, he reflected that "We seem to be near our finish, so near that the final, the perfect ... is forbidden us."[219] The poet Frank Bidart, Lowell's friend, occasional assistant, and editor of a posthumous 1,200-page volume of his collected poems, concluded that Lowell came to reject the assumption that there can be a perfect or definitive version of a work of art. Instead, there could be different versions of a poem, and *"we need not choose*. He often said that something is lost in revision even if something is gained. Each version is a journey: each occasion that he inhabited the material, slightly different."[220] In view of this belief, Bidart included several different versions of a number of poems when he edited Lowell's collected poems.[221]

Elizabeth Bishop understood Lowell's attitude. In her elegy for him, she wrote of the birds singing in Maine, always repeating but slightly changing their songs, then addressed Lowell:

> And now—you've left
> for good. You can't derange, or re-arrange,
> your poems again. (But the Sparrows can their song.)
> The words won't change again. Sad friend, you cannot change.[222]

Bishop thus portrayed Lowell's need to change his work as natural and instinctive, rather than pathological; she appears to have arrived at the view that what motivated him was the anticipation of change.[223]

A friend of Lowell's recalled that he might begin a poem in the fall and not finish it until the spring.[224] Bishop might take much longer. Like Lowell, Bishop was perennially dissatisfied with her poems: "All I can ever see is room for improvement. In fact I don't like anything I've written very much!" Unlike Lowell, however, she did not revise published work: "After a poem is published, I just change a word occasionally. Some poets like to rewrite, but I don't."[225] Early in her career, she decided "never to try to publish anything until I thought I'd done my best with it, no matter how many years it took— or never to publish at all."[226] One consequence was that she left many poems unfinished; another was that she might complete a poem only after a decade or more of work. In the case of "The Moose," based on an incident Bishop witnessed in 1946 in the course of a trip returning from a visit to relatives in Nova Scotia, a biographer noted that surviving drafts of the poem "appear in the script of nearly all Elizabeth's typewriters, indicating that she worked on it from time to time for more than twenty-five years."[227] In December 1956, Bishop wrote of "The Moose" to her Aunt Grace that she had written a poem that was dedicated to her, and that she would send her a copy when it was published.[228] In fact, it would be another sixteen years before Bishop's aunt received the poem. The wait might have been even longer, but in the spring of 1972, "Elizabeth showed version after version to [her friend] Frank Bidart, anxious and angry that she had let herself be pressed to finish a poem for a deadline." After reading the poem at Harvard's commencement, Bishop was still not satisfied with it. After more changes, she published it in *The New Yorker* later in the year, and sent the magazine to her aunt. After still more revisions, she published the final version in her next book of poems, in 1976.[229]

In a poem for Bishop, Lowell paid tribute to her patient search for the right language:

>   Do
>   you still hang your words in air, ten years
>   unfinished, glued to your notice board, with gaps
>   or empties for the unimaginable phrase—
>   unerring Muse who makes the casual perfect?[230]

Yet Bishop's extended process of composition was not simply a consequence of seeking the exact words to express an observation she had already formulated; her revisions in fact often involved changes in a poem's meaning. One scholar noted a recurring tendency for Bishop's revisions to effect a "move from greater to lesser security, optimism, or openness of possibility." So for example in the last line of the late "Poem," the "never-to-be-dismantled elms" changed into the "yet-to-be-dismantled elms," as time and its losses loomed over the trees portrayed in a great-uncle's painting.[231] In the title poem of *Questions of Travel*, published in 1965, the key line of the final stanza changed from "the choice perhaps is not great . . . but fairly free," to the final version, "the choice is never wide and never free," as in the course of revising the poem Bishop became more mindful of the restrictions that constrain travelers.[232] "One Art" changed significantly in meaning through its seventeen surviving drafts. So for example a declaration in the final stanza began as "above's all lies," then changed to the opposite—"above's not lies"—then further to "I haven't lied above," then to "these were not lies," and ultimately to "I shan't have lied." The changes demonstrate how Bishop used the process of revising the poem to think through how she felt about the greatest losses in her life. The first change reflected a change of mind: she began the poem believing the losses of the houses and places she had loved were too great to bear, but the change to "above's not lies" signaled her realization that she could in fact tolerate them. The final change, from past tense to future perfect, underscored the role of the writing of the poem in allowing her to bear her loss, for it suggested that as she wrote she had not yet come to terms with the loss of her lover, but that the process of completing the poem would allow her to do this.[233] The poem changed substantially in form as well as substance. Thus the poet Richard Tillinghast remarked that "'One Art' being among a handful of perfect villanelles in the language it's surprising that the poem began as a series of dispirited and formless reflections."[234]

Bishop explained in 1977 that her process of composition was open-ended: "At times I change horses in mid-stream. I begin a poem, but years later I see that I do not like it the way it was written. What started out being one poem frequently turns into another one."[235] Lowell referred to this process of exploration in the poem for Bishop quoted above:

> Have you seen an inchworm crawl on a leaf,
> cling to the very end, revolve in air,
> feeling for something to reach to something? . . .[236]

The speed with which Sylvia Plath produced her great *Ariel* poems in 1962 did not preclude revision; she simply composed and revised rapidly, so that in most cases a poem was begun and completed in a single early-morning session. She typically began by writing several drafts by hand, then typed several more.[237] The subjects of these poems were fixed from the start, as she rarely made changes in her poems' first stanzas in the course of revision. Many other lines also survived intact from first draft to final version. Most of her revisions served to sharpen the messages of the poems, rather than to change them. So for example the line in "Lady Lazarus," "I guess you could say I've a call," replaced the earlier version, "I guess I'm a natural," to emphasize that the speaker's suicide was a performance, rather than reality.[238]

The substantial differences in the processes of composition and revision among the poets considered here reflect significant differences in approach within as well as across the two basic categories of experimental and conceptual art. Yet the three experimental poets all demonstrated indecision about their work, as they all revised over extended periods. Frost composed largely from initial inspiration, but then hesitated to publish, as he made adjustments. Bishop often began with only a vague subject, then made major alterations that might change a poem's theme, or actually reverse its message, in a lengthy period of revision. Lowell wrote quickly, then revised repeatedly.

The very different revision practices of Eliot and Plath can equally be seen as consequences of their conceptual approaches to poetry, as both demonstrated their decisiveness in the process of composition in different ways. Eliot's belief that poems should be constructed rationally and impersonally allowed him fully to accept the major changes Pound made in his masterpiece. In contrast, Plath's certainty of her own convictions allowed her to complete each of her greatest poems within a single early-morning session of just a few hours.

4
Sculptors

Modern sculpture effectively began with Auguste Rodin. Alan Bowness explained Rodin's role:

> It has often been said of Rodin that he invented sculpture, or that he recreated a lost art—an understandable enough hyperbole, given the state of sculpture when he began to exhibit. It was not that there were no admirable sculptors at work in the mid-19th century, but simply that Rodin lifted sculpture on to an altogether more important plane of activity. To Baudelaire and his contemporaries, sculpture was a boring art, very limited in its expressive power. It was too often only a decorative adjunct to architecture, or a means of eternalizing the appearance or the memory of some distinguished personage. As a medium for the expression of ideas, it could scarcely be said to exist.
>
> Rodin changed all this; young men who fifty years earlier would have turned to painting now looked on sculpture as a more rewarding art.[1]

Sculpture thrived in the twentieth century, as its boundaries were radically extended into new forms and materials. And as in other arts, this occasioned a powerful struggle between experimental and conceptual approaches.

Auguste Rodin (1840–1917)

> The only thing is to *see*.
>
> Auguste Rodin[2]

As far back as he could remember, Auguste Rodin loved to draw. When it came time to begin preparing for a career, his parents sent him to a school of commercial art. There, he recalled, when he saw artist's clay for the first time, "I thought I had gone to heaven."[3]

Rodin's love for clay would endure: in time he would become the greatest sculptor of the modern era, and perhaps the greatest modeler of clay in the history of Western sculpture.[4] But his talent was not immediately apparent. In 1857, at 17, hoping to follow the surest path to a successful career as a sculptor, he applied to the prestigious Ecole des Beaux-Arts. Although he passed the drawing examination, he was rejected because he failed the sculpture test. After again failing this test in each of the following two years, Rodin resigned himself to an alternative route to his goal. For the next two decades, he worked as an assistant to a succession of restorers, jewelry-makers, and fabricators of ornamental sculpture. Throughout this extended period of apprenticeship, he continued to study on his own time, producing thousands of drawings and unknown numbers of sculptural studies.[5]

Rodin's surviving early work bears little resemblance to his great mature art. The poet Rainer Maria Rilke, a friend of Rodin's who worked briefly as his secretary, observed that his work "developed through long years. It has grown like a forest." Rilke contended that "it is an underlying patience in Rodin which renders him so great," and explained that patience was necessary because of the nature of his art: "His art was not built upon a great idea, but upon a minute, conscientious realization, upon the attainable, upon a craft." Rodin himself was committed to the belief that good art could only be made slowly: "Only slowly, little by little, by continual effort, can one make anything well."[6]

Rodin was an archetypal experimental artist. He consistently emphasized the visual goals of his art: his basic belief was that "art is only a close study of nature."[7] Observation must always precede ideas: "One must never try to express an idea by form. Make your form, make something, and the idea will come."[8] His inspiration came from the human body: "I can only work from a model. The sight of human forms feeds and comforts me."[9] Because his art was based on vision, Rodin worked without preconception: "when I have nothing to copy, I have no ideas; but when I see nature showing me forms, I immediately find something worth saying." This lack of planning meant that he sometimes ran into problems he could not immediately solve, but then he had a standard procedure: "I lay my work aside while it is yet unfinished, and for months I may appear to abandon it. Every now and then, however, I return to it and correct or add a detail here and there. I have not really abandoned it, you see, only I am hard to satisfy."[10] One result of this was that his sculptures could change as he worked: "I often begin with one intention and finish with another." Rodin recognized that pursuit of perfection could be the enemy of the good: "Wishing to do better, one sometimes demolishes even what one has done well; but one must be possessed by the demon of the best. If he guides us badly one day, he requites us another time, by leading us further."[11] The scholar Albert Elsen contended that Rodin's true love of sculpture was for the process rather than the products—"his passion [was] for the act of *making* rather than *completing* sculpture.... His personal problem was in setting for himself impossible absolutes of perfection toward which he dedicated a lifetime of striving. It is doubtful that at his death he would have pronounced any of his works finished or immutable."[12] The scholar Leo Steinberg believed that Rodin deliberately avoided finishing his sculptures, "his secret dream being to keep every work going like a stoked fire—forever, if possible.... For Rodin, a work of art is no longer the sort of work that can be finished. It can only be abandoned."[13] Looking at a Rodin sculpture "forces the viewer to acknowledge the work as a result of a process, an act that has shaped the figure over time."[14]

Unlike sculptors who made figures that were intended to be seen only from the front, or those who made figures from a single front and single back view, Rodin wanted to create figures that could be seen from any vantage point. He did not begin with drawings or other preparatory studies, but worked directly in clay. He developed a working process that was iterative and incremental:

> I place the model so that light, outlining it against a background, illuminates the contour. I execute it, I change my position and that of my model, and thus I see another contour, and so on successively all around the body.
>
> I begin again; I come closer and closer to the contours, and I refine them.
>
> Since the human body has an infinite number of contours, I multiply them as far as possible or so far as I think it useful.[15]

A key event in Rodin's development came in 1876, when he visited Italy for the first time. Michelangelo's Medici tombs in Florence left him "more profoundly impressed than anything I have ever seen."[16] The impact of Michelangelo's sculpture on Rodin's work was not immediate, but came gradually, after his return from Italy, when Rodin analyzed Michelangelo's poses. This eventually led Rodin to recognize that "movement existed in nature, and that I had only to avoid losing that in my models.... [M]ovement was something natural, not something I could impose artificially." For the rest of Rodin's life, capturing movement would be one of his primary goals, and he credited Michelangelo for this insight, explaining that "My liberation from academicism was via Michelangelo.... He is the bridge by which I passed from one circle to another."[17]

One of Rodin's greatest works originated in an 1880 commission for the bronze doors of a planned museum of decorative arts. Rodin decided to represent the gates of hell, based on Dante's *Inferno*, and told the government he would need at least three years to complete it. He made numerous sketches and maquettes for the project, but Elsen observed that he never settled on a single clear plan, preferring instead to concentrate on elements of the doors.[18] The critic Camille Mauclair, who saw Rodin at work, believed that the doors became "a theme for inspirations, and he brings into it a whole category of thoughts and works, never troubling himself about the architecture or the actual scheme. He will be for ever improvising some little figure ... and this he plants in his door, studies it against the other figures, then takes it out again, and if need be, breaks it up and uses the fragments for other attempts." Mauclair predicted that the doors would never be completed—"it could not contain all the figures destined for it by the artist"—and he proved to be correct.[19] Rodin did considerable work on the doors during 1880–1884, and obtained an estimate of the cost of casting it in bronze in 1884, but he nonetheless continued to make changes, and evidently never considered them finished; he first exhibited a plaster cast of the work in public only in 1900.[20] The idea of a separate museum building was eventually abandoned, so the government never called for the doors to be delivered. Rodin created nearly two hundred figures for the doors, some of which became independent works; probably the most famous of these was a nude male seated on a rock, leaning forward with its chin resting on one hand, that came to be titled *The Thinker*.[21] Whenever Rodin was reproached for not finishing the doors, he responded, "And were the cathedrals finished?"[22] After Rodin's death, a complete model of *The Gates of Hell* was assembled at his studio, and the first bronze cast of the doors was executed in 1926–1928.[23] Nearly 21 feet high and 13 feet wide, the *Gates* presents no clear narrative or theme: unlike Dante, Rodin provided no Virgil to guide the viewer, and he admitted that the work had "no scheme of illustration, or intended moral purpose."[24] But Mauclair contended that over time the *Gates* became "a storehouse of Rodin's creations," and effectively served as "the diary of his life as a sculptor."[25] After he had spent more than two decades on the project, Rodin himself offered a historical interpretation, describing the *Gates* as a record of his efforts to attain movement in his art: "It contains the whole history. There I have made movement yield all that it can."[26]

The single sculpture of Rodin's that is most frequently reproduced in art history textbooks is his *Monument to Balzac*.[27] In 1891 the novelist Emile Zola, as president of the Société des Gens de Lettres, awarded a commission to Rodin for a sculpture of the great novelist Honoré de Balzac, who had been a founder of the literary society. The commission was an important one, and Rodin agreed to deliver the sculpture in eighteen months. Yet the job presented Rodin with a series of problems. Rodin always worked from a model. Because Balzac had died in 1850, Rodin had to create a likeness of Balzac's face based on secondary sources—photographs, paintings, and written descriptions. In the belief that the place a man had been born would have similar physical types, Rodin traveled to Balzac's birthplace, near Tours, to find a suitable model for the body.

Rodin wanted not only to create a likeness of Balzac, but to represent the writer's triumph over adversity, and the enormous energy and creativity that had allowed him to invent more than 2,500 characters in nearly a hundred novels. Obviously identifying with the great realist writer, Rodin explained, "I think of his intense labor, of the difficulty of his life, of his incessant battles and of his great courage. I would express all that."[28] Rodin made a series of studies, some only of the head, others of the full figure, exploring possible poses, some naked, and others clothed. Predictably, the combination of Rodin's perennial dissatisfaction and the press of other projects caused him to miss the initial deadline, and despite many complaints by the Société, for years the commission remained incomplete, as Rodin refused to be hurried (he ignored the deadlines he had agreed to, scoffing, "As if it were possible, while one is searching, to be ready on a fixed date").[29] Finally, in 1898 he agreed to exhibit a plaster version of his *Balzac* at the annual official Salon. Even then, he confessed that he would have preferred to keep it longer: "I should prefer to contemplate it every day for a while, and wait until a sudden inspiration, such as occasionally flashes through the brain, came to flood my imagination and enable me to perfect and idealize my work. For a work, even when achieved, is never perfect; it is always susceptible to a modification that can increase its beauty."[30]

By 1898, the 58-year-old Rodin had been subjected to decades of criticism for his innovative art. But even he was shocked by the virulence of the public attacks on *Balzac* that began as soon as the Salon opened; not only was it ridiculed by critics, but a group of artists actually attempted to vandalize the statue. Shortly thereafter, the Société des Gens de Lettres announced its decision to refuse the sculpture, and annul its contract with Rodin. Wounded by the criticism, Rodin declined to sell *Balzac* to a group of his supporters who had raised a sum equal to the original commission, and had the plaster statue removed to his house near Paris. It was not cast in bronze until after his death. Interestingly, the importance of *Balzac* was a product not only of the sculpture's formal innovations, but also of the public furor it caused. Thus Albert Elsen observed that the attacks on the sculpture "confirmed not only the importance of Rodin, but of sculpture," as the intensity of the assault demonstrated to young sculptors that public sculpture had not lost its relevance to modern society.[31]

Much of the public outrage over *Balzac* was a result of the unconventionality of both its informal pose, with the writer not in formal dress but in the casual robe he wore in his study, and its rough execution. Rodin later defended his conception:

> By convention, a statue in a public place must represent a great man in a theatrical attitude which will cause him to be admired by posterity. But such reasoning is absurd. I submit there was only one way to evoke my subject. I had to show Balzac in his study, breathless, hair in disorder, eyes lost in a dream, a genius who in his little room reconstructs piece by piece all of society in order to bring it into tumultuous life before his contemporaries and generations to come.[32]

Evoking the real man further involved emphasizing the relationship of the figure to its environment, and Rodin did this with jagged contours and a rough surface that created sharp contrasts of light and shadow. In response to the resulting objection of the Société des Gens de Lettres that *Balzac* was only a "rough model," Rodin explained that he had sought "to render in sculpture what was not photographic.... My principle is to imitate not only form but also life. I search in nature for this life and amplify it by exaggerating the holes and lumps, to gain thereby more light."[33]

Rodin called *Balzac* "the sum of my whole life, result of a lifetime of effort."[34] He considered it a culmination of an artistic quest that began with his visit to the Medici Chapel two decades earlier. Seeing Michelangelo's sculptures had started him on a search for a means of animating his sculptures, which led to his discovery that capturing life in movement did not involve portraying a frozen, photographic pose, but rather showing bodies in transition: "Different parts of a sculpture represented at successive moments in time give an illusion of actual motion."[35] He believed he had attained this in *Balzac*, which "by its pose and look makes one imagine the milieu in which he walked, lived and thought. He is inseparable from his surroundings. He is like a veritable living being."[36]

Balzac also represented another important innovation of Rodin's late work, in its effective creation of a new aesthetic. George Heard Hamilton observed that with *Balzac*, Rodin had created "the first authentically 'ugly' work of modern art."[37] Rodin had previously treated subjects that were unattractive, but with *Balzac* the source of ugliness became not only the subject but the execution. The rough texture of the surfaces, the coarse modeling of the head, and the jagged profile of the face were shocking to contemporary viewers. But they were exciting to many later sculptors, who would increasingly privilege power over beauty in their art. Constantin Brancusi, one of the greatest sculptors of the twentieth century, called *Balzac* "indisputably the starting point of modern sculpture."[38]

The impact of *Balzac* also spread beyond sculpture. So for example when Pablo Picasso made a set of etchings to illustrate Balzac's *Unknown Masterpiece*, his portrait of the author was based on that by Rodin.[39] And in 1898, an account of the controversy over *Balzac* in a Milwaukee newspaper excited the young photographer Edward Steichen about going to Paris, "where artists of Rodin's stature lived and worked." When Steichen saw the newspaper photograph of *Balzac*, "it seemed the most wonderful thing I had ever seen. It was not just a statue of a man; it was the very embodiment of a tribute to genius. It looked like a mountain come to life." Steichen later spent an entire night photographing *Balzac* by moonlight at Rodin's estate, and these dramatic images so impressed Alfred Stieglitz that he bought them and donated them to New York's Metropolitan Museum.[40]

A final important innovation that emerged from Rodin's decades of work was his creation of partial figures. He began this practice as early as 1878, with the headless *Walking Man*, but the frequency with which he made partial figures increased later in his career. His attitude toward them changed as well, as he did not exhibit a partial figure until 1898. With time, he came to believe that the absence of heads and limbs could allow him better to concentrate on the planes of a torso, as he declared that "A well-made torso contains all of life."[41] The demonstration that the part could stand for the whole was an exciting revelation to many younger sculptors. Brancusi declared that "Without the discoveries of Rodin, my work would have been impossible," and a number of Brancusi's most important works were inspired by Rodin's fragmentary partial figures.[42]

Rodin understood that his greatest achievements were the result of his long years of work and study. When he visited Amsterdam for an exhibition of his sculpture in 1899, his first wish was to see the Rembrandts in the Rijksmuseum. He was most excited by the lifelike quality of the *Syndics of the Drapers' Guild*, and he asked when it had been painted. When he was told it was a late work he reflected, "Of course, this is not the work of youth.... [H]ere he was free, he knew what to keep and what to sacrifice." When a friend asked if he saw a parallel to his own *Balzac*, Rodin replied that he did: "I, too, was forced to stretch my art in order to reach the kind of simplification in which there is true grandeur."[43]

Umberto Boccioni (1882–1916)

> In the work of art the veristic details, I would say, are nothing else than the point of contact, the bridge the artist places between his idea and the world.
>
> Umberto Boccioni[44]

In Milan in 1907, the 25-year-old painter Umberto Boccioni confessed in his diary that "I do not know how to transfer a literary or philosophical vision into a pictorial one."[45] Boccioni would live less than another decade. Yet virtually all his artistic efforts during that period would go into remedying the problem he had identified in 1907, and in the process the young painter would create one of the most important sculptures of the twentieth century.

Boccioni was extremely ambitious, and was eager "to paint the new, the fruit of our industrial age."[46] He was consequently quick to take advantage of an opportunity that presented itself in 1909. In February of that year, a brash and charismatic young Italian poet, F. T. Marinetti, announced the founding of a new literary movement, Futurism, by publishing a manifesto in a leading Paris newspaper. Marinetti declared that the new movement was to be revolutionary: "Courage, audacity, and revolt will be essential elements of our poetry." A key goal was to erase the past: "We will destroy the museums, libraries, academies of every kind." A second was to celebrate speed: "the world's magnificence has been enriched by a new beauty: the beauty of speed." And a third was to glorify machines: "A racing car ... is more beautiful than the *Victory of Samothrace*." The movement's dynamism was a product of youth: "The oldest of us is thirty.... When we are forty, other younger and stronger men will probably throw us in the wastebasket like useless manuscripts—We want it to happen!"[47]

Within weeks Boccioni met Marinetti, and the two quickly became friends. Futurism was formally extended to painting, and in 1910 two manifestos of Futurist painting were published in Milan, with Boccioni as the lead author.[48] Following Marinetti's stress on speed, the manifestos emphasized the need to bring movement into painting. Boccioni wanted not merely to depict a momentary image, but to represent visually the entire experience of an object's motion—"the *dynamic sensation* itself."[49] Painting motion would furthermore require not only portraying the changes in an object's form as it moved, but also taking account of how it interacted visually with its environment: "The motor bus rushes into the houses which it passes, and in their turn the houses throw themselves upon the motor bus and are blended with it."[50]

Boccioni visited Paris in 1911, and his exposure to the recent work of Picasso and Braque had a profound impact on his art, as he quickly adapted the linear grid, the overlapping planes, and the stenciled letters and numbers of Cubism to his own Futurist ends.[51] Yet Boccioni was careful to differentiate his art from theirs, declaring that the Cubists "obstinately continue to paint objects motionless, frozen, and all the static aspects of Nature. ... To paint from the posing model is an absurdity, and an act of mental cowardice." Futurism would not be bound by this archaic practice: "the picture must be the synthesis of *what one remembers and of what one sees*."[52]

Boccioni's frequent references to the freedom of his Futurist art from the constraints of natural appearances underscore the conceptual nature of his practices and goals. In 1910 he wrote to a friend of his recent paintings, "It is done completely without models, and all the tricks of the trade are sacrificed to the ultimate cause of emotional expression. ... [T]he emotion will be presented with as little recourse as possible to the objects that have given rise to it."[53] He told an interviewer in 1911 that he was "always in continual struggle with myself to liberate myself from objective fact and arrive at an entirely spiritual expression: In me is the ultimate aspiration to try to reproduce the object as a sensation."[54] In a lecture he gave in Rome in 1911, he proclaimed a general principle: "*Art is not the copy of Nature*. The higher art raises itself, the more distant it becomes from Nature, and the more profound the artist, the more his subjective vision—that is, the world itself—is hopelessly unrecognizable at its first appearance."[55]

In the spring of 1912, Boccioni again visited Paris, on his way back to Milan after traveling to Berlin to prepare an exhibition of Futurist paintings. His host was Gino Severini, a fellow Futurist painter who was living in Paris, who had been one of Boccioni's closest friends since they had met as teenaged art students in Rome. Severini recalled that during this visit Boccioni had a new interest, in sculpture: "All day every day he would discuss the subject. To sate his appetite for exploring the problems of sculpture, I took him to visit Archipenko, Agero, Brancusi, and Duchamp-Villon, who were the most daring avant-garde sculptors of the moment."[56] During his stay in Paris, Boccioni wrote to a friend in Italy that "I am obsessed these days by sculpture! I think I can perceive a complete renewal of this mummified art."[57]

After a few frenetic days of visiting studios by day and artists' cafes by night, Boccioni returned to Milan. Severini was stung when, only weeks later, in Milan Boccioni published his *Technical Manifesto of Futurist Sculpture*: "During our discussions and visits to various sculptors in Paris, Boccioni had not once mentioned this manifesto, so it surprised and saddened me to have to acknowledge that these speed 'records,' these feverish searches for the sake of novelty itself, and a lack of sincerity on his part, would inevitably cause deep wounds in our relationship." In typical Futurist fashion, Boccioni's manifesto stridently condemned the sculpture of the time—"All the sculpture ... to be seen in all European cities presents such a pathetic spectacle of barbarism, ineptitude and tedious imitation that my Futurist eyes turn away from it with the deepest loathing"—so Severini felt deeply embarrassed before his colleagues in Paris: "it seemed to all my friends who had recently received him that I had been his accomplice, and I must confess that I found this very distasteful."[58]

Several of the sculptors Boccioni had visited in Paris were concerned with extending the innovations of Cubism to three dimensions, and he aimed to go beyond their efforts in several respects. One was systematically to incorporate motion into sculpture, as a dynamic process that was experienced over time. Another was to represent the tendency of both light and motion to destroy the concreteness of forms, by emphasizing the interplay between objects and their environment: "Let us fling open the figure and let it incorporate within itself whatever may surround it." Futurist sculpture would also be based on lines of force, whose "fundamental naked severity will symbolize the severity of steel in the lines of modern machinery."[59] John Golding suggested that what lay behind these plans was a realization that had dawned on Boccioni during his trip to Paris: "summing up the scene around him with an eye that was quick and competitive, [he] saw that there was as yet no such thing as a school of Cubist sculpture, and he sensed, very shrewdly, how he could best and most quickly make his mark."[60]

After publishing his manifesto of sculpture in April 1912, Boccioni began to make sculptures—something he had never previously done. Just over a year later, in June of 1913, he exhibited eleven plaster sculptures at a Paris gallery. Even Severini had to concede that this output was a tour de force—"such a desperate display of energy and a pressing sense of immediacy employed for the purpose of a maximum degree of expression."[61] Marinetti described the show's opening as "An unforgettable afternoon for the almost divine fervor of our devotion before the miracles of art and this supreme new beauty."[62]

Boccioni considered the last of the sculptures he had made, a work four feet high he titled *Unique Forms of Continuity in Space*, the most successful, and art scholars have agreed: it is illustrated in more textbooks of art history than any other conventional sculpture of the twentieth century.[63] The sculpture's title expressed Boccioni's belief that he had succeeded in representing speed as a continuous process: "To render a body in motion, I definitely do not present the trajectory, that is, the passage from one state of repose to another state of repose, but force myself to ascertain the form that expresses continuity in space."[64] A substantial figure, with a head and torso atop two powerful legs, strides forward at an angle that implies irresistible force. The forms of the body are divided into curved planes that suggest both bulging muscles and surging flames, and seem to flow in response to strong winds generated by the figure's rapid forward progress. The fragments are joined together at angles that produce open forms, creating dramatic contrasts of light and shadow, and suggesting the contact of the figure with its environment. The armless form echoes Greek sculptures even as it creates a superman of the future, whose human features are transformed into mechanical parts that have been shaped by the figure's violent contact with the atmosphere. Golding summarized the radical synthesis represented by *Unique Forms*: "The *Victory of Samothrace* and the speeding automobile have in a sense become one."[65]

The poet Guillaume Apollinaire, a close friend of Picasso and the leading critic of Paris' advanced art world, praised Boccioni's exhibition for successfully introducing movement into sculpture: "Varied materials, sculptural simultaneity, violent movement—these are the innovations contributed by

Boccioni's sculpture."[66] Elated, Boccioni reported to a friend that Apollinaire was "completely won over.... He says there is no one but me in modern sculpture." He went on to describe a dinner with Apollinaire and Marinetti: "We talked from seven until three in the morning. We came out drunk and exhausted." Oddly, however, his success left Boccioni despondent: "After these discussions, which are true conquests of magnetism, I end up sad and discouraged. I think about what I would have done by now if I had grown up with Paris or Berlin as my environment."[67]

Boccioni's brief foray into sculpture provides fascinating insights into both the abilities and attitudes of this brilliant young conceptual innovator. A few days of inspecting the most advanced sculpture in Paris were sufficient to provide a point of departure for Boccioni's own efforts to create innovative new sculptures. He then did this so successfully that in spite of the fact that he had never sculpted before, in a period of barely more than a year he produced a sculpture that ranks among the very most important works of art of the twentieth century. Yet beyond the remarkable speed of Boccioni's internalization of the state of the art, and the equally remarkable speed of his own contribution, the episode also gives a revealing glimpse into the psychology of the young artist, who was willing to embarrass a close friend in order to gain publicity for his own art, in pursuit of what Severini ruefully called "speed records"—"feverish searches for novelty." And finally, Boccioni's enormous ambition and impatience are witnessed by his surprising reaction to his critical success in Paris. Although he was only 31 years old, Boccioni could not simply enjoy Apollinaire's praise of his accomplishment, but instead immediately reflected that he could have made greater contributions even earlier if he had grown up in a center of the art world.

For reasons that remain unknown, Boccioni treated *Unique Forms* not as a beginning, but as an ending. He gave up sculpting after he executed it. Golding concluded that after making *Unique Forms*, "Boccioni seems to have realized that he had achieved the definitive masterpiece for which he had longed."[68] He returned to painting, with conservative works that analyzed the late Cézanne and Picasso's early Cubism, in the few years before he was killed in 1916, while serving in the Italian army. World War I effectively ended the Futurist movement, which became more influential for its ideas than for successful works of art. But John Golding declared that "Futurism did ... produce one major masterpiece," and perhaps it was appropriate that a movement initiated to celebrate the speed of modern life came to be represented by a sculpture created by an artist who devoted only one year to that art.

Alberto Giacometti (1901–1966)

> A sculpture is not an object, it is an interrogation, a question, an answer. It can never be finished or perfect.
>
> Alberto Giacometti[69]

Alberto Giacometti, the son of a successful painter in Italian-speaking Switzerland, was named for the great sixteenth-century German artist Albrecht Dürer. As a boy Alberto loved spending time in his father's studio, and he showed precocious artistic talent. Late in his life, he recalled that around the age of 10, when he first began to draw the world around him, he "was under the impression that I held such a command of the subject that I could do exactly as I pleased.... I had the feeling that there was no obstruction at all between seeing and doing." He remembered that feeling as "paradise." Yet it lasted only until he was 18 or 19, "when I got the feeling that I could no longer do anything at all.... Reality escaped me."[70] Struggling with perception throughout his training as an art student, first in Geneva and then in Paris, in 1925 Giacometti concluded that "it was impossible to create a painting or a sculpture exactly as I saw them," and he decided that "it was necessary to abandon the real."[71] His decision to work only from mental images dominated the next decade of his career.

Giacometti is a rare example of an artist who made important contributions both conceptually and experimentally. It has not been uncommon for artists to change over time from one approach to the other. In the nineteenth century, for example, it was standard for artists to be taught to make preparatory drawings before beginning their paintings. A number of artists then discarded this approach as they matured and became experimental painters. So for example early in his career Cézanne routinely made preparatory studies for his paintings, and he often drew his motifs from religion or mythology. Yet in Pontoise in 1872, at the age of 33, under Pissarro's guidance, he began to paint directly from nature, and he rarely if ever made preparatory drawings thereafter. Cézanne's significant innovations were made exclusively as an experimental painter: his early conceptual works had little impact on other artists, and today receive little attention from art scholars.[72] Other important experimental artists had careers like that of Cézanne, in which they discovered the experimental method as they matured artistically, having earlier produced undistinguished conceptual works. But Giacometti's experience differed, for he made significant early conceptual contributions before adopting the experimental approach that made him one of the most important sculptors of the modern era.[73]

After his decision to stop working from life, Giacometti began creating abstract forms, often with sexual symbolism. In 1930 his sculpture *Suspended Ball* attracted the attention of the Surrealist painter Salvador Dali, who declared it a prototype of a new kind of Surrealist object, for its expression of frustrated sexual desire.[74] The poet André Breton, who was the self-appointed leader of the Surrealist movement, bought *Suspended Ball* and formally invited Giacometti to join the group. He accepted, for Surrealism was then the most exciting group in Paris' advanced art world.[75] The basic principle of Surrealism was to draw on the unconscious, and during this time Giacometti worked strictly conceptually, from his imagination. In 1933 he wrote that "For years I have only made the sculptures that presented themselves to my mind in a finished state, merely reproducing them in space without changing any aspect of them or wondering what they could mean."[76] The sculptures were intended to be pure projections of thought, with no evidence of the artist's touch or manipulation, so Giacometti made plaster models and had the final works executed by a cabinetmaker.[77] During this period Giacometti made two works that are generally considered to be among the most important examples of Surrealist sculpture—*Woman with Her Throat Cut* (1932) and *The Palace at 4 A.M.* (1933).[78] Of the latter, Giacometti wrote that the image became so clear in his mind that its execution required no more than one day's work, and he later told a friend that in spite of the sculpture's complexity, "I knew to the millimeter how it ought to be. I didn't retouch a thing."[79]

Giacometti worked conceptually for a decade: "it was a more or less happy period. I strolled, I worked, the work in itself presented no difficulties, I did what I liked." Yet he knew this situation was temporary: "I knew that whatever I may do, whatever I may desire, one day I would feel obliged to sit on a stool facing the model, endeavoring to copy what I saw. Even if there were no hope at all of succeeding."[80] This day came in 1934, when Giacometti began to make portrait busts. Breton condemned this as reactionary, contemptuously declaring that "everybody knows what a head is," and formally expelled

Giacometti from the Surrealist movement. Giacometti stoically accepted his expulsion: "I lost all my friends. But now, in spite of everything I feel happy ... having decided anew to reproduce the human form as truly as possible, like a beginner."[81]

The last three decades of Giacometti's life became a quest to make art that corresponded to visual reality. When he returned to working from life, he immediately reencountered his earlier problem of perception: "The more I looked at the model, the more the screen between reality and myself thickened. You begin by seeing the person who is posing, but gradually every possible sculpture interposes itself between the sitter and you. The less clearly you actually see the model, the more unknown the head becomes."[82] The same problem dogged him when he painted, as he explained to a friend who was sitting for him: "One should draw and paint one's model the way one sees it—simply the way one sees it. Simply? That of all things is the most difficult! To draw something the way one sees it, not the way one knows it, not the way one thinks it looks, and not the way some others one may recall saw it! Only then, when one forgets what one does not actually see, can a resemblance—which is the essential thing—emerge."[83]

Giacometti's desire to achieve visual truth led him to reject Rodin's practice of sculpting busts by working from a succession of vantage points. He believed that Rodin's method did not yield "a total illusion of the reality, the appearance of a person in a particular position and a particular environment," because it depended on knowledge and calculation gained over time rather than simply on perception. Thus he told David Sylvester:

> Even Rodin still took measurements when he was making his busts. He didn't model a head as he actually saw it in space, at a certain distance.... He really wanted to make a parallel in clay, the exact equivalent of the head's volume in space. So basically it wasn't visual but conceptual. He knew it was round before he began.... [I]n the ordinary way it would never occur to me to get up and walk around you.... So, if I made a sculpture of you according to my absolute perception of you, I would make a rather flat, modulated sculpture.

He wanted to create a new sculpture based on vision: "I think we have for so long automatically accepted the received idea of what a sculptured head should look like that we have made ourselves completely incapable of seeing a head as we really see it."[84]

The artist whose work engaged Giacometti the most deeply was Cézanne. Giacometti studied Cézanne's paintings, and often made drawings from them. Giacometti's drawings, like Cézanne's, have no continuous lines—objects are never clearly outlined or delineated, but emerge tentatively and indistinctly from hazy bundles of smudged and blurred hatchings. Giacometti considered Cézanne the greatest artist of the modern era because he broke with classical conventions in pursuit of a truly visual art: "Cézanne ... only wanted to paint, to put down on canvas his own vision of reality—an apple, a head, a mountain—as close and as truthful to what he saw as possible." Giacometti echoed Cézanne in describing his own artistic goal, to "realize the vision I have of things." Like Cézanne, Giacometti struggled with the impossibility of portraying a subject in its entirety: "If I look at you full in the face, I forget the profile. If I look at the profile, I forget the full-face."[85] Like Cézanne, Giacometti was troubled by the gap in time between seeing and recording: "We may imagine that realism consists of copying ... a vase just as it appears on the table. In fact, one only ever copies the vision that remains of it at each instant, the image that becomes conscious.... You never copy the glass on the table; you copy the residue of a vision." And like Cézanne, Giacometti believed that his goal was not a fixed point, but a moving target—"I have the feeling, or the hope, that I am making progress each day ... knowing that the closer one gets to the goal, the further it retreats"—so resolution was not possible: "It's an endless search."[86]

A friend, the writer James Lord, posed for a portrait in 1964, and in the course of the sittings he asked Giacometti "the relation between your vision, the way things appear to you, and the technique that you have at your disposal to translate that vision into something which is visible to others." Giacometti replied, "That's the whole drama. I don't have such a technique." Lord pondered the response, and Giacometti's claim that it was essential "to work without any preconception whatever," for those statements appeared to belie the fact that Giacometti had long had a distinctive style, and was making new works that closely resembled those that preceded them. Lord concluded that Giacometti's assertions were "far more an expression of his total creative attitude than of his momentary relation to any single work in progress." Giacometti stated that "Cézanne discovered that it's impossible to copy nature.... But one must try all the same."[87]

Giacometti's attempt to create sculptures that would match the complexity of actual vision resulted in a working method based on irresolution, as he became known for repeatedly destroying his sculptures out of dissatisfaction.

He disputed this characterization, however, claiming that "What one calls destroying is simply undoing in order to improve, to continue."[88] His sculptures effectively became visual representations of uncertainty, as the smooth curves and decisive lines of his Surrealist works were replaced by jagged contours and mottled surfaces that retained the visible residue of countless nervous touches.

In 1948, Giacometti ended an interval of fifteen years without a one-man show, with an exhibition at a New York gallery. The tall, thin, isolated figures that emerged from his studio gave rise to an interpretation of his work that tied the sculptures' appearance to his already legendary working methods. This synthesis was provided by the existentialist philosopher Jean-Paul Sartre, a friend of Giacometti's, in a catalogue essay titled "The Search for the Absolute." Sartre declared that Giacometti and other contemporary sculptors were faced with the problem that "for three thousand years, sculpture modeled only corpses.... So one must begin again from scratch." Sartre credited Giacometti with perpetually starting afresh to animate his art: "I like what he said to me one day about some statues he had just destroyed: 'I was satisfied with them but they were made to last only a few hours.'... Never was matter less eternal, more fragile, nearer to being human." Sartre also connected Giacometti's art to the anxiety of his era, acknowledging of the thin figures that "At first glance we seem to be up against the fleshless martyrs of Buchenwald." Yet he noted that the appearance of the sculptures was not unrelievedly gloomy, but was more complex, for "a moment later we have a quite different conception: these fine and slender natures rise up to heaven ... they dance."[89]

The 1948 exhibition included *Man Pointing* (1947) and *City Square* (1948), the two sculptures by Giacometti that are most often reproduced in art history textbooks.[90] Both are prime examples of his mature perceptual art, in which he would model figures as they appeared to him—human beings, often in motion, situated at a specific distance, seen from a single viewpoint, and taken in as a unified whole, at one glance. Their uneven surfaces, thin limbs, and often leaning postures combine to give Giacometti's late sculptures not only a sense of motion, but also of nervous anxiety. The late sculptures became a source of inspiration for younger sculptors concerned with issues of perception, and also anticipated such later developments as the spatial installations that became popular among younger artists from the 1960s on, that included the viewer within the environment of the work of art.[91]

Giacometti wanted to create a three-dimensional art that would accurately represent the process of seeing. He recognized that he was pursuing an impossible objective—"the closer one gets to the goal, the further it retreats."[92] He wrote that "I don't know if I work in order to do something or in order to know why I can't do what I want to do."[93] Yet late in his life, like Cézanne, he based his effort not on attaining his goal, but on making progress toward it: "I now work only for the sensation I get during the process. And if I am then able to see better, if as I leave I see reality slightly differently, deep down, even if the picture doesn't make much sense or is ruined, in any event I have won."[94]

Robert Smithson (1938–1973)

> An object to me is the product of a thought.
> Robert Smithson[95]

When Robert Smithson was 10 years old, his father built him a museum in the basement of their New Jersey house, where Robert could display the fossils and shells he collected on family vacations and in local quarries. On weekend trips to New York City, Robert and his father visited the Metropolitan Museum only once, because Robert found it dull, but they frequently went to the Museum of Natural History, which he loved.[96] Robert had a number of early enthusiasms, including art, writing, and science fiction as well as geology, but these didn't coincide with his school courses, and he became hostile to school in general. As a junior in high school, he got permission to spend much of his time at the New York Art Students League, where he won a scholarship. After graduating from high school, he spent some time hitchhiking around the United States before moving to New York City.[97] Smithson had no interest in attending college, but he studied informally with several older painters, and worked with a number of young writers and artists. He quickly became known in New York's art world, as he not only exhibited his own paintings, but also curated several group shows and began to write art criticism. He was intense, articulate, and charismatic: a friend recalled that even at 18, "He never said, 'I am a genius,' but he spoke with such confidence and certainty that it was uncanny."[98]

Smithson came of age as an artist in the wake of the explosion of Pop on the art world in 1962. New York had become a magnet for ambitious young conceptual artists, and Smithson was as ambitious and iconoclastic as any. He developed a complex and convoluted set of beliefs that extended far beyond art to knowledge and culture more generally. He was a self-taught polymath, whose ideas and rhetoric were scintillating but undisciplined; he valued intuitive insights, but had little concern for logic. Summarizing his intentions and achievements is hazardous, because of the extraordinary variety of his means, and the elusive quality of his discourse. In 1969, Smithson declared that "I think the major issue now in art is what are the boundaries," and nearly all the important artists of the time would have agreed, but where Smithson went beyond most of his peers was in the number of different spheres in which he attacked the boundaries.[99]

Smithson initially set out to be a painter, and the Abstract Expressionists were among his early influences. In 1963, however, he came to the conclusion that he had to reject the art of Jackson Pollock, Willem de Kooning, and Barnett Newman on the grounds that their abstract images concealed an underlying symbolism that represented a continuation of an exhausted cultural tradition that was rooted deeply in the history of Western civilization. He later explained that "the real breakthrough came once I was able to overcome this lurking pagan religious anthropomorphism." He definitively gave up painting, and "began to develop structures based on a particular concern with the elements of material itself." His childhood passions reemerged, as "my early interest in geology and earth sciences began to assert itself over the whole cultural overlay of Europe." Smithson believed he had created a new conception of art: "out of the defunct ... class culture of Europe I developed something that was intrinsically my own and rooted to my own experience in America."[100]

In the years immediately following his breakthrough, which he considered the time of his "emergence as a conscious artist," Smithson developed a set of interrelated practices that changed the appearance and vocabulary of advanced art, and in the process he became recognized as the leader of one of the most audacious movements in the history of modern art. The most dramatic element of his innovations was a new genre of monumental outdoor art works. While consulting for an architectural firm that was designing a new air terminal for Dallas–Fort Worth, Smithson conceived of building large-scale sculptures on the fringes of the airport. Although his proposal was not executed, Smithson published his idea in an art journal in 1967, including the term *earthworks*, which became the name for the large objects he and other artists would create in—and from—the landscape, often in remote areas.[101]

In their size and location, earthworks exploded the traditional limits of the walls of art galleries. The enthusiasm with which a number of young artists embraced this practice was fueled by the political radicalism and anti-gallery sentiment that was widespread in the art world of the Vietnam War era.[102] Smithson wanted his works to demonstrate the process of entropy even as they served as metaphors for the ubiquity of dissolution: thus he introduced a 1968 essay on earth projects by observing that "One's mind and the earth are in a constant state of erosion."[103] Smithson effectively wanted to make time the basic creative principle of art, by producing structures that changed over time, witnessing the process of entropy.

Large projects in inaccessible locations might excite young conceptual artists, but they would not readily allow conventional exhibitions or market transactions. Smithson's innovations solved this problem, for while considering the initial project for the periphery of an airport, he pondered the question, "How can I transmit this into the center?"[104] His solution was to create "a dialogue between the indoor and the outdoor... a dialectic that involved what I call site and nonsite." The *nonsite* became a means "to transfer the land indoors," as Smithson displayed stones, maps, photographs, and other documentation of his earthworks.[105] While the outdoor sites allowed him to defy artistic tradition both in their remote locations and in their construction from dirt and stone, the indoor nonsites allowed him to show and sell his work in traditional settings. Characteristically, the entrepreneurial Smithson established Earth Art as a movement, and himself as its leader, by curating an exhibition titled *Earthworks* at a prominent New York gallery in 1968, that included his work with that of a number of established artists who followed his example of presenting photographs of projects they had executed outdoors.[106]

Written texts were another key element of Smithson's practice. In this he followed a vital tradition of modern art, for since Futurism the impact of nearly all significant conceptual art movements had been enhanced by manifestos. Smithson's texts rivaled or surpassed all such earlier documents in the wide range of subjects they touched on and the remarkable variety of the associations they cited for particular works. The verbal pyrotechnics of Smithson's writings increased the impact of his art by underscoring the intellectual basis of his work.[107]

Smithson made his earthworks in—and usually of—nature, but he was not an environmentalist, and he rejected as naive and nostalgic the desire of ecologists to preserve wilderness that did not reflect the impact of humanity.

A project he designed late in 1969 highlighted his clash with the values of ecologists. For *Island of Broken Glass*, Smithson proposed to dump 100 tons of industrial glass on a small rocky island near Vancouver, British Columbia, then to use a crowbar to shatter the glass, creating a "shimmering thing of beauty reflecting the light off the water." Over time, the sharp edges of the glass would be worn smooth, and in a few centuries the entire pile would turn to sand. The Canadian government initially granted Smithson permission for the project, but reversed this decision in the face of protests from environmentalists who contended the glass would harm birds and seals. Abandoning the project, Smithson charged "militant preservationists" with making him a scapegoat, using his art "as a symbol for their propaganda"; he considered them hypocrites, whose public protests cleared their consciences "while they continued to eat their bloody steaks and drive their poisonous cars."[108]

Smithson's greatest success came soon thereafter. In April 1970, a contractor from Ogden, Utah, provided a team of five workmen who used two dump trucks, a tractor, and a front loader to move 6,650 tons of mud, salt crystals, and rock at Rozel Point, at the north end of Great Salt Lake, to create a 1,500-foot-long promontory according to plans produced by Robert Smithson.[109] In the time since then, *Spiral Jetty* has been seen by relatively few visitors. From 1972 to 2002, a rise in the level of the lake caused it to be submerged almost continuously. Even now that it is visible above the lake's surface, it is separated from Utah State Route 83 by 16 miles of gravel roads, recommended for travel only by four-wheel-drive vehicles because of the many large embedded lava rocks. Remarkably, however, art scholars have resoundingly judged *Spiral Jetty* to be the dominant American work of art of the late twentieth century: it appears in more than 90 percent of art history textbooks that cover the century's last three decades, while in contrast no other work made by an American artist during that time appears in even half those textbooks.[110]

The importance of *Spiral Jetty* in spite of its inaccessibility is in large part a consequence of the supporting materials that Smithson created in other genres. A professional photographer filmed the construction of *Spiral Jetty*, following detailed plans Smithson made for a movie treatment, and Smithson painstakingly edited this, with his narration, into a 32-minute 16-mm film.[111] Many famous images of the jetty, including the aerial views that are most often reproduced in textbooks, are taken from this film. In 1972, Smithson also published an essay, "The Spiral Jetty," that described the development of the project and his perceptions of the landscape and the jetty. The text presents a dizzying array of references, in rapid-fire prose that seems intended to document Smithson's thought processes. So for example the curled shape of *Spiral Jetty* is associated variously with the solar system, the molecular structure of the salt crystals found in Great Salt Lake, Constantin Brancusi's sketch of James Joyce as a "spiral ear," the reels of the movie film used to document the work, a painting by Jackson Pollock titled *Eyes in the Heat*, the ion source of a cyclotron, ripples in the water of Great Salt Lake, and Vincent van Gogh painting ferns.[112] Smithson's film and essay together have greatly increased the appeal of *Spiral Jetty*, for the wide range of images and suggested symbolic meanings free viewers and readers from being constrained by any specific interpretation, and allow them to choose from a rich menu of images and ideas.

The advanced art of the 1970s and beyond is often characterized by scholars and critics with the terms "pluralism" and "postmodernism." These words are effectively art experts' confession that the proliferation of artistic genres, and the abandonment of trademark styles by many leading artists, have left them unable to produce coherent narratives of the art of this period.[113] Yet the absence of dominant genres and styles in fact does not mean there have been no systematic forces or trends. *Spiral Jetty*'s isolated location, its industrial execution, its simple but elegant form, and its existence in multiple genres made it a synthetic work for the conceptual art world of the late twentieth century, with its stress on innovative ideas, de-emphasis of individual style, and proliferation of genres. And Smithson himself appears as an emblematic figure, who remained an active member of New York's art world even as he devoted much of his time to exploring remote and desolate areas as possible sites for his trademark earthworks. His dynamic intellectualism made him a prototype of a new kind of artist, who could create great monuments out of raw materials in isolated areas that still echoed the raw American frontier even while he produced the dazzling new ideas that made him a dominant figure in New York's competitive art world. The critic Arthur Danto wrote in 2005 that Smithson

> has become the beau idéal of young artists, more than Picasso . . . the kind of figure they aspire to be—anti-institutional, in touch with the environment, hospitable to myth and ritual, alive to the poetry of the wilderness, ambitious in his desire to touch the public through a vision of monumentality that throws the world of the shopping mall and the parking lot into a moral perspective.[114]

Among many younger artists, the architect Maya Lin has cited Smithson as a central influence on her art: she told a critic that she was moved to tears by a Smithson retrospective exhibition in 1982, "because I thought it was so brilliant."[115]

Robert Smithson died in 1973, at the age of 35, when the small plane from which he was filming the staked-out plans for his latest earthwork crashed into a hillside, killing him, the pilot, and the owner of the West Texas ranch where the work was to be situated.[116] His career spanned barely more than a decade, but he nonetheless invented two distinctive new genres, became recognized as the leader of an art movement that continues today, and created a landmark of American art. The speed with which he accomplished all this was made possible by his highly conceptual approach to art, which is equally the source of his continuing fascination not only to younger artists but also to art scholars: as Kirk Varnedoe observed, "Smithson is the kind of artist who, if he didn't exist, would have to be invented by graduate students."[117]

Touch

Rodin brought a new modern aesthetic to sculpture, in which traces of the artist's touch remained visible in the finished work. Conservative critics made the same objection to his sculptures as they did to the innovative painting of the time, that they were not finished. Edmond de Goncourt wrote in 1889 that "Amid the present infatuation with Impressionism, when all of painting remains in the sketch stage, [Rodin] ought to be the first to make his name and *gloire* as a sculptor of unfinished sketches."[118] In time, admirers celebrated Rodin's distinctive working method, with his frequent, rapid modifications of the surface of a work in progress, as for example the poet Rainer Maria Rilke observed that "The maître works quickly ... adding touch after touch," and described his "quick hands, swooping down like birds of prey."[119] Rodin's greatness came to be specifically identified with his touch. George Bernard Shaw wrote an article about the experience of sitting for Rodin, declaring that "a succession of miracles took place as he worked," and remarking that "Rodin's hand worked, not as a sculptor's hand works, but as the Life Force works."[120]

Rodin considered the surface variation of his sculptures a key to their animation, according to what he called the "science of depression and relief." The many tiny projections and recessions on his sculptures created subtle effects of light and shadow, "For light serves, in conformity with depressions and reliefs, to give the eye the same sensation that the hand receives from touch." His ability to create surface texture was the source of his greatest pride: "The great concern of my life is the struggle I have maintained to escape from the general flatness. All the success of my sculpture comes from that."[121]

In his *Technical Manifesto of Futurist Sculpture*, Boccioni predicted that Futurist sculptures would contain "marvelous mathematical and geometric elements," including pieces of machinery embedded within the forms of a human body.[122] It is consequently not surprising that one study observed that in *Unique Forms of Continuity in Space*, "Human features made way for a synthesis of every kind of machine the Futurists ever depicted."[123] Boccioni specifically rejected "modeling with the thumb ... meant to imitate the lightness of Impressionist brushwork," and his sculptures generally mimic the smooth surfaces of modern machinery, with no suggestion of the touch of a sculptor.[124]

Giacometti exaggerated Rodin's practice of using his touch to create surface texture for visual effect. David Sylvester observed that his sculptures display "the reverse side of his gestures, the traces of his gestures" in their rough surfaces.[125] The discrete touches visible in these sculptures parallel the discrete brushstrokes that remain distinct in late works by Cézanne. Just as late Cézannes bear witness to the process of their own making, so late Giacomettis reveal the sculptor's process: Sylvester remarked of a late work, "He has mauled it, squeezed it, stretched it, gouged it, lacerated it, demolished it and seen it grow out of his hands over and over again, postponing the moment when it had to leave his hands, letting it go pitted and scarred with his gestures."[126] It was not a concern that his works' rough surfaces might make them appear unfinished, because Giacometti had ceased to believe in finished statements.

Robert Smithson's earliest published articles, in 1965, made it clear that he had no interest in the artist's touch. In an essay about the sculptor Donald Judd, Smithson described the boxes that Judd had had fabricated industrially from steel and Plexiglas, then observed that some art lovers were puzzled by Judd's objects: "They either wonder where the 'art' went or where the 'work' went, or both." Smithson explained that these observers didn't understand that "Judd is busy extending art into new mediums. This new approach to technique has nothing to do with sentimental notions about 'labor.' There is no subjective craftsmanship. Judd is not a specialist in a certain kind of labor, but a whole artist engaged in a multiplicity of techniques."

In another statement the same year, Smithson declared that "All kinds of engineering fascinates [sic] me, I'm for the automated artist."[127] Smithson judged art by the ideas it embodied, and his most celebrated works were executed by workmen operating bulldozers, trucks, and other heavy construction equipment.

For the experimental Rodin and Giacometti, the touch of their hands created the rough and irregular surfaces that brought their sculptures to life. For Rodin, vision and touch were closely connected: he described the experience of visiting France's great cathedrals, "in front of the stones themselves I feel them! I touch them everywhere with my gaze as I move around them to see from all directions how they soar into the sky."[128] Giacometti believed that "You have to learn to look and your hand will follow your eye."[129] In contrast, the conceptual Boccioni and Smithson had no interest in the artist's touch, for in different ways both embraced the use and appearance of machinery in their sculpture.

5
Novelists

William Faulkner believed that

> there's a period in a writer's life when he is . . . fertile and he just produces. . . . I think there's one time in his life when he writes at the top of his talent plus his speed, too. Later the speed slows; the talent doesn't necessarily have to fade at the same time. But there's a time in his life, one matchless time, when they are matched completely. The speed, and the power and the talent, they're all there . . . which of course can't last forever.[1]

Yet Faulkner didn't believe the timing of this period could be predicted: "Some write best when they are young, write themselves out. Some never reach their top speed until late in life. That's—you just can't say."[2]

F. Scott Fitzgerald disagreed. Just months before his death, he wrote to his college-aged daughter to offer advice on how to prepare for a career as a writer. He cautioned against impatience, noting that "the odds are against your having the type of talent that matures very quickly—most of my contemporaries did not get started at twenty-two, but usually at about twenty-seven to thirty or even later". He then offered a generalization about writers' life cycles: "The talent that matures early is usually of the poetic, which mine was in large part. The prose talent depends on other factors—assimilation of material and careful selection of it, or more bluntly: having something to say and an interesting, highly developed way of saying it."[3]

The difference in the perspectives of Faulkner and Fitzgerald is perhaps not surprising. Faulkner was a great experimental novelist, who wrote a series of important novels, no one of which is recognized as clearly superior to the others, and he produced these over an extended period. In contrast, Fitzgerald was a great conceptual novelist, who produced one great early novel that dominated his career.[4] When he completed that novel, with the confidence and certainty of a precocious conceptual innovator, the 28-year-old Fitzgerald wrote to his editor that "I think my novel is about the best American novel ever written."[5] In spite of his premature death at 44,

Fitzgerald had well over a decade to reflect on his inability to surpass, or match, the brilliance of *The Great Gatsby*. One poignant product of this was a confession by Fitzgerald, at the age of 33, to his friend Ernest Hemingway, that the outpouring of three novels and fifty stories he had written during his late 20s "may have taken all I had to say too early."[6]

The work of Faulkner and Fitzgerald also neatly illustrates the differences between the novels of experimental and conceptual writers. Faulkner is known for creating complex characters, who often surprised him in the process of effectively working out their own paths, for the open endings of his novels, which left the characters' destinies unresolved, and for the interdependence of his novels, in which characters and their descendants often reappeared. In contrast, Fitzgerald used lyrical prose, simplified figures, and symbolic stage props and settings in the service of elegant, allegorical plots.

Herman Melville (1819–1891)

I have swam through libraries and sailed through oceans.

Herman Melville[7]

In 1851, Herman Melville declared that "From my twenty-fifth year I date my life." By this reckoning, Melville's life began only when he started writing, thus excluding not only his childhood, but also the four years he had spent as a sailor on whaling ships in the South Seas. But in the midst of the intense intellectual effort he was making to complete *Moby-Dick*, Melville could value only the time he had devoted to becoming an artist, and so he considered that "Until I was twenty-five, I had no development at all."[8]

Melville had begun writing simply to earn a living. After returning to his native New York from his youthful travels, he needed a job, and he took the advice of his family and friends to write down the colorful stories he told them of his experiences in the tropics. His early books were narratives of these adventures, suitably embellished with titillating hints of exotic and licentious behavior among the native peoples of the South Seas. Melville's talent as a storyteller gained him a large audience of enthusiastic readers, a growing literary reputation, and a respectable income.

It was while he was writing his third book, *Mardi*, that Melville began to have higher aspirations. He considered his earlier books mere narratives of facts, and to the dismay of his publisher he explained that he had begun "to feel an incurable distaste for the same; and a longing to plume my pinions for a flight." Although *Mardi* was presented as the last novel of a Polynesian trilogy, its many literary allusions and obvious inventions were not well received by critics or the reading public, and sales were poorer than for his first two books. To make money, Melville quickly wrote two more realistic books, but with *Mardi* he had begun to explore "the world of mind," and he fully intended to return to it again.[9]

In early 1850, Melville began writing a new novel. At the end of June, he wrote to his publisher describing the book as a "romance of adventure" about a whaling voyage, which he expected to finish by the fall.[10] In August, however, these plans changed, as the result of a summer vacation Melville and his family took in the Berkshires. At a literary gathering organized by a neighbor, Melville met the older writer Nathaniel Hawthorne, and he was electrified. He immediately began reading Hawthorne's works, and within weeks he had written a review of Hawthorne's *Mosses from an Old Manse* in which he declared that "Hawthorne has dropped germinous seeds into my soul."[11] Melville would later dedicate *Moby-Dick* to Hawthorne, "in token of my admiration for his genius."

Melville's new friendship with Hawthorne inspired him to raise his artistic sights, and emboldened him to make the brash prediction that "if Shakespeare has not been equalled, he is sure to be surpassed, and surpassed by an American." The particular target was not chosen by chance, for while Melville explained that "it is that blackness in Hawthorne . . . that so fixes and fascinates me," it was this same blackness that Melville found so powerful in Shakespeare, particularly "the dark characters of Hamlet, Timon, Lear, and Iago."[12] Ahab, the central character of Melville's reconceived novel, was the product of this bewitchment with the dark underside of his literary predecessors.

Under this new inspiration, Melville returned to his book in progress, which had become "The Whale."[13] He clearly believed that—as Ishmael put it—"To produce a mighty book, you must choose a mighty theme," and his was certainly that: *Moby-Dick* was not merely about the largest of all living creatures, but an allegory of man against nature, and good against evil.[14] The revisions Melville carried out during 1851 made *Moby-Dick* into one of the greatest conceptual novels ever written.

The text of *Moby-Dick* begins with one of literature's most celebrated first sentences. Yet even before arriving at "Call me Ishmael," readers have already passed a page titled "Etymology [Supplied by a Late Consumptive Usher to a Grammar School]," with translations of "whale" into thirteen languages ranging from Hebrew to Erromangoan [sic], and a seven-page entry titled "Extracts [Supplied by a Sub-Sub-Librarian]," which quotes passages referring to whales from sources ranging from Genesis to Darwin's *Voyage of a Naturalist*. These facetious pseudoacademic introductory sections effectively alerted the reader that this would not be a conventional novel, in which the author would purport to recount an absorbing story based on actual events he has witnessed, but something with greater scholarly and philosophical ambitions.[15] And the reminders of the book's artificiality continued into the text. So for example a number of chapters include parenthetic stage directions for the characters, mimicking a play. And perhaps even more curiously, in the midst of a discussion of whale spouts, Melville recorded the precise time he was writing the words—"fifteen and a quarter minutes past one o'clock P.M. of this sixteenth day of December, A.D. 1850."[16]

The plot of *Moby-Dick* was in fact not based on events Melville himself had experienced, but was taken from a book he read about a whaling ship that had sunk after being rammed by a great sperm whale in the Pacific Ocean. The name and most distinctive characteristic of Melville's whale were similarly derived from an article he had read, about an enormous whale who was "white as wool," called Mocha Dick. Melville's fertile imagination transformed these factual accounts to his own purposes, as he routinely did: the enormous amount of factual information included in *Moby-Dick* about ships, whales, and their interaction was derived less from his own experience than from intensive research using books he purchased, or consulted at the New York Society Library.[17] Thus Nathaniel Philbrick commented that "The writing process for Melville was as much about responding to and incorporating the works of others as it was about relying on his own experiences."[18]

Melville not only based his story on earlier literature, but often borrowed its very language. He frequently drew on the Bible. So for example in Chapter 86, "The Tail," Ishmael concluded by pondering his inability to understand the whale: "if I know not even the tail of this whale, how understand his head? much more, how comprehend his face, when he has none? Thou shalt see my back parts, my tail, he seems to say, but my face shall not be seen." This was clearly based on the passage in Exodus in which God told Moses, "Thou canst not see my face: for there shall no man see me, and live.... And I will take away mine hands, and thou shalt see my back parts: but my face shall not be seen."[19] Melville also freely borrowed the language, and devices, of Shakespeare. So for example he read in a famous essay on *Hamlet* by Samuel Taylor Coleridge that "one of Shakespeare's modes of creating character is to conceive any one intellectual or moral faculty in morbid excess, and then to place himself... thus mutilated or diseased, under given circumstances." In reflecting on Ahab, Ishmael adapted Coleridge's observation: "For all men tragically great are made so through a certain morbidness. Be sure of this, O young ambition, all mortal greatness is but disease."[20] And Ishmael's range of reference also extended to Greek philosophy, as for example upon his first meeting with Queequeg, he remarked on the latter's "Socratic wisdom."[21]

Melville repeatedly heightened the power of his narrative by using formal and dramatic language to deliver conceptual messages. A famous example occurs in Chapter 36, "The Quarter-Deck," when the reasonable and sensible first mate Starbuck questions Ahab's irrational desire to seek vengeance on Moby Dick. Ahab categorically rejected the relevance of Starbuck's contention that Moby Dick had wounded him by acting purely on instinct:

> All visible objects, man, are but as pasteboard masks. But in each event—in the living act, the undoubted deed—there, some unknown but still reasoning thing puts forth the mouldings of its features from behind the unreasoning mask. If man will strike, strike through the mask!... Sometimes I think there's naught beyond. But 'tis enough. He tasks me; he heaps me; I see in him outrageous strength, with an inscrutable malice sinewing it. That inscrutable thing is chiefly what I hate: and be the white whale agent, or be the white whale principal, I will wreak that hate upon him. Talk not to me of blasphemy, man; I'd strike the sun if it insulted me.[22]

Ahab's contention that there is evil in nature was not expressed in the earthy and colloquial terms that would have been expected from the real captain of a Nantucket whaling ship, but rather with the formal language, vivid imagery, and abstract concepts that would have been declaimed by the obsessed and doomed tyrant in an Elizabethan tragedy. Melville thus again implicitly reminded his audience that this was not simply a story about a whaling voyage, to be read solely for the plot, but a much more ambitious artistic enterprise with higher philosophical intentions.

It is well known that *Moby-Dick* did not achieve early success: upon its publication in 1851 it received mixed reviews, and it sold poorly. Melville's earnings from it were less than from any of his previous books.[23] And although he lived another forty years, this was not long enough to see his greatest book become famous. It was not until the twentieth century that *Moby-Dick* came to be considered a masterpiece. Its eventual recognition was a consequence of both its form and its substance. During the 1920s, *Moby-Dick* became known for having anticipated many of the formal innovations of such leading contemporary novelists as James Joyce and William Faulkner, including long, rhythmic sentences, mixture of literary genres, changes in point of view, with abrupt transitions from first-person to omniscient narration, and mixture of formal speech with vernacular dialogue.[24] In 1923, the novelist D. H. Lawrence called *Moby-Dick* "one of the strangest and most wonderful books in the world ... an epic of the sea such as no man has ever equalled.... It moves awe in the soul."[25] And from the 1930s on, Melville's preoccupation with the destructiveness of human hate and the evils of tyranny came to be regarded as a prophecy of fascism, and an anticipation of the greatest political disasters of the twentieth century. Thus Ahab's triumph over the sensible but weak Starbuck seemed to foreshadow William Butler Yeats' complaint in 1920 that "the best lack all conviction, while the worst/Are full of passionate intensity," while by 1953 the writer C. L. R. James described *Moby-Dick* as "the biography of the last days of Adolf Hitler."[26]

The source of the decline of Melville's literary career after *Moby-Dick* is one of the perennial unsolved puzzles of American literary history. The puzzle was recognized even during his lifetime, as in 1889 an admirer noted that Melville had written *Moby-Dick* at 33, and observed that "It may seem strange that so vigorous a genius, from which stronger and stronger work might reasonably have been expected, should have reached its limit at so early a date."[27] Oddly, Melville anticipated his own loss of creativity even before he completed *Moby-Dick*, for in the summer of 1851, in a letter to Hawthorne describing his frantic efforts to finish his epic, he told his friend that he believed the extraordinary development he had experienced in the previous eight years was over: "I feel that I am now come to the inmost leaf of the bulb, and that shortly the flower must fall to the mould." In part, this foreboding may have been the product of frustration, for in the same letter he lamented that the greatest artistic accomplishments were never widely appreciated: "Try to get a living by the Truth—and go to the Soup Societies."[28]

In spite of generations of reappraisals of Melville's later fiction and poetry, there remains widespread agreement with a recent biographer's conclusion that by the mid-1850s Melville's powers of invention were definitely failing.[29] The three of his works given the greatest attention by recent literary scholars—*Moby-Dick*, *Mardi*, and *Pierre*—had all been completed by the time he was 33.[30] Biographers have pointed to a loss of confidence, as

Melville was discouraged and worn down by hostile critics, the loss of an audience for his books, and the vast efforts he made to create his early works.[31] Hawthorne apparently would have agreed, for when he saw his younger friend in 1856 after a hiatus of several years, he recorded in his journal that Melville "no doubt has suffered from too constant literary occupation, pursued without much success, latterly; and his writings, for a long while past, have indicated a morbid state of mind."[32] For a few brief years, Melville had written with both mastery and passion, and in 1851 he himself may have been the first to recognize that his passion had become a victim of the frustration of producing great literature for an indifferent public.

Mark Twain (1835–1910)

> A man who is not born with the novel-writing gift has a troublesome time of it when he tries to build a novel. I know this from experience.
> Mark Twain[33]

Samuel Clemens first used the pseudonym "Mark Twain" in 1863, while writing for the Virginia City *Territorial Enterprise*. He later claimed that it had been the nom de plume of a deceased riverboat pilot, whose death had allowed Clemens to lay "violent hands upon it without asking permission." In fact, however, the pilot in question did not die until 1864, so in this account, as was frequently the case, Mark Twain did not feel constrained by strict factual accuracy. Whatever the true proximate source for Clemens' appropriation, the call "mark twain" was a familiar one on the Mississippi River, for it was the riverboat leadsman's cry meaning the river was two fathoms deep, the minimum required for the safe passage of a typical steamboat.[34]

Mark Twain's development as a writer was not purposive: the scholar Bernard DeVoto remarked that "no man ever became a great writer more inadvertently."[35] During Twain's early career, he considered himself a journalist, travel writer, and humorist. He gained a considerable reputation in these roles, and he was hesitant to risk it by attempting to write novels. He published his first novel, *The Gilded Age*, at the age of 38, and this was co-authored with the older writer Charles Dudley Warner. Yet he had already begun to work on a more personal novel that took its subject matter from his childhood memories of Hannibal, Missouri, and the three years he had spent as a young man working as a steamship pilot on the Mississippi River. *The*

Adventures of Tom Sawyer, which Twain published in 1876, at the age of 41, marked an important step toward his greatest achievement.

Twain emphasized that his fiction grew out of things he knew directly—"life with which I am familiar"—so it is not surprising that he considered experience "an author's most valuable asset." Experience was what brought fiction to life—"the thing that puts the muscle and the breath and warm blood into the book"—and it could only be the product of deep knowledge: "Almost the whole capital of the novelist is the slow accumulation of unconscious observation." This required time: "the life, the genius, the soul of a people, are realized only through years of absorption." In addition to experience of life, the writer needed experience of his craft: "Every man must *learn* his trade—not pick it up. God requires that he learn it by slow and painful processes. The apprentice hand in blacksmithing, in medicine, in literature, in everything, is a thing that can't be hidden." Writers did not invent, they remembered: "I don't believe any writer ever invents a character; he draws from memory someone he has known."[36]

Twain was thus committed to realism, which he believed had to be based on experience and observation. He always sought to undermine stereotyped attitudes, and he consistently championed the individual who fought against social conventions. He did not believe in simple or universal moral statements. All of these convictions powerfully affected how he produced his novels. There is a consensus among scholars who have studied Twain's surviving manuscripts and methods of composition that he did not write his novels with a conclusion in mind, but rather discovered his plots as he wrote.[37] He once remarked that "I have noticed . . . that as the short tale grows into the long tale, the original intention (or motif) is apt to get abolished and find itself superseded by quite a different one."[38] The writer and editor William Dean Howells, who was Twain's closest friend, observed that "so far as I know, Mr. Clemens is the first writer to use in extended writing the fashion we all use in thinking, and to set down the thing that comes into his mind without fear or favor of the thing that went before or the thing that may be about to follow."[39] The scholar Franklin Rogers concluded that

> Twain was aware of implicit form and sought to discover it by a sort of trial-and-error method. His routine procedure seems to have been to start a novel with some structural plan which ordinarily soon proved defective, whereupon he would cast about for a new plot which would overcome the

difficulty, rewrite what he had already written, and then push on until some new defect forced him to repeat the process once again.[40]

The scholar Henry Nash Smith explained that Twain made discoveries in both meaning and method as he worked, and as he matured as an artist: "His development as a writer was a dialectic interplay in which the reach of his imagination imposed a constant strain on his technical resources, and innovations of method in turn opened up new vistas before his imagination."[41] Twain concluded a brief reflection on his methods of composition by observing that "Doubtless I have methods, but they beget themselves; in which case I am only their proprietor, not their father."[42]

One of Twain's greatest strengths as a writer, and perhaps his greatest source of pride, was his voice: the scholar Tom Quirk wrote of *Huck Finn* that "Nothing about the book commanded Twain's more minute attention than the sounds of its words."[43] To call attention to the subtlety of his work, Twain inserted a prefatory note in the book stating that it contained seven distinct dialects, then humorously admonished that the distinctions "have not been done in a hap-hazard fashion, or by guess-work; but pains-takingly, and with trustworthy guidance and support of personal familiarity with these several forms of speech."[44] Twain revised extensively and meticulously: as he once wrote, "the difference between the *almost right word* and the *right* word is really a large matter—'tis the difference between the lightning-bug and the lightning."[45]

Twain's interest in writing was in creating vivid characters, who in turn produced amusing incidents. These incidents were at best only loosely connected, and Twain's lack of concern with the coherence of his plots was such that he often did not bother to correct inconsistencies that occurred when he changed his mind about the direction of a narrative. So for example at the end of Chapter 16 of *Huck Finn*, Twain had a steamboat "come smashing straight through the raft." Scrambling for his life, Huck swam ashore, but he could not find Jim. Twain had clearly decided to move the narrative onto land, where Huck would travel by himself. Yet he evidently soon regretted this decision, and just two chapters later Huck happened across Jim, who informed him that in fact "dey warn't no great harm done" to the raft, whereupon the two returned to their adventures on the river.[46] Twain wrote himself a marginal note—"CHANGE—raft only *crippled* by steamer"—but in fact he never bothered to change the original description of the raft's demise, so that in this inconsistency *Huck Finn*, like an Abstract

Expressionist painting, visibly displays in its final version the record of its own making.[47]

Adventures of Huckleberry Finn was published in the United States in 1885, when Mark Twain was 50. Its greatness as an experimental novel is attested to by the fact that not only is it widely considered one of the greatest works of fiction ever written, but that Huck is considered one of the greatest characters ever created—worthy, according to no less a critic than T. S. Eliot, of standing with such others as Ulysses, Don Quixote, and Hamlet.[48] Twain's growth over time as an experimental artist can be seen clearly in the two key innovations of *Huck Finn*. One of these was in language, most famously and succinctly saluted by Ernest Hemingway in 1935: "All modern American literature comes from one book by Mark Twain called *Huckleberry Finn*."[49] Twain's mature command of language can be illustrated by a celebrated passage at the beginning of Chapter 19. Huck and Jim had to travel covertly, by night, so before sunrise they went ashore and set up their camp. That done,

> we slid into the river and had a swim, so as to freshen up and cool off; then we set down on the sandy bottom where the water was about knee deep, and watched the daylight come. Not a sound, anywheres—perfectly still—just like the whole world was asleep, only sometimes the bull-frogs a-cluttering, maybe. The first thing to see, looking away over the water, was a kind of dull line—that was the woods on t'other side—you couldn't make nothing else out; then a pale place in the sky; then more paleness spreading around; then the river softened up, away off, and warn't black any more, but gray ... and by and by you could see a streak on the water which you know by the look of the streak that there's a snag there in a swift current which breaks on it and makes that streak look that way; and you see the mist curl up off of the water, and the east reddens up, and the river....[50]

The eloquence of Huck's account can be placed in sharp relief by comparing it to another description of a sunrise on the Mississippi that Twain had written nine years earlier, in *Tom Sawyer*: "It was the cool gray dawn, and there was a delicious sense of repose and peace in the deep pervading calm and silence of the woods. Not a leaf stirred; not a sound obtruded upon nature's meditation."[51] The formal, stilted language and clichéd and mannered images of Twain's earlier description distance the reader from the actual scene. In contrast, the simple, descriptive words of the later passage take the reader into the river and let him see the sunrise through Huck's eyes. It is not surprising that Hemingway would pay homage to *Huck Finn*, for in passages like this one Twain pioneered the natural, colloquial prose that inspired much of modern American literature, including Hemingway's; the critic Harold Bloom considered it "the most beautiful prose paragraph yet written by an American."[52]

The second major innovation in *Huck Finn* was moral: as Ralph Ellison put it, "*Huckleberry Finn* projected the truth about slavery."[53] In what is widely considered the book's climactic moment, Huck was overcome by remorse at violating the South's social and religious values by helping a slave escape from his owner: he had a crisis in which he realized that "my wickedness was being watched all the time from up there in heaven, whilst I was stealing a poor old woman's [slave] that hadn't ever done me no harm." Filled with fear of "everlasting fire," Huck then wrote a letter to Jim's owner turning him in. After completing the letter, Huck felt cleansed of sin. But almost immediately he began to think back over his experiences with Jim, and found that he "couldn't seem to strike no places to harden me against him, but only the other kind." Realizing that Jim depended on him, just as he had so often depended on Jim, Huck held the letter, recognizing that "I'd got to decide, forever, betwixt two things." Then he made his decision, declaring "All right then, I'll *go* to hell," and tore the letter up.[54] Years later, Twain referred to *Huck Finn* as "a book of mine where a sound heart and a deformed conscience come into collision and conscience suffers defeat."[55] The opportunity for Huck's innate decency to triumph over the perverted morality of a society that sustained slavery was direct evidence of the growth of Twain's moral judgment, for the presence of Jim as a central character in *Huck Finn* stood in stark contrast to *Tom Sawyer*, in which Twain had carefully avoided the subject of slavery by almost completely excluding blacks.

These two great innovations are the central reasons for the vast importance of *Huck Finn* in American history and literature. Thus the critic Lionel Trilling considered the novel "one of the world's great books and one of the central documents of American culture," both for holding "the truth of moral passion" and establishing "for written prose the virtues of American colloquial speech."[56] Yet the two contributions have generally been considered to be unrelated. In fact, however, these innovations are integrally linked, not only by the fact that they were both products of Twain's growth over time as an artist, but because both were fundamental consequences of Twain's experimental method in producing *Huck Finn*. For the initial conception of the book did not anticipate the importance of either.

Twain's decision to make Huck the narrator of his own book appears to have been taken quite casually. In a letter to Howells in 1875, he reported that he had finished *Tom Sawyer*, but reflected that "I perhaps made a mistake in not writing it in the first person." Later in the letter, he mentioned that "By & by I shall take a boy of twelve & run him on through life (in the first person) but not Tom Sawyer."[57] Twain's composition of *Huck Finn* did not exhibit any obvious determination or dedication. He drafted the book over an elapsed period of eight years, in at least four discrete phases. He began writing what he called "Huck Finn's Autobiography" in 1876, but reported to Howells that he liked it "only tolerably well," and might "possibly pigeonhole or burn the manuscript." He returned to the novel sometime in 1879–1880, again put it aside, returned to it again sometime between 1881 and early 1883, again paused, then declared it finished after a final burst of writing in the summer of 1883.[58] Even then, he would not relinquish the manuscript until 1884, after he had worked over it for another six months.[59] The discontinuities in Twain's composition reflect major changes in the nature of the book, as Twain encountered unanticipated problems, and responded to each after taking time to think about how he might continue. The longest gap, for example, from 1876 until 1879, occurred just at the point in the manuscript where the raft was destroyed by the steamboat, and marked a shift from a light-hearted adventure narrative to pointed social satire. That Twain had begun *Huck Finn* as a continuation of the light entertainment of *Tom Sawyer* is apparent from the summary of the earlier book that Huck provided in the opening paragraphs of his own book. But after the destruction of the raft, the book's tone changed. It is likely that from the beginning Twain had intended to satirize the prewar South, but the break in his work after 1876 may imply that he found it more difficult than he had expected to reconcile social criticism with the book's adventure form. What Twain had almost certainly not anticipated was yet a further stage in the book's evolution, that led to Huck's internal struggle over whether to betray Jim or to continue to defy the South's most basic social conventions by aiding a runaway slave. And it was this unanticipated change that made *Huck Finn* a classic work.

Twain made a major literary innovation when he chose to use an uneducated boy as the narrator of *Huck Finn*. Earlier novels had included uneducated characters, but no novelist had ever narrated an entire book using such a character's vernacular speech, and this was a revolutionary decision.[60] Twain took full advantage of the opportunities this created, not only in the immediacy and concreteness of Huck's language, but also in his point of view: Huck's humorless innocence was a powerful tool for satirizing the pomposity and corruption of antebellum society and its institutions, and it proved an even more powerful vehicle for highlighting the struggle between social conformity and human decency. In a single character, Huck could combine such basic vernacular values as integrity and freedom with the values of the dominant social institutions, and this allowed Twain to create the collision between a sound heart and a deformed conscience. But Twain also conscientiously accepted the constraints imposed by Huck's narration. Huck's decision not to betray Jim was not the result of a moral conclusion that slavery was evil, because his age and lack of education did not give him the intellectual capacity to formulate the abstract proposition "slavery is wrong."[61] (As if to anticipate and contradict the interpretation of Huck's decision as a general statement of concern for slaves, in the very next chapter, when Huck invented a fictitious boat accident to explain his tardy arrival home and Aunt Sally exclaimed, "Good gracious! anybody hurt?," he replied, "No'm. Killed a [slave].")[62] Huck's decision was instead based on his feelings for Jim, and was expressed solely in emotional terms. Twain's experimental commitment to realism dictated this, for while it is realistic for a young boy to decide to protect a friend, it would not be realistic for him to base this decision on a generalization about an entire class of victims.[63]

Mark Twain's experimental approach is the source of a common error in the treatment of his greatest achievement, for although there is no definite article in the title *Adventures of Huckleberry Finn*, many critics and publishers have believed otherwise.[64] Twain concluded *Adventures of Huckleberry Finn*, but he did not resolve it, because he did not consider Huck's adventures finished. Few great novels end with a preview of coming attractions, but *Huck Finn* does just that, as in its final sentences Huck famously confided his plan to avoid having to go to school by going West: "But I reckon I got to light out for the Territory ahead of the rest, because aunt Sally she's going to adopt me and sivilize me and I can't stand it. I been there before."[65] Twain wrote nine chapters of a sequel but put it aside and never returned to it.[66] It is unlikely that the lack of resolution of *Huck Finn* bothered Twain. For him, the essence of art lay in the voyage, not the destination; as Huck said in his first chapter: "All I wanted was to go somewheres; all I wanted was a change, I warn't particular."[67] Both *Huck Finn*'s greatest moment and its greatest failing were products of Twain's experimental approach. The moral development of Huck's character, which Twain had not planned or anticipated, led to his noble decision not to betray Jim.[68] Yet the transition from the tale's comic origins to its serious climax left Twain uncertain how to close the novel, and his decision to return to comedy has baffled and dismayed generations of readers.[69]

The simplicity and clarity of Mark Twain's experimental prose helped to make him the first great American novelist who was also a popular writer; he was the first great writer who portrayed ordinary Americans realistically, using the language they themselves spoke.[70] He became the literary voice of American democracy, not only during his lifetime, but beyond. Franklin Roosevelt took his famous slogan, New Deal, from *A Connecticut Yankee in King Arthur's Court*; Harry Truman always kept on his desk the Twain inscription, "Always do right. It will please some people, and astonish the rest"; and in 2008, the presidential candidate Barack Obama quoted Twain's declaration that "Patriotism is supporting your country all the time, and your government when it deserves it."[71] And Bernard DeVoto observed that Twain's experimental approach made his greatest book a landmark for writers and readers who valued realism:

> [T]here is a type of mind, and the lovers of *Huckleberry Finn* belong to it, which prefers experience to metaphysical abstractions and the thing to its symbol. Such minds think of *Huckleberry Finn* as the greatest work of nineteenth-century fiction in America precisely because it is not a voyage in pursuit of a white whale but a voyage among feudists, mobbers, thieves, rogues, [slave]-hunters, and murderers, precisely because Huck never encounters a symbol but always some actual human being working out an actual destiny.[72]

Virginia Woolf (1882–1941)

> The novel is the only form of art which seeks to make us believe that it is giving a full and truthful record of the life of a real person.
> Virginia Woolf[73]

Virginia Woolf always knew she wanted to be a writer. At the age of nine she began producing a weekly newspaper for the entertainment of her family, and she stopped four years later only because of the death of her mother. Woolf did not go to university, because her father did not believe in higher education for women, and she resented this all her life. Yet her father, who was the editor of the *Dictionary of National Biography*, had her tutored in Greek and Latin, and encouraged her to use his sizeable library, where she read voraciously in literature, history, and biography.[74]

Woolf began writing professionally at 22, but for a decade she published only essays and reviews. After this extended, self-imposed apprenticeship, in 1915, at 33, she published her first novel, *The Voyage Out*. It had taken her six years to write, and went through at least seven drafts. Even then, Woolf was not satisfied with it, and she revised it considerably for an American edition in 1919.[75] With time, Woolf would publish her work with fewer revisions, but her writing would never settle into a formula or pattern.

Woolf's work constantly changed. Her inability to settle on a fixed form for her novels reflected her belief that the technique of a work of art implied a statement about its subject, and Woolf was never able to settle on a single view of the nature of life. She was frustrated that she could never reach any definite conclusion: "I have some restless searcher in me. Why is there not a discovery in life? Something one can lay hands on and say 'This is it'?"[76] Yet she recognized that it was not in her own nature to be certain of anything: "for after all, that is my temperament, I think, to be very little persuaded of the truth: what I say, what people say."[77] She believed that honesty in art would not allow the comfort of firm conclusions, but required the work to reflect the contingency of reality: "if honestly examined life presents question after question which must be left to sound on and on after the story is over."[78] As John Mepham observed of Woolf, "her integrity as an artist can be seen in her adoption of inconclusiveness as a principle."[79]

Woolf's agenda for the novel as an art form owed a large debt to her understanding of modern painting. Her sister Vanessa, who was one of Virginia's closest friends, not only was a painter herself, but married an eminent art critic, Clive Bell, who also became a close friend of Woolf's. Another friend, the art critic Roger Fry—the subject of Woolf's only biography—became perhaps the single most important intellectual influence on Woolf. Several key elements of Woolf's innovative analysis of the modern novel translate to literature Fry's distinctive interpretation of the development of modern painting.

In an essay published in 1925, Woolf described the desire of a number of contemporary novelists to free themselves from the constraints of conventional narrative, in order to capture their characters' inner lives. In a famous passage, she contended that life could not accurately be represented within the rigid structure of the traditional plot: "Life is not a series of gig-lamps symmetrically arranged; life is a luminous halo, a semi-transparent envelope surrounding us from the beginning of consciousness to the end. Is it not the task of the novelist to convey this varying, this unknown and uncircumscribed spirit, whatever aberration or complexity it may display . . . ?" This ambient envelope consisted of "an incessant shower of innumerable atoms." To capture the reality of life, "Let us record the atoms as they fall upon the mind in the order in which they fall, let us trace the pattern, however disconnected and incoherent in appearance, which each sight or incident scores upon the consciousness."[80] Woolf's account effectively transferred the perceptual concerns of Impressionist painting to literature, echoing Roger Fry's description of the movement's "representation of the totality of appearance," as well as Claude Monet's own characterization of his artistic goal as "the 'envelope' above all, the same light spread over everything."[81]

Yet although this recording of experience might describe "life itself," Woolf wanted to go still further, even if "we find ourselves fumbling rather awkwardly if we try to say what else we wish."[82] In an essay written in 1939, Woolf divided life into "moments of non-being"—the routine and mundane—and "moments of being." The former, "the cotton wool of daily life," generally conceal or obscure the latter, each of which is "a revelation of some order . . . a token of some real thing behind appearances." With characteristic caution, Woolf wrote that this was the basis for "what I might call a philosophy . . . that behind the cotton wool is hidden a pattern." She aimed to express these moments of being: "I make it real by putting it into words." This was her highest goal: "Perhaps this is the strongest pleasure known to me. It is the rapture I get when in writing I seem to be discovering what belongs to what; making a scene come right; making a character come together."[83] Both this conception and the language Woolf used to express it appear to echo Roger Fry's account of Cézanne's artistic goal, the uncertain objective that Cézanne himself had referred to as "realization," the pursuit of which gave rise to what Fry considered the most important oeuvre in modern painting—"this desperate search for the reality hidden beneath the veil of appearance, this reality which he had to draw forth and render apparent."[84] Just as Cézanne wished to penetrate beneath the descriptive forms of the Impressionists, to find a solid reality behind the surface veil of color, so Woolf wanted to dig beneath the stream of consciousness represented by James Joyce and other contemporary novelists, to uncover a deeper reality.

Late in her life, Woolf reflected that "I feel that by writing I am doing what is far more necessary than anything else."[85] Writing was not merely part of her life: in a real sense, it *was* her life. After her death a close friend, the novelist E. M. Forster, remarked that "She liked writing with an intensity which few writers have attained or even desired," and nearly everything she did contributed to her art.[86] When she wasn't writing novels, much of her time was devoted to writing in other forms: reviews, which allowed her to study other novelists' approaches; essays about the arts, which allowed her to develop her own theories; and myriad letters and diary entries, which allowed her to practice turning her ideas and perceptions into prose. And much of her time not spent writing was devoted to talking to the members of the luminous collection of distinguished writers, poets, artists, and scholars who comprised the Bloomsbury Group. These conversations were not only occasions to discuss and debate innovative theories about art, but also opportunities for study, for Woolf to learn more about how other people thought and behaved, in order to improve her ability to create characters in her novels. Writing novels, and preparing to write novels, thus took up the greater part of Woolf's life. For writing was not only a subject of intellectual interest to Woolf: for her, writing was a continuing effort to understand life in general, and her own life in particular.

Over time, Woolf's constant application made her a master of her art. Her prose is celebrated for its elegance and visual sensitivity, but this was the hard-won result of decades of experience. In an autobiographical essay of 1907, when she was 25, Woolf wrote of her mother: "Encompassed as she was by this solemn doubt her most trivial activities had something of grandeur about them; and her presence was large and austere, bringing with it not only joy and life, exquisite fleeting femininities, but the majesty of a nobly composed human being."[87] Thirty-two years later, the 57-year-old Woolf had completely outgrown the awkwardness of the ponderous and stilted Victorian prose that had reduced her mother to formal and abstract generalities, and she could write without affectation of one of her few specific memories of her mother, from an outing to the site of her mother's childhood home: "Once when we were children, my mother took us to Melbury Road; and when we came to the street that had been built on the old garden she gave a little spring forward, clapped her hands, and cried, 'That was where it was!' as if a fairyland had disappeared."[88] The simplicity and informality of the language make the latter portrait vivid and poignant, the verbal equivalent of a nostalgic faded snapshot from a cherished family album.

Woolf was well aware of the growth of her own powers. When she finished her third novel, *Jacob's Room*, she recorded in her diary, "There's no doubt in my own mind that I have found out how to begin (at 40) to say something in my own voice," though she recognized that she would never be fully satisfied: "I shall never write a book that is an entire success."[89] She was still plagued by her ambitious intentions, wondering the next year, "Have I the power of conveying the true reality?"[90] At 43, she was more pleased with *Mrs. Dalloway*, writing, "I wonder if this time I have achieved something?," before immediately qualifying the thought: "Well, nothing anyhow compared with Proust."[91] At 44, she recorded her opinion that *To the Lighthouse* was "easily the best of my books," and after another year of reflection, she affirmed that "With The Lighthouse I may just have climbed to the top of my hill."[92]

Scholars generally agree that *To the Lighthouse* was Woolf's most important novel.[93] It included both her attempt to come to terms with her memories of her parents and the creation of her own artistic self-portrait. Both of these were clearly major concerns. After the novel was published Vanessa, who was three years older than Virginia, wrote to her that "it seemed to me ... you have given a portrait of mother which is more like her to me than anything I could ever have conceived of as possible.... It was like meeting her again with oneself grown up and on equal terms and it seems to me the most astonishing feat of creation to have been able to see her in such a way."[94] Woolf was elated, responding that "I'm in a terrible state of pleasure that you should think Mrs. Ramsay so like mother.... [S]he has always haunted me."[95] Woolf's satisfaction stemmed from the fact that one of her greatest ambitions had always been to create characters who were true to life. In a memoir written near the end of her own life, she reflected that "if one could give a sense of my mother's personality one would have to be an artist. It would be as difficult to do that, as it should be done, as to paint a Cézanne."[96]

Interestingly, in *To the Lighthouse* Woolf chose to make her fictional self not a writer but a painter. Lily Briscoe was an experimental painter. She persevered even though she feared that her art was bad; she did not consider it honest to tamper with the colors of nature; she could not plan her paintings in advance but found inspiration only in the act of painting.[97] Like Cézanne, Lily wanted to go beneath surface appearances. She saw what she was seeking only after studying her subject: "Then beneath the color was the shape. She could see it all so clearly, so commandingly when she looked." Yet also like Cézanne, Lily suffered from the difficulty of recording this vision: "it was when she took her brush in hand that the whole thing changed. It was in that moment's flight between the picture and the canvas that the demons set on her."[98] Lily's goals for her painting paralleled those of Woolf for her novels, to capture both surface appearances and underlying structures, both the ephemeral and the enduring: "Beautiful and bright it should be on the surface, feathery and evanescent, one color melting into another like the colors on a butterfly's wing; but beneath the fabric must be clamped together with bolts of iron."[99]

Joan Bennett explained that Woolf "was not content with the record of a single mind. She wanted also to communicate the impression made by one individual upon others and to reveal human personality partly through its own self-consciousness and partly through the picture projected by it upon other minds." So in each of her later novels, "a small group of people is selected, and through their closely interrelated experience the reader receives his total impression." Her art served the ensemble: "The method is cumulative, and it is therefore impossible to isolate from her books a portrait which epitomizes a particular character." Because of the organic nature of her books, "the embryo of the book about to be made could not be expressed by defining a part of the content.... Each book seems to evolve rather than to be planned and then made. She never fully foresees the shape it will take."[100]

To the Lighthouse has been described as the finest example of Woolf's innovative technique of multiple points of view, with frequent shifts among narrators—the literary equivalent of the multiple vantage points Cézanne used in his late still lifes.[101] Although Woolf told Roger Fry she had not dedicated the book to him because she feared it was inadequate, the book's text provides evidence of her sense of her accomplishment.[102] Woolf struggled with the novel's ending: on September 5, 1926, she noted in her diary that she was "casting about for an end . . . I am feathering about with various ideas." Among the problems was the painting Lily had been working on throughout the book: "what becomes of Lily and her picture?" Eleven days later, Woolf wrote the novel's final paragraph, in which Lily's effort ended. "she looked at her canvas; it was blurred. With a sudden intensity, as if she saw it clear for a second, she drew a line there, in the center. It was done; it was finished. Yes, she thought, laying down the brush in extreme fatigue, I have had my vision."[103] Lily was 44 at the novel's end, as was Woolf herself. It is difficult to resist the conclusion that this ending was Woolf's statement of her belief that in *To the Lighthouse* she had succeeded in realizing her own clear artistic vision.

Woolf's work, and life, affected many later writers, particularly those interested in innovative narrative strategies and representations of consciousness.

One notable example is that of Sylvia Plath. In 1957, struggling with an early version of *The Bell Jar*, she wrote in her diary that "Virginia Woolf helps. Her novels make mine possible."[104] In her desire to capture "the *psychic* equivalent" of experience, Plath wondered "how does Woolf do it?" and marveled at Woolf's "*luminousness* . . . a shimmer of the plasm that *is* life."[105] Plath felt "my life linked to her, somehow," even to Woolf's suicide, which Plath felt she was "reduplicating in that black summer of 1953," when Plath had first attempted suicide.[106] Another important case is that of Doris Lessing. Unlike Plath, Lessing did not write about her debt to Woolf, but scholars have found Woolf's impact in her fiction. They have traced this not least to *The Golden Notebook*, published in 1962, in which Lessing created a novelist named Anna Wulf, who resembled the real Woolf in a number of respects, including living in London, keeping a detailed diary in a series of notebooks, repeatedly revising her work, and struggling with psychological breakdown while writing about suicide.[107]

Ernest Hemingway (1899–1961)

> From things that have happened and from things as they exist and from all things that you know and all those you cannot know, you make something through your invention that is not a representation but a whole new thing truer than anything true and alive, and you make it alive, and if you make it well enough, you give it immortality. That is why you write and for no other reason that you know of.
> Ernest Hemingway[108]

After graduating from high school in suburban Oak Park, Illinois, Ernest Hemingway chose not to go to college, but instead took a job as a reporter for the *Kansas City Star*. He was anxious to see World War I, however, and within less than a year the 18-year-old Hemingway was driving an ambulance for the Red Cross in Italy. After barely five weeks, he was seriously wounded when a shell exploded near him in the trenches. The injury ended Hemingway's war, and after several months convalescing in a Milan hospital, he returned to journalism. By the end of 1921, Hemingway was in Paris, working as a correspondent for the *Toronto Star*.

In Paris, under the tutelage of the poet Ezra Pound and the writer Gertrude Stein, Hemingway developed a distinctive new way of writing fiction. His understated and laconic artistic voice projected an attitude of nihilism and fatalism that soon became associated with the disillusioned generation that had fought World War I—an association that Hemingway fostered by quoting in an early novel a remark made to him by Gertrude Stein, "You are all a lost generation."[109] Hemingway's trademark style was embodied most notably in an early collection of stories, *In Our Time* (1925), and the two novels *The Sun Also Rises* (1926) and *A Farewell to Arms* (1929). He later explained that in his early writing his goal "was to put down what really happened in action; what the actual things were which produced the emotion that you experienced." He called this goal "the real thing, the sequence of motion and fact which made the emotion and which would be as valid in a year or ten years or, with luck and if you stated it purely enough, always."[110] Following Mark Twain, Hemingway's prose used only spoken American language. His short declarative sentences stressed simple nouns. Longer sentences were made by compounding these, usually with the connective *and*, often without commas or other punctuation, so there was no subordination of clauses.[111]

An example of an ostensibly realistic technical innovation that was in fact based on artifice was Hemingway's celebrated writing of dialogue. In a review of *The Sun Also Rises*, the poet Conrad Aiken declared that "the dialogue is brilliant," and described it as "alive with the rhythms and idioms, the pauses and suspensions and innuendos and shorthands, of living speech."[112] Yet, as Philip Young later observed, "for all the impression of authenticity Hemingway's dialogue gives, it was no simple reproduction of actual human talking.... Instead, Hemingway's dialogue strips speech down to the essentials which are typical of the speaker. He built a pattern of mannerisms and responses which give an illusion of reality that, in its completeness, reality itself does not give."[113]

Hemingway's style was not based solely on technical devices, however. It also had a pronounced moral dimension. Hemingway declared that "A writer's job is to tell the truth." Yet for him this did not necessarily mean factual accuracy, as he explained that the writer's "standard of fidelity to the truth should be so high that his invention, out of his experience, should produce a truer account than anything factual can be."[114] The writer's imagination was key, for "If he gets so he can imagine truly enough people will think that the things he relates all really happened."[115] Falsification was consequently not incompatible with Hemingway's conception of truth: "If you invent successfully, it is more true than if you try to remember it. A big lie is more plausible than truth."[116] Hemingway's practice of inventing in order to create an illusion of truth explains the frequent observation by critics that his fiction described a world simpler, more brilliant, and more vivid than reality. As Hemingway commented in an early short story, "The only writing that was any good was what you made up, what you imagined. That made everything come true."[117]

Hemingway's stories were written from the vantage point of a first-person narrator. Through their objective, uninflected, and unemotional accounts, these narrators revealed a moral code that unified most, if not all, of Hemingway's fiction. The narrator was honest, brave, stoic, and graceful under pressure. He was, or became, disillusioned, and distrustful of abstractions. So for example amidst the carnage of World War I Frederic Henry, the narrator of *A Farewell to Arms*, reflected that

> I was always embarrassed by the words sacred, glorious, and sacrifice and the expression in vain . . . I had seen nothing sacred, and the things that were glorious had no glory and the sacrifices were like the stockyards at Chicago if nothing was done with the meat except to bury it. There were many words that you could not stand to hear and finally only the names of places had dignity. Certain numbers were the same way and certain dates and these with the names of the places were all you could say and have them mean anything. Abstract words such as glory, honor, courage, or hallow were obscene beside the concrete names of villages, the numbers of roads, the names of rivers, the numbers of regiments and the dates.[118]

Henry thus respected soldiers, but not the abstract ideals that caused their deaths, and this was consistent with Hemingway's code that valued only real things and sensations. He later explained that "I know only that what is moral is what you feel good after and what is immoral is what you feel bad after."[119] Hemingway's narrators fought valiantly and honorably, but they shared a fatalistic resignation to the knowledge that there are no ultimate victories. Well before the tragic ending of *A Farewell to Arms*, Frederic Henry bitterly pondered his pessimistic ideology:

> If people bring so much courage to this world the world has to kill them to break them, so of course it kills them. The world breaks every one and afterward many are strong at the broken places. But those that will not break it kills. It kills the very good and the very gentle and the very brave

impartially. If you are none of these you can be sure it will kill you too but there will be no special hurry.[120]

Hemingway heightened the intensity of the moral climate in his works through the stylistic device of severe compression. One of his trademark practices, from the time of his earliest writing as a journalist, derived from his theory of omission: "If a writer of prose knows enough about what he is writing about he may omit things that he knows and the reader, if he is writing truly enough, will have a feeling of these things as strikingly as though the writer had stated them. The dignity of movement of an iceberg is due to only one-eighth of it being above water."[121] Both the understatement and the severely abbreviated exposition of Hemingway's narrators mirrored the rigid restraint of action that was a basic element of their code of conduct.[122]

Hemingway's use of his narrators to express a consistent moral philosophy revealed a conceptual novelist at work. His methods were equally conceptual. His early novels are celebrated for their careful construction and planning. In *A Farewell to Arms*, which scholars generally consider his greatest novel, every major action was foreshadowed.[123] This was often done symbolically, as for example every disaster was anticipated by rain.[124] The book was dominated by two themes—love and war—that have not often been joined together by novelists. Yet the scholar Philip Young observed that the progress of these two themes ran exactly, though subtly, parallel: "In his affair with the war Henry goes from desultory participation to serious action and a wound, and then through his recuperation in Milan to a retreat which leads to his desertion. His relationship with Catherine Barkley undergoes six precisely corresponding stages—from a trifling sexual affair to actual love and her conception, and then through her confinement in the Alps to a trip to the hospital which leads to her death."[125]

Hemingway's innovative early writing gained him not only critical success as the leading writer of his generation but also, with *A Farewell to Arms*, considerable popular and financial success. Over time, he multiplied both his fame and fortune by carefully crafting a public image as a fearless man of action—war correspondent, boxer, big game hunter, deep sea fisherman, bullfighting aficionado, bon vivant, and playboy. Although a biographer observed that "virtually all the drinking, boxing, hunting, fishing, and fornicating stories are exaggerations or fantasies," Hemingway's swashbuckling persona extended his influence far beyond the literary world, but it also created skepticism among critics, and led to even greater scrutiny of the changes in his work.[126] He himself contended that writers did not have to deteriorate artistically with age: "People who know what they are doing should last as long as their heads last."[127] Yet in the month that Hemingway celebrated his fortieth birthday Edmund Wilson, a prominent critic, published a detailed analysis of his artistic decline, including the charge that "The master of that precise and clean style now indulges in purple patches which go on spreading for pages on end."[128] Although this topic was for many years a popular subject of vigorous debate between Hemingway's admirers and detractors, over time it became generally recognized that his most innovative work had ended with *A Farewell to Arms*.[129]

A number of critics have attributed Hemingway's failure to grow as a writer to his inability to develop a more complex and subtle philosophy.[130] This is in turn often traced to his repeated use of a single theme. Hemingway's early achievements were all based on the use of violence as a subject: as he explained, "I was trying to learn to write, commencing with the simplest things, and one of the simplest things of all and the most fundamental is violent death."[131] Because he never gave up this practice, his characters were never placed in new situations, where they might display more nuanced and complex reactions. Hemingway wrote repeatedly about a simple and narrow world, and his characters never transcended the limits of this environment. A longtime rival, William Faulkner, criticized Hemingway for not challenging himself, but instead "having taught himself a pattern, a method he could use and he stuck to that without splashing around to try to experiment."[132] Even more bluntly, in an obituary for Hemingway, the novelist Alberto Moravia declared that throughout his life he had remained in an "infantile and precocious state of arrested development." Noting that Hemingway had written his best books during his 20s, Moravia concluded that "he was incapable of developing or adding anything of value to his early, naïve nihilism."[133]

Over time, Hemingway's prose style clearly changed. In the process, it lost the purity that had made it such a strong influence on younger writers. A prime example of Hemingway's early prose can be taken from *The Sun Also Rises*, published when he was 27. Jake Barnes and two friends were sitting in a Pamplona café on the day the fiesta of San Fermin was to begin:

> Before the waiter brought the sherry the rocket that announced the fiesta went up in the square. It burst and there was a gray ball of smoke high up above the Theatre Gayarre, across on the other side of the plaza. The ball

of smoke hung in the sky like a shrapnel burst, and as I watched, another rocket came up to it, trickling smoke in the bright sunlight. I saw the bright flash as it burst and another little cloud of smoke appeared. By the time the second rocket had burst there were so many people in the arcade, that had been empty a minute before, that the waiter, holding the bottle high up over his head, could hardly get through the crowd to our table. People were coming into the square from all sides, and down the street we heard the pipes and the fifes and the drums coming.[134]

An example of Hemingway's late prose comes from *Across the River and into the Trees*, published when he was 51. Colonel Richard Cantwell has gone duck hunting:

He watched the sky lightening beyond the long point of marsh, and turning in the sunken barrel, he looked out across the frozen lagoon, and the marsh, and saw the snow-covered mountains a long way off. Low as he was, no foothills showed, and the mountains rose abruptly from the plain. As he looked toward the mountains he could feel a breeze on his face and he knew, then, the wind would come from there, rising with the sun, and that some birds would surely come flying in from the sea when the wind disturbed them.[135]

In the earlier passage, in pursuit of "the real thing" Hemingway carefully restricted himself to "what really happened . . . what the actual things were." The excitement and commotion of the sudden beginning of the fiesta was implied rather than asserted, communicated concisely through declarative sentences describing actual things. Hemingway avoided narrating the assembly of the crowd by having it appear while Jake's view was on the rockets, and avoided describing the speed of the crowd's movement by observing that it had entirely filled the arcade during the brief interval in which Jake's attention was averted. The surge of the crowd was not directly described, but was implied by the waiter's difficulty in reaching the table. In contrast, the later passage was not restricted to what really happened. Twice Hemingway gave explanations—of why Cantwell could not see foothills, and how he knew birds would arrive—rather than descriptions: the third-person narrative now provided analysis, rather than merely description.[136] Several scholars have observed that, at its best, Hemingway's prose was cinematic, presenting a succession of visual images.[137] In the present examples, the rockets, the waiter, the crowd, and all the things described by Jake Barnes could be fully captured by a sequence of filmed images, whereas Richard Cantwell's judgment that he would soon see birds flying could not. The effect on the quality of the prose is subtle; Hugh Kenner suggested that Hemingway might not have even been aware of it, noting that by the time he wrote *Across the River*, he "had composed so many sentences around primary nouns that he no longer noticed when he was cheating."[138] Late in his life, when he had become a legendary figure, Hemingway liked to hold forth on the difficulty of the writer's craft, and in one interview he declared that "The most essential gift for a good writer is a built-in, shock-proof, shit detector."[139] As he grew older, Hemingway's own detector may have lost its sensitivity, as his simple, sharp early prose lost its precision and clarity, and with them much of its power. As Irving Howe wrote in an obituary, "Much of the late work was bad, Papa gone soft."[140]

Joan Didion wrote that Hemingway "in his time made the English language new, changed the rhythms of the way both his own and the next few generations would speak and write and think. The very grammar of a Hemingway sentence dictated, or was dictated by, a certain way of looking at the world, a way of looking but not joining, a way of moving through but not attaching, a kind of romantic individualism distinctly adapted to its time and source."[141] Using metaphors that reflected his debt to Hemingway, Norman Mailer explained that "Hemingway's style affected whole generations of us, the way a roomful of men are affected when a beautiful woman walks through—their night is turned for better or worse. His style has the ability to hit young writers in the gut, and they weren't the same after that."[142] Mailer recognized that Hemingway's colorful persona, which effectively embodied the philosophy of his narrators, was also a powerful element of his legacy: "The way to save your work and reach more readers is to advertise yourself, steal your own favorite page out of Hemingway's unwritten *Notes From Papa On How The Working Novelist Can Get Ahead.* Truman Capote did it bravely when he began, and my hat is off to him. James Jones did it, and did it well."[143] For Mailer, the combination made Hemingway a vital figure: "I would say that he occupies the very center of American writing."[144]

Plots and Endings

Conceptual novelists are more likely to plan their novels carefully in advance, so their plots often lead to closed endings, in which a narrative has reached a definite conclusion, and its suspense has been resolved. These endings often have a moral, which ties the specific story of the novel to a larger concept. In contrast, experimental novelists generally do not plan their stories. Their novels often have ambiguous or open endings, in which the narrative is incomplete, leaving readers to wonder what will happen to the characters.

In 1929, Lewis Mumford praised the complex and skillful construction of *Moby-Dick*:

> *Moby-Dick* is a symphony; every resource of language and thought, fantasy, description, philosophy, natural history, drama, broken rhythms, blank verse, imagery, symbol, are stylized to sustain and expand the great theme. The conception of *Moby-Dick* organically demands the expressive interrelation, for a single total effect, of a hundred different pieces....
>
> Melville's instrumentation is unsurpassed in the writing of the last century: one must go to a Beethoven or a Wagner for an exhibition of similar powers: one will not find it among the works of literature.[145]

Another critic, Lincoln Colcord, observed that Melville's skill allowed him to make the book's ending its climax, by creating "purposeful suspense which flows through the tale from beginning to end in a constant swelling current."[146] And Van Wyck Brooks explained that the presumptuous challenge of man to nature made the book's ending, with the destruction of Ahab and his ship, inevitable: "He is fate, this Moby Dick, and the terrible old Captain Ahab is the tragic will of man which defies it and tracks it down, only to be overwhelmed and to perish by it."[147]

The ending of *Huck Finn* has long been considered a glaring weakness. Henry Nash Smith's tactful comment was that "It has become a commonplace of criticism that the drastic shift in tone in the last section of *Huckleberry Finn* ... poses a problem of interpretation," while Bernard DeVoto's less circumspect judgment was that "In the whole reach of the English novel there is no more abrupt or more chilling descent."[148] Ernest Hemingway had a simple solution. After his famous tribute to *Huck Finn* as the source of all modern American literature, he continued: "If you read it you must stop where the [slave] Jim is stolen from the boys. That is the real end. The rest is just cheating."[149]

As Smith observed, Twain's decision to have Tom Sawyer reappear, and join Huck in tormenting Jim, "was certain to produce an anticlimax."[150] Why Twain did this continues to be debated today, with no sign of consensus or even widespread agreement. Interestingly, however, perhaps the single most sophisticated defender of Twain's open ending effectively based his defense on the experimental nature of the novel, and its structure as a series of loosely related episodes rather than a logical progression leading to a climax or resolution. Thus T. S. Eliot pointed out that "*Huckleberry Finn* is not the kind of story in which the author knows, from the beginning, what is going to happen." Eliot contended that Huck, like the Mississippi River, could have no beginning or end: like the river, which changed its pace and shifted its channel unpredictably, and at some indeterminate point simply disappeared into its delta, the character of Huck could not have a purposeful design or career. So in Eliot's opinion the unresolved ending of *Huck Finn* was appropriate, because for Huck "neither a tragic nor a happy ending would be suitable.... Huck Finn must come from nowhere and be bound for nowhere."[151]

Eliot's rationalization of *Huck Finn*'s open ending may not satisfy all readers who have worked their way through more than four hundred pages of text, and had expected to be rewarded with an edifying resolution. Yet any readers dissatisfied for this reason have only themselves to blame. At the front of the book, on the page immediately following the copyright, there is a "NOTICE" that declares: "Persons attempting to find a motive in this narrative will be prosecuted; persons attempting to find a moral in it will be banished; persons attempting to find a plot in it will be shot." Twain's Notice could almost serve as a universal credo for experimental novelists, informing their readers that their books are not intended to have hidden meanings or motivations, moral imperatives or symbols, or carefully planned and orchestrated story lines. Lacking these elements, readers will understand that they are not entitled to coherent plots or fully resolved endings; they may receive them as a special bonus from considerate and conscientious authors who are willing to make extraordinary efforts, but they are not intrinsic to the works. Victor Doyno wrote of *Huck Finn* that it is "a supreme misreading of the novel to read for plot as plot." He explained that Twain discovered his plot as he worked, "writing without a definite final resolution or plan in mind. His real interests were elsewhere—in writing memorable episodes and frequently in doubling the incidents or repeating the basic situation in varied forms."[152] Tom Quirk wrote simply that *Huck Finn* "is sustained by its rendering of life rather than by a formal narrative coherence."[153]

Virginia Woolf clearly understood her strengths and weaknesses as a novelist: in 1927, the year she published *To the Lighthouse*, she noted in her diary that "I can make up situations, but I cannot make up plots."[154] The issue of planning plots was one she had pondered for years. So for example in 1922, after finishing *Jacob's Room*, she recorded in her diary her desire to plan her next book more carefully: "I want to think out *Mrs. Dalloway*. I want to foresee this book better than the others and get the utmost out of it. I expect I could have screwed *Jacob* up tighter, if I had foreseen; but I had to make my path as I went."[155] In the event, her goal was not achieved. *Mrs. Dalloway* was published in 1925, and three years later, in 1928, Woolf wrote an introduction for a new edition. She remarked that authors should accept criticism in silence, but that occasionally critics made statements that were simply mistaken:

> One such statement has been made sufficiently often about *Mrs. Dalloway* to be worth perhaps a word of contradiction. The book, it was said, was the deliberate offspring of a method. The author, it was said, dissatisfied with the form of fiction then in vogue, was determined to beg, borrow, steal, or even create another of her own. But, as far as it is possible to be honest about the mysterious process of the mind, the facts are otherwise. Dissatisfied the author may have been; but her dissatisfaction was primarily with nature for giving an idea, without providing a house for it to live in.... The novel was the obvious lodging, but the novel it seemed was built on the wrong plan. Thus rebuked the idea started as the oyster starts or the snail to secrete a house for itself. And this it did without any conscious direction. The little note book in which an attempt was made to forecast a plan was soon abandoned, and the book grew day by day, week by week, without any plan at all, except that which was dictated each morning in the act of writing. The other way, to make a house and then inhabit it, as Wordsworth did and Coleridge, is, it need not be said, equally good and much more philosophic. But in the present case it was necessary to write the book first and to invent a theory afterwards.[156]

After finishing *Mrs. Dalloway*, Woolf had in fact wondered in her diary whether the book would have been better without several of its chapters, and commented that "Always I think at the end, I see how the whole ought to have been written."[157] In *To the Lighthouse*, Lily Briscoe was unable to answer a question about what she was trying to make of her work in progress: "She could not show him what she wished to make of it, could not see it even herself, without a brush in her hand."[158] Allen McLaurin explained: "It is only in the making of the work of art that she realizes what she wants to 'say.'"[159]

Woolf's desire to plan her plots and to fashion structures that illustrated theories was also consistently foiled by her characteristically experimental distrust of stable beliefs or firm conclusions. Late in *To the Lighthouse*, Lily Briscoe rested for a moment from her work of painting and reflected, "What is the meaning of life? That was all—a simple question; one that tended to close in on one with years. The great revelation had never come. The great revelation perhaps never did come. Instead there were little daily miracles, illuminations, matches struck unexpectedly in the dark." These achievements were not definitive, but they were nonetheless significant: "In the midst of chaos there was shape."[160] As noted earlier, Woolf resolved the narrative of *To the Lighthouse* by allowing Lily to finish her painting, and to conclude that she had had her vision. But as if to undercut the scope of Lily's achievement, immediately before this ending, Lily looked at her painting, with "its attempt at something. It would be hung in the attics, she thought; it would be destroyed." Lily persevered nonetheless, asking herself "what did that matter?," but it is difficult not to see this late denigration of her project as a qualification of her final vision, suggesting that it was not a great revelation but rather a little illumination.[161] The experimental Woolf could not give her novel a definitive resolution because she did not believe that life had definitive resolutions; there were achievements and victories, but they were minor and transitory.

In an interview for the *Paris Review*, Ernest Hemingway told George Plimpton that he had rewritten the last page of *A Farewell to Arms* thirty-nine times.[162] Bernard Oldsey concluded that this was probably not an exaggeration: his study of Hemingway's papers at the John F. Kennedy Library revealed that there are "between thirty-two and forty-one elements of conclusion" of the book. Yet Oldsey found substantial common ground among these endings, for "All of the conclusions in the Hemingway Collection presuppose Catherine's death." The five holographic versions of what became the actual ending all shared "the descriptive element of the rain, [Frederic Henry's] dramatic action of clearing the hospital room and taking leave of Catherine's corpse, and the narrative reflection that none of it is any good. All include the most important sentence in the actual conclusion: 'It was like saying goodbye to a statue.'"[163] But they all expressed these matters slightly differently. When Plimpton asked what problem had occasioned the revisions, Hemingway answered, "Getting the words right."[164] Thus although Hemingway had not completely planned the ending of *A Farewell to Arms*, the variation in the events of the possible endings occurred within a relatively narrow range. This can be understood as a consequence of Hemingway's desire to provide a definite resolution, by making the ending a logical result of what preceded it. So for example the rain that accompanied Frederic's final walk back to his hotel was foreshadowed by Catherine's earlier confession to him that "I'm afraid of the rain because sometimes I see me dead in it."[165] And most basically, as Philip Young explained, Catherine's death was the final element "in the point that is made very clear, lest there be any sentimental doubt about it, that life, both social and personal, is a struggle in which the Loser Takes Nothing."[166] Hemingway completed his demonstration of the novel's ideology in its final paragraph, with Frederic's failure to achieve any catharsis from his final farewell to Catherine. There could be no separate peace, so Henry was left with nothing from his efforts to achieve one. It is perhaps worth emphasizing that this example demonstrates that repeated revision—to get the words right—is not inconsistent with the careful advance planning of plot, with preconception of all important actions and emotions.

Huck Finn and *To the Lighthouse* are great novels, by great novelists. Yet their greatness is a function of elements other than the structure of their plots and their endings. In contrast, *Moby-Dick* and *A Farewell to Arms* are great novels for which the elegance of their construction and the power of their endings are among their most celebrated strengths. The endings of these novels serve very different functions. *Moby-Dick* and *A Farewell to Arms* build toward tragic endings, and conclude with powerful images and language that fully resolve their narratives. In contrast, the ending of *Huck Finn* is left open, with a promise to continue on another occasion. *To the Lighthouse* is more fully resolved, as Lily finishes her painting, but the meaning of this is not as clear, nor certainly as dramatic, as the destruction of a ship and the deaths of all but one of its crew, or the death of a narrator's true love. The conceptual Melville and Hemingway clearly wanted readers to remember their novels' endings as climaxes, whereas the experimental Twain and Woolf equally clearly did not consider their endings this important.

6
Architects

In his influential survey of the development of modern architecture, Sigfried Giedion provided a dichotomy:

> Throughout history there persist two distinct trends—the one toward the rational and the geometrical, the other toward the irrational and the organic: two different ways of dealing with or of mastering the environment. These contrasting approaches to the problem have been evident in all cultures, both early and late. Since the beginning of civilization there have been cities planned according to regular schemes and cities which have grown up organically like trees....
>
> The difference between organic and geometrical perceptions is present even today in contemporary painting and contemporary architecture. They are constantly recurrent ways of approach; one cannot be considered superior to the other.

Giedion's analysis appears neatly to separate rational, conceptual architects from their organic, experimental peers. He immediately proceeded to an application of his scheme: "From the beginning Frank Lloyd Wright faced toward an organic perception of the world."[1] This chapter examines the careers and contributions of Wright and two other great experimental modern architects, and of a conceptual architect who revolutionized a particular branch of modern architecture.

Frank Lloyd Wright (1867–1959)

> The architect has a hard road to travel and far to go.
> Frank Lloyd Wright[2]

In a speech to his fellow architects, 33-year-old Frank Lloyd Wright declared that "The education of the architect should commence when he is two days old (three days is too much), and continue until he passes beyond, leaving his experiments by the wayside to serve his profession as warning signs or guide posts." He cautioned that the dedicated architect was likely to "see his wife and children suffer for ideals that may seem ridiculous," and this was true for his own three wives and numerous children, for throughout his tumultuous life Wright consistently placed his profession ahead of his family.[3] But Wright never wavered, for he knew that "architecture is life; or at least it is life itself taking *form*.... So architecture I know to be a Great Spirit."[4]

Wright claimed that for him architecture was congenital, for even before he was born, his mother "intended him to be an Architect." Her goal for him was simple: "The boy, she said, was to build beautiful buildings."[5] To inspire him, she hung engravings of great cathedrals in his bedroom. Wright later recalled that he had "grown up from childhood with the idea that there was nothing quite so sacrosanct, so high, so sacred as an architect, a builder."[6] He spent most of his childhood in Wisconsin, and it was during summers he spent working on an uncle's farm that he discovered the aesthetic that was to have a profound impact on his art: "I loved the prairie by instinct as itself a great simplicity."[7] His embrace of nature fulfilled another element of his mother's philosophy, for her favorite quotation was from Shakespeare's *As You Like It*: "And this our life, exempt from public haunt,/Finds tongues in trees, books in the running brooks,/Sermons in stones, and good in everything." Thus architecture—"sermons in stones"—would be based on nature, which was the source of all that was good.[8] Wright had little interest in college, and spent barely a year at the University of Wisconsin before leaving Madison for Chicago. There, at the age of 19, he found work as an architect and began a career that would last more than seventy years.

Wright became by far the greatest American architect of the twentieth century. A poll of its members taken in 2000 by the American Institute of Architects (AIA) determined that Wright designed four of the ten greatest American buildings of the twentieth century—three more than any other architect. Wright designed one of these buildings at the age of 41, two at 69, and one at 76. This remarkable age profile was a result of both the nature of Wright's goals and the methods he devised to pursue them.

In 1908, Wright stated six principles of what he called *organic architecture*. The first was simplicity. The second was individuality: people differ, so houses should differ to suit them. The third was harmony with surroundings: "A building should appear to grow easily from its site." The fourth was to use the colors of nature, particularly the "warm, optimistic tones of earths and autumn leaves." The fifth was to bring out the true nature of materials, by revealing their natural textures and appearance. And the sixth was character: like people, buildings should have sincerity and integrity.[9] Throughout his career, Wright would insist that his architecture was *organic*, but he would never make the concept more precise. Sigfried Giedion observed that "It was clear, finally, that no explanation was possible in words, that what he meant by organic architecture could be revealed only in his work."[10]

In 1887 Wright joined Adler and Sullivan, the leading Chicago firm for commercial architecture. Among the commissions assigned to Wright were those for any private residences the firm could not avoid. This led to his first major contribution, the Prairie House. Wright designed a series of homes that culminated in Chicago's Robie House (1908), the earliest of the four Wright buildings cited by the AIA poll. In these houses he developed a distinctive style, with strong horizontal planes that made the buildings "belong to the ground," a long, low roof, cantilevered out to create an overhang that extended the horizontal, and open, flowing interior spaces produced by minimizing walls, doors, and other internal partitions.[11] The Prairie Houses were generally cruciform in shape, their spaces projecting from a great central fireplace; these plans, and their many full-height glass doors, meant that the primary family rooms could all have light and views on three sides. The Prairie Houses were often located not at the center of their sites, as was the normal practice, but instead at the edges, thus increasing the importance of the landscape and its interdependence with the house. This close connection to nature, a major benefit for families moving to the suburbs, was Wright's primary inspiration for the Prairie Houses.[12] When a catalogue of Wright's work was published in Germany in 1910–1911, the Prairie House had a large impact on the work of a number of younger European architects, including Walter Gropius, Le Corbusier, and Mies van der Rohe, who used elements of Wright's style in ways that he would bitterly resent.[13]

During the construction of Robie House, Wright altered the contractor's blueprints to make an opening in the floor of the balcony at each end of the building, creating dramatic views from the ground to the roof.[14] This was an example of a lifelong practice that stemmed from Wright's highly experimental approach to his art. He believed that plans should grow slowly—"the plan is the gist of all truly creative matter and must gradually mature as such." Yet the drawing by no means completed the design: "The original plan not as an idea but as a piece of paper may be thrown away as the work proceeds. Probably most of those for the most wonderful buildings in the world were because the concept grows and matures during realization, if the master mind is continually with the work." The importance of the master mind's control implied that no process would be acceptable "that does not give to the architect complete control of his design and assure control to him until final completion of the building."[15] Wright regularly altered buildings under construction, and this inevitably caused delays and increased costs. He also consistently used his charm and charisma to mollify disgruntled contractors and outraged clients. So for example the construction of the Johnson Wax Company's administration building in Racine—another of the AIA's greatest buildings—stretched from a scheduled one year to three, and its final cost rose to more than ten times the initial estimate, as Wright performed what a friend and biographer described as "a succession of near-miraculous improvisations on an essentially simple theme." In one letter to the long-suffering client, Wright actually attributed his failure to provide complete working drawings for the building to the difficulty of anticipating its appearance: "You see the building grows as it is built and is none too easy, therefore, to keep up with."[16]

As he gained recognition, Wright preached to his fellow architects the need for extended training, with apprenticeships and conscientious study, to acquire artistic integrity. He spoke of his own departure into the field of domestic architecture, in which he had broken with tradition to make new forms, and explained that the work of two decades had allowed him to achieve an individuality "as irrevocably mine as the work of any painter, sculptor, or poet who ever lived was irrevocably his." He condemned "the feverish ambition to get fame or fortune 'quick' . . . and consequent unwillingness to wait to prepare thoroughly." The architect's goal should be a distinctive individual style, which could not be adopted or borrowed, but could emerge only from devotion to a disciplined process: "*Style* is a by-product of the process and comes of the man or the mind in the process. The style of the thing, therefore, will be the man—it is his." The highest achievement would be to bring to architecture "the integral simplicity of organic nature," to create "a beautiful building beautifully, as organically true in itself, to itself and its purpose, as any tree or flower."[17]

By 1910, Wright was widely considered the most important architect alive, but during the next two decades he was eclipsed by several younger European rivals. By 1930, with Wright past the age of 60, many assumed his career was finished. But Wright disagreed, as in that year he declared that "not only do I fully intend to be the greatest architect who has yet lived, but the greatest who will ever live."[18] Commissions were scarce during the Depression, but in 1934, the Pittsburgh department store owner E. J. Kaufmann asked Wright to design his weekend house near a stream at Bear Run, Pennsylvania. Given this opportunity to revive his career, Wright succeeded spectacularly.

Wright traveled from his home in Wisconsin to visit the site at least three times over a period of nine months before producing his first plans for the house. These contained a major surprise, for instead of siting the house across the stream from a 30-foot waterfall, Wright placed the house above the waterfall, creating the visual illusion that the stream runs through the house: he explained to his startled client that "I want you to live with the waterfall, not just to look at it."[19] Instead of a view of the waterfall, residents heard the sound of the water roaring beneath them. Wright gave the house an elegant profile, but he insisted that its visual effects "are entirely consistent with the Prairie Houses of 1901–10," notably in the visual dominance of the long, low, horizontal roof and terraces.[20] One of the house's most famous features, the upper balcony that dramatically oversails the living room below it, was a daring use of the cantilever that in less extreme form had been a staple of the Prairie Houses. The building's conformity to the landscape around it has been attributed to Wright's subtle use of the diagonal axis as an organizing force, a skill he had acquired from long experience in using diagonals ever since the early Prairie Houses of the 1890s.[21] Fallingwater's rooms were not arranged in a rectilinear progression but were offset, and its exterior walls were not straight but zigzagged. The house's strong horizontal lines set it firmly in the sedimentary rock on which it was based, and its visual integration into the setting was increased by its construction from sandstone quarried just 500 feet from the site.[22] As usual, Wright made major alterations during construction, including tearing down the three massive concrete bolsters that served as the building's main support, in order to remake them with a sleeker shape.[23] Fallingwater was both beautiful and dramatic, and carried to a new level Wright's career-long ideal of integrating domestic architecture with the surrounding landscape.

Fallingwater received an enormous amount of publicity when it was completed in 1937, with feature articles in hundreds of newspapers and magazines, and an exhibition devoted to the house at New York's Museum of Modern Art. Wright's fame rose to new heights, far beyond the world of architecture; at the age of 70, he became the first architect to appear on the cover of *Time* magazine, standing in front of his color rendering of Fallingwater, and *The New Yorker* seconded *Time's* judgment that he was the world's greatest living architect.[24] Fallingwater also had an immediate impact on other architects, as within months of its completion it influenced the Finnish architect Alvar Aalto's approach to the Villa Mairea, with projecting balconies, open interior spaces, and the use of stone, wood, and broad windows to emphasize the house's setting in the forest.[25] In time, Aalto would be recognized as one of the century's greatest architects, and the Villa Mairea would be considered his greatest achievement.[26]

Fallingwater is often considered Wright's greatest achievement: so for example it ranked first in the AIA poll in 2000. Yet by another measure, Wright's greatest work was done still later, for Fallingwater ranks second among Wright's buildings in frequency of illustration in art history textbooks, behind New York's Guggenheim Museum.[27]

Wright was commissioned to design the Guggenheim in 1943. Two years later, he had settled on its distinctive design, featuring a circular spiral that widened as it rose.[28] The building was not completed until 1959, because of delays in acquiring the site and permissions for construction. Yet in January 1959, the 92-year-old Wright made his last trip to New York to settle such final details as the proper finish for the floors, and less than a week before his death in April he wrote to protest the construction of a fence to keep crowds away from the building. Wright's concern—that the vertical posts of the fence would clash with the building's horizontal lines, and thus destroy "the overall character of the building"—was, as always, visual.[29]

The Guggenheim drew heavily on Wright's many decades of experience. Its fundamental organization, with a large building, the focus of primary activity, dominating a smaller connected building that housed supporting services, can be traced through all of Wright's public projects, beginning with Buffalo's Larkin Building (1906), and including the Johnson Wax Building (1936), making these seemingly diverse buildings "variations on a single remarkably specific architectural device."[30] The larger building in each project had a central skylight and one or more mezzanines ringing a central open space. (One familiar echo of this design is the towering atrium that became the visual trademark of Hyatt Regency hotels, taken by the architect John Portman from Wright.)

Wright devoted a substantial part of his final two decades to designing what he called Usonian Houses. Intended for middle-class families, these were modest in both size and cost, and were designed to be extremely energy-efficient, with solar warming in winter, and cooling by shade and cross-ventilation in summer.[31] Although these were constructed largely from standardized components, Wright wanted to tailor each one for the client: an assistant recalled that even for a $5,000 house, "Mr. Wright would always closet himself with [the client] in his office because he liked to work with them in person."[32] Wright built more than one hundred Usonian Houses, which he also called Natural Houses, because they were intended to be integral to their sites, their environments, and the lives of their inhabitants. He considered them among his greatest achievements, because he believed the family house, specifically designed for the needs of individuals, was a fundamental basis of American democracy: to Wright, the individuality of a building was a complement to the dignity of the individual.

Wright had a lasting influence on the design of American single-family homes, in creating more open floor plans, in which kitchens, dining rooms, and living rooms were no longer separated by walls and doors, but were instead parts of a continuous living space. He also opened up houses to their surrounding gardens, using more windows to make houses lighter and airier, and to create greater continuity between interior and exterior. More generally, Wright is a continuing source of inspiration to experimental architects who are committed to making functional buildings that are attractive and enjoyable places to live and work, rather than to producing startling novelties motivated by abstract ideas.[33]

Frank Lloyd Wright's quest, which he named organic architecture, was to create buildings that were inspired by nature. Donald Hoffman observed that his "progress was slow and unsteady and often far from evident.... At first, he liked to say, he had only been feeling his way, knowing that some better relation between buildings and the land had to be possible."[34] He recognized that it would never be possible to match the perfection of natural forms, so "The complete goal of the ideal of organic architecture is never reached." But this did not trouble him: "What worthwhile ideal is ever reached?"[35] Wright considered creating buildings a "searching process," in which a progressive simplification would bring him ever closer to his elusive goal: "Nothing is more difficult to achieve than the integral simplicity of organic nature."[36] Because this process had no end point, "no organic building may ever be 'finished,'" and Wright not only changed his buildings during their construction but also often returned to old drawings in his archives, revising them and using them as the basis for new commissions.[37] His commitment was to improving his art through experimentation, and he produced his greatest masterpieces after five decades of work. At the age of 66, he recorded his faith in the experimental life cycle of creativity: "Any work of any lifetime truly animated by principle will leave fresh ideas on the drawing board every morning.... And the later work of any such spirit will be the greatest work; ripened by the only valuable tests on the only real proving ground; the proving ground of intimate experience."[38]

Le Corbusier (1887–1965)

Creation is a patient search.

Le Corbusier[39]

Charles-Edouard Jeanneret-Gris was born and raised in La Chaux-de-Fonds, a Swiss town in the Jura mountains dominated by watchmaking. He attended art school, intending to follow his grandfather and father into the craft of engraving watch cases, but he rebelled, and for a time remained undecided between architecture and painting. He found his calling in 1911, at the age of 24, on a trip around Europe. He recalled that "The essential moment came for me at Athens," as among the temples of the Acropolis, he discovered that architecture could have an emotional impact: "everything was a shout of inspiration."[40] Studying the Acropolis daily for three weeks, he decided that its power came from the relation of the buildings to their setting: "For all the majesty of the natural surroundings, the focal point was an amalgam of buildings perfectly placed on their sites by human beings."[41]

Edouard subsequently renamed himself Le Corbusier, and in time became the greatest architect of the modern era—the only twentieth-century architect whose work is more frequently illustrated in architecture and art history textbooks than that of Frank Lloyd Wright.[42] He never did formal studies in architecture, and he always considered his youthful journey to the East his "school of architecture . . . his education, opening doors and windows for him."[43]

Le Corbusier moved to Paris permanently in 1917. In addition to his architectural practice, he wrote for a magazine he founded with the painter Amédée Ozenfant. In 1923, he published a collection of his articles as a book, under the title *Vers une architecture* (*Toward an Architecture*). This quickly became one of the most influential books ever published by a modern architect. With its stark declaration that "A house is a machine for living in," *Vers une architecture* was generally regarded as a radical functionalist manifesto for the new age of machinery. This view appeared to be supported by the book's many pictures of elegant modern ocean liners, airplanes, and automobiles, and the assertion that "We must create the mass-production spirit." Yet this interpretation overlooked such statements as "Architecture goes beyond utilitarian needs," and "there is no art without emotion." It also ignored Le Corbusier's definition of architecture in visual terms, as "the masterly, correct and magnificent play of masses brought together in light."[44] As the architect Peter Blake later observed, "by and large, Corbu has been less concerned with the technology of architecture than with its art. The confusion about Corbu's true objective stems from the single, simple fact that he found his major sources of *aesthetic* inspiration in the *technology* of our time."[45]

In *Vers une architecture*, Le Corbusier stressed the challenge of reconciling modern technology with the art of architecture. In a key passage, he noted that "in the last fifty years steel and concrete have brought new conquests, which are the index of a greater capacity for construction, and of an architecture in which the old codes have been overturned."[46] Ferroconcrete, or reinforced concrete, had begun to be widely used in the early twentieth century, and Le Corbusier had learned of its potential value when he worked briefly for Auguste Perret, the French architect who pioneered its use. Le Corbusier early adopted ferroconcrete as a basic material, and he devoted much of his career to creating a new architecture that exploited its capacities.

During the 1920s, Le Corbusier designed a series of houses, and these led to his first masterpiece. The Villa Savoye (1928) in Poissy, near Paris, is challenged only by Fallingwater for the position of the most innovative private residence of the twentieth century.[47] Villa Savoye's pristine white surfaces and simple geometric forms further contributed to the image of Le Corbusier as a functionalist, and led to its contemptuous dismissal by Frank Lloyd Wright as a "box on stilts."[48] In fact, however, the building's taut contours were inspired not only by modern machines, but also by Le Corbusier's recollection of the perfect lines of the marble columns of the Parthenon, on which the sections were connected so smoothly that he could not find the joints even by running his fingernail over them.[49] The Villa's elevation on stilts was also inspired by the Acropolis, for its raised position allowed it to look out over nature like the Greek temples that commanded the surrounding land and sea. The reinforced concrete structure of the Villa made possible the long horizontal windows that opened it up to light to a greater extent than had previously been possible.[50]

Le Corbusier's architecture never stopped changing. One landmark result of his extended continued evolution was a celebrated apartment building, the vast, eighteen-story Unité d'Habitation Marseille (1945–1952). Le Corbusier declared that "Twenty years of research are written into this building," as the smooth white facades of the Villa Savoye were replaced by rough, dark expanses of raw concrete that appear to have been inscribed or scraped.[51] These were made of unfinished concrete that bears the irregular imprint of the wood grain of the boards used to form it. At the building's inauguration, Le Corbusier observed that ferroconcrete treated in this way might be considered "a natural material of the same rank as stone, wood or terra cotta. It seems to be really possible to consider concrete as a reconstructed stone worthy of being exposed in its natural state."[52] The 65-year-old architect declared that "The defects shout at one from all parts of the structure!," and contended that this gave it dignity and sincerity: "in men and women do you not see the wrinkles and birthmarks, the crooked noses, the innumerable peculiarities? . . . Faults are human; they are ourselves, our daily lives."[53] The coarse appearance of the enormous Unité made it a popular target for ridicule by the press and public, giving rise to what Le Corbusier called "Five years of storm, spite, and uproar ... despicable, ugly."[54] Yet Le Corbusier's peers quickly appreciated the building's new aesthetic. Even Walter Gropius, a leading practitioner and proponent of functionalist architecture who generally gave little weight to a building's appearance, remarked that "Any architect who does not find this building beautiful had better lay down his pencil."[55] And less than a decade after the completion of the Unité, it inspired the New Brutalism, a movement created by a group of young English architects.

While working on the Unité, Le Corbusier designed a very different structure that art scholars consider the greatest building of the twentieth century. Thus the Chapel of Notre-Dame-du-Haut (1950–1955) at Ronchamp is more frequently illustrated in textbooks than any other building of the century.[56] When the Protestant Le Corbusier was first approached to design a Catholic church he declined, saying he had no time for a "dead institution." Yet Le Corbusier agreed to visit Ronchamp, and the priest who accompanied him recalled that the architect was "seduced by the site," high atop a hill, with uninterrupted views of nature in all directions, and that he immediately began to draw.[57] His immediate goal was to make the building "a visual echo of the landscape."[58] The appeal of the commission was enhanced by the promise that he would have free rein to do what he pleased, a rare opportunity to create what he called "Completely uninhibited architecture."[59]

The shape of the chapel's most celebrated feature, its bulging, curved roof, originated from a crab shell Le Corbusier had found on a beach three years earlier, then evolved gradually over time: he explained that "Perception is a series of visual events.... Time, duration, succession, continuity are the constitutive features of architecture."[60] The roof was constructed from untinted reinforced concrete, in its raw state. Immediately after the chapel's inauguration, Le Corbusier triumphantly wrote to a friend that "The architecture of reinforced concrete has entered into the history of pure architecture."[61] His claim was fully justified by events, for the roof at Ronchamp would inspire scores of younger architects to create what Vincent Scully called "such eccentric and active shapes as architects had hardly imagined."[62] Charles Jencks observed that the irregular, curved form of the roof at Ronchamp initiated a new "tradition of fractal design . . . that moves from [Eero] Saarinen's TWA Terminal to [Jorn] Utzon's Sydney Opera House and, later, to Gehry's Guggenheim Bilbao."[63] The chapel at Ronchamp was also a white building on top of a hill, yet another reference to Edouard Jeanneret's essential moment in Athens more than forty years before.

Over time Le Corbusier grew bitter at the constant criticism of his work, and lack of official support: he was sorely disappointed that he never received a major commission in either Paris or New York.[64] After the architect's death, his friend André Malraux declared in a eulogy that "no one else has so forcefully signified the architectural revolution, for no one else has been so long and so patiently insulted. It is through disparagement that his glory has attained its ultimate luster."[65] Le Corbusier worked tirelessly toward a goal he formulated early in his career, of reconciling modern technology with beauty in architecture. Late in his life he declared that "I have achieved a position throughout the world thanks to my researches concerning the structures of a machine civilization."[66] The products of his research inspired generations of architects: in a typical tribute, Tadao Ando wrote that at his first sight of the chapel at Ronchamp, "I was overwhelmed by this architecture celebrating the joy of creation and human freedom."[67] Frank Gehry, who first saw the chapel at Ronchamp shortly after it was completed, still visits it at least once a year for inspiration. When Gehry was asked about Le Corbusier's influence on him, he responded, "Corb is the lightbulb. Number one on my hit parade."[68] Le Corbusier's complete commitment to his art was also an inspiration to his successors: Louis Kahn explained that "Every man ... has a figure in his work who he feels answerable to. I often ... say to myself, 'How'm I doing, Corbusier?'"[69]

Le Corbusier's legacy was that of a great experimental artist: in a memoir written just a month before his death, he described himself as "A visual man, working with his eyes and his hands." In that memoir, he reflected that "my philosophy could be summed up in this way: in life one must act . . . with modesty, correctly, with precision. The only possible atmosphere conducive to artistic creation is steadiness, modesty, continuity, perseverance."[70] He constantly studied his own work: "An awareness of one's evolution is the springboard of progress."[71] Because of his conviction that architecture required judgment, he warned aspiring architects that they must be patient: "One can be a poet at twenty, a virtuoso at fifteen; but architects and urban planners are late bloomers."[72] This was not mere rhetoric on his part, for among his many achievements, at the age of 68 he had completed the greatest building of the twentieth century.

Le Corbusier was given the title "Architect of the Century" by a centennial exhibition in London in 1987. The critic Martin Filler went further, calling Le Corbusier the most influential architect since Andrea Palladio, the sixteenth-century Italian whose architecture represents the height of Renaissance harmony.[73] And the scholar Vincent Scully went further still, naming Le Corbusier the most influential architect since Imhotep, the Egyptian who is considered to have created the basis for all later Western architecture. In Scully's opinion, since the pyramids Le Corbusier was the architect most responsible for "changing the environment as a whole and having it built up around his own cosmic schemes." Scully was at best ambivalent about Le Corbusier's impact, for although he admired many of his forms individually, he regretted the effect of his enormous late buildings, in forbidding raw concrete, as a violation of the context of the traditional city: in his opinion, the primitive masses of these vast giants inspired Le Corbusier's brutalist followers to create buildings that threatened "the ultimate destruction of the old urban fabric through their exaggeratedly anti-contextual and aggressive design."[74] Le Corbusier has thus remained a highly controversial figure: many admirers, including prominent practitioners, consider him to have given architects license to create artistic monuments that stand apart from their surroundings, whereas detractors bemoan his role in allowing architecture to become coarse and overwhelming, and to disrupt and even destroy the physical unity and harmony of the modern city. Yet whatever the attitude of the observer, there is little disagreement about Le Corbusier's motivation: as Scully wrote, "His loyalty, unswervingly given, was to his own vision, his primal search."[75]

Frank Gehry (1929–)

> My working process is an evolution, like watching paint dry.
> Frank Gehry[76]

Frank Goldberg was born and raised in Toronto, Ontario. His family was never secure economically, and when Frank was 18 they moved to Los Angeles. Frank attended the University of Southern California, and when he left school in 1954 he changed his last name to Gehry, to avoid being identified as Jewish.[77] He has spent virtually his entire professional life in Los Angeles, where he started his own firm in 1962. A survey in 2008 of recent textbooks of the history of art and architecture found that Gehry's work was reproduced more frequently than that of any other living architect, implying that art scholars consider him the greatest architect of the late twentieth and early twenty-first centuries.[78]

Gehry studied both fine art and architecture in college, and he was determined to combine the two to improve cities. He decided early on that large-scale urban planning was impracticable, so his goal was to design individual buildings that would beautify their neighborhoods, and he aimed to do this by importing visual qualities from painting and sculpture into architecture.[79] Gradually, he developed a distinctive new aesthetic.

One of Gehry's central concerns has been to create architecture for the modern city that incorporates movement:

> It's modern life, the real experience of living in this world, that's fueled my work.... The real world today comes hurtling at you like a runaway truck.... That's the energy I try to harness in my work.... I'm intrigued by the sense of movement.[80]

A model for this came from modern sculpture:

> It's hard to sustain the feeling of life from a first model to the final work.... Giacometti just got it. It's all about surface, and it takes a lifetime to know how to do it. And Giacometti figured it out.[81]

A related element of Gehry's aesthetic is his preference for buildings that appear incomplete:

> I am interested in the work not appearing finished. . . . I prefer the sketch quality, the tentativeness, the messiness if you will, the appearance of in-progress rather than the presumption of total resolution and finality.[82]

Here again, an inspiration came from experimental visual artists, particularly those whose finished works visibly retain the marks of their own creation: "I was interested in the unfinished—or the quality that you find in paintings by Jackson Pollock, for instance, or de Kooning, or Cézanne, that look like the paint was just applied."[83] Gehry has long believed in the aesthetic redemption of commonplace materials. One prominent example of this is metal fencing: "That's the populism in my work, as opposed to the art. What's wrong with chain link? I hate it, too, but can we make it beautiful? I said, 'Maybe . . . if you're going to use it in huge quantities, you can use it beautifully.'"[84]

Gehry has pointed to many artistic influences, but in a 1994 lecture at London's Royal Academy he identified his models in architecture as Frank Lloyd Wright, Le Corbusier, Mies van der Rohe, and Alvar Aalto—all great experimental architects.[85] More recently, he explained that what he valued in the architecture of Wright, Corbusier, and Aalto was "the touch . . . the humanity of it."[86]

Gehry stresses that his work is done gradually: "I am a *slow* architect, I take a long time to create."[87] He designs by an extended process of trial and error, with intensive visual examination at every stage:

> I sketch it out, and once we know it'll function, sometimes with the crumpled paper but mostly with other materials, and we build model after model after model. We agonize about every little part of it, and I stare for hours and then I move something just a little bit, and I stare some more, and then slowly it starts to take shape.[88]

He needs to engage not only with the site, but with the client: "I need to fall in love with the people, the client, the site. Establishing that trust gives me the time to explore. Place is the crucial starting point."[89] If his relationship with the client deteriorates, so does his interest in the project: "The building is a building, but it has lost its soul."[90]

Gehry recognizes that his seemingly endless process of searching eventually frustrates even sympathetic clients, because they don't understand that their agreement with Gehry on a design does not mean he will stop changing it:

> They think I'm doing four different schemes. "I like the first one, the second one, I liked the third one—now you're doing it again?" So they think you're pulling the carpet out.... I don't know where I'm going. I just explain the issues. Is it better not to do that? Is it better to come in at the end, and say, "This is it"?[91]

Gehry's need to keep changing his designs even at the cost of alienating clients appears to parallel Roger Fry's description of Cézanne, approaching his motif "with infinite precautions, stalking it, as it were, now from one point of view, now from another, and always in fear lest a premature definition might deprive it of something of its total complexity."[92] The critic Paul Goldberger recently observed that what Gehry likes about the design process is "the sense of endless possibilities that existed when a design was still in formation. Once any design was finalized, all possibilities but one went away, and Frank did not like giving up the feeling that a project had multiple solutions and could go in multiple directions."[93]

Gehry enjoys the pursuit of the unattainable: he thinks of the final product of his work "as a dream image, and it's always elusive. You can have a sense of what the building should look like and you can try to capture it. But you never quite do."[94] Forms can't be created systematically: "Architecture's intuitive, it's a magic trick. I don't know where it comes from."[95] It's magic "when all of the ideas, all of the thoughts, all of the time devoted to a project come together and produce something that the world thinks is beautiful," but this is rare: "We're lucky when it happens."[96]

An example of Gehry's experimental approach and its consequences is afforded by the case of a Malibu guest house he designed for the art collector Norton Simon in 1976. After much of the construction was done, Gehry attempted to create a novel visual effect:

> I decided to make a trellis that looked like a pile of wood that had been laid on the roof, caught up in the wind blowing off the ocean, as if the wind had caught it and flung it in mid-air. The trellis would have captured this movement, and every time you looked at it, it would look different. That's what I was trying to do. I didn't know how to do it. I knew how to draw it, but I didn't know how to build it.

Gehry decided to build the trellis incrementally, drawing a layer, building it, looking at it, then repeating the process. This ended with the client's intervention:

> I think we even got the third layer built, and Norton said, "Stop," because it was getting too expensive. . . . [I]t offended him that he was paying for this experiment and he didn't know where it was going to go. . . . He said to me, "There have been many great artists over time who have not been able to finish their masterpieces. I'm going to add you to the list." And so we stopped.[97]

Gehry first attracted widespread attention in 1978, when he was 49, as a result of his renovation of his own home in Santa Monica. His transformation of a conventional wood bungalow, by wrapping the ground floor in corrugated steel and screening the upper floor with chain-link fencing, shocked and angered many of his neighbors, who were quoted in the *Los Angeles Times* describing it variously as "anti-social," a "monstrosity," a "prison," and "a dirty thing to do in somebody else's front yard." In addition to numerous official protests and legal actions, on two occasions bullets were fired through a window.[98] Gehry was philosophical about the attacks, reflecting that life was not a "chocolate sundae—people bite each other."[99] Yet he felt he had accomplished something, by creating ambiguity: "You were never sure what was intentional and what wasn't. It looked in progress. . . . There was something magical about the house. And I know that the thing a lot of people hated or laughed at, was the magic."[100] Nor did he consider the house a final product: it was, he said, "a sketchbook for future projects."[101]

Gehry's reputation grew over time, and his style evolved. His early projects were rectilinear—he explained that "we have to take small steps"—but during the 1990s he became famous for his novel use of curved forms. In 1991, Gehry was awarded the commission to design a new satellite of the Guggenheim Museum in the Basque city of Bilbao. The city was struggling economically, and Gehry was told that the Basque regional government "needed a 'hit' there. . . . They needed the building to do for Bilbao what the Sydney Opera House did for Australia." This need led them to choose Gehry's unconventional proposal—what even he called his "weird-looking scheme."[102]

Faced with the challenge of creating not only a tourist attraction for a depressed region, but also a work of art worthy of becoming a younger sibling

162 INNOVATORS

to Frank Lloyd Wright's New York Guggenheim, Gehry stretched the bounds of architecture to produce a masterpiece that succeeded on both counts. As Gehry accurately and succinctly summarized the building's economic impact, "After it was built people started going to Bilbao and that changed the economics of the city. It was wildly successful."[103] Indeed, the building's economic success prompted the architect Peter Eisenman to coin the term "Bilbao Effect," which quickly gained currency to describe the economic stimulus a dramatic new building could give a community.[104] Artistically, the abstract sculptural forms of the Bilbao Guggenheim quickly made it the second most frequently illustrated building of the twentieth century in textbooks of architecture and art history, narrowly behind Le Corbusier's chapel at Ronchamp, and well ahead of Wright's Guggenheim.[105] When the Bilbao Guggenheim was completed in 1997, Frank Gehry was 68 years old.

The radical curved and abstract forms of the Bilbao Guggenheim were the result of decades of gradual development of Gehry's art. His long-standing interest in fluid forms dated back at least as far as his early love of Le Corbusier's chapel at Ronchamp. In the early 1980s, in search of a way to add movement to architecture, Gehry began studying fish:

> I started drawing fish. And then they started to have a life of their own. I started to really look at fish. I began going to the library and looking at pictures of all the fish that were there, learning how the scales work. I looked at fish in ponds—the sense of movement fascinated me. The Greeks did it, and Rodin did it.[106]

Gehry's study of fish eventually led to the graceful curved contours of the Bilbao Guggenheim as well as the building's sinuous titanium surface that shimmers like the scales of a fish. Interestingly, a recent comment by Gehry suggests that the necessary growth during the preliminary process of developing a design may not be only to the form of the final work, but also to his recognition of a successful design. Thus he recounted that the very first sketch for the Guggenheim, made on his first day in Bilbao,

> incorporates all of the issues that are in the final building, but I didn't know that, so I only looked at that first drawing after the building was finished. I said "Oh my God, why did it take so long?" I could've had it all from the beginning; but you don't recognize it, I think, in the beginning.[107]

One often-discussed aspect of the process by which the Bilbao Guggenheim was designed is the use by Gehry's firm of the CATIA program (Computer Aided Three-Dimensional Interactive Application), originally developed for the aerospace industry.[108] Yet Gehry did not design the building by computer, for he feared it would restrict his architecture to simple and symmetric geometric forms. Instead, he produced the design in his usual way, with drawings and models, and only then was the software used to translate the design into specifications that allowed its construction. An assistant who helped adapt the computer program for this purpose explained that Gehry's complex curved forms were effectively made possible in practice only by computers: "Bilbao could have been drawn with a pencil and straight-edge, but it would take us decades."[109] Gehry contends that the computer gives the architect greater control over his design: "I think that it makes the architect more the parent and the contractor more the child—the reverse of the twentieth-century system."[110]

The importance of the Guggenheim Bilbao is a function not only of its economic impact on the Basque region, but also of its influence on many younger architects. Martin Filler wrote that "Gehry opened the way for Zaha Hadid, Rem Koolhaas, Daniel Libeskind, Thom Mayne, and many others whose careers blossomed in the afterglow of Bilbao. Gehry also opened the way for Santiago Calatrava, the most conspicuous impresario of what has been called the architecture of spectacle."[111] Filler also reflected that "in 1976, when America's Bicentennial prompted countless predictions, no one would have bet that Gehry, pushing fifty and with no major buildings to his credit, would become the country's, let alone the world's, dominant architectural figure by the new millennium." (Interestingly, Filler noted that "Amid the Bilbao ballyhoo, I admitted to [Gehry] that even his most fervent early supporters could never have foreseen such a triumph, to which he replied, 'How do you think *I* feel?'")[112] Gehry's extended evolution throughout his career, produced by his unfailing belief in an experimental approach, explains this puzzle. The opening of the Bilbao Guggenheim in 1997 made him an instant celebrity, but it did not affect the humility of his approach to his art. Thus in 1998, when the clients for a new project asked Gehry how to break their old habits so they could accept a radical new design for their offices, he replied, "Well, you try things; you start things."[113] This is an open-ended process: in Gehry's words, "I always say that if I knew in advance where I was going, I wouldn't go there."[114]

Maya Lin (1959–)

> My idea arrives very quickly and is fully formed when it arrives.
> Maya Lin[115]

Maya Lin's father was a ceramicist, and as a child she loved to play in his studio. In college she studied both art and architecture, and she was unsure whether she could work as both a sculptor and an architect. She did not resolve her concern over this problem until much later, when Frank Gehry advised her not to worry about the distinction and simply make her work.[116]

During her senior year at Yale, Lin took a seminar in funereal architecture. When a national competition was announced for a Vietnam veterans memorial, the class adopted this as an appropriate assignment for its final project. Lin and a few of her classmates traveled to Washington, DC, to see the proposed site for the monument on the Mall, and "it was at the site that the idea for the design took shape," in what she described as "an instantaneous idea." She later recalled that:

> I had a simple impulse to cut into the earth.
>   I imagined taking a knife and cutting into the earth, opening it up, an initial violence and pain that in time would heal.[117]

Lin's plan was to have two long walls of polished black granite, arranged in a V shape, placed in the ground to form an embankment. One of the walls was to point to the Lincoln Memorial, the other to the Washington Monument: "By linking these two strong symbols for the country, I wanted to create a unity between the nation's past and present." The names of the dead soldiers would be inscribed chronologically, beginning and ending at the monument's apex. The design was extremely simple, but Lin quickly realized that its strength lay in its simplicity:

> On our return to Yale, I quickly sketched my idea up, and it almost seemed too simple, too little. I toyed with the idea of adding some large flat slabs that would appear to lead into the memorial, but they didn't belong. The image was so simple that anything added to it began to detract from it.[118]

After Lin had completed the design, she decided to enter it in the national competition. She found that the most difficult part of the entry was writing a description:

It took longer, in fact, to write the statement that I felt was needed to accompany the required drawings than to design the memorial. The description was critical to understanding the design since the memorial worked more on an emotional level than a formal level.[119]

One of the conditions of the competition for the memorial was that the design must include the names of all 57,000 Americans killed and missing in Vietnam, but Lin had in fact decided to do this even before she learned of the requirement, as a result of studying earlier memorials. The one that impressed her most was Sir Edward Lutyens' 1932 monument to the missing soldiers of the World War I Battle of the Somme. Lin recalled that one of her professors at Yale, Vincent Scully, was puzzled by her claim that Lutyens' memorial had influenced her, because its form had nothing in common with her design for the Vietnam memorial. Yet what inspired Lin wasn't the brick pyramidal form of Lutyens' memorial, or its interlocking arches, but rather its listing of thousands of names of soldiers, which allowed his monument to avoid making any political statement about the war.[120] Thus the influence of Lutyens' memorial on Lin was not visual, but conceptual. And contrary to the general assumption that the names of the dead would be ordered alphabetically, Lin insisted that they be placed chronologically, so their relatives could find their names alongside those of the soldiers they died with.

The designs submitted for the memorial were presented to the competition's jurors without the authors' names, and one juror remarked of #1026—Lin's submission—that "He must really know what he's doing to dare to do something so naïve." When Lin's identity was revealed, the juror Pietro Belluschi, former dean of architecture at MIT, argued that the excellence of her design was a product of her inexperience: "It is very naïve ... more what a child will do than what a sophisticated artist would present.... It has the sort of purity of an idea that shines."[121]

Lin's design was chosen unanimously by an eight-person selection committee from among 1,421 entries—the largest number of entrants in any American design competition; among the losing entrants were Frank Gehry and the famous architectural firm Skidmore, Owings and Merrill.[122] She instantly became a national celebrity, and violent debates ensued over her unorthodox design, both within the government agencies that had to approve the project and among the public at large. Criticisms included objections to the monument's black color, its lack of a profile above ground level, and its non-representational form. In an eventual compromise, a sculpture of three soldiers was placed near Lin's monument, over her vehement protest (Lin told the *Washington Post*, "I can't see how anyone of integrity can go around drawing mustaches on other people's portraits").[123] Yet when the *Memorial* was dedicated in the fall of 1982, barely a year and a half after the selection of her design, Lin found it did reflect her original intention: "the place was frighteningly close to what I thought it should be."[124]

Lin's incorporation of names into the *Vietnam Veterans Memorial* was not an isolated solution but rather the first instance of her use of texts—a practice she has followed throughout her career, that reflects her belief that "writing is the purest of art forms." Her goal is to communicate ideas, and "Words can be the most direct means of sharing our thoughts." She does not want people simply to look at her work: "My incorporation of text ... requires a viewer to read the work." And many of her projects, like the *Vietnam Veterans Memorial*, involve chronologies, so that "Time becomes the object of the works; the form dematerializes ... so that the text, the information, becomes the object."[125]

Lin's account of her practice in making art is highly conceptual. She begins her projects in a library: "I spend months reading, researching and studying a project before I try to find the form." She likes the fact that each is a new departure: "each project allows me to learn about a new subject." She is not initially concerned with structures: "Instead, I try to think about it as an idea without a shape." At some point, the form appears: "I just wake up one morning and, without even thinking about it, I just make a model of it." The final form arrives so suddenly that she compares the process to laying an egg: "It is a rather strange metaphor, but an accurate one." She does not iterate: "I do not work and rework the idea." Nor does she control the timing: "I am never sure when I am going to find the form. Or, more accurately, when the form is going to find me." Lin attributes her immediate use of a model, without preliminary sketches or drawings, to the influence of her early experiences in her father's ceramics studio.[126]

Vincent Scully has contended that "In terms of popular response, and in its general effect on the national consciousness, the *Vietnam Veterans Memorial* has to be seen not only as the most important monument but also as the single most significant work of architecture to be constructed in the United States during the second half of [the twentieth] century." He explained that the *Memorial*

> changed things, changed the way the country felt, and is supremely a work of modern art. It was Hemingway who wrote, angrily, that the old rhetoric

no longer worked and only names and numbers counted anymore. Here, without comment, the names of 57,000 dead are strung along a wall.

Scully described a popular photograph of a man leaning forward to touch the *Memorial*, and contended that the reflection of the man's image in the wall's shiny black granite represented not merely a reflection, "but a soldier of Vietnam who is coming out of the darkness.... It is literally a communion with the dead." Scully believed that survivors of the Vietnam War intuitively understand the power of the *Memorial*:

> They... recognize the fundamental truth of the wall beyond the usual rhetoric of memorials. It does not glorify or exalt. It neither apportions guilt nor claims victory. It simply affirms the massive fact, far more real than any political idea, of being there and dying there.[127]

Lin's design changed the course of modern architecture and sculpture. The *Vietnam Veterans Memorial* was the first major non-representational memorial, drawing on the simplified forms of 1960s Minimalism and Earth Art to produce a new archetype for future memorials.[128] In so doing, Lin successfully healed a rift that had originated with Rodin. As Albert Elsen explained,

> Until Rodin, great sculptors throughout history provided images by which their sponsors obtained a sense of identity. Statues and reliefs were eternal reminders of those who had founded and defended the religion, laws, and culture of a society.... What has been broken in [the twentieth] century is that part of the tradition in which great sculptors played a role. Ironically, the change focuses on Rodin ... Rodin came to epitomize, at modern sculpture's beginning, the clash between sculpture made from private values, and expectations based on public norms.[129]

Rodin's *Monument to Balzac* was the prime early example of innovative modern sculpture disappointing the expectations for a monumental public work; Lin's *Vietnam Veterans Memorial* was the first major demonstration that advanced modern sculpture could successfully be adapted to public purposes. Although her design was initially enormously controversial, and was bitterly attacked by traditionalists, it has become so successful that it is now simply assumed that memorial monuments will be minimal abstractions in form.

The importance of the *Vietnam Veterans Memorial* for the history of art is witnessed by the fact that a recent survey of forty art history textbooks published since 1994 found it to be illustrated in sixteen books, which placed it in a tie with Richard Serra's *Tilted Arc* as the most frequently illustrated work made by an American artist during the 1980s.[130] Inevitably, the fame Lin gained from the *Memorial* led to a series of important commissions for public and private projects.[131] Remarkably, however, no other work by Lin is illustrated in even a single one of the forty textbooks surveyed.[132] Lin has acknowledged her fear that one early inspiration would overshadow all her later efforts: "How do you compete with a work that has become so public, so well received, so widely accepted?"[133]

Drawing and Persistence

In his autobiography, Frank Lloyd Wright recalled that as a boy he was "perpetually making designs. Drawing always. Always making drawings for fun. Especially by lamplight, evenings."[134] Le Corbusier recalled that he had left school to study art at the age of 13, "Because I had been very interested by drawing ever since I could remember. I drew on the table, everywhere, nonstop."[135]

As an adult, Wright never lost his passion for drawing: "Now regard this pure white sheet of paper! . . . T-square, triangle, scale—seductive invitation lying upon the spotless surface. Temptation!"[136] Le Corbusier never went anywhere without sketch pads; for him drawing was seeing, and creating:

> When one travels and works with visual things—architecture, painting or sculpture—one uses one's eyes and *draws*, so as to fix deep down in one's experience what is seen. . . . To draw oneself, to trace the lines, handle the volumes, organize the surface . . . all this means first to look, and then to observe and finally perhaps to discover . . . and it is then that inspiration may come.[137]

Frank Gehry refers to sketching as a way of "thinking aloud."[138] He has explained his process:

> I start drawing sometimes, not knowing exactly where it is going. I use familiar strokes that evolve into the building. . . . Sometimes it seems

directionless, not going anywhere for sure. It's like feeling your way along in the dark, anticipating that something will come out usually. I become a voyeur of my own thoughts as they develop, and wander about them.[139]

In classic experimental language, Gehry describes his drawings as "a searching in the paper. It's almost like I'm grinding into the paper, trying to find the building."[140]

Gehry's reference to grinding into the paper suggests that for these experimental artists the act of drawing may have been not only visual, but also tactile. The architect André Wogenscky, who worked with Le Corbusier for many years, noted that Le Corbusier had first been trained as a manual worker, engraving watch cases, and observed that "The track of manual work remained in all his works: forms felt and shaped by the hand." Wogenscky believed that for Le Corbusier, drawing was always informed by his early experience in engraving: "The hand drew, but it did not draw on a flat surface. To engrave is to draw in three dimensions. It means to dig into things or to make them jut out, to see the volume."[141]

Maya Lin's relationship to drawing contrasts sharply with those of Wright, Le Corbusier, and Gehry. For her, works of art do not begin as visual images, but as verbal ideas: "I first try to imagine an artwork verbally. I try to describe in writing what the project is, what it is trying to do. I need to understand the artwork without giving it a specific materiality or solid form."[142] Even after the idea appears, Lin often does not make drawings, preferring instead to proceed directly to models: "drawings other than plans are harder for me to see.... [O]ftentimes I will make a model of a work without trying to draw it up or plan how to make the model—it is made instantaneously."[143]

Wright, Le Corbusier, and Gehry all used drawing both as a way of initially finding a form, and then of exploring possible variations on that form that might improve upon it. In contrast, the conceptual Lin does not use drawings for either of those purposes—she finds forms more abstractly, with language, and she often proceeds directly to a final model of the work without experimentation.

The contrast between the experimental desire for iteration and the conceptual disdain for it can equally be seen in these architects' attitudes toward sequential projects. Wright discovered early in his career, while developing the Prairie House, that he learned as he worked, and this made each project a point of departure for the next: "ideas had naturally begun to come to me as to a more natural house. Each house I built I longed for the chance to build

170   INNOVATORS

another."[144] Le Corbusier similarly learned from his own experience: "It is helpful... to study one's own work constantly."[145] For Gehry, no building is an end in itself: each house, for him, is "a sketchbook for future projects."[146] Over time, he has become reconciled to the need to stop working on individual projects, but he understands his experimentation will continue:

> at some point I stop, because that's it. I don't come to a conclusion, but I think there's a certain reality of pressures to get the thing done that I accept. It's maturity, or whatever you want to call it, to say, stop, go, finish. I've got other ideas now, and the door is open for the next move, but it's not going to happen on this building, it's going to happen on the next one.[147]

For the experimental Wright, Le Corbusier, and Gehry, each project led to a desire to do another, with the eager anticipation that their growing knowledge would allow them to do even better. Lin's attitude again contrasts starkly. For her, the *Vietnam Veterans Memorial*—her first project—was not a point of departure, but a definitive end point that she had no interest in developing further. Thus in her memoir, she wrote that "I used to dread it whenever some large-scale disaster would happen because I inevitably would get a fax whether I could design a memorial to... which I would politely decline."[148]

7
Photographers

In 1960, the critic Siegfried Kracauer divided photography broadly into two groups, "on the one side a tendency toward realism culminating in records of nature, and on the other a formative tendency aiming at artistic creations." He explained that realists "enhance the camera's recording and revealing abilities and . . . consider it their task as photographers to make the 'best statement of facts.'" These photographers were concerned with recording "unstaged reality." In contrast, formative photographers wanted "to work the given raw material into creations of an expressive rather than reproductive order." They deliberately departed from realism, mixing the real and the artificial in order to create images that would constitute subjective expressions of their own imaginations.[1]

The division Kracauer identified is that between experimental and conceptual photographers. The realists are experimental, with visual goals, while the formative are conceptual, whose work expresses ideas and emotions. Important examples of both types can be found in the history of photography.

Eugène Atget (1857–1927)

> I can truthfully say that I possess all of Old Paris.
> Eugène Atget[2]

Jean-Eugène-Auguste Atget was born in a small town near Bordeaux. We know little about his early life, and less about his life as a whole than is perhaps the case for any other important modern artist.[3] He was orphaned at an early age, and lived with an uncle; he went to sea as a cabin boy, and later a sailor. By 1879, Atget was in Paris, and spent as much as a decade acting in a touring theatrical troupe. During this time he met an actress who remained his companion until her death in 1926.

Atget's lack of success as an actor forced him to consider other occupations. He was a serious amateur painter, but did not have the formal training that might have allowed him to make this a career. He probably took up photography during the 1880s; by 1892 he had set up a studio in Paris offering photographs of "landscapes, animals, flowers, monuments, documents, foregrounds for painters, reproductions of paintings," that were intended as models for painters. Atget had a late start in his profession, and did not have the large stock of some other photographers, but he was willing to accept commissions, and he was ambitious. Thus an art magazine observed in a note about him in 1892 that "He wants to see, photograph, and sell everything!"[4] He continued to sell photographs to painters throughout his career—Maurice Utrillo was among those who often painted from his pictures—but over time Atget's primary clientele changed.[5]

On a calling card from around 1900, Atget described himself as "Creator and Purveyor of a 'Collection of Photographs of Old Paris.'"[6] Photographs of facades, doors, railings, and other architectural details could be sold to architects and building craftsmen seeking historical sources for their designs, while these motifs and street scenes could be sold to museums, libraries, and archives, as well as to private collectors. Atget eventually sold thousands of prints to the Bibliothèque Historique de la Ville de Paris, the Bibliothèque Nationale, London's Victoria and Albert Museum, and other large institutions.

Atget's sales almost completely stopped during World War I, and after the war the modern reconstruction of Paris prevented a strong revival of his market. His reaction was to offer to sell the bulk of his negatives to the French government. The letter in which Atget made this proposal in 1920 contained his most detailed statement about his life's work:

> For more than twenty years, through my own labor and individual initiative, in all the venerable streets of Old Paris, I have been making photographic negatives measuring 18 × 24 cm., artistic documents of beautiful civil architecture from the 16th to the 19th century: the old mansions, houses historical or curious; beautiful facades, doorways, wainscots; door knockers, old fountains, period staircases (in wood and wrought iron); the interiors of all the churches of Paris....
>
> This enormous artistic and documentary collection is today complete....

> Now that I am approaching old age—that is to say, 70 years—and have neither heir nor successor, I am worried and tormented about the future of this beautiful collection of negatives....[7]

Atget transferred more than 2,500 negatives to the national archive in the resulting sale, but his work did not stop. He was in fact very productive in his remaining years, and students of his work contend that in this time he worked with a new freedom to produce some of his greatest photographs, as his subjects broadened and his style became more subjective.[8]

Friends described Atget as thrifty, abstemious, reserved, and independent.[9] He sold his photographs for pennies, so he earned little and lived modestly. From 1899 on, he and Valentine lived in a Montparnasse neighborhood where many painters and sculptors lived and worked. Yet Atget had little real contact with artists, and did not consider himself one. His impact on the art of photography came only after his death, as a consequence of a chance meeting late in his life.

In 1922, the American photographer Man Ray rented a studio on the street where Atget lived. The two met, and Man Ray began buying Atget's photographs: by 1926, he had accumulated more than forty.[10] The images Man Ray selected were those he considered to "have a Dada or Surrealist quality about them," often because they isolated ordinary objects from their usual settings, freeing them of conventional associations.[11] In 1926, Man Ray reproduced an Atget photograph—a group of pedestrians shading their eyes as they looked up at the sky, watching an eclipse—on the cover of a Surrealist magazine. When he told Atget of his intention, the older man replied, "Don't put my name on it. These are simply documents I make." Nearly fifty years later, the self-promoting Man Ray was still amused by Atget's modesty as he told this story, explaining, "You see, he didn't want any publicity." Man Ray described Atget as "a very simple man, almost naïve, like a Sunday painter, you might say, but he worked every day."[12]

The real advocacy of Atget's work came from another source. Berenice Abbott, a young American sculptor, began working as Man Ray's studio assistant in 1924. Under his tutelage, she quickly became a successful portrait photographer. Abbott later recalled first seeing Atget's photographs in Man Ray's studio in 1925:

> Their impact was immediate and tremendous. There was a sudden flash of recognition—the shock of realism unadorned. The subjects were not

sensational, but nevertheless shocking in their very familiarity. The real world, seen with wonderment and surprise, was mirrored in each print. Whatever means Atget used to project the image did not intrude between subject and observer.[13]

Abbott visited Atget, and bought several of his prints. She returned many times, and asked him many questions about his techniques and goals, as the two became more friendly, and Atget grew less reticent. Abbott not only bought more prints from Atget, but showed them to everyone she knew, and urged them to visit his studio and buy prints for themselves. In 1927, Abbott persuaded Atget to come to her studio to sit for his portrait. The exposures she made in that session are the only formal portraits ever made of Atget. When Abbott went to Atget's home to show him the prints, she was shocked to discover he had died.[14]

Seeking out the friend of Atget who had inherited his possessions, Abbott purchased what remained of his work, almost 1,500 glass negatives and 8,000 prints.[15] She then began a remarkable campaign, that she would continue for the rest of her life, to gain attention for Atget's art. A scholar recently observed that "It is hard to find a similar example of one artist spending so much of her life and career conserving and promoting the work of another."[16] Abbott wrote poignantly of Atget's commitment:

> This man of violent temper and of absolute ideas had all the patience of a saint with his photographing. No time was too long to spend over a print, no material too good. Vain to say that his métier paid only with misery. The last twenty years of his life he ate nothing but bread, milk, and pieces of sugar. He was as absolute in his art.[17]

Within a year after purchasing Atget's estate, Abbott had given up studio photography and returned to the United States. She embarked on a cumulative, composite portrait of New York City, clearly motivated by Atget's portrait of Paris, that established her as an important documentary photographer. She believed her goal was the same as that of Atget: "How can anybody but a photographer hope today to fix for posterity the image of the modern city?"[18]

Through Abbott's efforts, Atget's work was exhibited and published, and a series of important experimental photographers were influenced by him. In 1930, Edward Weston wrote of Atget that "What I admire most of all is the man's simple honesty. He has no bag of tricks."[19] The next year, Ansel Adams praised Atget for his "revelation of the simplest aspects of his environment. There is no superimposed symbolic motive, no tortured application of design, no intellectual axe to grind. The Atget prints are direct and emotionally clean records of a rare and subtle perception, and represent perhaps the earliest expression of true photographic art."[20]

Walker Evans, perhaps the greatest American documentary photographer, was another early admirer of Atget, writing in 1931 of his "lyrical understanding of the street, trained observation of it, special feeling for patina, eye for revealing detail, over all of which is thrown a poetry."[21] In 1964, in an autobiographical lecture that he titled "Lyric Documentary," Evans named Atget as the "supreme lyric documentary photographer."[22] And in 1975, just two days before his death, Evans spoke of his initial reaction to Atget's work and of the concern it had caused him:

> I don't like to look at too much of Atget's work because I am too close to that in style myself. I didn't discover him until I had been going for quite a while; and when I did, I was quite electrified and alarmed.... It's a little residue of insecurity and fear of such magnificent strength and style there. If it happens to border on yours, it makes you wonder how original you are.[23]

In 1977 the critic James Stern contradicted Evans' account, reporting that he and Evans had in fact first seen Atget's prints at Berenice Abbott's apartment in New York in 1929, nearly at the beginning of Evans' career, and added, "Surely it is not invidious to wonder what kind of Evans we would have, which way his art would have developed, had there never been an Atget?"[24] In 2000, the photographer and curator John Szarkowski called Evans "Atget's greatest student," and observed that "It seems now that Evans worked his way through Atget's whole iconographical catalogue."[25]

Atget effectively became a visual historian of Paris: his notebooks list the names of "amateurs of Old Paris," who no doubt advised him in selecting buildings, streets, ruins, and works of art to photograph. He captured not only the city's structures, but also its vanishing ways of life, as he photographed rag-pickers, street vendors, and manual workers. His Paris was an ancient city of small scale. He rarely photographed great buildings or famous landmarks, and he avoided such modern monuments as the Eiffel Tower, the Arc de Triomphe, and Garnier's Opera. He saw the city from close up; he did not photograph panoramic views or wide landscapes. He photographed subjects in detail, and no detail was too small or insignificant.

Every building, every shop sign, even every cobblestone was sharp, clear, and distinct in his images.

A recent survey of textbooks of the history of photography found that Atget ranks fifth in importance among all photographers of the twentieth century. Like many great experimental artists, Atget did not produce any single famous masterpiece, but is known for a large body of work. He often made multiple views of the scenes he photographed, and returned to the same subjects over periods of years, always making changes and adjustments. The single year from which his photographs are most often reproduced in the surveys of the history of photography was 1901, when he was 44, while his second best year, with only one fewer illustration, was 1925, when he was 68.[26] Szarkowski observed that "Much of Atget's most beautiful and original work was done in his last years, as he approached seventy. This is exceptional in the history of photography."[27] Scholars have commented on changes over time that made Atget's late work more profound. His use of light grew subtler. Whereas early in his career he worked primarily in the middle of the day, to make factual and unemotional records of his subjects in strong, direct light, later he also worked in early morning and late afternoon, using shadows and atmospheric conditions more prominently to create moods. Sharp contrasts between light and dark produced dramatic chiaroscuro effects. His shift over time from frontal, direct views of buildings and streets to oblique perspectives tended to create more complex effects. In some late images Atget effectively made time a visual element, as the angles of his compositions not only drew the viewer back into space, but also suggested a passage back into the past, to old buildings and pathways, through open doorways or winding alleys.[28] His late images also often moved back into shadow, creating an enigmatic and mysterious quality, prompting the viewer to look more closely, to see what lies behind the image.

In 1968, New York's Museum of Modern Art bought Berenice Abbott's collection of Atget's photographs, and the next year the museum drew from these to present an exhibition. John Szarkowski, the director of the museum's department of photography, later recalled that the photographs were not dated, and that at the time little was known about the chronology of Atget's oeuvre, so he and a colleague had simply selected what they considered the most interesting and successful photographs for the exhibition. Twelve years later, Szarkowski noted that a dissertation completed at Columbia University in 1980 allowed the pictures in the 1969 exhibition to be dated with a high degree of accuracy, and that this revealed that half of the images came from the first 25 years of Atget's career, and the other half from his last six years of work. The two years most heavily represented in the exhibition were 1925–1926, Atget's last two full years of work before his death in 1927. Szarkowski contended that this evidence of selection demonstrated that Atget's work changed substantially, and grew stronger, with time.[29]

For nearly four decades, Eugène Atget traveled daily by bus and subway all over Paris, carrying a bellows camera, wooden tripod, and glass plates that together weighed more than 40 pounds, in a relentless and painstaking effort to capture the appearance of the vanishing old city. He was a pioneer: Berenice Abbott noted that in his time photography was so new a medium that few thought to adopt it as a profession. He did not see Paris as a vast modern metropolis, but rather as a series of individual ancient streets, buildings, and ways of life, and he recorded his vision with infinite care and patience, for little material reward and less recognition. His quest was that of a great experimental innovator, whose work inspired younger photographers by providing a visual vocabulary on which they could base their own efforts to portray the world around them. Berenice Abbott, the first of many to do this, recognized at first sight that "Atget's photographs ... somehow spelled photography to me."[30]

Alfred Stieglitz (1864–1946)

Photography is my passion. The search for Truth my obsession.
Alfred Stieglitz[31]

Alfred Stieglitz grew up in New York, the eldest son of a prosperous merchant who had immigrated to the United States from Germany. When Alfred was 17, his father took the family to Europe for five years, to give his children the benefit of an Old World education. Alfred went to Berlin to study engineering. He loved the city's culture, but disliked his courses, which he found too abstract. One day in 1883 he bought a camera. He later wrote that "The camera was waiting for me by predestination, and I took to it as a musician takes to the piano or a painter to the canvas."[32] He was drawn to photography "first as a toy, then as a passion, then as an obsession."[33]

His new enthusiasm prompted Alfred to switch his university studies to photochemistry. The lectures were again too theoretical, but he enjoyed working in the laboratory. Dorothy Norman, later a close friend and biographer of Stieglitz, observed that his early distaste for theory set a pattern: "He preferred instead to make constant experiments. Throughout his career he varied accepted practices both when photographing and when preparing negatives and prints. He liked best to judge for himself what he should do, to follow his intuition based on ever increasing experience."[34]

An important event occurred in Berlin, when his teacher showed Stieglitz's work to a group of painters. Although several admired his prints, they all agreed that photographs could not be art because they were not made by hand. Stieglitz believed this attitude ignored modern technological progress: "I found it difficult to understand how, with society supposed to be 'in the hands of the engineers,' machine-made objects were looked down upon." The encounter caused Stieglitz to write to his father that he planned to dedicate his life to seeing that photographs were accepted as works of art.[35]

Stieglitz returned to the United States in 1890. Except for several vacations in Europe, he would spend the rest of his life in New York City and at his family's summer home at Lake George, in the Catskills. During that time, he became a central figure not only in photography, but in the American art world: in addition to making photographs, Stieglitz founded and edited several pioneering journals of photography, and founded and operated a series of art galleries devoted to innovative photography, painting, and sculpture. His most basic commitment always remained that of establishing photography as an independent art. But his means in this campaign changed over time, as his understanding and practice of photography evolved.

Stieglitz's earliest interest in photography was scientific: "I began to make mechanical drawings with [the camera], and gradually switched over to the art side."[36] Much of his early effort went into solving technical problems, to expand the boundaries of photography. His early work included innovative photographs made under conditions photographers had previously avoided, notably in rain, in snow, and at night. His success strengthened his conviction that photography was capable of artistic expression. As he matured artistically, Stieglitz rejected the work of photographers who mimicked painting with romantic scenes of posed, artificial subjects, and became a proponent of "straight" photography: clear, sharp images made with natural light in the open air, using rapid exposures to capture unposed models. He considered simplicity "the key to all art," and embraced realism: "There is a reality—so subtle that it becomes more real than reality. That's what I'm trying to get down in photography."[37] He wanted to use photography to make people aware of the beauty all around them, contending that "the camera is one of the most effective means of teaching people to distinguish between what is beautiful and what is not."[38]

In 1892, Stieglitz began taking a hand camera on his walks around New York. One of his goals was to make atmosphere a feature of his images, for he contended that "Atmosphere is the medium through which we see all things." His street photographs captured the steam rising from carriage horses in the cold, the smoke from chimneys, and the dirt and grit of a city at work. His formula for using a handheld camera was to find a subject, study the lighting, then "await the moment in which everything is in balance; that is, satisfies your eye." With the movement of people and vehicles, this visual process "often means hours of patient waiting," but for Stieglitz it was what separated a great photographer from a casual snap-shooter, allowing him to produce excellent pictures with consistency as opposed to an occasional lucky effort.[39]

Stieglitz also began to study modern painting, for he believed that comparison to other arts could demonstrate photography's unique qualities.[40] His education led to a series of exhibitions in which his small gallery introduced Paris' most advanced art to New York: these included the first American shows of Cézanne, Matisse, and Picasso.[41] In 1912, Stieglitz coined a new term to underscore his argument for a division of labor between painting and photography. Recognizing the leadership of Matisse and Picasso in painting, he characterized their approach as *antiphotographic*: "It is this antiphotography in their mental attitude and in their work that I am using in order to emphasize the meaning of photography."[42] In Stieglitz's view, this recent development of advanced painting allowed photography to take over the role of creating realistic, representational works of art. In contrast to the conceptual painting of Matisse and Picasso, Stieglitz's art of photography was fundamentally experimental. He was committed to visual goals, as he wrote in 1892 that "My sole aim in making pictures is to reproduce what I see," and more than 30 years later he complained, "Could I but photograph what I *see*!"[43] Visual art was not subject to verbal expression: "if the artist could explain in words what he has made, he would not have had to create it."[44]

Stieglitz fought against the common belief that photography was easy. He wrote in 1899 that "the ability to make a truly artistic photograph is not acquired offhand, but is the result of an artistic instinct coupled with years of labor." Nearly two decades later, he declared that in his opinion "the most difficult problem in photography is to learn to see." True vision was not innate: "Seeing needs practice." Real achievement was difficult: "Everything worthwhile means continuous struggle and concentration of effort—even in photography."[45]

In 1921, at the age of 57, Stieglitz summarized his philosophy for the catalogue of a major exhibition of his work. He offered a succinct experimental credo: "My teachers have been life—work—continuous experiment." He stressed that his experimentation was constant: "Every print I make, even from one negative, is a new experience, a new problem. For, unless I am able to vary—add—I am not interested."[46]

Stieglitz never ceased experimenting. In some cases, this involved photographing the same motif repeatedly, while in others it involved making variations on a single photograph. An example of the latter was *Winter on Fifth Avenue*, which he made in 1893 in a snowstorm, to refute the traditional belief that there was not enough light to make photographs in bad weather. A biographer recently wrote of this photograph:

> The original negative was horizontal, but almost every print Stieglitz made from it was vertical, cutting out pedestrians to the left and right, eliminating as many signs of life as possible, with the effect that the snow seems heavier and the horse and driver more isolated in the storm. The railroad ties visible at the left of the original image were laid down on snowy days so passengers could alight from carriages more easily. As Stieglitz printed and reprinted this negative over the course of years, he got rid of these entirely, until in the 1920s or 1930s his aesthetic changed and he printed the whole negative horizontally, including all the random details his early taste had rejected.

The biographer commented that it is difficult to find "such a good example of an artist working over the same material at different ages. These early New York images were Stieglitz's companions for decades, changing as he changed."[47]

Stieglitz made his photograph that is most often reproduced in textbooks of the history of photography in 1907, when he was 43.[48] Although it is often used to represent immigrants bound for the United States, *The Steerage* was in fact taken on a ship bound for Europe, and Stieglitz's interest in the image lay more in its formal properties than its subject. He explained that as he looked down from first class to the passengers below in steerage, he was captivated by the visual effects of the interaction of the shapes of the ship's fittings and the positions of the passengers: "To me it is a study in mathematical lines, in balance, in a pattern of light and shade."[49]

Stieglitz discovered the art of Georgia O'Keeffe in 1917, and immediately exhibited it in his gallery. The two were soon romantically involved, and they married in 1924. Their marriage was one of the most remarkable in the history of modern art, and profoundly affected the work of both. When they met, Stieglitz was 53 and the most famous photographer alive, while O'Keeffe, age 30, was an unknown painter who taught art at a teachers' college in West Texas. During their marriage she rose to a position as one of the most important American artists of her time. Stieglitz began photographing O'Keeffe in 1917, and during the next twenty years made more than three hundred images of her.[50] This was one of the most important composite portraits ever made, and one of the most significant serial works ever made by a modern artist; Edward Steichen called the entire series "certainly the most comprehensive and intimate portrayal of a single person that has ever been realized by any of the visual arts."[51] The experimental Stieglitz had always liked to work in series, and O'Keeffe explained that his idea of a portrait was a sequence that followed a person throughout an entire life: "As a portrait it would be a photographic diary."[52]

Stieglitz affected O'Keeffe's art in a number of ways. She commented that the portraits made her aware of her own individuality: "I can see myself, and it has helped me to say what I want to say—in paint."[53] A striking feature of many of Stieglitz's photographs of her was his use of close-ups, in which a part of her body—often her hands or her torso—stood for the whole. In 1919, he explained that these images were "so sharp that you can see the pores in a face—yet it is abstract."[54] O'Keeffe adopted this understanding of abstraction, and some of her most celebrated paintings of flowers and other motifs combined clarity with extreme close-up views. Thus she told an interviewer in 1922 that "It is only by selection, by elimination, by emphasis, that we get at the real meaning of things."[55] Stieglitz's persistent experimentation also became a source of inspiration for O'Keeffe. She wrote to a friend that his work "is always a surprise to me—one feels there can be nothing more for him to do—and then away he goes—shooting way ahead just like the last time."[56] She was impressed by his ability to find motifs for his art wherever he was: "I never knew him to make a trip anywhere to photograph. His eye was in him, and he used it on anything that was nearby."[57]

Stieglitz and O'Keeffe were both visual seekers, who shared a basic commitment to open-ended experimental art. In 1910, Stieglitz declared that the American artists of his gallery—who prominently included John Marin and Arthur Dove as well as O'Keeffe—were "seeking for the unknown.... [The artists] do believe in themselves... but they do not believe they have reached... will ever reach—the point for which they are striving." In 1923, O'Keeffe wrote that in creating artistic form, "Making your unknown known is the important thing—and keeping the unknown always beyond you."[58] Works of art were never ends in themselves, but were part of a process; Stieglitz often told critics, "You are interested in the fruit. I am interested in the tree."[59] Stieglitz disliked the very idea of finality: "Any conclusion is for me a dead thing—unaesthetic, a tombstone. Where there are no contradictions, there is no life."[60]

Stieglitz's personal flamboyance and messianic agenda made him a controversial figure: O'Keeffe conceded that "He was either loved or hated—there wasn't much in between."[61] One critic called him "the Napoleon of pictorial photography," who "put into the movement for internal progress and external recognition the fanaticism of a Mad Mullah, the wiles of a Machiavelli, the advertising skill of a P. T. Barnum, the literary barbs of a Whistler, and an untiring persistence and confidence all his own."[62] His impact on the development of photography was great. Edward Steichen wrote in 1941 that "forty years or so ago, Alfred Stieglitz began to be called the Father of American Photography, and I am speaking here as a son in this movement."[63] Walker Evans, who came to resent Stieglitz's rhetorical excesses, described him as "photography's missionary" and argued that his significance "may have lain in his resounding, crafty fight for recognition, as much as it lay in his *oeuvre*. Recognition for fine photography as art." Yet Evans recognized that Stieglitz was a master as well as a prophet of the great "straight" tradition in photography.[64] A recent survey of textbooks of the history of photography revealed that Evans placed second among all twentieth-century photographers in total illustrations of his work, well behind only Stieglitz.[65] In 1969, Evans acknowledged that "There *is* a ground-swell ... of arresting still photography at this time, and it may perhaps be traced to the life work of one man: Alfred Stieglitz."[66] Stieglitz would have been pleased, but probably not surprised, for he believed that his enterprise could go on indefinitely. In 1923 he wrote to a friend that "my photography is different. Something new. A classical reality—direct—an understanding of the life of nature—an endless field. And the means are simple—but it means work, work, and still more work—step by step."[67]

Man Ray (1890–1976)

> I do not photograph nature, I photograph my fantasy.
> Man Ray[68]

Emmanuel Radnitzky was the son of Russian immigrants to the United States. When he was seven his family moved from Philadelphia to Brooklyn, where his father worked in a garment factory.[69] That same year, the battleship *Maine* was sunk in Havana harbor. Emmanuel carefully drew the ship from a newspaper photograph, then "colored it with my crayons in a most arbitrary manner, using the whole spectrum at my command." He was not fazed by his family's objections: "I felt that since the original pictures were in black, I was perfectly free to use my imagination."[70] This was a practice Emmanuel would often follow, of favoring imagination over accepted conventions.

Emmanuel loved to draw and paint. Later he recalled that "I wanted to paint, it was a passion.... It seemed like a disease; the smell of turpentine and oil would intoxicate me as alcohol intoxicated others."[71] He stole tubes of paint from an art supply store, and had no remorse because of the nobility of the cause: "I considered the painting of a picture the acme of human accomplishment; even today, the conviction still persists.... I consider all artists as privileged and sacred beings."[72]

In high school Emmanuel excelled at mechanical drawing. He was offered a scholarship to study architecture at New York University, but to his parents' dismay he rejected this to become an artist. He supported himself by designing maps for a commercial publisher. During lunch hours he went to art galleries, notably that of Alfred Stieglitz, where he was introduced to both photography and advanced painting. He became friendly with Stieglitz—on one visit Stieglitz took his portrait—and their conversations led Emmanuel to consider the role of photography: "I could not help thinking that since photography had liberated the modern painter from the drudgery of faithful representation, this field would become the exclusive one of photography, helping it to become an art in its own right."[73] Emmanuel was thus a good student of Stieglitz. In time, he would develop his own, very different, view of the role of photography.

In 1911, Emmanuel and his family discarded their ethnic surname, shortening it to "Ray." Emmanuel also shortened his first name. With characteristic nonconformism, he considered both elements of his new name a single unit.[74]

In 1915, Man Ray was commuting to New York City from a small artists' colony in New Jersey. Friends visited on weekends, and one day the art collector Walter Arensberg brought a young French artist, Marcel Duchamp, whose *Nude Descending a Staircase* had caused a furor at the Armory Show two years earlier. Although Man Ray spoke no French, and Duchamp no English, the two immediately hit it off: "I brought out a couple of old tennis rackets, and a ball which we batted back and forth without any net, in front of the house. Having played the game on regular courts previously, I called the strokes to make conversation: fifteen, thirty, forty, love, to which he replied each time with the same word: yes."[75] The two artists would be close friends for more than fifty years, until Duchamp's death in 1968. It was fitting that they would begin their relationship by playing tennis without a net, for Duchamp, perhaps the most iconoclastic and subversive of modern conceptual innovators, would consistently support Man Ray's irreverent violations of artistic conventions.[76] His early contact with Duchamp combined with his dissatisfaction with the current state of American art to prompt Man Ray to a declaration of intent: "I shall from now on do the things I'm not supposed to do."[77]

Man Ray also began making photographs in 1915. Although he did this initially merely to document his paintings, he was surprised how quickly he mastered the techniques, and he soon began to earn money by taking portraits. For the rest of his life, Man Ray would carry on two careers simultaneously, as a photographer and painter. He would always maintain that there was no conflict between the activities. So for example in 1952 he explained that "Depending on the subject and the intended treatment, I make my choice between painting and photography."[78] Nor need the choice be difficult: "I paint what cannot be photographed, something from the imagination or a dream, or a subconscious impulse. I photograph the things I don't want to paint, that are already in existence."[79]

In fact, however, Man Ray suffered considerably from his joint practice. Most troubling was his failure ever fully to reconcile himself to the fact that he was vastly more successful, artistically as well as financially, in the activity he favored less: in his 1963 autobiography, he reflected that "Despite my respect for Stieglitz's efforts, and my aroused interest in photography, painting remained my guiding passion," and in an interview a decade later he claimed that "I wasn't really interested in photography, I never was, as an artist."[80] The rhetoric of the latter statement is clearly exaggerated, but it appears to reflect his bitterness at what he considered the lack of recognition of his painting.[81] A persistent irritation was the refusal of others to accept his two professions: "It irked me when I was asked, according to my activity at the moment, whether I had given up the one for the other. There was no conflict between the two—why couldn't people accept the idea that one might engage in two activities in his lifetime, alternately or simultaneously?"[82] Man Ray's innovations were in fact products of his training in both arts: he often made paintings that looked like photographs, and photographs that looked like paintings.[83] As he wrote in 1963, "one of the principal accusations against me by sticklers for pure photography... was that I confused painting with photography. How true, I replied, I was a painter: it was perfectly normal that one should influence the other."[84]

An early example of Man Ray's blending of the arts occurred in 1916, when he began to use airbrushing, a technique he learned in his commercial job, to make paintings. This freed him from conventional tools: "It was thrilling to paint a picture, hardly touching the surface—a purely cerebral act."[85] With stencils, the airbrush created a photographic precision and allowed him to work quickly: "I was more interested in the idea I wanted to communicate than in the aesthetics of the picture, and here was a way to express my ideas more rapidly than by a painting."[86] His conceptual departure into the mechanical process of making aerographs was not welcomed by New York's collectors: "we began to use our brains, to use the painting medium to express ideas and not just to demonstrate our virtuosity. The Americans couldn't grasp that."[87]

In 1921, Man Ray fulfilled a childhood dream by going to Paris, "that Mecca of art."[88] His friend Duchamp met him at the Gare St. Lazare, and took him to meet the leading lights of Paris' Dada movement. They immediately embraced Man Ray, as would the Surrealists when that movement superseded Dada. Although the anti-art Dadas and the Surrealist champions of the subconscious would be divided by doctrinal disputes, Man Ray was accepted by both groups, perhaps because he was not one of a large number of poets or painters, but instead the sole photographer in either group. The Dada poet Georges Ribemont-Dessaignes called Man Ray "the subtle chemist of mysteries," and wrote that "He invents a new world and photographs it to prove that it exists."[89]

Man Ray earned a living in Paris as a professional photographer. In addition to photographing the Surrealist poets and painters, he photographed Picasso and Braque in their studios, such other painters as Matisse, Kandinsky, and Léger, and the sculptors Brancusi and Giacometti. Gertrude Stein would let only Man Ray photograph her, and James Joyce was photographed by him when *Ulysses* was published. Man Ray photographed Marcel Proust on his deathbed, Paris resident writers Ezra Pound and Ernest Hemingway, and visitors Virginia Woolf and T. S. Eliot.[90] He justifiably described himself as "an official recorder of events and personalities," and many of his portraits were among the most celebrated images of their famous subjects.[91] He produced penetrating character studies by working quickly and informally, allowing sitters to move as they wished, filming them from a distance with a long-focus lens, then often cropping and enlarging his portraits.[92] His skill as a studio photographer educated and inspired others, as four of his assistants from the 1920s—Berenice Abbott, Bill Brandt, Jacques-André Boiffard, and Lee Miller—went on to become important photographers after their apprenticeships.[93]

In 1921, Man Ray discovered that he could create images without a camera, by placing objects on wet photographic paper, then exposing it to the light: the objects appeared as white areas, where no light reached the paper, while exposed areas of the paper turned black. This was not a new process, for photograms had earlier been made in this way, but Man Ray achieved novel effects by moving the light source, shifting the objects, and making multiple exposures, to produce illusions of depth and movement.[94] These ghostly images, eerie and unpredictable, were immediately hailed by the Surrealists as a means of drawing directly on the subconscious, and thus the visual equivalent of their literary device of automatic writing.[95] Man Ray wrote to a friend that "I have finally freed myself from the sticky medium of paint, and am working directly with light itself. I have found a way of recording it. The subjects were never so near to life itself as in my new work."[96] Triumphantly, he christened his innovation the *Rayograph*.[97]

Early in his stay in Paris, Man Ray became romantically involved with a celebrated artists' model, known as Kiki of Montparnasse. One of his many pictures of her, made in 1924, became his single most frequently reproduced photograph.[98] Titled *Le Violon d'Ingres*, the photograph showed the nude back of Kiki, on which Man Ray stenciled the two curved *f*-holes of a violin. Both Kiki's pose and the turban she wore were references to the central figure in one of the most famous paintings by the nineteenth-century master J. A. D. Ingres, *The Turkish Bath*.[99] The title added enigma. Ingres was so avid an amateur violinist that even today the phrase *violon d'Ingres* is a French expression for "hobby." The title therefore suggested that photography, or Kiki, or perhaps both, were hobbies of Man Ray. The elegant and imaginative visual quotation of earlier art, and the symbolism added by the title, made *Le Violon d'Ingres* a classic conceptual work. The obvious resemblance of the shape of Kiki's back to a violin, and the added imagery of the *f*-holes that emphasized this, also made it a classic Surrealist work.

Man Ray painted and photographed until late in his life. Yet no photograph he made after the age of 46 was illustrated in any recent textbook of the history of photography, and his most frequently illustrated photographs were made when he was in his early 30s.[100] He is known above all as the iconoclastic photographer of Surrealism, praised by the leader of that movement, André Breton, for having used photography for "the thorough exploration ... of that region which painting imagined it was going to be able to keep to itself."[101] Marcel Duchamp wrote that his old friend's achievement was "to treat the camera as he treated the paint brush, a mere instrument at the service of the mind."[102] Man Ray's goals were completely conceptual: "I would photograph an idea rather than an object, and a dream rather than an idea."[103]

Late in his life, Man Ray declared, "I have no style." This was deliberate: he wanted to be "contradictory and irrational," so that "each succeeding work, or series of works, shall be entirely different from preceding works."[104] This became an important part of his legacy. So for example Bruce Nauman, one of the most influential artists of the late twentieth century, puzzled critics by working in many different genres, with no consistent style. He explained that this practice was a result of seeing a Man Ray retrospective exhibition early in his career: "To me Man Ray seemed to avoid the idea that every piece had to take on a historical meaning. What I liked was that there appeared to be no consistency to his thinking, no one style."[105] Man Ray would have been pleased to have inspired Nauman and other young artists to reject stylistic consistency, to change genres at will, and to ignore conventional boundaries between genres, for as he remarked late in his life, "Perhaps the final goal desired by the artist is a confusion or merging of all the arts, as things merge in real life."[106]

Cindy Sherman (1954–)

[T]he one thing I've always known is that the camera lies.
Cindy Sherman[107]

As a child growing up on Long Island, Cindy Sherman loved make-believe. She had a trunk full of old clothes, some inherited from her grandmother, that she used to play dress-up—"it was fun because it was artificial."[108] She loved putting on makeup.[109] She "was always glued to the television," and she loved watching movies: "There was one show, *The Million Dollar Movie*, that played the same film over every night for a week, so you could really know it by heart."[110] And even when she was watching television, Cindy was always drawing.[111]

Art was Cindy's best subject in school. Her family couldn't afford a private college, so she chose to go to SUNY Buffalo, which offered a bachelor of fine arts degree. She began the program expecting to be a painter, but "suddenly realized I couldn't do it any more, it was ridiculous, there was nothing more to say." Mastering the techniques of painting involved copying earlier art, and Sherman "realized I could just use a camera and put my time into an idea instead."[112] Her major required a course in photography, and Sherman failed it as a freshman "because I couldn't quite grasp the technology of it. I just couldn't understand what shutter and speed and all of that had to do with making the print." When she repeated the course, "I finally had this teacher who said, 'Don't worry about the technology—just concentrate on your ideas.'"[113] Sherman was instantly converted: "right away that made so much more sense to me."[114] Photography was simply a faster way of achieving what she had been attempting by painting, and this would remain her attitude, as nearly two decades after her original conversion she explained that "I think of myself as using the camera in the same way as someone could be using a paint brush although it takes a lot less time. I'm just recording everything in a split second."[115]

Her choice of a subject grew out of her childhood love of make-believe. She later explained that when she was at college, "every time I would feel depressed or confused, I would lock myself in my room and just make myself into someone else.... [I]t was just some kind of cathartic thing I needed to do at the time, that made me feel kind of good afterwards." Her partner suggested she should use this for her art: "it wasn't even my idea to record it, it was my friend Robert Longo's idea, who just said, you know, 'Why don't you do something about that and just document this.' And I did and that seemed to put together a lot of the frustrations about where I was going to go, in making art."[116]

Sherman moved to New York in 1977, the year after she graduated from college. From 1977 through 1980 she made a series of sixty-nine photographs, collectively called the *Untitled Film Stills*, that is generally considered her most important work, and accounts for more than half of all the illustrations of her photographs in recent textbooks of art history.[117] Each of the black-and-white photographs portrayed Sherman as a character in what appeared to be B-movies from the 1940s, 1950s, and 1960s. Sherman explained that they were modeled after real film stills: "I had friends who worked at Barnes & Noble who would bring home cheap film books. Barnes & Noble had millions of books about the movies—whole books on Garbo, Eastern European films, silent films, horror movies, film fads. These books were my textbooks, my research."[118] She wanted her pictures "to seem cheap and trashy, something you'd find in a novelty store and buy for a quarter. I didn't want them to look like art." She numbered them, instead of giving them titles, to increase their ambiguity.[119] Above all, she wanted her art to be widely accessible—"something that people could relate to without having to read a book about it first. So that anybody off the street could appreciate it.... That's the reason why I wanted to imitate something out of the culture, and also make fun of the culture as I was doing it."[120]

The *Untitled Film Stills* have become very important for contemporary art, and their ambiguity has prompted numerous scholars and critics to offer explanations for them. Sherman has rejected many of these. So for example she has denied that her intent came from feminism: "I know I was not consciously aware of this thing the 'male gaze.' It was the way I was shooting, the mimicry of the style of black-and-white grade-Z motion pictures that produced the self-consciousness of these characters, not my knowledge of feminist theory."[121] She has also denied that they are self-portraits: "people seem to think that I must be revealing something of a personal or autobiographical nature, and they are constantly looking for it."[122] She has explained that she enjoyed making the *Stills* "because throughout my childhood I had stored up so many images of role models. It was real easy to think of a different one in every scene."[123] She was anxious to demystify art: "I can't stand the idea of art as a precious object."[124] She was surprised by the enthusiastic reception of the *Stills*: "I'm doing one of the most stupid things in the world which I can't even explain, dressing up like a child and posing in front of a camera trying to make beautiful pictures. And people seem to fall for it."[125] This has contributed to her conclusion about the *Stills*: "The role-playing was intended to make people become aware of how stupid roles are, a lot of roles, but since it's not all that serious, perhaps that's more the moral to it, not to take anything too seriously."[126]

Sherman has enjoyed enormous success. In 1987, at the age of 33, she had a full-scale retrospective exhibition at New York's Whitney Museum, and in

1997 the Museum of Modern Art presented an exhibition, sponsored by the pop singer Madonna, in honor of the museum's acquisition of a complete set of the *Untitled Film Stills*. Sherman's prominence in the art world as a whole is unprecedented for a photographer: a recent survey of textbooks of art history published in 2000 or later found that Sherman ranked first among all artists in total reproductions of works made in 1975 or later, ahead of such major painters as Gerhard Richter and Jean-Michel Basquiat, and such leading sculptors as Jeff Koons and Damien Hirst.[127] Sherman's work has elevated the position of photography in the art world. In 1987 the curator of her Whitney Museum exhibition declared that "She has accomplished what photographers have been pursuing for a century—true parity with the other two arts."[128] And in 1995, a dealer offered evidence in support of this, commenting that "Cindy Sherman has performed some sort of modern-day alchemy. She has convinced the art market that her photographs should be priced like paintings."[129]

Sherman's success has been widely analyzed. As early as 1990, the critic Arthur Danto remarked that "Sherman's brilliant appropriation, in the late 1970s, of the format of the 'still,' with its implied narrative in which she was the nameless starlet, became the focus of so much neostructuralist, radical feminist, Frankfurt School Marxist and semiological hermeneutics that one is convinced there must be whole programs of study in institutions of higher learning in which one can major, or even earn a doctorate, in Sherman Studies."[130] Characteristically, Sherman does not embrace these formal analyses: "I have never been a fan of criticism or theories, so that actually none of that affected me and still doesn't."[131] But Sherman likes ambiguity, so she concedes that "I have to accept that there will be this range of interpretations that I can't control, and don't want to control, because that's what makes it interesting to me."[132] In 2000, the critic Calvin Tomkins commented on the extent of Sherman's influence on contemporary artists in multiple genres:

> She has reclaimed the oldest trick in the book, storytelling, and given it new life in visual art. An amazing number of younger artists have followed her lead; the galleries are full of what has come to be called setup photography, in which complex and often highly enigmatic scenarios are plotted, constructed, and photographed, and much of the newer painting and sculpture on view these days has a strong narrative content.[133]

Sherman has achieved her high standing in the art world by using photography in novel ways. The critic Peter Schjeldahl observed that Sherman and several contemporaries "have diverted the official course of the history of photography by rejecting its most revered conventions: the sacredness of the photographic paper, of the camera, the perfect exposure, and the immaculate print."[134] The preparation of her scenes is so much more important than the execution of her photographs that Sherman does not need to take her own photographs: she took many of the *Untitled Film Stills* with a delayed shutter release, but she had Robert Longo and other friends snap some, and the most celebrated single image in the series was taken by her father, a retired engineer.[135] Sherman's indifference to these traditional concerns is a product of her conceptual approach to photography. She has described her feelings toward photography as a love/hate relationship, "because I hate the technology of it. I hate people who are obsessed with the technology of it."[136] She freely admits to ignorance of the history of photography: "Of course I've seen Atget and Stieglitz for years but just didn't pay much attention."[137] Sherman's distaste for the conventions of photography is such that she has declared that she is not a photographer, but an artist whose medium is photography.[138] For her a camera is not a powerful vehicle for pursuing lofty aesthetic goals, but simply a convenient means of making whimsical statements by recording the make-believe she loves.

The Real World

Eugène Atget hung a sign outside his door that read *Documents pour Artistes*—documents for artists.[139] Edward Weston agreed with the description: "Atget was a great documentary photographer."[140] Weston praised Atget's "simple, very understanding way of seeing . . . with direct honesty."[141] Berenice Abbott stressed that "For Atget, the subject was the important thing. The structure, the composition, was dictated by the subject. His compositions, so consistently flawless, were merely a means to clarify and express that subject as simply as possible." Comparing him to a great literary realist, she called Atget "a Balzac of the camera."[142]

Alfred Stieglitz campaigned tirelessly to make photography an art that would portray the beauty of the real world directly and honestly. His goal for his own work was to portray reality: "I try to show life as it is, not as it should be or as I would like to have it."[143] His art aimed at perception rather than interpretation: "I am interested in putting down an image only of what I have seen, not what it means to me."[144] He predicted that photography's greatest achievements lay in realism: "It is to the men who understand nature and love it, and who love photography, that the future will bring about revelations little dreamed of today."[145]

Early in his career, Man Ray realized that "not only would I cease to look for inspiration in nature; I would turn more and more to man-made sources."[146] In his photography as well as in his painting, Man Ray's goal was to transform the real world through his own thoughts. Thus he declared that "After all photography is not restricted to the mere role of a copyist. It is a marvelous explorer of aspects that our retina will never register."[147] Although Man Ray rejected Stieglitz's aesthetic goals, his efforts were nonetheless inspired by their early conversations, for a lesson he learned from Stieglitz was never to accept what others considered the limits of photography. Man Ray consequently worked to devise new means of extending the technical boundaries of the camera and film.[148] Unlike Stieglitz, however, Man Ray worked to extend photography into the world of the imagination.

When she began studying art in college, Cindy Sherman was "the kind of painter who would copy things," but with her own atmosphere: "I was just interested in reproducing a picture with somewhat surrealistic overtones."[149] She has stressed that her photographs are not documentary: "I tend to prefer staged imagery that contrasts reality from fiction."[150] The *Untitled Film Stills* were not realistic: "the women aren't being lifelike, they're acting. There are so many levels of artifice."[151]

Atget and Stieglitz were experimental photographers, who considered the camera a powerful tool for capturing the beauty of the real world. Man Ray and Sherman are conceptual photographers, who use the camera as a powerful means of creating artificial images that express their ideas and fantasies. There is irony in the great success Sherman has achieved, for although Stieglitz would have been delighted that a photographer could become the preeminent visual artist of her generation, he would probably have been bitterly disappointed that she did this by creating artificial images, and rejecting the aesthetic values that he regarded as photography's mission.

8
Filmmakers

During the 1950s, the eminent French film critic André Bazin proposed a division of directors into two groups: "Those . . . who put their faith in the image and those who put their faith in reality." He explained that he defined *image* very broadly, as "everything that the representation on the screen adds to the object there represented," comprising a variety of means that allow the cinema "to impose its interpretation of an event on the spectator." Bazin considered these two groups to represent basically opposing tendencies that challenged the aesthetic unity of film.[1] His insight was a striking one, that appears to have anticipated the division analyzed here between conceptual and experimental innovators. It might have served as an analytical framework for study of the history of film, but unfortunately it received little attention and this did not occur. This chapter effectively expands upon Bazin's insight.

The division between experimental and conceptual filmmakers can be traced back to the earliest practitioners of the new art. A short history of French film began with the observation that "Louis Lumière (1864–1948) has as strong a claim as anyone to the title of inventor of the cinema." Shortly thereafter, the volume continued:

> The second great figure in the French cinema, Georges Méliès (1861–1938), forms such a striking contrast to Lumière that their names are often used to define two major tendencies in the cinema. Where Lumière is concerned to portray life as it really is, Méliès deals with fantasy and imagination. He replaced his predecessor's sober concern for everyday reality with his own taste for spectacle.[2]

Similarly, Gerald Mast and Bruce Kawin later wrote that

> If Lumière documented the world, Méliès transformed it. If Lumière established that the camera could record a factual record of an event, Méliès proved that the camera could create an event that never happened. Lumière

set the pattern for realism; Méliès opened the door to the impossible. Méliès gave the cinema the tools of fantasy, illusion, and distortion.[3]

Interestingly, when the conceptual Orson Welles made a genealogical chart to trace the major branches of cinema, he identified as his own ancestors Méliès and two later great conceptual directors, D. W. Griffith and Sergei Eisenstein.[4]

John Ford (1894–1973)

> Pictures, not words, should tell the story.
>
> John Ford[5]

John Martin Feeney was born in Cape Elizabeth, Maine, the son of immigrants from County Galway, Ireland. Over the years he would convince more than a few interviewers that he had been baptized Sean Aloysius O'Fearna, though the records of St. Dominic's Church in Portland reveal that to have been, in the words of a biographer, "a load of Fordian blarney."[6] Yet he never lost his pride in his Irish heritage, or the identification with the less privileged that came from his childhood as the son of an immigrant saloonkeeper. Late in his life, he declared, "I am of the proletariat. My people were peasants." But he also never lost the belief in the American dream that he gained from his family's experience, as he continued, "They came here, were educated. They served this country well. I love America."[7]

As a boy, John was fascinated by nickelodeons, and the glamour of the movies. After graduating from high school, instead of attending college he went to Hollywood, where his older brother Francis, who had earlier run off to join the circus, had become a successful movie actor and director. Francis had taken the surname Ford, and John followed him. Sponsored by his brother, John worked in a number of different jobs, including stuntman, actor, property man, cameraman, and assistant director. In 1917, just three years after his arrival in Hollywood, Ford began directing his own films—mostly low-budget Westerns, starring Harry Carey.

Ford and Carey became good friends, and made more than two dozen Westerns together during the next five years. Their movies were based on a number of elements that Ford would develop into a distinctive experimental style. He preferred images to words: "Scripts are dialogue, and I don't like all that *talk*. I've always tried to get things across visually."[8] Action was the best way to accomplish this: "When a motion picture is at its best, it is long on action and short on dialogue. When it tells its story and reveals its characters in a series of simple, beautiful, active pictures, and does it with as little talk as possible, then the motion picture medium is being used to its fullest advantage." His favorite genre best fitted this approach: "I don't know any subject on earth better suited to such a presentation than a Western."[9] He always preferred to leave the studio, and film outdoors in rugged and picturesque settings; the dramatic buttes and mesas of Utah's Monument Valley later became important in creating atmosphere in his films, and Ford believed "the real star of my Westerns has always been the land."[10] A comparison of the final shooting script to the actual film of *The Searchers*, which Ford made in Monument Valley in 1956, revealed that "every time he has the opportunity, Ford chooses to reduce or eliminate altogether the dialogue and exposition, substituting lyrical ambiguity for the prosaic clarity of the script."[11] Ford defined technique as "what you don't see on the screen," and he disliked any method that called attention to itself, such as camera movement: "It says, 'This is a motion picture. This isn't real.' I like to have the audience feel that this is the real thing. I don't like to have the audience interested in the camera."[12] Alfred Hitchcock paid tribute to Ford's success in this regard: "A John Ford picture was a visual gratification—his method of shooting, eloquent in its clarity and apparent simplicity."[13] The director William Friedkin contended that the popularity of Ford's art would be lasting because of his mastery of the use of action to tell stories: "I really believe that when people have colonized the moon they'll [still] be watching John Ford pictures."[14]

What mattered most to Ford were the actors: "After all, you've got to tell your story through the people who portray it. You can have a weak, utterly bad script—and a good cast will turn it into a good picture."[15] He used many of the same actors in one film after another: "Well, it's natural to use people whose capabilities one knows and also they know my method of work."[16] The critic and director Peter Bogdanovich observed that this was just one of the elements of continuity in Ford's films: "Every Ford movie is filled with reverberations from another—which makes his use of the same players from year to year, decade to decade, so much more than just building 'a stock company'—and one film of his cannot really be looked at as separate from the rest."[17]

As early as 1920, an interviewer reported that "'In everything I want realism' is Ford's continual cry," and this remained central to his films; Orson

Welles observed that "With Ford at his best, you feel that the movie has lived and breathed in a real world."[18] Striking testimony to Ford's realism came from the novelist John Steinbeck. In 1938, Steinbeck traveled through migrant camps in California, and the next year he published *The Grapes of Wrath* to dramatize the tragedy of the victims of the Dust Bowl. When the novel became a bestseller, the producer Darryl Zanuck purchased the film rights and offered it to Ford, who accepted: "The whole thing appealed to me—being about simple people—and the story was similar to the famine in Ireland."[19] Steinbeck was apprehensive, fearing a Hollywood studio would weaken the novel's harsh indictment of the exploitation of the migrants in California. Yet when he was given a pre-release screening in December 1939, he wrote to his agent in amazement, describing the film as "a hard, straight picture in which the actors are submerged so completely that it looks and feels like a documentary film and certainly it has a hard, truthful ring."[20]

Contemporaries recognized that Ford's work gained in power as he grew older. He won Oscars as best director for *The Informer*, which he made at the age of 41, *The Grapes of Wrath* (46), *How Green Was My Valley* (47), and *The Quiet Man* (58). Conspicuously absent from this list, however, were Ford's Westerns. He considered these his greatest achievement—two years before his death he declared that "I want to be remembered as 'John Ford—a guy that made Westerns'"—but he believed they were unfairly slighted by critics out of snobbery.[21] Time has corrected this injustice. In a 2002 poll taken by *Sight and Sound*, the journal of the British Film Institute, in which an international panel of critics were each asked to list the ten best movies ever made, the three of Ford's films that received the most votes were all Westerns: *The Searchers* ranked first, followed in order by *The Man Who Shot Liberty Valance* and *Stagecoach*.[22] These were made when Ford was 62, 68, and 45, respectively, and all three starred John Wayne.

These three great Westerns shared several themes that reflected Ford's basic beliefs about American history. In each, civilization ultimately triumphed over chaos and lawlessness. Yet in no case was this a simple epic tale of conquest of good over evil. In each instance the victory of civilization was made possible only by the actions of a "good bad man"—all played by Wayne—who violated the rules of civilized society, taking the law into his own hands to eliminate an evil that stood in the way of the establishment of a society based on law. And in each case, Wayne's unlawful actions disqualified him from a place in the society he had brought into existence: ironically, his very conquest of anarchy had made his own values obsolete, and unacceptable, in a civilized world.[23]

Ford's great Westerns were thus not simple morality tales, for in each some degree of irony undercut the simple opposition between good and evil. This reflected Ford's belief that "Westerns have been most inaccurate in overglamorizing and overdramatizing the heroes and villains of the period.... [I]t is true that much of the conversion to law and order was accomplished by reformed criminals.... It is equally wrong for the heroes to have been made out to be pure Sir Galahads in so many cases, which is nonsense."[24] Nonetheless, in Ford's last major reflection on the West, in 1962, a frontier newspaper editor chose to suppress the truth of the heroism and magnanimity of John Wayne's good bad man, and in so doing to perpetuate the lie by which Wayne had allowed Jimmy Stewart's character to take the credit, and reap the rewards, for being the man who had civilized his territory by killing the outlaw Liberty Valance. The movie was presented as a flashback: Stewart had returned from Washington, DC, where he was a senator, for the funeral of Wayne, who had died in obscurity and poverty. After listening to Stewart's retrospective account of the true story, the editor tore up the notes of Stewart's confession, famously declaring, "This is the West, sir. When the legend becomes fact, print the legend."[25] Ford explained that he agreed with the editor's decision, "because it's good for the country. We've had a lot of people who were supposed to be great heroes, and you know damn well they weren't. But it's good for the country to have heroes to look up to."[26] Yet the irony of Ford's statement in defense of myth lies in the fact that his film, *The Man Who Shot Liberty Valance*, told precisely the story the editor had chosen to suppress. Confronted with the judgment that his obvious sympathy for Wayne's character over Stewart's reflected a tendency for his Westerns to have become sadder over time, Ford grudgingly conceded, "Possibly—I don't know—I'm not a psychologist.... Maybe I'm getting older."[27] But the elderly Ford knew that the impact of Westerns had diminished, and that by the 1960s even as good a movie as *Liberty Valance* would not significantly affect American myth.

The great popularity of Ford's films spread his influence widely into popular culture. In one example, Buddy Holly saw *The Searchers* in Lubbock, Texas, in 1956, and seized on the ironic catchphrase of John Wayne's character as the title for a new song. "That'll Be the Day" became the breakthrough hit for Buddy Holly and the Crickets, as it rose to number one in both the United States and Britain the following year.[28] Ford's simple and powerful visual technique influenced many younger movie directors. So for example Akira Kurosawa acknowledged Ford as the greatest influence on his own movies, and Orson Welles declared that at the beginning of his film career, *Stagecoach* was his "movie textbook."[29] Welles recalled that "Every night for more than a month, I would screen [*Stagecoach*] with a different technician from RKO and ask him questions all through the movie."[30] What Welles wanted was not a message but a language: "I didn't need to learn from somebody who had something to say, but from somebody who would show me how to say what I had in mind; and John Ford is perfect for that."[31] Later filmmakers responded not only to Ford's technique, but also to the irony and darkness of his late Westerns. Martin Scorsese included a clip from *The Searchers* in *Mean Streets* (1973), and the plot of *Taxi Driver* (1976) parallels that of *The Searchers*, as Robert DeNiro's obsessional quest to destroy the pimp who corrupted a young girl is a contemporary urban version of John Wayne's long search for the Comanche chief who massacred his brother's family and kidnapped his niece.[32] The experimental Scorsese wanted to capture the look and feel of Times Square as authentically as his predecessor had captured Monument Valley; he declared that "John Ford made Westerns. We make street movies."[33]

Ford disdained pretension, and characteristically he told Bogdanovich that "I have never thought about what I was doing in terms of art.... To me, it was always a job of work—which I enjoyed immensely—and that's it."[34] Shortly before his death, he remarked that "I do think there is an art to the making of a motion picture. There are some great artists in the business. I am not one of them."[35] The critic and director François Truffaut understood Ford's humility, writing that "Ford was an artist who never said the word 'art.'" Truffaut explained his admiration for Ford's great experimental art: "His camera is invisible; his staging is perfect; he maintains a smoothness of surface in which no scene is allowed to become more important than any other. Such mastery is possible only after one has made an enormous number of films."[36]

Alfred Hitchcock (1899–1980)

> It is no use telling people; they have got to SEE.
> Alfred Hitchcock[37]

Growing up in east London, Alfred Hitchcock loved the theater and movies. He was also an avid reader, and at 16 he found the works of Edgar Allan Poe. He never forgot a discovery he made while reading "The Murders in the Rue

Morgue": "Fear, you see, is a feeling that people like to feel, when they are certain of being in safety." This had a lasting effect on him:

> Without wanting to seem immodest, I can't help but compare what I try to put in my films with what Poe put in his stories: a perfectly unbelievable story recounted to readers with such a hallucinatory logic that one has the impression that this same story can happen to you tomorrow. And that's the rule of the game if one wants the reader or spectator to subconsciously substitute himself for the hero.[38]

Early in his career, Hitchcock explained the persistent demand for thrillers as a basic human need for jolting emotional disturbances: "Our nature is such that we must have these 'shake-ups' or we grow sluggish and jellified; but . . . our civilization has so screened and sheltered us that it isn't practicable to experience sufficient thrills at firsthand. So we have to experience them artificially, and the screen is the best medium for this."[39] And so Hitchcock devoted his career to mastering cinematic shock therapy.

In Hitchcock's films, a thin veneer of civilization is constantly in danger of being pierced to reveal dark hidden depths: at any moment, even the most ordinary lives can be inexplicably threatened by powerful unidentified forces of evil. The critic Robin Wood described Hitchcock's cinematic world as "quicksand, unstable, constantly shifting, into which we may sink at any step in any direction, illusion and reality constantly ambiguous, even interchangeable."[40] In recognition of this, François Truffaut called Hitchcock an "artist of anxiety," alongside Kafka, Dostoevsky, and Poe.[41]

Hitchcock first got a job in the movie industry in 1920, when a company in London hired him to design title-cards for silent movies. He worked his way up through a series of technical jobs, learning all the details of how movies were made, and by 1925 he had begun directing. In 1929 he made the first English film with sound. During the next decade he directed a number of popular thrillers, and he came to be considered the leading director in England. In 1939 he moved to Hollywood, where he became an immediate success, as his first American film, *Rebecca*, won an Oscar for best movie. He continued to make movies in Hollywood for the rest of his life. In 1972, he explained his devotion to the industry, in terms that echoed his early excitement: "I've always believed in film as the newest art of the twentieth century because of its ability to communicate with the mass audiences of the world."[42]

Throughout his career, Hitchcock presented a consistent vision of his goals and philosophy. Late in his life, he stressed that "you have to remember that as well as being a creative person I am a very technical person. The actual exercise of technique is very important to me."[43] Skillful technique was to be used to accomplish the goal of "getting audiences on the edge of their seats" through the creation of suspense.[44] This required involving the audience: "Watching a well-made film, we don't sit by as spectators; we participate." The best technique was therefore unobtrusive: "The mark of good technique is that it is unnoticed."[45]

Even after the introduction of sound, Hitchcock maintained that "films must still be primarily a medium for telling a story in pictures."[46] Accordingly, he praised montage—the juxtaposition of images to create emotions or ideas—as "pure film," and scoffed at "photographs of people talking" as irrelevant to film.[47] Hitchcock believed that "in all artistic domains we attempt to create an emotion. The importance of a work of art, no matter what sort, is to evoke a reaction."[48] The story of a film was not of primary importance, for in his opinion the power of movies—what made them most effective in evoking a reaction and creating emotion—was "the manner and style of telling the story." This was the director's job: "what gives an effect of life to a picture [is] the feeling that when you see it on the screen you are watching something that has been conceived and brought to birth directly in visual terms."[49] Hitchcock considered this his strength: "my craft is that I handle the camera."[50]

Hitchcock valued images over words, and form over content: "though sound helps and is the most valuable advance the films have ever made they still remain primarily a visual art."[51] Tellingly, the great experimental director compared himself to a great experimental painter: "Cézanne is one of the precursors of the modern movement in art and ... the most important thing for him was to translate visual sensations. Similarly for me, when I take on a screenplay I feel the same needs."[52] This parallel explained Hitchcock's exasperation at the frequent criticism of his films for their unimportant subjects, which he likened to "looking at a painting of a still life, say by Cézanne, and wondering whether the apples on the plate are sweet or sour. Who cares? It's the way they're painted."[53] Hitchcock wanted to tell his story so much in pictures "that if by any chance the sound apparatus broke down in the cinema, the audience would not fret and get restless because the pictorial action would still hold them."[54] His goal was never to make his audience think, but rather to make them react to the suspense, excitement, and shocks he provided.

Over time, Hitchcock developed a set of practices that collectively constituted his trademark style. He often spoke of "building up a picture," and these components were effectively fitted together to achieve his primary goal of creating suspense. Distractions should be eliminated—"beauty, the virtuosity of the camera, everything must be sacrificed or compromised when it gets in the way of a story."[55] He frequently used "subjective treatment"—close-ups of a character and point-of-view shots of what the character saw—to increase the audience's identification with the character.[56] He favored simple, clear narratives that "hold the attention of any audience and won't puzzle them."[57] His films often featured the pursuit of an innocent man, who was falsely accused, because he believed it gave the audience a greater sense of danger: "It's easier for them to identify with him than with a guilty man on the run."[58] He sought realism in behavior—"When characters are unbelievable you never get real suspense"—and in settings—"looking so natural that the audience gets involved and believes, for the time being, what's going on up there on the screen."[59] One of Hitchcock's visual signatures was an eerie high-angle shot with empty space around the main character, that emphasized his isolation and vulnerability to an unseen lurking threat.[60]

Hitchcock distinguished between *surprise*—the sudden unanticipated explosion of a bomb—and *suspense*—a hidden bomb that the audience knows is set to explode in fifteen minutes but of which the characters in the film are unaware. The former gives the audience a fifteen-second jolt, whereas the latter provides fifteen minutes of discomfort "because the public is participating in the scene. The audience is longing to warn the characters." The extended anxiety of suspense was far more important to Hitchcock's films than the brief shock of surprise, so his guiding principle was that "whenever possible the public must be informed."[61]

Hitchcock considered that "the whole art of the motion picture is a succession of composed images, rapidly going through a machine," and his virtuosity in creating these sequences produced many individual scenes famous for their visual impact. Prominent examples include Cary Grant being chased across a bare midwestern prairie by a crop-dusting plane in *North by Northwest*, Jimmy Stewart struggling to control his vision—and mind—in the staircase of a tower in *Vertigo*, and Janet Leigh being stabbed and killed in the shower in *Psycho*.[62] Leigh's murder occupied only forty-five seconds in the completed film, but used fifty-two separate cuts, and required seven days to film.[63] (Hitchcock was proud that his bold use of montage in the scene actually made audiences scream, in spite of the fact that "the whole thing is purely an illusion. No knife ever touched any woman's body in that scene. Ever." For this he called *Psycho* "one of the most cinematic pictures I've ever made."[64]) The tower sequence in *Vertigo*, in which Hitchcock created a visual representation of dizziness and disorientation by having a camera simultaneously track away from the staircase and zoom in on it, drew on years of deliberation:

> I always remember one night at the Chelsea Arts Ball at Albert Hall in London when I got terribly drunk and I had the sensation that everything was going far away from me. I tried to get that into *Rebecca*, but they couldn't do it.... I thought about the problem for fifteen years. By the time we got to *Vertigo*, we solved it by using the dolly and zoom simultaneously.

When he was told that the heavy machinery needed to lift the camera at the top of the stairs would cost $50,000, Hitchcock pointed out that since there were no characters in the scene, they could use a model of the stairway, laid on its side. The scene was filmed in this way, with the camera tracking on the ground, at a cost of less than $20,000.[65] (In a tribute to Hitchcock, Martin Scorsese later used the "Vertigo shot" in *Goodfellas*.[66])

Like many experimental artists, Hitchcock struggled with endings. The psychology lecture at the end of *Psycho*, added to the filming schedule at the last minute to explain Norman Bates' murders, is a case in point.[67] In choosing books to film, Hitchcock looked not for a strong narrative, but for engaging characters and situations. Samuel Taylor, who wrote the screenplays for *Vertigo* and *Topaz*, explained that Hitchcock's vision focused on parts rather than the whole: "He was the master of the situation, the master of the vignette, the master of the small moment. He always knew what he wanted to do with those. He did not have so much of an overall view of the story he was going to tell." Working on a script, Hitchcock pitched many unconnected ideas: "when he told you about a picture, he never told you the story. He told you his favorite scenes." Taylor compared Hitchcock's ideas to pieces of a mosaic. But the job of organizing these pieces into a coherent narrative with a final resolution fell to the writer: "Now, if he didn't have a good writer, there were going to be pieces missing."[68]

Hitchcock was a shrewd businessman. He gained wealth as well as artistic independence through contracts that gave him percentages of his films' profits, he created a popular television series, and he eventually became one of the largest stockholders in Universal Studios. He was known to be the wealthiest Hollywood director, and he owned an art collection that included a Rodin sculpture and paintings by Klee, de Chirico, and Soutine.[69] For much of his career, most critics regarded Hitchcock as a commercially successful director whose work had no artistic merit; in a typical judgment, in 1949 the English critic and director Lindsay Anderson remarked that "Hitchcock has never been a 'serious' director. His films are interesting neither for their ideas nor for their characters."[70] This perception began to change during the 1950s, with the reevaluation of Hitchcock by a group of young French critics who later became important directors. François Truffaut designated Hitchcock as a filmmaker *auteur*, whose work was worthy of serious artistic analysis.[71] In 1957, Eric Rohmer and Claude Chabrol published a monograph on Hitchcock's films, in which they called him "one of the greatest inventors of form in the entire history of cinema."[72] Jean-Luc Godard later dropped the qualification, calling Hitchcock "the greatest creator of forms of the twentieth century."[73]

Truffaut identified a key reason for Hitchcock's importance, noting that "In Hitchcock's work a film-maker is bound to find the answer to many of his own problems, including the most fundamental question of all: how to express oneself by purely visual means."[74] Truffaut's belief in the importance of Hitchcock's technique was so great that in 1962, after Truffaut had already become a successful director, he traveled from Paris to Hollywood and recorded fifty hours of interviews with Hitchcock that were published as a book, in 1966 in French and the following year in English. Truffaut explained that he did this because while editing his film *Jules and Jim*, he had "started to realize that there must be laws of directing that are never really expressed, and that Hitchcock must be the one who had created his laws and that it was with him that I had to speak."[75] This instructional value of his films helped to spread Hitchcock's influence from Paris to Hollywood. A childhood friend of Steven Spielberg recalled that the director the young Spielberg most revered was Hitchcock, to whom he referred as "the Master" in recognition of his technical excellence. Spielberg also admired Hitchcock for his success in reaching a mass audience: "[Spielberg] said, 'The movies reach out and grab you.' That's what he thought was great about Alfred Hitchcock."[76] Martin Scorsese recalled that *Vertigo* had been an early inspiration to him and many of his contemporaries: "For such a personal work with such a uniquely disturbing vision of the world to come out of the studio system when it did [1958] was not just unusual—it was nearly unthinkable." Scorsese paid tribute to Hitchcock's visual mastery, telling an interviewer that he watched Hitchcock's films "repeatedly, repeatedly, repeatedly, often without the sound."[77] In 2002, a panel of experts polled by *Movie Maker* magazine ranked Hitchcock as the most influential director in history. The magazine observed that Hitchcock was "inarguably the most imitated motion picture artist of all time."[78]

In the 2012 *Sight and* Sound poll of critics, *Vertigo* was named the greatest film ever made. The next Hitchcock film on the list, ranked 35th overall, was *Psycho. Vertigo* and *Psycho* were also the two Hitchcock films included in the American National Society of Film Critics' 2002 list of the 100 most important films.[79] Hitchcock directed *Vertigo* and *Psycho* at the ages of 59 and 61, respectively. He would not have been surprised at the appreciation of his late work, for he considered his career a steady process of improvement. On the first day of shooting *Strangers on a Train* in 1950, after he had directed two dozen films in England and a dozen more in Hollywood—including the Oscar-winning *Rebecca*—the 51-year-old Hitchcock "announced to his cast and crew that none of his previous pictures counted—today was the real beginning of his film-making career."[80] In 1962 he told Truffaut that "your evolution does follow a systematic pattern of consistent amelioration from film to film. If you're not sure an idea has been properly carried out in one picture, you'll work it out in the next one."[81] In comparing the first version of *The Man Who Knew Too Much* he had made in England in 1934 with the second version of the same film he made in Hollywood in 1956, Hitchcock commented, "the first version is the work of a talented amateur and the second was made by a professional."[82] The difference lay in the development of his style, for "the most significant and individually important thing about a director is his style." Hitchcock believed that "Style in directing develops slowly and naturally as it does in everything else." It could not be produced deliberately but had to evolve from experience: "It must be the result of growth and patient experimentation with the materials of the trade, the style itself emerging eventually almost unconsciously."[83] What was true of a film was also true of a career: "It takes so long, and so much work, to achieve simplicity."[84]

Late in his career, Hitchcock publicly professed to be amused by tributes to him as an important innovator: when Truffaut described him as the doyen of the French New Wave, he joked that he hated to be the doyen of anything because it made him sound old, and he flatly told Peter Bogdanovich that he did not consider himself an artist.[85] But privately he had in fact long been annoyed by critics who did not recognize the skill and seriousness with which he made his films.[86] Truffaut wrote of Hitchcock that "In examining his films, it was obvious that he had given more thought to the potential of his art than any of his colleagues."[87] Hitchcock entered the movie industry in its infancy, and saw it grow enormously during his five decades as a director. In 1963, he commented that "I believe we still have in our hands the most powerful instrument, cinema, that's been known." He marveled at the fact that with film, unlike any other medium, "different audiences of different nationalities can be shocked at the same moment at the same thing." This created a unique opportunity, and carried with it a responsibility: "I enjoy the fact that we can cause, internationally, audiences to emote. And I think this is our job."[88]

Orson Welles (1915–1985)

> I know that in theory the word is secondary in cinema but the secret of my work is that everything is based on the word. I do not make silent films.
>
> Orson Welles[89]

Orson Welles joked that "The word *genius* was whispered into my ear the first thing I ever heard while I was still mewling in my crib, so it never occurred to me that I wasn't until middle age!"[90] Welles was the extremely precocious son of a prosperous family in Kenosha, Wisconsin, and his mother's desire to give him an artistic upbringing included having him make his stage debut in the Chicago Opera at the age of three. When Orson was 10, a Madison newspaper became the first to publish the epithet that would follow him throughout his life, as an article titled "Cartoonist, Actor, Poet and Only 10," referred to his "apparent genius."[91] Welles recognized that his family's encouragement had a major effect on his development: "I never heard a discouraging word for years, you see.... And there just seemed to me no limit to what I could do."[92]

In high school Welles devoted most of his time to theater, directing as well as acting. He was not interested in college, and at 16 he set out on a walking tour of Ireland. Running low on cash, in Dublin he auditioned for the Gate Theatre, a repertory company. The theater's co-director, Mícheál MacLiammóir, later wrote that Welles' audition was "an astonishing performance, wrong from beginning to end but with all the qualities of fine acting tearing their way through a chaos of inexperience." Even at first encounter, MacLiammóir saw that Welles had "some ageless and superb inner confidence that no one could blow out. It was unquenchable. That was his secret. He knew that he was precisely what he himself would have chosen to be had God consulted him on the subject at his birth."[93] Welles' first professional performance at the Gate was praised by the *New York Times* as "amazingly fine."[94] He remained there less than a year, but the Gate had a lasting influence on Welles, for his exposure to the theories of Hilton Edwards, the theater's other co-director. Edwards believed that the theater should not conceal its artifice: his directing was designed never to allow the audience to forget that they were in a *theater*, where *actors* were *performing*. As a director himself just a few years later, Welles would emulate Edwards' antinaturalistic approach to the theater, and not long thereafter he would extend Edwards' theory to a different art, and apply the same theatricality and stylization to film.[95]

By the age of 20, Welles became established in New York as one of the most successful actors on radio; he was in so many shows that he often commuted from one to another by ambulance.[96] Among his many successful roles, Welles played Lamont Cranston, whose double identity as The Shadow in the eponymous radio program made him the prototype for such later split personalities as Batman and Superman.[97] In 1935 he joined the theater division of the federal Works Progress Administration as a director, and made an immediate sensation with the "Voodoo *Macbeth*," an all-black version of the play, staged in Harlem, with its action transposed from Scotland to Haiti. A study of Welles' early theatrical productions concluded that foremost among his qualities was his "delight in sharing not only illusion but the mechanics of illusion with his audience"; Welles himself wrote in this period that the director's job was "to make his playhouse a kind of magic trick in which something impossible comes to be."[98] Welles' growing fame as a director and actor landed him on the cover of *Time* magazine on his twenty-third birthday in May of 1938, with a headline that celebrated the range of his art— "Shadow to Shakespeare, Shoemaker to Shaw"—called him a "Marvelous Boy," and declared that "The sky is the only limit his ambitions recognize."[99] Later that year, his Halloween-eve adaptation of H. G. Wells' *The War of the Worlds* caused mass hysteria over a supposed landing of armed Martians at Grover's Mill, New Jersey, and became perhaps the most famous of all radio broadcasts. (In 1940, Princeton University Press published *The Invasion from Mars* by the Princeton sociologist Hadley Cantril, the first study to use modern techniques of survey research to understand the sources of a public panic. In the book, Cantril observed that "Probably never before have so many people in all walks of life and in all parts of the country become so suddenly and so intensely disturbed as they did on this night."[100]) Newspaper headlines identifying Welles as the source of the hoax that panicked America increased his celebrity, and greatly raised his value to Hollywood.[101] In 1939, Welles agreed to make two movies for RKO, and his contract received extensive publicity both for his large salary and for the unusual artistic freedom he would enjoy, as writer, producer, director, and actor—a degree of control matched at the time only by Charlie Chaplin, who was the world's most popular film star.[102]

François Truffaut pointed out that *Citizen Kane* was unique, in being the only first film made by a man who was already famous: unlike other great directors, who became famous after making several films, Welles arrived in Hollywood with a national reputation.[103] Welles' lucrative contract and his reputation as a boy wonder made many in Hollywood hostile to the newcomer. F. Scott Fitzgerald published a short story in *Esquire*, "Pat Hobby and Orson Welles," in which an unemployed screenwriter bitterly warned a studio executive that "Orson Welles is the biggest menace that's come to Hollywood for years. He gets a hundred and fifty grand a picture and I wouldn't be surprised if he was so radical that you had to have all new equipment and start all over again like you did with sound in 1928."[104] Truffaut later contended that the combination of Welles' reputation and Hollywood's hostility posed a challenge: "Welles in 1939 must have felt that it was necessary to offer the public not only *a good film*, but *the* film, one that would summarize forty years of cinema while taking the opposite course to everything that had been done ... a declaration of war on traditional cinema and a declaration of love for the medium."[105] Welles' careful preparation for *Citizen Kane* attests to his ambitious goals. So for example both his chief cameraman, Gregg Toland, and the film's composer, Bernard Herrmann, later wrote of the considerable time they were given to plan their novel contributions before filming began, contrary to standard Hollywood practice.[106]

Welles deliberately set out to create a masterpiece, and there is remarkably widespread agreement that he did—and at the age of 26 created what many have considered the greatest movie ever made. *Citizen Kane* ranked first as the best movie ever made in each of the five decennial polls of film critics *Sight and Sound* took from 1962 through 2002.[107] *Kane* was also named the greatest American movie of all time in a poll taken by the American Film Institute in 1997, and again when the AFI repeated its poll 10 years later. And it also placed first in a poll of French film scholars and critics published in 2008 by the journal *Cahiers du Cinéma* to determine the *cent plus beaux filmes du monde*—the hundred most beautiful films in the world.[108] Decades after he made *Kane*, when Welles was asked if he had been aware of creating such an important film, he replied, "I never doubted it for a single instant."[109] Despite his youth and inexperience, he gave no sign of being intimidated: shortly after arriving in Hollywood, in an interview with a national magazine he described the RKO studio as "the greatest railroad train a boy ever had."[110] He later recalled that he had recognized no constraints—"I thought you could do anything with a camera, you know, that the eye and the imagination could do"—so he made radical innovations "Simply by not knowing that they were impossible, or theoretically impossible." His lack of expertise didn't faze him: "You know, the great mystery that requires 20 years doesn't exist in any field. Certainly not in a camera."[111] And he was encouraged in this attitude by Toland, one of Hollywood's best cinematographers, who assured Welles he could teach him all he needed to know in a few days, "So we spent the next weekend together and he showed me the inside of that bag of tricks, and like all good magic, the secrets are ridiculously simple."[112]

Citizen Kane startled the film world with innovations in both sight and sound. Among the most celebrated visual effects was what Toland called "human-eye focus," with wide-angle lenses that gave much greater depth of field than movies normally afforded, so action could occur simultaneously at different distances from the camera.[113] In sound, *Kane* used what Herrmann called "radio scoring"—musical bridges to foreshadow transitions—and overlapping dialogue tracks that mimicked the interruptions of real conversation.[114] Truffaut observed that these and other *Kane* trademarks, including deep contrasts of light and shadow, achieved by the use of spotlights, and low camera angles that showed the action to viewers as if they were seated in the front of a theater for a play, were imported from Welles' earlier artistic activities: "Welles' thoughts as he embarked on the cinema could be summed up as follows: I'm going to make a film that will present all the advantages of radio and theatre without their disadvantages, with the result that my film will be unlike any other that has been made."[115] Peter Bogdanovich similarly stressed the synthetic nature of *Kane* for Welles: "All his passions—theatre, magic, circus, radio, painting, literature—suddenly fused into one." Welles might polish his style in later films, but Bogdanovich explained that *Kane* remained transcendent because seeing it is "watching a consummate artist grappling for the first time with the intoxication of his found vocation."[116]

One of *Kane*'s most striking achievements was its powerful marriage of form and content. Jorge Luis Borges explained that the film's subject was "the discovery of the secret soul of a man," and observed that "In astonishing and endlessly varied ways, Orson Welles exhibits the fragments of the life of the man, Charles Foster Kane, and invites us to combine and reconstruct them. Shapes of multiplicity and diversity abound in the film."[117] The film's conspicuous fragmentation of both images and sounds echoed and underscored the fragmentation of the portrait of Kane that emerged from the divergent accounts of him given by a series of different witnesses. Welles' prominent use of stage tricks was not universally applauded: detractors have criticized his technique as heavy-handed, as for example Jean-Paul Sartre contended that "all too often, in *Citizen Kane*, one has the feeling that the image is too much in love with itself.... Just like a novel whose style keeps forcing itself into the foreground and in which we keep forgetting the characters."[118]

François Truffaut declared that *Citizen Kane* "has inspired more vocations to cinema throughout the world than any other [film]." Martin Scorsese agreed: "he was responsible for inspiring more people to be film directors than anyone else in the history of cinema."[119] Welles' youth played a part in this, as Truffaut explained that "his genius seemed closer to us than the talents of the traditional American directors.... [He was] a friend to discover, an accomplice to love, a person we felt close to in heart and mind." Truffaut loved *Kane*'s exuberance and the freedom of Welles' imagination, and likened the movie director to the film's rambunctious protagonist: "When Thatcher challenges him, 'So, that's really how you think a newspaper should be run?,' the young Kane answers, 'I have absolutely no experience in running a newspaper, Mr. Thatcher. I just try out all the ideas that come into my head.'" Truffaut reflected that after he became a director, it was *Kane*'s "twofold aspect as fairy tale and moral fable that strikes me most forcefully."[120] The scholar David Bordwell traced *Kane*'s influence through the greatest conceptual filmmakers of the following decades: "As the ancestor of the works of Godard, Bergman, Fellini, Bresson, and Antonioni, *Kane* is a monument in the modern cinema, the cinema of consciousness."[121] Even more simply, the conceptual Truffaut wrote in 1972 that "everything that matters in cinema since 1940 has been influenced by *Citizen Kane*."[122]

Welles relished discussing his artistic philosophy. He believed movies should make personal statements: "I have a passion for films that ... are made of opinions, the expression of the personality and ideas of the director."[123]

Directors should be artists: "A film is never really good unless the camera is an eye in the head of a poet."[124] Movies were magic: "A film is a ribbon of dreams."[125] Judging films by their visual impact alone was a mistake, "like judging a novel only by the quality of its prose."[126] Directors should consequently control both content and form: "I don't recognize a film as being completely a man's work unless he's also its author."[127] This was the only way Welles could work: "I'm sure I can't make good films unless I also write the screenplay."[128] Language was primary: "I always begin with the dialogue. And I do not understand how one dares to write action before dialogue.... I must know what [the characters] say before seeing them do what they do."[129] For Welles, what mattered most was concepts: "I am a man of ideas...above all else."[130] Welles wanted to make movies as deep and complex as great novels, that would be studied as closely as important literature.

The focus of virtually all analyses of Welles' career has been his failure to surpass, or equal, *Citizen Kane* in the more than four decades that remained in his life: as the critic Andrew Sarris succinctly observed, "The conventional American diagnosis of his career is decline, pure and simple."[131] Attacks on the former boy wonder began early, as for example when Welles was just 36, the critic Walter Kerr described him as an "international joke, and possibly the youngest living has-been."[132] Many of Welles' admirers blamed Hollywood: *Kane* failed to make money, and Welles never again enjoyed the full support of a major studio, forcing him to take unflattering acting roles and make television commercials to raise money for his own films. Late in his life, Welles himself reflected that "I think I made essentially a mistake in staying in movies," and lamented his lost time and effort: "I've wasted a greater part of my life looking for money and trying to get along, trying to make my work from this terribly expensive paintbox which is a movie."[133]

Welles did direct films of high quality after *Kane*.[134] Admiring critics have praised the excellence not only of *The Magnificent Ambersons*, which Welles directed the year after *Kane*, but also of such later films as *Touch of Evil* (1958) and *Chimes at Midnight* (1966).[135] But even Welles could not deny that the trajectory of his work was a disappointment. What haunted him for decades was that he could no longer make films that were as abundantly and manifestly innovative as *Kane*. In 1960, when an interviewer asked how he had had the confidence to make *Kane* at such an early age, Welles replied, "Ignorance, ignorance, sheer ignorance—you know there's no confidence to equal it. It's only when you know something about a profession, I think, that you're timid or careful."[136] Welles claimed to believe that directors did their best work both early and late in their lives—before 30 and after 70—but in fact it is likely that he understood that his youthful ignorance, and with it his boundless confidence and creativity, had been irretrievably lost to the inevitable accumulation of experience. His true feelings about old age were probably reflected most accurately in a comment he made more than once late in his life: "'Old age,' said Charles de Gaulle, 'old age is a shipwreck'—and he knew whereof he spoke."[137] Many who knew Welles agreed with Ingrid Bergman's judgment that "it must have been a great burden for him to have made a masterpiece when he was twenty-five years old. And it must have been very hard to live up to it all those years."[138] Yet with *Citizen Kane* Welles had changed the cinema: Jean-Luc Godard declared in 1963, "All of us will always owe him everything."[139]

Jean-Luc Godard (1930–2022)

To me, especially since talking pictures were invented, the film is no longer a visual art.

Jean-Luc Godard[140]

In June of 1950, while enrolled as an anthropology student at Paris' Sorbonne, Jean-Luc Godard began to write for a small magazine, *La Gazette du cinema*, that would survive for less than a year. Godard wrote under a pseudonym, in order not to interfere with his loftier ambition of eventually publishing a novel with a prestigious publisher.[141] Yet these articles betrayed Godard's true destiny. In a review of an obscure documentary, he declared that "At the cinema we do not think, we are thought."[142] Godard thus revealed that he had already been captured by film, because of his conviction that it could guide not only the vision of its audience, but also their thought.[143]

Godard soon joined a group of young cinephiles who became known initially as critics for a much more successful new journal, *Cahiers du cinéma*, that was founded in 1951. Under the inspiration of the older critic André Bazin, these younger writers—notably François Truffaut, Claude Chabrol, Jacques Rivette, and Eric Rohmer in addition to Godard—dedicated themselves both to improving cinema by raising the quality of criticism and to establishing film as an art form as respectable as painting or literature. Their success was remarkable: in 1959, Godard could justly declare that "We won the day in having it acknowledged in principle that a film by Hitchcock, for example, is as important as a book by [the poet Louis] Aragon. Film *auteurs*, thanks to us, have finally entered the history of art."[144]

Having revolutionized film criticism, in the late 1950s the young Turks set out to revolutionize film itself. In 1957, Truffaut had predicted a new kind of cinema: "The film of tomorrow appears to me as even more personal than an individual and autobiographical novel, like a confession, or a diary."[145] In 1959 he fulfilled his own prophecy, by directing the autobiographical *Les Quatre cents coups* (*The 400 Blows*). The film became the first hit for what quickly became known as the *Nouvelle Vague*—New Wave—film directors. In 1960, Godard effectively took over leadership of the movement by directing his own first feature film. To Godard, the transition from critic to director was a natural one: "I think of myself as an essayist... only instead of writing, I film them.... For there is a clear continuity between all forms of expression."[146] Decades later, Godard recognized that the whole movement had been a conceptual one: "The New Wave was a relationship with the imaginary."[147]

Godard's first feature, *A bout de souffle* (*Breathless*), was a sensation even before it opened in Paris early in 1960. Its reputation sprang primarily from technical innovations that made a radical break from basic Hollywood conventions. One of these was its *faux raccords*—false matching shots—that conspicuously violated normal continuity and narrative development: characters might wear different clothes in successive shots within a single scene, and sudden exaggerated shifts in angles of vision called attention to the camera. Another prominent device was its many jump cuts, which abruptly advanced the action while disrupting the logic of the plot.[148] Susan Sontag compared Godard's violation of such established film rules as the unobtrusive cut, consistency of point of view, and clarity of story line to the challenge of the Cubist painters to realistic figuration and three-dimensional pictorial space, and Godard stressed that the magnitude of the challenge was deliberate, explaining that "What I wanted was to take a conventional story and remake, but differently, everything the cinema had done. I also wanted to give the feeling that the techniques of film-making had just been discovered or experienced for the first time."[149] Godard's revolution was immediately embraced by the next generation. So for example the Italian director Bernardo Bertolucci, who was 19 in 1960, recalled that "I saw *A bout de souffle* during the early summer of 1960 in Paris, and I had the feeling that something was starting from zero there, that all the films I had seen up to then constituted the cinema before *A bout de souffle*."[150] The critic Georges

Sadoul recognized that *Breathless* was a technical revolution, writing in a review that "Godard has consigned all of the existing grammatical and syntactical rules of the cinema to the dust-heap."[151]

Although *Breathless* became famous for its technical innovations, it was in fact the first in a series of remarkable films in which Godard displayed his fundamentally new conception of cinema. In the 2002 *Sight and Sound* poll of critics, six films by Godard received two or more votes, and all were made within a span of seven years, from *Breathless* in 1960, through *My Life to Live* (1962), *Contempt* (1963), and *Pierrot le Fou* (1965) to *Masculine/Feminine* and *2 or 3 Things I Know about Her* (both 1966).[152] The three of Godard's films that were ranked among the 100 "most beautiful films in the world" in a poll of French experts published by *Cahiers du cinéma* in 2008—*Breathless*, *Contempt*, and *Pierrot*—were a subset of this same group.[153] Godard's films of this period constitute the most important statement of his complex philosophy of film.

A cornerstone of Godard's philosophy was a conception of montage far more encompassing than the usual definition of the term as a sequence of separate images. Early in his career, Godard explained why he had given up literature for film:

> I wrote, "The weather is nice. The train enters the station," and I sat there for hours wondering why I couldn't just as well have written the opposite: "The train enters the station. The weather is nice" or "it is raining." In the cinema, it's simpler. There is something ineluctable about it.[154]

For Godard, the simultaneity of film's recording of disparate elements made cinema both unique and superior to literature.[155] The camera also recorded the passage of time, and therefore life: "The cinema is the only art which, as Cocteau says... 'films death at work.' Whoever one films is growing older and will die. So one is filming a moment of death at work. Painting is static: the cinema is interesting because it seizes life and the mortal side of life."[156]

Godard in fact believed that film alone among the arts not only recorded life, but was in effect life itself: "Cinema is not a dream or fantasy. It is life. I see no difference between the movies and life. They are the same."[157] The cinema was privileged by the camera's automatic recording of reality: "Art is not only a mirror. There is not only the reality and then the mirror-camera.... I discovered you can't separate the mirror from the reality."[158] For Godard, there was consequently no division between filming and other activities: "I make my films not only when I'm shooting but as I dream, eat, read, talk."[159] For him everything was cinema: "I want to include everything.... Everything should be put into a film."[160]

Godard believed movies should be personal: "I only like films which resemble their creators."[161] His films expressed his ideas: "What I have to say, I don't say myself but I have my characters say it and that's why they talk abundantly."[162] The ideas were embodied in the script: "contrary to popular belief, there cannot be good direction without a good script."[163] Plots were merely vehicles: "I don't really like telling a story. I prefer to use a kind of tapestry, a background on which I can embroider my own ideas."[164] It was not important for audiences to suspend their disbelief: "I think it's good to say to the audience... 'This is a movie.'"[165] A friend of Godard's, the philosopher Youssef Ishaghpour, compared Godard's conceptual vision to that of Andy Warhol: "for Godard, as for the Pop painters, reality was already image."[166]

Godard's cinema has always drawn heavily on earlier art. He noted that at the start of his career this was inevitable: "I knew nothing of life except through the cinema, and my first efforts were 'films de cinéphile'... I didn't see things in relation to the world, to life or history, but in relation to the cinema."[167] He had intended *Breathless* to be a gangster film, but later realized it wasn't: "I thought it was a realistic film, but now it seems like *Alice in Wonderland*, a completely unreal, surrealistic world."[168] Godard's films are filled with countless references not only to earlier movies, but also to the other arts: the critic Peter Wollen commented that "Godard treated Hollywood as a kind of conceptual property store from which he could serendipitously loot ideas for scenes, shots, and moods," and a collaborator of Godard's, Jean-Pierre Gorin, summarized Godard's entire career as "an assault on the notion of intellectual property."[169] Godard did not dispute the characterization, explaining that "It's very good to steal things. Bertolt Brecht said art is made from plagiarism."[170]

Written texts have played a large role in Godard's films. A biographer observed that for Godard, "writing is the privileged element which breaks the classic unity of the cinema.... Writing is used to comment on the action and to distance the viewer from the immediacy of the image."[171] Godard traces this to the primacy of expressing ideas: "I'm someone whose real country is language, and whose territory is movies."[172] The poet Louis Aragon declared in 1965 that "I love language, and it's for that reason that I love Godard. Who is completely language."[173]

Godard's films have always highlighted the accidental. In 1963, he made a short movie he called an "Action-Film," and the cameraman recalled that to achieve spontaneity, "I filmed it like a real event, as if it were a piece of documentary reality." An artist in the film made what he called "action sculpture"—"I take pieces of metal, I throw them, and the way they fall, I weld them."[174] Godard's use of spontaneity prompted comparisons of his art to the action painting of the Abstract Expressionists.[175] Yet Godard did not use chance like Jackson Pollock, as a point of departure, but instead as an end in itself. Like the sculptor in his film, for Godard chance occurrences were final products, and in this he resembled not the experimental Abstract Expressionists, but rather the earlier conceptual Dada painters and poets, who embraced chance as a means of eliminating style.[176] Like the Dadas, Godard rejected consistency: "I have no 'style,' I just want to make films."[177] As early as 1968, the critic Manny Farber commented on the protean nature of Godard's art: "Each Godard film is of itself widely varied in persona as well as quality.... At the end of this director's career, there will probably be a hundred films, each one a bizarrely different species.... [T]he form and manner of execution changes totally with each film."[178] Three decades and fifty films later, Peter Wollen observed that "just as Farber predicted, each film seems to be *sui generis*, quite unlike any of his previous work, the same only in being so unpredictably, inconsistently different."[179]

In 1967, Godard concluded the movie *Weekend* with two title cards: the first read "End of Film," and the second "End of Cinema."[180] He participated in the student protests of May 1968, and subsequently continued to make films, promoting such causes as Maoism and anti-Semitism.[181] But as noted above, his influential work ended in the 1960s. In 2008, a biographer complained that Godard's later work had been unduly neglected: "Godard is an artist as dominant, as crucial, as protean, and as influential as Picasso, but he is a Picasso who vanished from public consciousness and from the encyclopedias after the first heady flourish of Cubism."[182] In assessing the biography, however, a *New York Times* reviewer declared that "Now we know how one of the greatest of all filmmakers—the man who so radically changed cinema in 1959 with his debut feature, *Breathless*—became an intolerable gasbag."[183]

Godard's films of the 1960s spearheaded a conceptual revolution in film. Not surprisingly, his innovations were not embraced by his elders. Orson Welles, for example, conceded that Godard was "the definitive influence" of the 1960s, but objected that "I just can't take him very seriously as a *thinker.*"[184] But scores of younger filmmakers followed Godard's lead. The German director Volker Schlöndorff recalled that "The older generation said that Godard didn't know how to edit pictures, but . . . Godard just edited his films in a different style, and today nearly every film is edited in the way that Godard cut *A bout de souffle.* Godard invented the craftsmanship of the future."[185] Like other radical conceptual innovations, Godard's technique thus appeared incompetent to older practitioners even as it immediately appeared superior to younger ones. Quentin Tarantino, who named his production company A Band Apart in honor of Godard's *Bande à part* (1964), reflected that "Godard did to movies what Bob Dylan did to music: they both revolutionized the forms."[186] In a revealing characterization of conceptual innovation, Peter Wollen observed that "Godard's films showed a contradictory reverence for the art of the past and a delinquent refusal to obey any of its rules."[187] Godard attributed the urgency of *Breathless* to his early insecurities: "Adolescence, youth, fear, despair, solitude." But he admitted that it also displayed the brashness of youth: "We barged into the cinema like cavemen into the Versailles of Louis the Fifteenth."[188]

In a celebrated article published in 1948, the writer and director Alexandre Astruc predicted a new era in cinema, that he called "the age of *caméra-stylo*" (camera-pen). He contended that the maturation of the cinema was making it a language—"a form in which and by which artists can express their thoughts, however abstract they may be"—and asserted that if Descartes were alive at that time, he would use a 16 mm camera to write his philosophy on film.[189] In 1960, the critic Gérald Devries declared that *Breathless* had fulfilled Astruc's prophecy: "Here is, in fact, the first work authentically written with a caméra-stylo."[190] In 2005, the scholar Douglas Morrey judged that Godard's oeuvre had in fact created a new kind of cinema, that consistently treated abstract ideas that mirrored central concerns of contemporary philosophy. But Morrey went further, arguing that "Godard's cinema is not simply cinema *about* philosophy or cinema *with* philosophy, rather it is cinema *as* philosophy. The cinematograph is a machine for thinking, for propelling thought."[191]

Directors and Audiences

John Ford's attitude toward making movies was pragmatic: "This is a business. If we can give the public what it wants, then it is a good business and makes money. The audience is happy and we're happy."[192] He didn't consider it dishonorable to make popular movies: "I've got a whole lot of respect for the people who go to see motion pictures. I think we ought to make pictures in their language."[193] Ford didn't feel superior to his viewers—"I am a peasant, and my pride is to remain one"—so he saw no conflict between his taste and that of his audience: "I like, as a director and as a spectator, simple, direct, frank films. Nothing disgusts me more than snobbism, mannerism, technical gratuity (that the spectators pay for) and, most of all, intellectualism."[194] His criterion for accomplishment was straightforward: "For me, a film is a success if the spectators leave the theater satisfied, if they identify with the characters, if they get joy or energy."[195]

Ford's films were consistently profitable, but Alfred Hitchcock's were even more so. In view of this, it is not surprising that he believed that "in the world of films and film production it is the public's appetite that must first be appeased."[196] That appetite was for entertainment: "people go to the movies to be aroused." His work was made for the pleasure of his viewers: "I'm a professional. I don't put my personal feelings into my pictures. I don't indulge myself—I don't make pictures to please me. I make them to please audiences."[197]

Unlike Ford, Hitchcock believed that the need for commercial success acted as a constraint on art, as he told one interviewer that "it is harder to make a film that has both integrity and wide audience appeal than it is to make one that merely satisfies one's own artistic conscience." Satisfying his own conscience while fulfilling his responsibility to his employers made Hitchcock consider his job "a kind of constant tight-rope walking."[198] Hitchcock also acknowledged that his trademark genre identification had an economic source: "If I were to make films for my own satisfaction they would certainly be very different from those you see.... The reason why I have specialized, so to speak, in suspense is strictly commercial."[199] Hitchcock vowed never to preach to his audience: "People don't go to the movies to listen to sermons. If that were the case, then instead of buying a ticket they'd put a coin in the collection plate and make the sign of the cross before taking a seat in the stalls."[200] He never forgot why he made movies: "I never think of the films I make as being *my* films. I'm not that vain or egotistical."[201]

Orson Welles disagreed with Ford and Hitchcock on the purpose of making movies. From the very beginning of his career in theater, Welles had believed that the arts should raise the taste of their audiences. The critic David Thomson contended that *Citizen Kane*'s lack of commercial success stemmed in part from its complexity: "Kane was the first American movie so dense that it needed to be seen more than once."[202] Welles believed that Hollywood aimed at a lowest common denominator: in a speech at the Edinburgh Festival in 1953, he argued that the quality of movies was deteriorating because directors were expected to reach mass audiences. Welles declared that "The biggest mistake we have made is to consider that films are primarily a form of entertainment. The film is the greatest medium since the invention of movable type for exchanging ideas and information, and it is no more at its best in light entertainment than literature is at its best in the light novel."[203] Films should have moral value: "I have never made a film without having a solid ethical point of view about its story. Morally speaking, there is no ambiguity in what I do."[204] Late in his life, Welles insisted that "I would *love* to have a mass audience," and claimed that he had actively pursued that goal: "You're looking at a man who's been searching for a mass audience."[205] Yet this effort apparently did not extend to compromising on his choice of subjects: in Edinburgh he had observed that one way of escaping from banality was to return to the classics, and his projects in later years included Kafka's *The Trial*, adaptations of Shakespeare including *Falstaff* and *The Merchant of Venice*, and *Don Quixote*.[206] Welles' true feelings toward compromising to increase the size of his audience may in fact be revealed by the advice he gave a friend who was an independent filmmaker: "never make a movie for anyone else, or on some idea of what other people will like. Make it *yours*, and hope that there will be others who will understand. But never compromise to *make* them understand.... Make the movies you want to make. On your own. And be free."[207]

Even early in his career as a director, Jean-Luc Godard's attitude toward the popularity of films was closer to that of his fellow conceptual innovator Welles than to those of the experimental Ford and Hitchcock. In a 1961 interview, he commented that "There is certainly no reason why the films I make should not displease some people," and declared that "I no longer believe that cinema should be aimed at the masses."[208] The next year, he distinguished his practice from that of Hitchcock in moderate terms: "If Hitchcock ... thinks that people will not understand something, he will not do it. At the same time I feel that one must sometimes go ahead—light may dawn in a few years time."[209]

By the pivotal year of 1968, Godard's moderation had vanished. Thus he told an audience that his goal of creating an art that was both popular and intellectual would not be easily achieved: "We have to fight the audience."[210] Effectively making himself an heir of Sergei Eisenstein and other conceptual directors who had believed film should be devoted to propaganda, Godard declared that "We should abandon drama and psychology and go in more for politics." Defending his recent work against the charge that he had abandoned emotion for tedious intellectual exposition of ideas, Godard explained that he had no interest in telling a love story in La Chinoise (1967): "What's important is to know what Marxism-Leninism is and how it helps them in their love." He admitted that "I don't want people to come see my movies the way they go to see other movies. This has to be changed." When he was asked if he was trying to change the audience, Godard replied, "I am trying to change the world."[211] Later in his career, Godard echoed Welles' objection to the use of film as entertainment. In 1995 he described cinema as "a tool that we've misused," and explained that "In the beginning, it was thought that cinema would impose itself as a new instrument of knowledge, like a microscope or a telescope, but very quickly it was prevented from playing its role and was turned into a toy. Cinema has not played its role as an instrument of thought."[212] The contrast is stark: the experimental Ford and Hitchcock loved film for its ability to entertain with realistic works, whereas the conceptual Welles and Godard valued it as a means of creating and disseminating knowledge.

Welles and Godard are examples of important conceptual filmmakers whose techniques and subjects limited the sizes of their audiences, but this is not necessarily true of conceptual films. Steven Spielberg and George Lucas are recent examples of conceptual directors whose films have reached large audiences by creating fantastic worlds that highlight moral issues. Their allegorical morality tales, in which simplified characters carry out battles between good and evil, were deliberately aimed at the largest possible audiences, because of their creators' desire to disseminate their moral values as widely as possible.[213] Although small audiences are thus not necessarily characteristic of conceptual films, didactic messages generally are: conceptual directors are typically distinguished from their experimental counterparts by their desire to educate or instruct their audiences, rather than merely aiming to engage and entertain them. Welles and Godard sacrificed audience size to create works that conveyed their particular messages, whereas Spielberg and Lucas embodied their messages in films designed to reach large audiences. Ford and Hitchcock were not primarily concerned with messages—Hitchcock quipped that "messages are for Western Union"[214]—but with entertainment, and for them large audiences demonstrated that they had succeeded.

9

Songwriters

During the early twentieth century, the primary source of innovations in popular songwriting was the musical theater. Composers and lyricists took ideas from the librettos of musical comedies as the starting point for ballads that were then tailored for the particular situations and characters of those plays. These songs were generally experimental in nature, for they dealt with the lives and (especially) loves of realistic characters in terms that were intended to be universal—readily understood and enjoyed by a wide audience, who could see them as relevant to their own lives.

The second half of the century saw rock and roll replace the theater as the primary source of innovative popular songs. These songs were intended to stand alone. No longer constrained by the plots of specific plays, writers could treat any subject they wished. In this new, freer setting, the greater speed with which their innovations could be made gave conceptual songwriters a decided advantage, and from the mid-1960s on popular music became a predominantly conceptual art.

This chapter examines the careers and contributions of two of the greatest songwriters of what came to be considered the Golden Era of popular song, in the second quarter of the twentieth century, of the three rock songwriters who created a conceptual revolution in popular music, and of a great contemporary experimental songwriter.

Irving Berlin (1888–1989)

> A verse with simple words will always linger,
> A tune that you can pick out with one finger.
>
> Irving Berlin[1]

Israel Baline arrived in the United States at the age of five, with his parents and four older siblings. His only lasting memory of his native Russia was of watching his home burn down during a pogrom.[2] His family settled on

New York's Lower East Side, where they lived in extreme poverty. His father had been a cantor in Russia, and Izzy enjoyed singing with his father in a synagogue on holy days.

His father died when Izzy was 13. His family was desperately poor, and out of shame at not being able to contribute more to the family's income—in the words of Berlin's friend and first biographer, Alexander Woollcott, "sick with a sense of his own worthlessness"—Izzy decided to leave home. For the next few years he lived in dormitories. These charged ten cents a night for a bed, and Izzy earned this as a busker: he would "sidle through the swinging doors of some cheerful saloon, lift his voice in a woeful ballad of the day and see what pennies would shower on the floor around him." At 16, he got a regular job as a singing waiter in a Chinatown dance hall. After three years, the owner suggested that Izzy and the café's pianist write a song, to attract customers. Izzy wrote the lyrics and the pianist the melody to "Marie from Sunny Italy." To their surprise, a music publisher bought it. At 19, Izzy signed his first published song with a new name he considered more formal; four years later, he legally changed his name to Irving Berlin.[3]

Berlin began to earn money writing songs for vaudeville, and at 21 he quit waiting tables and went to work as a staff lyricist at a music publishing firm. There he began working without a collaborator. Although he had no formal training, and never learned to read or write music, Berlin would subsequently work alone, both writing lyrics and composing music, and having his songs transcribed by an assistant. He produced songs at a rapid rate. In 1913, a journalist reported that Berlin wrote an average of three songs a week, but published only one in ten: "He is willing to waste nine efforts for the sake of evolving one good tune."[4]

Berlin was often described by his peers as the master of *American* songwriting: in 1925, for example, Jerome Kern declared that "Berlin has entrenched himself in shell-proof, impregnable position as commander-in-chief of all the purveyors of American music," in 1936 Cole Porter reflected that "Berlin comes closest to writing real American music," and in 1946 Richard Rodgers called him "America's folk song writer."[5] One source of this characterization was Berlin's first great popular success, "Alexander's Ragtime Band," in 1911. He did not intend "Alexander" to be a rag, but rather a song about ragtime music. Yet to a white American audience largely unfamiliar with the music of Scott Joplin, Eubie Blake, and other black composers, "Alexander" caused Berlin to be labeled the "King of Ragtime."[6] Berlin embraced this identification. In a 1915 interview, he accused other composers of being ashamed of American music, and of imitating European music. He portrayed himself as unsophisticated but patriotic: "Ignorant as I am, from their standpoints, I'm doing something they all refuse to do: I'm writing American music!"[7]

It might appear ironic that a native Yiddish speaker who had no formal training in music would come to be considered the quintessentially American composer, but in fact there is no necessary contradiction. One of Berlin's greatest innovations was to bring common language, which had previously been restricted to folk music, to the commercial popular music of Tin Pan Alley. Late in his life, he reflected that the simplicity for which his music was celebrated was a product of his early educational deficiencies: "The reason I wrote simply is just that I wasn't clever when I started. . . . By the time I sharpened the tools of my trade, I found I wrote simple songs because that's how they came out of my head."[8] Berlin's importance was also a result of the fact that he was the first Tin Pan Alley composer to embrace America's greatest indigenous music. In 1929, George Gershwin paid tribute to Berlin for showing him what became the key to his own music: "I have learned many things from Irving Berlin, but the most precious lesson has been that ragtime—or jazz, as its more developed state was later called—was the only musical idiom in existence that could aptly express America. And so, when I was eager to compose something larger and more permanent than mere songs, I did not for a moment think of abandoning the jazz idiom."[9]

Berlin aimed at the largest possible audience, and measured success accordingly: "The mob is always right. It seems to be able to judge instinctively what is good, and I believe that there are darned few good songs which have not been whistled or sung by the crowd."[10] Achieving this required a song to be universal: "Your lyric must have to do with ideas, emotions, or objects known to everyone." It must also be simple: "Simplicity is achieved only after much hard work, but you must attain it." And the lyric had to be "*euphonious*—written in easily singable words and phrases."[11] Combining these features was always his goal: "'Easy to sing, easy to say, easy to remember and applicable to everyday events' is a good rule for a phrase."[12] Berlin's practice was never to try to change public opinion, but to echo it: "A song to become popular should not establish new ideas—it must be a means of expression for sentiments already in vogue."[13] The song's theme should be stated in the title, then repeated frequently: "The title, which must be simple and easily remembered, must be '*planted*' effectively in the song. It must be emphasized, accented again and again, throughout verses and chorus."[14] Berlin rejected as pretentious the idea that songwriters were artists, instead maintaining that they were craftsmen and (his highest term of praise) professionals. He scoffed at "this legendary stuff about great inspiration in popular songwriting. If you're a professional, you sit down and write."[15] He was enormously productive—his complete works include more than 1,250 songs—but he attributed this to hard work rather than facility: "The melody doesn't come to you. You sweat it out."[16] He considered songwriting a job, declaring that "This is a business and I'm in it to make money."[17] Having depended on music to earn a living from a very early age, Berlin was never embarrassed to say that he wrote for money: he told his friend Cole Porter, "Never apologize for a song that sells a million copies."[18]

Berlin had no doubt that his skills improved over time. In 1960, he dismissed his early songs: "I call 'em bad. They were not only bad, they were amateurish."[19] It is also clear that Berlin in fact had artistic goals that were not limited exclusively to making money. As early as 1910, he complained that "we are not producing any living songs. These songs I am writing are only for the brief career of the vaudeville stage. They will be a hit for a week or two.... But I cannot think of a song in years that has come to stay."[20] Berlin produced hits throughout his career, but his most lasting songs came only with his maturation as a craftsman.

In Berlin's novice work, the narrator of "Marie from Sunny Italy" (1907) implored his beloved to

> Meet me while the summer moon is beaming,
> For you and me the little stars are gleaming.
> Please come out tonight, my queen,
> Can't you hear my mandolin?[21]

The language is stilted and formal, the rhyme between *queen* and *mandolin* forced, and the latter is hardly an everyday instrument. Berlin worked assiduously at his craft, however, and soon adopted a simpler vocabulary. In 1911, the narrator of the song that first made Berlin both rich and famous invited listeners to

> Come on and hear, come on and hear
> Alexander's Ragtime Band.

> Come on and hear, come on and hear,
> It's the best band in the land.[22]

The song's use of dialect—it opened by addressing "ma honey"—its rapid tempo, and its insistent repetition all suited it to vaudeville, where it had its great success.

Over time, Berlin's songs became slower and more thoughtful. In 1927, "Blue Skies" was the first song Al Jolson sang in the legendary early talkie *The Jazz Singer*:

> Never saw the sun
> Shining so bright,
> Never saw things
> Going so right.
> Noticing the days
> Hurrying by—
> When you're in love
> My, how they fly![23]

As is often the case in Berlin's ballads, the sweetness of the lyric is tempered by a hint of fragility, here the narrator's observation of how quickly happy times pass.

Berlin often put aside unfinished songs in the hope of improving them later. A famous example was "God Bless America," which he wrote in 1918 for a stage review at his Army base, but did not use because he felt it was too serious for a comedy. In 1938, alarmed by the Munich pact, Berlin revised both the melody and lyrics, transforming it from a war song into a patriotic prayer for peace—eliminating, for example, "Make her victorious on land and foam." In other cases he salvaged elements from failed songs. Berlin considered "To My Mammy," that he wrote for Al Jolson in 1929, "a true horror" and scrapped it. But he liked several of its lines: "How much does she love me? / I'll tell you no lie / How deep is the ocean? / How high is the sky?" Three years later, he made a new song from these lines. Berlin considered "How Deep Is the Ocean?" one of his best songs: it was an immediate hit and has subsequently been recorded dozens of times, by such luminaries as Frank Sinatra, Charlie Parker, Billie Holiday, Bob Dylan, and Barbra Streisand.[24]

Berlin was a thoroughgoing New Yorker. (Even Los Angeles was too rustic for him: "There's no Lindy's in Los Angeles. No paper at two in the morning. No Broadway. No city."[25]) "There's No Business Like Show Business," which Berlin wrote when he was 58, became a theatrical anthem because it captured both the romance of the theater and the excitement of a Broadway production. Yet Berlin insisted that it was not his own taste that should be reflected in his songs, but rather that "A good song embodies the taste of the mob."[26] Jerome Kern declared that Berlin "honestly absorbs the vibrations emanating from the people, manners and life of his time, and in turn gives these impressions back to the world—simplified—clarified—glorified."[27] One of Berlin's most enduring songs, "God Bless America" (1938), embodied popular tastes by ignoring urban America and glorifying the country's natural beauty—"From the mountains, to the prairies,/To the oceans white with foam."[28] Much easier to sing than "The Star-Spangled Banner," during World War II Berlin's song became a popular alternative to the official national anthem and has remained so to the present; its performance at public events increased dramatically in the wake of 9/11.[29]

In 1942, Bing Crosby sang "White Christmas" in the movie *Holiday Inn*. The song became a hit in that year, spending ten weeks in first place on the Lucky Strike Hit Parade. More significantly, however, "White Christmas" became a preeminent example of what the young Irving Berlin had called a living song. It is the top-selling popular song in history, with record sales of over 125 million copies. It is also one of the most frequently recorded popular songs: since Crosby's famous version, "White Christmas" has been recorded by scores of other musicians, including Louis Armstrong, Frank Sinatra, Nat King Cole, Charlie Parker, Elvis Presley, Aretha Franklin, the Beach Boys, the Supremes, the Jackson 5, Willie Nelson, Barbra Streisand, Bob Marley and the Wailers, and U2.[30]

The long life of "White Christmas" was the result of Berlin's success in fully achieving his goal of writing simple, universal songs. "White Christmas" evokes the associations of a rural New England winter holiday simply and vividly. And it makes these associations more poignant by having them expressed by a speaker who now can only remember them wistfully. The song's visual imagery reminds the listener of Christmas cards, to which the lyric refers explicitly. When "White Christmas" was released, Irving Berlin was 54.[31] After decades of painstaking effort, he had succeeded in writing "in the simplest way ... as simple as writing a telegram."[32] A biographer tellingly compared Berlin's masterpiece to the greatest work of another great experimental writer: "'White Christmas' is the counterpart to Robert Frost's 'Stopping by Woods on a Snowy Evening,' which uses the simplest of rhymes and the barest of imagery to evoke a beautiful but melancholy scene."[33] In an era of American popular music that produced a number of great experimental songwriters, Berlin came to be widely considered the most important of the group. The scholar Alec Wilder described him as "the best all-around, over-all songwriter America has ever had," and when one of his greatest peers, Jerome Kern, was asked what place Berlin held in American music, he replied, "Irving Berlin has *no* place in American music. He *is* American music."[34]

Cole Porter (1891–1964)

> Poets always speak of youth
> With such admiration,
> But we all must face the truth,
> Age has many a compensation.
>
> Cole Porter[35]

If Irving Berlin was the immigrant who grew up to represent traditional American values, Cole Porter was the small-town boy who grew up to epitomize the glitter and elegance of New York high society. Born and raised in Peru, Indiana, Porter was the grandson of a very wealthy landowner, and enjoyed a privileged youth. His mother's dream was for Cole to be a great musician, and by the age of six he had instructors for both piano and violin, and practiced music two hours a day. Cole wrote an operetta at the age of 10, and when he wrote "The Bobolink Waltz" a year later, improvised from the notes of a bird's song, his mother had it published in Chicago.[36]

A friend and biographer concluded that Porter's childhood taught him he could use music to gain affection and acceptance, and observed that he carried this lesson with him throughout his life.[37] He attended prep school in Massachusetts and went on to Yale, and throughout his school career he used his wit and musical skills to be popular: many parties revolved around Cole playing piano and singing, and at Yale he wrote not only productions for the drama society and songs for the glee club, but also fight songs for the football team. A reviewer of one glee club performance described Cole as "one of those musical geniuses to whom music is second nature," and predicted that

"He could make his fortune on the vaudeville stage," singing "topical songs to his own accompaniment or giving imitations."[38]

Porter did intend to conquer Broadway, and in 1916 he wrote the score for a musical comedy, *See America First*. The lyrics gave signs of Porter's ability as a phrasemaker, as in the alliterative "lazy hazy crazy" (that would reemerge nearly fifty years later in the title of one of Nat King Cole's greatest hits), but this was embedded in an awkward tribute to his native state: "I simply quiver—to drive my flivver/Along that lazy hazy crazy Wabash River."[39] Porter also liberally displayed his expensive education—one song contained references to Browning, Ibsen, Maeterlinck, and Shelley. The play was heavily indebted to Gilbert and Sullivan, and one critic described it as "something that college boys might have done in the way of entertainment." The play was a flop—another critic advised "Don't *See America First*"—and it closed within two weeks.[40]

Porter's successes throughout his school years had not prepared him for failure, and he was humiliated. Uncertain of his future, the next year he went to Paris, apparently to try to forget the self-doubt that followed his failed New York debut. In 1919 he married Linda Lee Thomas, a beautiful and wealthy American divorcee. The Porters entertained lavishly and frequently at their Paris mansion and their Venice palazzo. Among their guests were minor European royalty and major theatrical and musical royalty, including Noël Coward, John Barrymore, Serge Diaghilev, George Bernard Shaw, Igor Stravinsky, Irving Berlin, George Gershwin, Richard Rodgers, and Lorenz Hart. During this time, Berlin advised Porter to stop trying to imitate other composers and write in his own style.[41] Richard Rodgers was entertained by the Porters in Venice, and he later recalled that he was stunned when Porter played a few of his new songs, which "fairly cried out to be heard from a stage. Why, I asked Cole, was he wasting his time? Why wasn't he writing for Broadway?"[42]

When Porter did return to New York in 1928, appropriately as the composer of the score of *Paris*, he received rave reviews. Among the songs was his first hit, "Let's Do It, Let's Fall in Love," which escaped being banned from radio play only because of the title's second phrase.[43] The song is a prime example of Porter writing with supreme confidence—sophisticated, clever, suggestive, and irrepressible:

> Electric eels, I might add, do it,
> Though it shocks 'em, I know.

> Why ask if shad do it?
> Waiter, bring me shad roe.

The lyrics are filled with double entendres, alliteration, and verbal surprises: one phrase, for example—"So does ev'ry katydid do it"—contains three forms of a single verb within the span of just six words.[44]

During the next few years Porter wrote a series of hits, and in the process he became not only the toast of New York's high society, but for many listeners elsewhere the personification of that tribe—the wealthy, urbane aristocrat who wrote songs that offered amusing, sophisticated glimpses of love as it was practiced in the café society of Fifth Avenue. In 1934, "You're the Top" provided an irreverent rhymed catalogue of the chic and the excellent, from a Bendel bonnet and a Shakespeare sonnet, the National Gallery and Garbo's salary, an O'Neill drama and Whistler's mama, to a Waldorf salad and—in tribute to his friend Irving—a Berlin ballad.[45] Porter's achievement was appreciated by Ethel Merman, who sang the song in *Anything Goes*: "What Cole had done was to analyze my voice and turn out songs which showed off its variety. 'You're the Top' brought audiences to their feet because it was a new kind of love song. There had never been a song like it before."[46] In the same score, Porter displayed his verbal virtuosity by including five rhymes within a single sentence of "I Get a Kick Out of You"—"Flying too high in the sky with some guy/Is my idea of nothing to do."[47]

The two Porter songs that have been most often recorded were both written after he had passed the age of 40: "Night and Day" (1932) and "Begin the Beguine" (1935).[48] Both are love songs, with insistent rhythms that have helped make them standards for jazz musicians. In "Night and Day," repetitive sounds the narrator hears—the beat of a drum, the tick of a clock, the drip of raindrops—echo the repeated thought he has of his beloved, and the thought becomes a physical sensation:

> Night and day under the hide of me
> There's an, oh, such a hungry yearning burning inside of me,
> And its torment won't be through
> Till you let me spend my life making love to you
> Day and night, night and day.[49]

In "Begin the Beguine," hearing the music of a popular dance powerfully evokes the memory of a lost love:

> When they begin the beguine
> It brings back the sound of music so tender,
> It brings back a night of tropical splendor,
> It brings back a memory ever green.[50]

In these songs Porter used his mastery of language and rhythm to express love and passion, free of satire or irony.

F. Scott Fitzgerald made the Jazz Age into short stories and novels; Cole Porter made it into songs and musical comedies. Porter succeeded early in becoming a member of the social elite, but he did not begin to achieve artistic and professional success until he understood that his true audience was not his own circle, but a much larger population of those who were entertained by the lives of the rich and famous. Late in his life, Porter told a biographer that one of the few people who had sought him out to give him encouragement after his early failure on Broadway, the playwright Harrison Rhodes, told him that if he wanted to take advantage of his talent, working hard was not enough: Rhodes' advice, Porter recalled, was to "Learn about life."[51] Porter's eventual success was the result of doing that, and of developing a vocabulary that communicated the glamour and excitement of his own life to anyone who heard his songs. In 1955, Porter reflected that as a young composer he was overly concerned with what he called tricky rhymes: "In Yale, I was rhyme crazy. That was due to the fact that I was Gilbert and Sullivan crazy." With time, however, he had made his music simpler: "My songs are easier than they used to be musically and lyrically. I've never been able to get complete simplicity the way Berlin does."[52] Although Porter's songs never did become as simple as Berlin's, he had learned to write sophisticated songs that were widely accessible. In his humorous songs, his early bookish references were replaced by more familiar people and places. And in "Night and Day" and "Begin the Beguine," he altogether eliminated the flippancy of his early work, and used his technical skills to create passionate love songs.

Porter's greatest work was almost certainly truncated prematurely by a devastating horse-riding accident in 1937 that broke both his legs, and left him in pain for the rest of his life. The pain did not stop him from producing work of high quality; the songs he wrote for *Kiss Me, Kate* in 1947, for example, are generally considered the best complete score he ever wrote.[53] Yet no individual song Porter wrote after 1937 matched the best of those songs he had written in the years just before the accident, and Porter himself believed there was a permanent loss in the quality of his work.[54] At his best, Porter's

230   INNOVATORS

songs expressed a carefree optimism and joy in living, as a mature experimental artist used his craft to describe the thrill of being talented and in love. After 1937, however, the constant pain he suffered appears to have left him unable to recapture the exhilaration and excitement that animate every phrase of his best songs.

Bob Dylan (1941–)

> Take me on a trip upon your magic swirlin' ship,
> My senses have been stripped, my hands can't feel to grip,
> My toes too numb to step, wait only for my boot heels
> To be wanderin'.
>
> Bob Dylan[55]

In 1955, James Dean's performance in *Rebel without a Cause* gave 14-year-old Bobby Zimmerman a formative model of the artist as defiant non-conformist.[56] Bobby's chosen art, however, was not movies, but popular music. Among the singers Bobby revered were Elvis Presley, Buddy Holly, and Hank Williams, he played in bands called the Golden Chords and the Satin Tones, and when he graduated from Hibbing (Minn.) High School, in the yearbook he listed his ambition in life as "To join the band of Little Richard."[57] *Zimmerman* wouldn't do for a rock musician, so in 1958 Bobby decided his new name would be *Bob Dylan*.[58] He knew that he wanted to be exceptional: "I wanted to do something that no one else did or could do, and I wanted to do it better than anyone else had." [59]

Bob's background was solidly middle class: his father was a partner in a family electrical appliance store, and his mother worked part-time at a department store. As a concession to his parents, he enrolled at the University of Minnesota. Acquiescence did not come naturally to him, however, and he did not complete his freshman year. Yet his time in Minneapolis had a profound impact, for the university's bohemian neighborhood was not dedicated to rock and roll, as he'd expected, but rather to folk music. The folk ethos appealed to Bob's individualism, and he quickly became a disciple. His conversion was cemented by his discovery of *Bound for Glory*, the memoir of the folk singer Woody Guthrie. Guthrie's book presented a philosophy that championed the individual, the dispossessed, and the downtrodden, and his songs made this philosophy into anthems of protest and hope. Dylan instantly had a new role model, as he adopted wholesale Guthrie's ideas, his music, and even his bad grammar: "when I heard Woody Guthrie, that was it, it was all over."[60]

When Bob Dylan arrived in New York early in 1961, his first concern was to visit Woody Guthrie, who was suffering from the degenerative disease Huntington's chorea in a New Jersey state hospital. Dylan then set out to conquer folk music. He was inspired by an innovator from another discipline, who was still in the news at the age of 80: "Picasso had fractured the art world and cracked it wide open. He was revolutionary. I wanted to be like that."[61]

Dylan immersed himself in the Greenwich Village folk music community, learning from more experienced singers and performing in coffeehouses. He cultivated people who could advance his career, among them a *New York Times* critic. On September 29, 1961, a *Times* review described Dylan as "bursting at the seams with talent," a newcomer with "originality and inspiration all the more noteworthy for his youth." Like others in the folk community, the reviewer was struck by the speed with which Dylan's music was developing, commenting that "He has been sopping up influences like a sponge."[62]

Dylan immediately used the *Times*' rave to obtain a recording contract.[63] He also began to write his own songs. In 1962, he wrote "Blowin' in the Wind." Its simple tune and lyrics placed it clearly in a line of descent from Guthrie's "This Land Is Your Land" and Pete Seeger's "Where Have All the Flowers Gone," and its criticism of indifference to social injustice made it an instant civil rights standard:

> Yes, 'n' how many years can some people exist
> Before they're allowed to be free?
> Yes, 'n' how many times can a man turn his head,
> Pretending he just doesn't see?[64]

In 1963, a recording of the song by Peter, Paul and Mary reached number two on the *Billboard* charts. When Peter, Paul and Mary performed their hit at the 1963 Newport Folk Festival, Peter Yarrow introduced it by saying "This song was written by the most important young folksinger in America today."[65] Dylan had recently become romantically involved with Joan Baez, who was already a major star, and they became the king and queen of folk music.[66] In barely more than two years in New York, at the age of 22, Bob Dylan had become a leader of the folk music revival. He had also done something that Guthrie and Seeger never had, by writing a popular hit song that effectively combined folk and pop music.

Declaring that "the times cry for the truth," Dylan's avowed mission was to channel the power of tradition: "There's mystery, magic, truth, and the Bible in great folk music. I can't hope to touch that. But I'm goin' to try."[67] He created a persona, liberally adopting elements of Woody Guthrie's past as his own in casting himself as an itinerant troubadour who had ridden the rails "all around the country, to the southlands."[68] In spite of his inventions, he asserted that "if I haven't been through what I write about, the songs aren't worth anything."[69] Yet in 1963, when *Newsweek* magazine exposed the clash between his autobiographical fictions and his quest for authenticity, he angrily countered that all that mattered was his art: "I am my words." Dylan told the journalist that he'd lost contact with his parents, and hadn't seen them in years, when in fact they were in New York to hear him sing at Carnegie Hall. His father explained that "My son is a corporation and his public image is strictly an act."[70]

Among the songs Dylan wrote during 1962–1963 were his "finger-pointing" songs—"You know—pointing to all the things that are wrong."[71] Some of these, like "A Hard Rain's Gonna Fall" (1962), contained such apocalyptic images as "a dozen dead oceans" and "the roar of a wave that could drown the whole world," while others, like "Masters of War" (1963), had angry messages of protest, as the speaker vowed to "stand o'er your grave/'Til I'm sure that you're dead."[72] The hallucinatory imagery and bitter vitriol of these songs went well beyond the traditional bounds of folk music: as Noel Stookey (Paul of Peter, Paul and Mary) observed, "Dylan was stretching the folk idiom and traditionalists were no longer going to be upheld. A new spirit had come."[73] In the summer of 1963, at the invitation of the singer Theodore Bikel, Dylan accompanied Bikel and Pete Seeger to a voter registration rally in Greenwood, Mississippi, where songs the three sang included "Blowin' in the Wind," "We Shall Overcome," and a song Dylan had written about the murder of the civil rights leader Medgar Evers.[74]

In 1964, Dylan made another abrupt transition. He emphatically resigned as a leader of folk music—"I don't want to write *for* people anymore. You know—be a spokesman"—and he bluntly denied being a civil rights activist: "I'm not part of no Movement." He would no longer write about the external world: "From now on, I want to work from inside me."[75] Dismissing his earlier songs as one-dimensional, Dylan declared in 1965 that his new songs were "more three-dimensional, you know, there's more symbolism, they're written on more than one level."[76] He added a blues sound to folk music, and his lyrics were inspired by Arthur Rimbaud and other Symbolist poets (the "magic swirlin' ship" in "Mr. Tambourine Man" [1964] has been seen as Dylan's nod to Rimbaud's famous drunken boat).[77] His new music was quickly labeled "folk-rock," though he objected to that name, explaining that "I like to think of it more in terms of vision music."[78] As suddenly as he had earlier become a leader of folk music, Dylan now became a leader of popular music: he was booed by folk audiences, who felt spurned, even as he became a pop superstar, transforming rock and roll with a radical new synthesis. Ever the rebel, however, he would not admit this. In 1966, he complained that he would never achieve the same critical acceptance as the Beatles, and he scoffed at their music as "a cop-out"—"There are millions of songs like 'Michelle' and 'Yesterday' written in Tin Pan Alley." When asked if he influenced young people because he broke the rules, Dylan protested, "It's not a question of breaking the rules, don't you understand? I don't break the rules, because I don't see any rules to break. As far as I'm concerned, there aren't any rules."[79]

Dylan identified his breakthrough song as "Like a Rolling Stone" (1965)—"I'd never written anything like that before and it suddenly came to me that this is what I should do.... Because it was a whole new category."[80] Although Dylan described the song as "a long piece of vomit," it was firmly rooted historically: its title alluded to "Rollin' Stone" (1950) by the legendary blues singer Muddy Waters, and its form owed a clear debt to the chanting rhythms of Allen Ginsberg's poem "Howl" (1956).[81] The song was a vindictive and vituperative attack on a woman identified only as Miss Lonely, sneering at her arrogance, reveling in her fall from prosperity, and repeatedly taunting,

> How does it feel...
> To be on your own...
> Like a complete unknown
> Like a rolling stone?[82]

"Rolling Stone" convinced Dylan he could fit whatever he had to say into songs: "I didn't care anymore after that about writing books or poems or whatever."[83] As a single, it peaked at number two, giving Dylan his own first hit, in spite of the fact that at six minutes it was more than twice as long as most singles. Yet it marked a clear shift, for although Dylan might be settling his own scores (and debates raged over the identity of Miss Lonely), he was no longer writing about anyone else's problems. To leave no doubt about this, in the vicious sequel "Positively 4th Street" (1965), Dylan jeered,

> You say I let you down...
> You say you lost your faith...
> Don't you understand
> It's not my problem.[84]

At the end of 1965, Dylan declared "'Rolling Stone's the best song I wrote," and four decades later, *Rolling Stone* magazine named it the greatest rock song of all time, explaining that "No other pop song has so thoroughly challenged and transformed the commercial laws and artistic conventions of its time."[85]

"Like a Rolling Stone" became the first track on *Highway 61 Revisited* (1965), which Dylan followed with *Blonde on Blonde* (1966). These two albums, completed by the time he was 25, were the two highest-rated of Dylan's albums in two major recent rankings of the greatest rock albums of all time, based on surveys taken by cable network VH1 in 2003 and *Rolling Stone* magazine in 2005. *Rolling Stone* wrote that *Highway 61* "quite simply, changed everything," while VH1 commented that in *Blonde on Blonde* Dylan "brought an intelligence and emotional sophistication to pop music that blew listeners' minds and daunted those who tried to match him."[86] On the occasion of Dylan's induction into the Rock and Roll Hall of Fame in 1988, the rock singer Bruce Springsteen gave a succinct summary of the impact of these albums that neatly captured both the immediacy and the durability of their influence:

Without Bob, the Beatles wouldn't have made *Sgt. Pepper* [1967], the Beach Boys wouldn't have made *Pet Sounds* [1966], the Sex Pistols wouldn't have made "God Save the Queen" [1977], U2 wouldn't have done "Pride in the Name of Love" [1984], Marvin Gaye wouldn't have done *What's Going On?* [1971], the Count Five would not have done "Psychotic Reaction" [1966], Grandmaster Flash might not have done "The Message" [1982], and there never would have been a group named the Electric Prunes [1965–1969]. To this day, wherever great rock music is being made, there is the shadow of Bob Dylan.[87]

In the summer of 1966, a motorcycle accident left Dylan seriously injured, and he did not release another album until 1968. He has made dozens of albums since then, but none has repeated his early impact on popular music: in 1986, Mikal Gilmore could write in *Rolling Stone* that "for about twenty years now Bob Dylan hasn't produced much music that transfigures either pop style or youth culture," and in 2003 Quinton Skinner observed that *Blonde on Blonde* had been "the last of Dylan's great mid-sixties mind-bombs."[88] Nor did it take decades to recognize the disappearance of Dylan's inventiveness: as early as 1970, in a review of Dylan's album *Self Portrait*, the critic Greil Marcus observed that "In a real way, Dylan is trading on the treasure of myth, fame, and awe he gathered in '65 and '66."[89] Dylan himself remarked in 1971 that "Until the accident, I was living music twenty-four hours a day.... If I wrote a song, it would take me two hours, or two days, maybe even two weeks. Now, two lines." And in 1978, he said that "Right through the time of *Blonde on Blonde* I was doing it unconsciously. Then one day I was half-stepping, and the lights went out."[90] The two rankings referred to earlier both reflect the decline in Dylan's creativity. Of his four albums among the 100 ranked by VH1, three were made in 1965–1966, and one in 1975. Of his five albums among the top 100 in the *Rolling Stone* ranking, four were made during 1963–1966, and one in 1975. Another two of his albums were among the top 300; these were made in 1967 and 1976. Two other Dylan albums, made in 1997 and 2001, both ranked below the top 400.

Dylan has pondered his loss of creativity. In his memoir, he wrote of a visit he made to New Orleans in 1989 to work with a celebrated producer, Daniel Lanois, in the hope of reviving his recording career. As they worked together, Lanois repeatedly remarked—"nagging at me, just about every other day"— that they could use some songs like those Dylan had written in the mid-1960s. Dylan had no answer:

> I would have liked to been able to give him the kinds of songs that he wanted, like "Masters of War," "Hard Rain," "Gates of Eden," but those kinds of songs were written under different circumstances, and circumstances never repeat themselves. Not exactly. I couldn't get to those kinds of songs for him or anyone else. To do it, you've got to have power and dominion over the spirits. I had done it once, and once was enough. Someone would come along eventually who would have it again—someone who could see into things, the truth of things—not metaphorically, either—but really see,

like seeing into metal and making it melt, see it for what it was and reveal it for what it was with hard words and vicious insight.[91]

Throughout his career, Dylan has maintained that he had no control over his creativity. In 1962, for example, he told an interviewer that his songs were given to him: "The songs are there. They exist all by themselves just waiting for someone to write them down. I just put them down on paper. If I didn't do it, somebody else would."[92] At the age of 44, Dylan could only marvel at the songs he had written twenty years earlier: "I can't write those songs today. No way. But I look at those songs, 'cause I sing 'em all the time, I wonder where they came from and how they came.... I couldn't do them now, and I don't even try, I'd be a fool to try."[93] Two decades later, in 2004, the source of "Like a Rolling Stone" was still a mystery: "It's like a ghost is writing a song like that. It gives you the song and it goes away.... You don't know what it means."[94] In a rare television interview in 2004, Dylan told Ed Bradley he didn't know how he'd done it: "Those early songs were almost magically written."[95] Yet when he looked back, it was with pride as well as bemusement: "I've written some songs that I look at, and they just give me a sense of awe. Stuff like 'It's Alright, Ma' [1965], just the alliteration in that blows me away. And I can also look back and know where I was tricky and where I was really saying something that just happened to have a spark of poetry in it."[96] In 1995, Dylan offered an explanation for why his muse had deserted him: "As you get older, you get smarter and that can hinder you because you try to gain control over the creative impulse.... If your mind is intellectually in the way, it will stop you. You've got to program your brain not to think too much."[97]

Just as his idol James Dean had been a rebel without a cause, in the mid-1960s Bob Dylan became the strident and angry voice of protest for an era marked by political assassinations, race riots, a polarizing war, and widespread student demonstrations. At the same time, his novel synthesis of folk music, the blues, and Symbolist poetry created a radical new model for popular music, as the clear, simple language that generations of songwriters had used to express universal emotions suddenly gave way before an onslaught of cryptic and enigmatic verses that expressed the thoughts and feelings only of the musicians who wrote and sang them. In the process, he transformed rock and roll from entertaining dance music to biting social commentary. As Bruce Springsteen recognized, Dylan created a conceptual revolution in popular music: "Bob freed your mind the way Elvis freed your body. He showed us that just because the music was innately physical did not mean that it was anti-intellectual."[98]

John Lennon (1940–1980) and Paul McCartney (1942–)

> Let me take you down,
> 'Cause I'm going to Strawberry Fields.
> Nothing is real,
> And nothing to get hung about.
> John Lennon–Paul McCartney[99]

John Lennon and Paul McCartney first met on July 6, 1957, at a neighborhood festival in a Liverpool suburb, after one of the first performances by Lennon's band, the Quarry Men. The two teenagers discovered that they shared a passion for American rock and roll, particularly that of Elvis Presley, Little Richard, Chuck Berry, and Buddy Holly, and Paul soon joined John's band.[100] By 1962, the Quarry Men had become the Beatles (the insect reference a tribute to Buddy Holly's band, the Crickets, and the spelling John's homage to the Beat Generation), the personnel consisted of Lennon, McCartney, and two other Liverpudlians, the guitarist George Harrison and the drummer Ringo Starr, and they had been voted the top band in Liverpool in the first annual *Mersey Beat* poll.[101] In 1962 the Beatles released their first single, "Love Me Do," which became a top twenty hit in England and started the meteoric recording career that would make them the most famous and influential band in the history of rock music.[102]

George Harrison described the Beatles' original goal as "just to be in a band as opposed to having a job."[103] But Paul McCartney noted that "It went beyond that pretty quickly," as he and John Lennon began doing something more ambitious, and unusual for rock and roll singers, by writing some of the songs they performed.[104] From the start, they agreed to share credit for all their songs.[105] Unlike earlier songwriting teams, however, which typically paired a composer and a lyricist, Lennon and McCartney both performed both tasks. Their styles were quite different, as Lennon observed that McCartney "provided a lightness, an optimism, while I would always go for the sadness, the discords, the bluesy notes."[106] Sometimes they worked separately, but Lennon stressed that "We wrote a *lot* of stuff together, one-on-one, eyeball to eyeball."[107] The Beatles' producer, George Martin, explained that the collaboration changed over time, as initially "It was more a question of one of them trying to write a song, getting stuck, and asking the other: 'I need a middle eight. What have you got?'... But as they developed their art, each moved on to writing songs entirely on his own. Collaboration became rare, apart from the odd word or line: it was either a John Lennon song or a Paul McCartney song." (And Martin added a comment to remember whenever you hear a Beatles song: "We established the working format that whoever wrote the song generally sang it.")[108]

Initially, Lennon and McCartney aimed to emulate Tin Pan Alley songwriters: "first of all Paul and I wanted to be the Goffin and King of England."[109] Gerry Goffin and Carole King were leading New York songwriters, who in 1961 had written a number-one hit for the Shirelles, and another in 1962 for Little Eva, and whose "Chains," originally recorded by the Cookies, was included on the Beatles' first album in 1963. In early Lennon–McCartney songs, John explained that "lyrics didn't really count as long as we had some vague theme: 'She loves you, he loves her, and they love each other.' It was the hook and the line and the sound we were after."[110] These early songs used simple and direct language to express the heady and urgent experience of young love. A song's speaker, typically identified as "I," declared his love for the object of his affection, usually "you," in simple rhymes, with repetition, as in "Love Me Do":

> Love, love me do
> You know I love you.
> I'll always be true
> So please love me do
> Whoa-ho love me do.[111]

On *A Hard Day's Night* (1964), the Beatles' first album that consisted exclusively of their own compositions, the three words *I*, *love*, and *you* accounted for 18.3 percent of the total words in the album's songs.[112]

From late 1962 through mid-1965, the Beatles recorded nearly sixty original songs, every one of which was concerned with boy–girl romance.[113] Rapid tempos and lyrical melodies further contributed to a music that millions of fans found exciting and exhilarating ("We sing about love," Lennon explained, "but we mean sex, and the fans know it."[114]) These early love songs, in Lennon's words "pop songs with no more thought to them than that—to create a sound," became the basis for a popular enthusiasm so widespread and so intense that it would add a new word—*Beatlemania*—to the *Oxford English Dictionary*.[115]

The Beatles' music changed over time, largely in response to the music of Bob Dylan. The Beatles first met Dylan in New York in 1964, and again the next year when he visited England. Lennon recalled that at "the early meetings with Dylan, he was always saying 'Listen to the words, man' and I said 'I can't be bothered, I listen to the sound of it, the overall sound.'"[116] Soon, however, Dylan's emphasis on lyrics took effect, as Lennon reflected that

> I think it was Dylan helped me realize that—not by any discussion or anything but just by hearing his work—I had a sort of professional songwriter's attitude to writing pop songs.... But to express myself I would write [the books] *Spaniard in the Works* [1965] or *In His Own Write* [1964], the personal stories that were expressive of my personal emotions. I'd have a separate songwriting John Lennon who wrote songs for the sort of meat market, and I didn't consider them—the lyrics or anything—to have any depth at all.... Then I started being me about the songs, not writing them objectively, but subjectively.[117]

In 1965 Lennon wrote "In My Life," which he considered "my first real major piece of work.... [T]hat was the first time I consciously put my literary part of myself into the lyric."[118] The narrator wistfully remembered people he had loved in the past, reflecting that "Some are dead and some are living," before resolving his emotions in favor of the present:

> Though I know I'll never lose affection
> For people and things that went before
> I know I'll often stop and think about them
> In my life I love you more. [119]

Included on *Rubber Soul*, "In My Life" broke with earlier rock and roll songs in its nostalgia and melancholy, and its open acknowledgment of death. *Rubber Soul* (1965) marked a turning point: the Beatles would no longer sing only about young love, but would also make statements about their own lives and their society, and they and their engineers would develop new sounds and recording techniques to reinforce their more complex verbal statements. Paul McCartney described *Rubber Soul* as "the beginning of my adult life."[120]

In 1967, Lennon drew on his childhood, real and imagined, in "Strawberry Fields Forever." To emphasize the element of fantasy, the chorus included the statement, "Nothing is real." The enigmatic lyrics included the line, "No one I think is in my tree," which Lennon later explained was an expression of his early feelings of isolation: "what I was trying to say in that line is 'Nobody seems to be as hip as me, therefore I must be crazy or a genius.' . . . And it's scary when you're a child, because there is nobody to relate to."[121] McCartney explained that Strawberry Fields had been a magical childhood place for Lennon, and that "We transformed it into the sort of psychedelic dream, so it was everybody's magic childhood place."[122] McCartney drew on his own childhood memories for "Penny Lane." He explained that the song's images served artistic goals: "the 'fireman with the hourglass' and all that sort of stuff was us trying to get into a bit of art, a bit of surrealism."[123] The fireman and the song's other eccentrics, characterized simply and clearly and described as "very strange," were inspired by the incongruous imagery and limpid technique employed by the Surrealist painter René Magritte, whose art Paul had recently begun to collect.[124] Lennon emphasized his debt in this period to Dylan's example:

> In those days I was writing obscurely, à la Dylan, never saying what you mean, but giving the *impression* of something. Where more *or* less can be read into it. It's a good game. . . . [T]here has been more said about Dylan's wonderful lyrics than was ever in the lyrics at all. Mine too. But it was the intellectuals who read all this into Dylan or the Beatles. Dylan got away with murder. I thought, Well, I can write this crap, too.

Lennon described the process: "You know, you just stick a few images together, thread them together, and you call it poetry. Well, maybe it *is* poetry."[125] McCartney wanted the music to be mystical: "I'd like a lot more things to happen like they did when you were kids, when you didn't know how the conjuror did it, and were happy just to see it there and say, 'Well, it's magic.'"[126]

The impact of the Beatles' new music on their peers was both great and sudden. Brian Wilson of the Beach Boys, one of the preeminent songwriters of the time, had earlier been stunned by the beauty of *Rubber Soul*, and had taken it as a challenge.[127] Just months later, his response was *Pet Sounds*, which combined sensitive and introspective lyrics with beautiful melodies to express the hopes and insecurities of coming of age; it eventually came to be recognized as Wilson's masterpiece. Paul McCartney declared *Pet Sounds* "the album of all time," and played it during breaks from recording *Sgt. Pepper*, as a spur to the Beatles to equal it.[128] But when Wilson first heard "Strawberry Fields Forever," he was devastated: he told a journalist that he had pulled his car over and cried, because he knew he could not match Lennon's nostalgic, evocative dream of childhood.[129]

Lennon summarized the change in the Beatles' music: "The *depth* of the Beatles' songwriting . . . in the late Sixties was more pronounced; it had a more mature, more intellectual . . . approach." He explained that "We were different. We were older."[130] Yet they were not much older, for the change occurred quickly. In 1964, the word "love" appeared fifty-three times in the lyrics of their album *Hard Day's Night*, but just three years later it appeared only thirteen times in *Sgt. Pepper*; the three words *I*, *love*, and *you* accounted for only 7.4 percent of the total words of *Sgt. Pepper*. And as the Beatles' themes expanded, so did their vocabulary: *Sgt. Pepper* had only 13 percent more total words than *Hard Day's Night*, but it contained fully 76 percent more *different* words than the earlier album.[131] In just a few years, the Beatles had departed decisively from the restricted subjects and language of conventional popular music.

In 2003, VH1 ranked the Beatles' *Revolver* as the greatest album ever made ("Music changed the day that *Revolver* was released, forever and for better"); in 2005, *Rolling Stone* gave this honor to *Sgt. Pepper's Lonely Hearts Club Band* ("an unsurpassed adventure in concept, sound, songwriting, cover art and studio technology by the greatest rock and roll group of all time"). In spite of this disagreement, both rankings clearly agreed on the greatest period of the Beatles' career, for VH1 placed five of their albums—*Rubber Soul* (1965), *Revolver* (1966), *Sgt. Pepper* (1967), *The Beatles* (aka *The White Album*) (1968), and *Abbey Road* (1969)—among its top eleven, and *Rolling Stone* placed these same five among its top fourteen.[132] No other album by the Beatles, or by Lennon or McCartney after they left the Beatles, made the top twenty in either ranking. At the end of the period spanned by these five landmark albums, John Lennon was 29 years old, and Paul McCartney was 27.

Sgt. Pepper was the first album the Beatles made after deciding to retire from performing live. Its songs could not have been performed on stage, but were elaborate studio productions, involving novel and complex recording techniques. The chief engineer, Geoff Emerick, recalled racking his brain "to come up with ways to make things sound different," and his solutions included "unusual signal routings, different combinations of limiters and compressors, new miking techniques, even using bathrooms and other areas of the Abbey Road complex as echo chambers."[133] Many of these novel effects were intended to create sounds that would match the album's psychedelic verbal imagery (as Paul McCartney later explained, "*Sgt. Pepper* was a drug album").[134] The Beatles' first album, in 1962, had used less than twenty hours of studio time; just four years later, *Sgt. Pepper* used seven hundred hours, over a span of six months.[135] *Sgt. Pepper* introduced Indian instruments and melodies to popular music, under the influence of Ravi Shankar, and electronic music, under the influence of Karlheinz Stockhausen. For "A Day in the Life," which John Lennon wanted to end with "a sound like the end of the world," forty-two classical musicians—half a symphony orchestra—were brought to the Abbey Road studio; George Martin, the producer, recorded them four times and used all four recordings, at slightly different intervals, in the final version.[136] The musicologist Michael Hannan described *Sgt. Pepper* as "a breakthrough album in the history of popular music because of the inventive ways the studio equipment was used and of the new processes that were pioneered."[137] Even the cover of *Sgt. Pepper* was innovative, for it was created not by a designer but by an important contemporary artist, Peter Blake, who made an enormous collage that included photographs of scores of the Beatles' heroes, from H. G. Wells, Lewis Carroll, and Dylan Thomas to Mae West, W. C. Fields, and Bob Dylan.[138]

Paul McCartney had wanted *Sgt. Pepper* to have a theme—to be not a collection of songs but "a complete thing ... a little magic presentation."[139] His original plan was to have the whole album played like a stage show by the fictitious Lonely Hearts Club Band, but this was quickly abandoned. John Lennon later pointed out that *Sgt. Pepper* was not a true concept album, because many of its songs were not related to Sgt. Pepper's band. Yet the album nonetheless became known as the first concept album, because by beginning and ending with Sgt. Pepper, and eliminating banding—the usual silences between songs—it gave an illusion of unity: in Lennon's words, "it works 'cause we *said* it worked.'"[140] And as Michael Frontani observed, *Sgt. Pepper* inspired later theme albums because it was "a conceptual work: it is self-consciously and unapologetically Art."[141] The artistry of *Sgt. Pepper* equally caused its extraordinary reception, with not only the frenzied excitement of pop music fans and journalists, but also much more unusual praise from highbrow critics and musicologists. So for example the literary scholar Richard Poirier wrote in *Partisan Review* that *Sgt. Pepper* established the Beatles "not merely as a phenomenon of entertainment but as a force of historical consequence," and the classical composer Ned Rorem, in the *New York Review of Books*, compared the Beatles' songs favorably to those of Monteverdi and Poulenc.[142] The ubiquity of the sounds of *Sgt. Pepper* during the summer of 1967 prompted the writer Langdon Winner to declare it the closest Western civilization had come to unity in the modern era: "for a brief moment, the irreparably fragmented consciousness of the West was unified."[143]

The Beatles have been the subject of a great deal of writing, scholarly as well as popular. Yet relatively little attention has been devoted to the dramatic time profile of their creativity—the abrupt transition from the early work to the peak period of 1965–1969, and the loss of creativity by both Lennon and McCartney in their solo careers after the dissolution of the Beatles in 1970. Both may have been consequences of their conceptual approach to their art.

Lennon and McCartney had no formal training in music. They learned to play guitar together, listening to records, and neither learned to read or write musical notation.[144] Their producer George Martin, who was formally trained in classical composition, wrote in his memoir that he was often asked if he could have written any of the Beatles' songs, "and the answer is definitely no: for one basic reason. I didn't have their simple approach to music." He attributed their creativity to the absence of constraints:

> I think that if Paul, for instance, had learned music "properly"—not just the piano, but correct notation for writing and reading music, all the harmony and counterpoint that I had to go through, and techniques of orchestration—it might well have inhibited him.... Once you start being taught things, your mind is channeled in a particular way. Paul didn't have that channeling, so he had freedom, and could think of things that I would have considered outrageous.[145]

McCartney agreed: "People say now, 'Oh, the Beatles were breaking all the rules.' But we didn't know what the rules were. We had no knowledge whatsoever of musical theory. We just did what felt right."[146]

The Beatles' sudden breakthrough in 1965 into their most innovative period was the immediate result of a decision by Lennon and McCartney to draw on their own experiences and emotions in writing songs.[147] Neither Lennon nor McCartney claimed to understand where the creativity of the next few years came from. Lennon recalled that on one occasion he'd "struggled for days and hours to write clever lyrics. Then I gave up and 'In

My Life' came to me." Similarly, he explained that the lyrics for "Across the Universe" (1969) "were given to me as *boom*! I don't own it, you know, it came through like that. I don't know where it came from.... It's like being *possessed*; like a *psychic* or a *medium*."[148] "Yesterday" (1965) came to McCartney suddenly and completely: "I had a tune in my head. It was just all there, a complete thing. I couldn't believe it. It came too easy. In fact, I didn't believe I'd written it. I thought maybe I'd heard it before, it was some other tune, and I went around for weeks playing the chords of the song for people, asking them, 'Is this like something? I think I've written it.'"[149] In one of his last interviews, Lennon was asked whether musicians' creativity disappeared early in their lives, and responded: "I can't believe it goes away forever... but you can never be twenty-four again. You can't be that hungry twice." In the same interview, he explained that he had given up music for much of the 1970s because of what he wanted to avoid: "Let's use Picasso as an example. He just repeated himself into the grave. It's not to take away from his great talent, but his last forty years were a repetition. It didn't go anywhere."[150]

A common explanation for the loss of creativity of Lennon and McCartney after the Beatles era attributes it to the end of their collaboration.[151] Perhaps, however, the end of the collaboration was not the real problem: perhaps, like Bob Dylan, Lennon and McCartney had passed the time when innovative lyrics and melodies would simply be given to them, as if by spirits. Much like the aging Dylan, at 62 McCartney could only look back at his own early work with a mixture of wonder and pride: "you can't go on making *Pepper* all your life. It just can't be done. *Pepper* was a peak.... It hit the right notes, the right moment in time. It was strange. It was weird. It was hugely popular. It embraced all the things you want to embrace as an artist.... But it was always going to be impossible to top."[152]

Together with Bob Dylan, during the mid-1960s the Beatles created a conceptual revolution in popular music. Dylan and Lennon and McCartney broadened the subject matter and vocabulary of popular music: thus in 1968 Jean-Luc Godard declared that the Beatles "are very important because they are popular and intellectual at the same time. That is good. That is what I am trying to do in the movies."[153] In the process, Dylan and the Beatles transformed rock and roll from dance music into something to be listened to, carefully and attentively, by adults as well as teenagers, and for the first time made it something to be studied intensively by scholars—"a music of introspective self-absorption, a medium fit for communicating autobiographical intimacies, political discontents, spiritual elation."[154] Dylan and the Beatles also definitively eliminated the division of labor between songwriters and performers. Beyond the legacy they shared with Dylan, the Beatles changed the sound of popular music, by introducing novel production techniques, instruments that had not previously been used for pop songs, and electronic music: the critic Elijah Wald observed that the Beatles' later albums "were not just written but produced and directed with a degree of effort and thought that had previously been reserved for filmmaking—in George Martin's words, they were 'making movies in sound.'"[155] With *Sgt. Pepper*, the Beatles also introduced the concept album, which made a record a single extended statement rather than a collection of individual songs. Their music has been recorded by countless other musicians: the *Guinness Book of World Records* ranks "Yesterday" as the most frequently covered song ever written. They changed the appearance of albums, by having prominent English pop artists Peter Blake and Richard Hamilton create the covers of *Sgt. Pepper* and the *White Album*, respectively. And for a vast audience in the 1960s and afterward, the Beatles created the sound of an era: as the American classical composer Aaron Copland observed, "When people ask to recreate the mood of the sixties, they will play Beatle music."[156]

Paul Simon (1941–)

> I've been working on my rewrite, that's right
> I'm gonna change the ending
> Gonna throw away my title
> And toss it in the trash
>
> Paul Simon[157]

When 14-year-old Paul Simon first heard Elvis Presley on the radio, "I wanted to be Elvis." That dream ended abruptly when he saw Elvis on *Ed Sullivan*—tall, handsome, with a deep voice, an exotic name, and the magical birthplace of Tupelo, Mississippi: "I realized I had to get as far from what Elvis was doing as I could with my music.... I knew I couldn't beat him. But I still felt I could make it. I just had to go softer."[158]

Paul began writing songs in his early teens, but he didn't have a success until "The Sound of Silence" became a hit for him and Art Garfunkel in 1965—the same year Bob Dylan released "Like a Rolling Stone." Simon would spend much of his career in the shadow of Dylan's conceptual revolution, as critics would consistently use Dylan's music as a counterpoint to his. The earliest instance of this came in 1966, when the first issue of *Crawdaddy*—the first magazine devoted to criticism of rock music—hailed Simon and Garfunkel's album *Sounds of Silence* as "easily the best American album since [Dylan's] *Bringing It All Back Home*." The review was a rave, but it sounded a hesitant note: "It's not quite rock 'n' roll, nearly but never folk."[159] In the *New York Times*, Robert Shelton contrasted Dylan's "rough, natural, dirty sound" with Simon and Garfunkel's "timid contrived side," and disparaged Simon as "a suburban type of Dylan."[160]

Simon and Garfunkel sang at the Monterey Pop Festival in 1967, but they were overshadowed by more raucous performances, including the raw emotion of Janis Joplin, the guitar smashing of The Who, and the guitar incineration of Jimi Hendrix. *Newsweek* commented that although Simon and Garfunkel "sounded nice enough, they seemed sadly left behind."[161] When the great success of Simon's soundtrack for Mike Nichols' surprise hit film *The Graduate* launched Simon and Garfunkel to two consecutive number-one albums on the *Billboard* pop charts in 1968, *Rolling Stone* conceded that Simon's songs were "nice enough," but still objected that they were "not rock and roll, whatever that is."[162] Jann Wenner, the founder of *Rolling Stone*, later explained that Simon and Garfunkel were never on the magazine's cover in the 1960s because their sound was "too soft." They did make the cover in the '70s, with the rise of folk rock, but invidious Dylan comparisons persisted. A hostile *New York Times* review of a 1975 concert contended that Simon's songs had a "polished, commercially packaged side that shared much with the tradition of American cabaret and show tunes," and that "Mr. Simon never seems to be risking as much as the rawer sort of folk and folk-rock singer epitomized by Bob Dylan."[163]

Although Simon bridled at the claim that his music was not rock and roll, he conceded that his sensibility differed from Dylan's: "What he represents is the rebel poet, the darkness.... I couldn't be Dylan any more than I could be Elvis."[164] Late in his career, he reflected on the contrast between his lyrics and Dylan's: "I've tried to sound ironic. I can't. Dylan, everything he sings has two meanings. He's telling you the truth and making fun of you at the same time. I sound sincere every time."[165] Clive Davis, the president of Columbia Records in the heyday of Simon and Garfunkel, observed that Simon "fit in with the greats before him, the Cole Porters and Irving Berlins, as someone who combines an incredible feel for melody with a literate lyric sense." A poll taken in 2004 by the American Film Institute ranked "Mrs. Robinson" sixth among the best songs ever included in a movie, behind classics from the Great American Songbook: "Over the Rainbow," "As Time Goes By," "Singin' in the Rain," "Moon River," and "White Christmas."[166] Simon resented the sharp line that was routinely drawn between rock and earlier popular music. In a 1984 interview he complained that rock musicians were expected to be "unsophisticated, working class, nonintellectual." Noting that "the idea that rock would be an art form that people with a brain might work at was always treated with derision," he pointed out that "there are a lot of smart guys in this profession, but they don't express that side."[167]

Simon remarked that "I write about the things I know and observe."[168] His music was not didactic: "I'm not a fan of songs that tell you 'And my point is. . . .'"[169] He wanted his writing to be a process of searching: "I don't consciously think about what a song should say. In fact, I consciously try *not* to think about what a song should say. . . . I like to discover what it is that's interesting to me. I like to *discover* it rather than plot it out."[170] In 1967, Simon described songwriting as "an excruciating process," noting that he had been working on one song for three months. He might spend days or even weeks trying to find the right word. One of his most famous lines—"Where have you gone, Joe DiMaggio?"—was a product of revision: Simon used DiMaggio instead of the idol of his teen years, Mickey Mantle, because it had the right number of syllables. He also spent many long sessions experimenting in the recording studio. When he was accused of being a perfectionist, "My response is I'm looking for something in the studio and I'm not hearing it. . . . I'll think 'No, that's not right' or 'That's not the way I want it to sound.'"[171]

In 2011, Simon characterized songwriting as exploring: "It's like you're wandering down a path and you don't know what the destination is. Somewhere, toward the end, you can sort of see what the destination is and you can understand what the journey is about."[172] The sound was more important than the subject: "the music always precedes the words. The words often come from the sound of the music and eventually evolve into coherent thoughts. Or incoherent thoughts." Aesthetics were important in developing themes—"Rhythm plays a crucial part in the lyrics-making as well"—so writing the lyrics involved searching for a fit for the music: "It's like a puzzle to find the right words to express what the music is saying."[173]

Simon has inspired younger songwriters with his literate and melodic songs. The musician Sting, for example, became a fan when he heard "The Sound of Silence"—"He was the kind of songwriter I wanted to be."[174]

Simon always had wide-ranging musical tastes, and he was always alert to connections. Gospel music reminded him of the 1950s rock 'n' roll he had grown up with, and it became an influence on "Bridge over Troubled Water." Throughout his career, Simon reached out to find sounds that would enhance his music—to Jamaica for ska and reggae, Muscle Shoals for Southern soul, Puerto Rico for plena, Louisiana for zydeco, South Africa for mbaqanga. *The Times* of London called Simon the godfather of world music, noting that although Dylan had the prophet's vision, "it was Simon who looked beyond the music of his own country and found a way to utilize styles from all over the world in a way that made them palatable to rock audiences."[175]

Dating the high point of Simon's career is not straightforward. In 2005, *Rolling Stone* placed *Bridge over Troubled Water* (1970) ahead of *Graceland* (1986) as Simon's two best albums, but in the magazine's 2020 ranking the positions of the two albums were reversed. The change in order may reflect the growing importance of globalization in popular music, as in 2020 *Rolling Stone* commented that *Graceland* "opened up South African music to the world, and in particular launched the international career of Ladysmith Black Mambazo."[176] Today there appears to be widespread agreement that *Graceland* was Simon's most important album, followed by *Bridge over Troubled Water*, implying that his best work spanned at least the sixteen years from ages 29 to 45.

In a 2021 audiobook based on dozens of hours of interviews with Paul Simon, the author Malcolm Gladwell paid particular attention to his creative process. He concluded that "Paul Simon isn't a conceptual innovator. He doesn't embark on long journeys with his destination clearly in sight. He just embarks on long journeys and hopes for the best. He's an experimentalist, and ... for the experimentalist, the production of the work is a process of searching."[177] Several critics have contrasted the progression of Simon's career to those of his conceptual peers. In 1972 Stephen Holden wrote in *Rolling Stone* that "Unlike Dylan, who executed a series of dramatic stylistic changes, Simon's evolution has been subtle, but in the long run almost as significant." Holden described the change in Simon's music as "a triumphant movement away from folk rock formalism and an academic poetic style toward a more relaxed, more assured narrative style with greater depth and range of expression."[178] And Robert Hilburn noted that "Simon kept reinventing himself, but it wasn't in the shifting persona adopted by, say, David Bowie, who shook up his fans by moving from one carefully plotted role to another ... Simon's changes were organic, dictated largely by his constant pursuit of new musical expression."[179]

Malcolm Gladwell marveled at Paul Simon's creative longevity: "Paul Simon writes 'Sound of Silence' when he's 23. And what's his creative peak, probably *Graceland*, right? It comes out in 1986, 22 years later." Nor did Simon stop there, making *The Rhythm of the Saints* in 1990 and *So Beautiful or So What* in 2011: "Wherever you land on the question of what Paul Simon's greatest album is, the point is the same, that his career has been astonishingly long." Gladwell's explanation: "He's Cézanne. He's the experimental innovator. That's why his creative peaks extend for so long, because he's constantly trying new things, and testing out ideas, and taking one kind of creative flyer after another."[180]

Craftsmen and Artists

The practices and attitudes of Golden Era songwriters stemmed in large part from their recognition of the role of their work, for their songs were nearly always created in response to the needs of musical comedy scripts that had been written before composers or lyricists ever became involved. Early on, these songwriters accepted as a test of quality that their songs should not disrupt the continuity of the play, and over time the integration of songs into the plot, and their role in developing characters, came to be considered increasingly important criteria for a songwriter's success. Irving Berlin and Cole Porter were among the experimental master songwriters who produced songs intended for the voices of specific actors. Even as an undergraduate in college, when he was writing the score for a fraternity musical, Porter asked the director: "Tell me whom you select for different parts, and I can write fitting songs."[181] In 1932, Fred Astaire hesitated to accept a role in *The Gay Divorce*, because he was unsure of singing "Night and Day" successfully, but Porter convinced him that the song was tailored to his strengths. As Gerald Mast explained, "One reason 'Night and Day' uses a single note eighty-one times is that G was a particularly good note for Astaire. One reason the song uses its insistent rhythms and half-tone modulations is that Astaire was a master of rhythmic punctuation and melodic modulation."[182] Porter's judgment was vindicated by the great popular and critical success of his score, as Astaire acknowledged that *Gay Divorce* "came to be known as the 'Night and Day' show," and Irving Berlin wrote to Porter that "I am mad about 'Night and Day' and I think it is your high spot."[183] A few years later, while writing the score for the movie *Top Hat*, Berlin's appreciation for Astaire's exceptional delivery and diction prompted him to write "Cheek to Cheek" without an opening verse, instead beginning with the chorus. Songwriters normally used a verse to ease the transition from dialogue to song, but Berlin realized Astaire could make this change by beginning to sing as if he were talking.[184]

Philip Roth facetiously saluted the ingenuity of a Jewish songwriter in writing hit songs about both Easter and Christmas: "The two holidays that celebrate the divinity of Christ ... and what does Irving Berlin brilliantly do? He de-Christs them both!"[185] But that Berlin's songs were not personal is even more powerfully demonstrated by one of these songs. Berlin did not dream of Christmas; he hated it. His only son, Irving Berlin Jr., died from crib death on Christmas Day in 1928. Every Christmas thereafter, Berlin and his wife left flowers on their son's grave. It was the one day of the year they both dreaded.

Bob Dylan, John Lennon, and Paul McCartney were the leading figures in creating a new model, in which the conceptual writer of popular songs would also be the performer. Instead of a craftsman producing material to be interpreted by an artist, the creation of the song would now be an integral part of the final work of art. In 1978, when asked to define what he did, Dylan declared, "I'm an artist. I try to create art."[186] He was not concerned with anyone else's voice: "My songs were written with me in mind."[187] Mindful that most of popular culture was ephemeral, he aimed higher: "I wanted to do something that stood alongside Rembrandt's paintings."[188] Lennon considered his mature songs to be intellectual contributions, not mere decorations: "I'm interested in concepts and philosophies. I am not interested in wallpaper, which most music is."[189]

Dylan had not initially devoted much thought to songwriting, but early in his time in New York he was jolted when he heard a performance by Pete Seeger's brother, Mike. Seeger played many different folk instruments and sang in a wide range of traditional styles; he wasn't just a good folksinger, he was "the supreme archetype.... [H]e played these songs as good as it was possible to play them." Seeger had folk music "in his genes.... Before he was even born, this music had to be in his blood." Dylan knew he couldn't compete—"to be as good as that, you'd just about have to be him"—and realized he would have to do something different: "The thought occurred to me that maybe I'd have to write my own folk songs, ones that Mike didn't know. That was a startling thought." He decided he would have to innovate: "if

I wanted to compose folk songs I would need some new kind of template, some philosophical identity that wouldn't burn out." He would need "to change my inner thought patterns.... I might have to disorientate myself." He needed a new conceptual method: "I needed to learn how to telescope things, ideas."[190]

In keeping with their view of themselves as craftsmen, Golden Era songwriters prided themselves on their humility and avoidance of pretension. The highest tribute Jerome Kern could pay to his fellow composer Irving Berlin was to explain that "He doesn't attempt to stuff the public's ears with pseudo-original, ultra modernism, but he honestly absorbs the vibrations emanating from the people, manners and life of his time, and in turn, gives these impressions back to the world—simplified, clarified, glorified."[191] Similarly Porter, whose work was routinely described as sophisticated, would protest that "I've worked like a dog to keep all that ['sophisticated'] implies out of my music."[192] The Golden Era songwriters thus considered their greatest obligation to be to their audience, but the same would not necessarily be true of their conceptual successors. When asked in 1965 whom he was writing and singing for, Dylan responded, "Not writing and singing for anybody, to tell you the truth."[193] His obligations were limited: "I have no responsibility to anybody except myself."[194] Lennon confessed that "I always wrote about me when I could.... I like first person music."[195] Eschewing false modesty, Lennon explained that he was a genius: "It isn't egomania. It's a fact. If somebody gave me a pair of glasses that makes me see through walls, I can't help it.... I just see and hear *differently* from other people." He wrote about what he knew: "I like to write about me; 'cause I *know* me."[196]

Berlin's approach to composing was to strive for simplicity through a repeated process of refinement. The writer Anita Loos recalled sitting with Berlin as he worked: "He would go over and over a lyric until it seemed perfect to my ears. Then he'd scrap the whole thing and begin over again. When I asked Irving what was wrong, he invariably said, 'It isn't *simple* enough.'"[197] Dylan's method of composition during his peak years owed little to revision, but was instead indebted to Rimbaud's belief that the artist should systematically derange his own senses.[198] He would smoke marijuana and write as quickly as possible: "The best songs to me—my best songs—are songs which were written very quickly.... Just about as much time as it takes to write it down is about as long as it takes to write it."[199] Paul McCartney explained that *Sgt. Pepper*, which he considered the Beatles' greatest achievement, was not the product of drudgery: "Whatever *Pepper* amounted to, call it wisdom, call it a vision, call it what you like, it didn't come out of a great struggle. It came out of a great party we were having."[200] One critic observed that Dylan "was not pursuing refinement, sophistication, and clarity of expression, those ideals of the Cole Porter generation of songwriters, but their near opposites: kinetic energy, instinct, and ambiguity," while another noted that the approach pioneered by Dylan and the Beatles became characteristic of the best rock music—"the sound of surprise: not the surprise of virtuosos improvising in new ways to play (the thrill of jazz), but rather the surprise of untrained amateurs . . . finding a voice of their own—and sometimes even elaborating new song forms unthinkable to more highly skilled musicians."[201]

Berlin and his fellow Golden Era songwriters dismissed Dylan and the Beatles with their strongest term of contempt, referring to them as the "unprofessionals."[202] Yet in light of the contrasting aesthetic of the younger songwriters, the insult held little sting, for the very qualities Berlin and the other experimental songwriters derided as amateurish were prized by the younger conceptual songwriters as the secret of their success. When an interviewer in 1986 referred to the epoch-making music he had created in the mid-1960s, Dylan responded, "I did that accidentally."[203] Dylan consistently maintained that his songwriting was not a career: "In my mind it's never really been seriously a profession. . . . It's been more confessional than professional."[204] And in his best Liverpudlian diction, John Lennon explained why he often composed at the piano, which by his own admission he played worse than the guitar: "I surprise meself, you know."[205]

Paul Simon was often called a poet—no less an authority than Derek Walcott remarked that Simon's lyrics reminded him of Hart Crane—but he rejected the label, explaining that "the lyrics of pop songs are so banal that if you show a spark of intelligence they call you a poet. But the people who call you a poet are people who never read poetry."[206] He was also uncomfortable with the label of artist: "I really didn't like being called an artist until I was in my forties." He eventually accepted it: "when I was in my forties, which of course is around the time of *Graceland*, I said, 'Well, actually I am an artist.' It doesn't mean I'm a good artist. . . . You could be a bad artist; you could be a great artist. But it's a kind of type of person."[207]

In 1975, Simon told an interviewer that he regretted the lost craftsmanship exemplified by earlier experimental songwriters, declaring that "Pop music is in a terrible state right now. . . . There's nothing that goes back to the richest, most original form of American popular music—Broadway and Tin Pan Alley—in which sophisticated lyrics are matched by sophisticated melodies." And he recognized his kinship with his Golden Age predecessors: "It's no fluke that me, Berlin, Gershwin and Kern are all Jewish guys from New York who look alike." [208]

10
Scientists and Entrepreneurs

The analysis presented in this book was developed through the study of artists. Yet as I studied each of the disciplines treated in the preceding chapters, it became increasingly clear that the analysis was applicable more widely, to virtually all intellectual activities. This chapter illustrates how it can be applied to the careers of scientists and entrepreneurs.

Charles Darwin (1809–1882)

> My industry has been nearly as great as it could have been in the observation and collection of facts.
>
> Charles Darwin[1]

Charles Darwin was born into a distinguished and prosperous family. His father was a successful physician; his maternal grandfather was Josiah Wedgwood, the famous potter and industrialist. His family's wealth would allow Charles to follow his interests without ever having to work for a living. Charles always loved the outdoors; he believed that he "was born a naturalist."[2] He was less interested in school, and was a mediocre student. The biographer Gavin de Beer observed that "Darwin was a striking example of the fact that in educational matters the race is not always to the swift; he was an outstanding late developer."[3] Late in his life, Darwin recalled that "To my deep mortification my father once said to me, 'You care for nothing but shooting, dogs, and rat-catching, and you will be a disgrace to yourself and all your family.'"[4]

His father sent Charles to Edinburgh University to study medicine, but Charles hated his studies, and left without a degree. His father then sent him to Cambridge, to prepare for a career as a clergyman. Charles again had little enthusiasm for his courses, but became passionately interested in collecting beetles in the local fens, and met several professors of natural history. Shortly after he graduated, one of these professors offered him passage on a ship bound for a voyage around the world.

When the *Beagle* sailed in 1831, Darwin was the companion to the captain on a projected two-year voyage to chart the southern coasts of South America for the British Admiralty. In fact, the voyage stretched to five years, and Darwin soon became the ship's naturalist. In the course of the voyage, he was able to spend a considerable amount of time on land, collecting a wide variety of samples and recording his impressions of what he saw. His productivity was remarkable, as he wrote 770 pages of a diary, 1,383 notebook pages on geology, 368 pages on zoology, collected 1,529 samples of species in spirits, and 3,907 labeled animal skins and bones.[5] Darwin wrote in his autobiography that "The voyage of the *Beagle* has been by far the most important event in my life and has determined my whole career." It was his school: "I owe to the voyage the first real training or education of my mind. I was led to attend closely to several branches of natural history, and thus my powers of observation were improved."[6] Darwin would devote the rest of his life to questions that first occurred to him during the voyage.[7] His reading on the trip also contributed to his education. Charles Lyell's book on geology stressed the substantial consequences of the gradual accumulation of many incremental changes; Darwin would fruitfully extend to biology the idea that over extremely long periods, small changes could add up to large cumulative effects. The biographer Janet Browne observed that "In Darwin's mind, it became a powerful way of thought that could be applied to the whole of the natural world.... This one idea became the touchstone of Darwin's scientific approach."[8]

Darwin recalled that his industry on the *Beagle* was due to "the mere pleasure of investigation," but added that "I was also ambitious to take a fair place among scientific men."[9] After his return to England in 1836, he turned his diary into a book. The biologist Edward Wilson called this "intellectually the most important travel book of all time"; upon publication it sold well, was favorably reviewed, and established Darwin as a serious scientist.[10]

In 1837, Darwin became convinced of the existence of evolution—then called "transmutation." A key contribution to his belief was the determination by the ornithologist John Gould that the mockingbirds Darwin had found on three different islands in the Galapagos were actually three different species.[11] Janet Browne stressed the empirical basis of Darwin's belief: "where other men pledged themselves to the idea of transmutation because of their philosophical commitment to progress in cultural spheres, Darwin mostly arrived at it through the organisms themselves."[12] As Darwin began to collect evidence of transmutation, he also began to suffer from health problems, including persistent nausea and vomiting, that would plague him for decades. He would try many treatments, but would never find a cure. Scholars have debated the source—perhaps a disease contracted in South America, or psychiatric causes, from anxiety over the reception of his research—without reaching a definite conclusion.[13]

In his autobiography, Darwin recalled that in 1838,

> I happened to read for amusement Malthus on Population, and being well prepared to appreciate the struggle for existence which everywhere goes on from long-continued observation of the habits of animals and plants, it at once struck me that under these circumstances favorable variations would tend to be preserved, and unfavorable ones destroyed. The result of this would be the formation of new species. Here, then, I had at last got a theory by which to work.[14]

This was the theory Darwin would later call *natural selection*, that explained by natural causes all the adaptations of living organisms that had previously been attributed to divine design.[15] Yet Darwin's recollection overstated the suddenness of the discovery. Study of Darwin's research notebooks led M. Hodge and David Kohn to conclude that during 1837–1839 Darwin was "working knowingly with a comprehensive structure of argument . . . and that the theory of natural selection emerges toward the end of this period in a series of steps such that no one can be picked out as taking Darwin from lacking to possessing the theory."[16]

Darwin married his cousin, Emma Wedgwood, in 1839. Three years later, with two (of an eventual nine) children, the family moved to Downe, a small town 16 miles southeast of London, where they settled in an old parsonage. Darwin took refuge in Down House for the rest of his life, devoting himself to writing and research, avoiding travel as damaging to his fragile health. In 1842, Darwin wrote "a very brief abstract of my theory in pencil in 35 pages"; in 1844, he expanded this to a manuscript of 230 pages, of which he had a fair copy made. He had no intention of publishing this, but left instructions to have it published in case of his death.[17]

In 1844, Darwin wrote to a friend, the botanist Joseph Hooker, that "I am almost convinced (quite contrary to the opinion I started with) that species are not (it is like confessing a murder) immutable."[18] The melodramatic language may help to explain the puzzling gap that scholars have named "Darwin's Delay"—two decades between his formulation of natural selection and publication of *On the Origin of Species*. The biologist Stephen Jay Gould argued that "fear must have played at least as great a role as the need for additional documentation.... He was not about to compromise a promising career by promulgating a heresy that he could not prove."[19] The Nobel laureate James Watson stressed the magnitude of Darwin's contribution: "Copernicus, Galileo and Newton had removed the Earth from its central position in the universe.... But the position of man, as the image of God on earth, was left unchanged by their revisions of the received cosmology. Darwin changed this." Hence the delay: "Extraordinary claims require extraordinary evidence, so Darwin began a long process of accumulating fact after fact that could be explained better from an evolutionary perspective than any other."[20] James Secord agreed that Darwin did not want his book to be speculative, and merely to suggest a possible future basis for research, but rather wanted it to be definitive: "He wanted all the supporting evidence and argument to be in place, so that contemporaries could be convinced that a scientific way of going forward could be found in a theory of evolution. Darwin wanted his revolution to be a fait accompli, total and irrefutable."[21] And Darwin understood that accumulating more evidence would never merely buttress an existing framework, but would inevitably cause extension and adjustment of his theories. Thus he commented in his autobiography that "I gained much by my delay in publishing from about 1839, when the theory was clearly conceived, to 1859."[22] And much of what he gained was unanticipated.

In 1846, Darwin began to study the last specimens that remained from the *Beagle* voyage, of small crustaceans. He enjoyed the work—dissecting tiny barnacles under a microscope, he wrote happily to Hooker that "there is extraordinary pleasure in pure observation"—but he expected to spend only a few months, to write a few papers.[23] Yet important discoveries caused him to expand the project: Darwin eventually spent eight years making a complete survey of all known species of barnacles, during which he examined ten thousand specimens, published four volumes, and earned the Royal Society's Royal Medal for Natural Science.[24]

The barnacles added key elements to Darwin's understanding of evolution. He was excited to discover direct evidence for his belief that transmutation progressively occurred away from self-fertilization, as he observed a series of forms, from hermaphrodite to an intermediate bisexual stage of incomplete sexual differentiation, to two distinct sexes. The barnacles thus provided powerful confirmation for the existence of evolution.[25] Darwin had also previously assumed that most species were normally stable and uniform, posing the problem of why and how organisms varied. But the barnacles revealed that variation within a species was pervasive: he told Hooker that he was "struck...with the variability of every part in some slight degree of every species." This led Darwin to the "principle of divergence," which held that natural selection would favor those chance variants of a species that were best suited to particular geographic niches, which would systematically cause diversification from original forms.[26] This provided a central element of the theory of evolution—Darwin later called the principle of divergence "the key-stone of my Book"—for it meant that neither major environmental change nor prolonged isolation was necessary for speciation, but that new species could appear under normal circumstances within a single continental habitat.[27]

Both the great expansion of the barnacle project and its serendipitous results were products of Darwin's inductive method, for he never focused narrowly on any aspect of a problem, but tried to learn all he could about any subject he touched. And Janet Browne noted that the barnacles in turn increased his commitment to direct observation: "his barnacles had shown him—as no reading or thinking could have done—the sheer impact of looking at organisms directly." This would spur him to become "one of the most original experimental scientists of the Victorian era."[28] The historian Sandra Herbert recognized that Darwin's experimental forays often yielded unexpected benefits: "Darwin's entrance into new fields altered his theory in a direction and to an extent which he could not have imagined beforehand."[29]

In 1856, Darwin began writing a technical treatise on evolution that he projected to run to three volumes. This was never completed, for in 1858 he received by mail an unpublished essay from the naturalist Alfred Russel Wallace, who was in Malaysia. To Darwin's horror, "this essay contained exactly the same theory as mine."[30] Several of Darwin's friends arranged for Wallace's paper to be published together with extracts from Darwin's previously unpublished 1844 essay, so that Darwin would not lose priority, but Darwin now recognized that he must proceed more quickly. Abandoning his treatise, he wrote a shorter monograph, aimed not at specialists but at the general public.[31] In 1859, when Darwin was 50 years old, this was published as *On the Origin of Species by Means of Natural Selection, or: The Preservation of Favoured Races in the Struggle for Life.*

Edward Wilson recently wrote that "I believe we can safely say that the *Origin of Species* is the most important book of science ever written.... No work of science has ever been so fully vindicated by subsequent investigation, or has so profoundly altered humanity's view of itself and how the living world works."[32] The first edition sold out within days of publication; five revised editions eventually followed. Today, its copyright long expired, *Origin* is available from more than two dozen publishers in English alone, and its annual sales worldwide are estimated at 75,000–100,000 copies.[33] Its impact on science was both rapid and profound: in 1871, the zoologist T. H. Huxley declared that "in a dozen years, the *Origin of Species* has worked as complete a revolution in biological sciences as the *Principia* did in astronomy."[34]

In the *Origin of Species*, Darwin argued that all organisms are the product of a long, gradual process of development from simpler forms. The mechanism causing this is natural selection: only a few organisms survive to reproduce, and success in this process depends on organisms' distinctive features. Over time, this leads to change, and to adaptation.[35] (Darwin first substituted the phrase "survival of the fittest" for "natural selection" in the fifth edition of the *Origin*, at the urging of Alfred Wallace, who argued that selection implied a selector.[36]) Initially intended by Darwin as an article, the *Origin* grew into a book of five hundred pages. One reason for this was its complexity. Although Darwin often referred to his theory in the singular, Ernst Mayr observed that it comprised five distinct theories—evolution, common descent, multiplication of species, gradualism, and natural selection—and that the last of these was itself a package of theories.[37] Even more, *Origin*'s considerable length was a consequence of the enormous amount of evidence it contained. Shortly before he drafted the book, Darwin wrote to a friend that "I am like Croesus overwhelmed with my riches in facts, and I mean to make my Book as perfect as ever I can."[38] The philosopher David Hull observed that "Although there is, broadly speaking, a deductive core to the *Origin*, by and large it is one long, involved inductive argument conducted in the midst of a mass of very concrete facts. Darwin's argument as presented in the *Origin* is a genuinely inductive argument."[39] The great empirical contribution of the *Origin* was emphasized in a letter from Darwin to one of his closest friends, Charles Lyell, at a time when he was devastated by the thought that Wallace's manuscript on evolution had cost him priority in publishing the theory. He acknowledged that "all my originality, whatever it may amount to, will be smashed." But he continued: "Though my Book, if it will ever have any value, will not be deteriorated, as all the labour consists in the application of the theory."[40]

Darwin generated many of his facts himself, as he constantly experimented at his home in Downe with both plants and animals. Although his time on the *Beagle* figures more dramatically in accounts of his career, Janet Browne contended that "these home-based researches were the hidden triumph of his theory of evolution."[41] (These continue even today: a geneticist recently observed that Darwin's measurement at Down House of the sinking of a millstone due to the burrowing of worms is currently the longest-running biological experiment in the world.[42]) Darwin also took advantage of the knowledge of others on a scale that must have had few if any precedents. Browne noted that "Darwin wrote or received some fourteen thousand letters that are still in existence in libraries the world over, and there must have been as many again now lost to posterity." The greatest numbers of these were exchanged with scientists, but Darwin found a wide range of others, including farmers, breeders, civil servants, and army officers, scattered around the world, to send him specimens or answer queries. Browne contended that Darwin's completed theory of evolution might best be seen as "the interplay between the creative vision residing in a single mind and a mass of information gathered from many different hands, including his own."[43]

In part, Darwin's delay in publishing his theory was a result not only of his search for answers, but for a clear view of the questions. After he published the *Origin*, in a letter to a friend he mused that "I suppose that I am a very slow thinker, for you would be surprised at the number of years it took me to see clearly what some of the problems were, which had to be solved.... Looking back, I think it was more difficult to see what the problems were than to solve them ... & this seems to me rather curious." The extended effort involved in identifying relevant problems was a consequence of the inductive nature of the project, as Darwin had to construct a complex argument from a series of many interrelated propositions.[44]

In one respect, Darwin's cautious delay continued even after 1859, for the *Origin* famously contained no analysis of human evolution, cryptically commenting only that in the future, "Light will be thrown on the origin of man and his history."[45] It was not until 1871 that Darwin published *The Descent of Man, and Selection in Relation to Sex*. The psychologist Howard Gruber consequently described Darwin's career as a strategy involving not one but two delays; he argued that the second delay was caused by "a great deal of additional hard work, much of it highly original, done in the years 1867–71," as Darwin passed the age of 60.[46]

Great scientists must explain things, so no important scientist can be purely an observer. Darwin himself was sensitive to this; in his autobiography, he responded to critics who "said, 'Oh, he is a good observer, but has no power of reasoning,'" by contending that "the *Origin of Species* is one long argument.... No one could have written it without having some power of reasoning." He noted that useful observation necessarily had to be guided by theory: "How odd it is that anyone should not see that all observation must be for or against some view if it is to be of service!" Yet he stressed that he had always "endeavored to keep my mind free, so as to give up any hypothesis, however much beloved ... as soon as facts are shown to be opposed to it. Indeed ... I cannot remember a single first-formed hypothesis which had not after a time to be given up or greatly modified. This has naturally led me to distrust greatly deductive reasoning in the mixed sciences."[47]

Darwin was modest in assessing his own talents, but he admitted that "I think I am superior to the common run of men in noticing things which easily escape attention, and in observing them carefully."[48] Yet he was never content simply with observation: "From my early youth I have had the strongest desire to understand or explain what I observed—that is, to group all facts under some general laws. These causes combined have given me the patience to reflect or ponder for any number of years over any unexplained problem."[49] The philosopher Antonello La Vergata concluded that Darwin was "continuously readjusting, or rather constructing, his bold theoretical framework and struggling with hard facts."[50] The geneticist Steve Jones believed that Darwin "became a better scientist as he grew older for he began to test ideas with experiments, many far ahead of their time, rather than collating the results of others."[51] In his autobiography, which he began writing at 67, Darwin provided a succinct and striking characterization of himself as an inductive experimental scholar: "My mind seems to have become a kind of machine for grinding general laws out of large collections of facts."[52]

Darwin's impact on biology was fundamental. The geneticist Theodosius Dobzhansky declared that "Nothing in biology makes sense except in the light of evolution."[53] Edward Wilson observed that "Evolution by natural selection is perhaps the only one true law unique to biological systems, as opposed to nonliving physical systems."[54] And Darwin's impact extends far beyond biology: Stephen Jay Gould contended that "Darwin changed our intellectual world perhaps more than any other person in the history of science."[55]

Darwin received many honors in his lifetime. The one he probably valued most highly was an honorary doctor of laws from his alma mater, Cambridge University, in 1877. He traveled to Cambridge for a special ceremony; cheering undergraduates crammed Senate House and gave Darwin a deafening ovation that drowned out the Latin oration conferring the degree.[56] Although he was too controversial during his lifetime to be honored with a knighthood, after his death an outpouring of appreciation by scientists and the press insisted on official recognition for Darwin: in a typical tribute, *The Times* declared that "The impetus he has given to science ... can only find a parallel in Newton."[57] Darwin had wanted to be buried in the churchyard of his beloved Downe, but his family reluctantly agreed that he should be honored by burial in Westminster Abbey, where his grave was placed near that of Isaac Newton. A specially commissioned hymn for the occasion took its opening line from Proverbs: "Happy is the man that findeth wisdom and getteth understanding."[58]

Albert Einstein (1879–1955)

> Imagination is more important than knowledge.
> Albert Einstein[59]

One of Albert Einstein's earliest memories was the sense of wonder he experienced at the age of four or five when his father gave him a compass. That the needle moved without being touched left "a deep and lasting impression. Something deeply hidden had to be behind things."[60] This early fascination with the invisible magnetic field may have been a harbinger, for Einstein would devote much of his career to theorizing about the impact of unseen fields—magnetic, electrical, or gravitational—on physical objects.[61]

At 12, Einstein "experienced a second wonder of a totally different nature," from what he later referred to as "the holy geometry book": he was "thrilled to see that it was possible to find out truth by reasoning alone, without the help of any outside experience." He loved the "clarity and certainty" of the book's contents. This provided a foundation for a basic conviction: "I became more and more convinced that nature could be understood as a relatively simple mathematical structure."[62]

In the history of science, the name *annus mirabilis* has long been given to 1666, when the 24-year-old Isaac Newton developed calculus, an analysis of the light spectrum, and the laws of gravity. Today, that honorific is also given to Einstein's work of 1905. Prior to 1905, Einstein had published a total of five little-known papers. He had completed four years of studies in physics in Zurich, but his dissertation had been rejected, so he had not yet earned a PhD. After failing to find an academic job of any kind, he was working in an entry-level position in the Swiss Patent Office in Bern. But during 1905, the 26-year-old Einstein wrote five papers that transformed the discipline of physics.[63]

Both the diversity of the *annus mirabilis* papers and the timing of their production are a continuing source of amazement to scholars. On March 17, Einstein sent to the German journal *Annalen der Physik*, Europe's leading physics journal, an article on the quantum theory of light. (This was the work for which he would later receive his only Nobel Prize.) On April 30, Einstein completed a paper on the size of molecules, which he later submitted to the University of Zurich as his dissertation. On May 11, his paper on Brownian motion was received by *Annalen der Physik*. On June 30, *Annalen* received his first paper on the special theory of relativity. And on September 30, *Annalen* received a second, shorter paper on relativity. (This contained the link between energy and mass—$E = mc^2$—that would become the most famous equation in the history of science.)[64]

In spite of their extremely diverse subjects, the *annus mirabilis* papers shared a basis in Einstein's highly conceptual approach. The physicist Gerald Holton observed that the three epochal papers—on the quantum theory of light, Brownian motion, and special relativity theory—shared a common structure: "Each begins with a statement of formal asymmetries or other incongruities of a predominantly aesthetic nature (rather than, for example, a puzzle posed by unexplained experimental facts), then proposes a principle . . . which removes the asymmetries as one of the deduced consequences, and at the end produces one or more experimentally verifiable predictions." Holton stressed that these papers all represented attempts "to solve problems by the *postulation* of appropriate fundamental hypotheses and to restrict those hypotheses to the most *general kind* and the *smallest number* possible—a goal on which Einstein often insisted."[65] The physicist Abraham Pais stressed the definitiveness of these early papers: "They exude finality even when they deal with a subject in flux. For example, no statement made in the 1905 paper on light-quanta needs to be revised in the light of later developments."[66]

The physicist Peter Bergmann described Einstein's 1905 paper on special relativity as "revolutionary because it was formally simple, yet conceptually deep."[67] Its first sentence stated an apparent contradiction in the electrodynamics of moving bodies, then the article proceeded to resolve this paradox without a single citation to any earlier publication. John Rigden explained that this was possible because in developing his special theory of relativity, "Einstein did not draw from or build upon the work of others. He adopted two principles as axiomatic, and by means of his intellectual prowess, he brought the unseen consequences of the two principles into full view."[68] The physicist Kip Thorne agreed: "Not only was experiment unimportant in Einstein's construction of a new foundation of physics, the ideas of other physicists were also unimportant." Einstein was guided by his own beliefs: "His conviction that the Universe loves simplicity and beauty, and his willingness to be guided by this conviction, even if it means destroying the foundations of Newtonian physics, led him, with a clarity of thought others could not match, to his new description of space and time."[69]

Einstein sometimes claimed that the origins of his work lay in empirical evidence. So for example in 1921 he contended that relativity theory was "not speculative in origin," but was "conditioned by observed facts."[70] Holton disputed this characterization, however, noting that the 1905 relativity paper was based on "two thematic hypotheses (one on the constancy of light velocity and the other on the extension of the principle of relativity to all branches of physics), two postulates for which there was and can be no direct empirical confirmation." Holton further observed that over time, "Einstein more and more openly put the consistency of a simple and convincing theory or of a thematic conception higher in importance than the latest news from the laboratory."[71] In 1931 Einstein conceded that his pursuit of a unified field theory was motivated not by empirical evidence but by mathematical elegance: "I have been guided not by the pressure from behind of experimental facts, but by the attraction in front from mathematical simplicity."[72] In a lecture at Oxford in 1933, Einstein criticized Newton and other scientists of earlier times for believing "that the fundamental concepts and postulates of physics ... could be deduced from experience by 'abstraction.'" He instead argued "that the axiomatic basis of theoretical physics cannot be extracted from experience but must be freely invented." This was not a problem, however, because of a lesson from history: "Our experience hitherto justifies us in believing that nature is the realization of the simplest conceivable mathematical ideas." Evidence would be necessary for testing theories, but "the creative principle resides in mathematics." In a sweeping affirmation of belief in the power of reasoning, he declared that "I am convinced that we can discover by means of purely mathematical constructions the concepts and the laws connecting them with each other, which furnish the key to the understanding of natural phenomena."[73] In 1936 he again declared that "There is no inductive method which could lead to the fundamental concepts of physics."[74] And in time he admitted that this recognition had actually come to him very early. Thus in 1946 he recalled that in the process of creating the special theory of relativity of 1905, "I despaired of the possibility of discovering the true laws by means of constructive efforts based on known facts. The longer and more despairingly I tried, the more I came to the conviction that only the discovery of a universal formal principle could lead us to assured results."[75] He became convinced that "there is no way from experience to the setting up of a theory"; the theorist's key concepts could only be "free creations of thought which cannot inductively be gained from sense experiences."[76] Looking back at Einstein's struggle to create his general theory of relativity in the decade after 1905, the Nobel laureate Paul Dirac reflected that "Einstein seemed to feel that beauty in the mathematical foundation was more important, in a very fundamental way, than getting agreement with observation."[77]

Einstein's theories often originated in visualized thought experiments. His special theory of relativity began when Einstein imagined what it would be like if a person could run after a light wave at the same speed as light (186,000 miles per second); would the light beam appear to be standing still?[78] His generalization of the special theory began one day while he was sitting in a chair in the patent office at Bern, "when all of a sudden a thought occurred to me. If a person falls freely, he will not feel his own weight." He later called this "the happiest thought in my life."[79] Einstein's peers marveled at the power of his intuition. The Nobel laureate Louis de Broglie likened Einstein's early papers to "blazing rockets," products of "the originality and genius of a mind which can perceive in a single glance, through the complex maze of difficult questions, the new and simple idea which enabled him to elicit their true significance and suddenly to bring clarity and light where darkness had reigned."[80] The physicist Gino Segrè similarly stressed Einstein's "extraordinary ability to look at simple concepts and see them as nobody else had." Segrè considered this a product of Einstein's "apartness"—the willingness to stand apart from others in his discipline, even when they were unanimous in some belief.[81]

After he created the special theory of relativity in 1905, Einstein realized it was incomplete. He devoted most of the next decade to developing a new field theory of gravity and to generalizing his relativity theory. He now discovered that more sophisticated mathematics was necessary to derive the results. He enlisted a mathematician to help him, and wrote to a fellow physicist that with this assistance he expected to reach his goal, adding that "I have gained enormous respect for mathematics, whose more subtle parts I considered until now, in my ignorance, as pure luxury!"[82] Einstein persevered in spite of enormous skepticism within his discipline. In 1913 the eminent physicist Max Planck, who had been an important early supporter of Einstein's 1905 theory of relativity, warned him against his current research on general relativity, saying that "As an older friend I must advise you against it for in the first place you will not succeed; and even if you succeed, no one will believe you."[83] Yet after intensive effort, Einstein declared victory, stating definitively on November 25, 1915, that "Finally the general theory of relativity is closed as a logical structure."[84] In spite of his exhaustion, and even amidst the carnage of World War I and the acrimony of his own failing marriage, Einstein was elated, writing to a friend that "My boldest dreams have now come true." At the age of 36, Einstein immediately knew that he had achieved "the most valuable discovery of my life"; he exulted that "The theory is of incomparable beauty."[85] His peers soon agreed. Paul Dirac called general relativity "probably the greatest scientific discovery ever made," while another physics Nobel laureate, Max Born, considered it "the greatest feat of human thinking about nature, the most amazing combination of philosophical penetration, physical intuition and mathematical skill."[86]

The story of Einstein's later intellectual life is inextricably tied to his unyielding resistance to quantum mechanics, a revolution created by younger physicists, which ironically was built in part on Einstein's own quantum theory of light of 1905. These new advances of the 1920s held that the properties of objects could not be discussed without reference to how those properties were observed or measured. This implied that nature has no single underlying reality independent of our observations; nature was no longer seen as deterministic, but probabilistic. Einstein was never able to accept this formulation, for he was committed to classical notions of determinism, and to a belief in an objective external world, independent of the person observing it.[87] In one instance of what had become a familiar refrain, in 1944 Einstein wrote to his friend Max Born, a central figure in the development of quantum mechanics, that "We have become Antipodean in our scientific expectations. You believe in the God who plays dice, and I in complete law and order in a world which objectively exists, and which I, in a wildly speculative way, am trying to capture." He acknowledged his recalcitrance: "I am aware that our younger colleagues interpret this as a sign of senility."[88]

In defiance of the quantum mechanics revolution, Einstein spent decades pursuing the holy grail of a unified field theory. In 2005, the Nobel laureate physicist Steven Weinberg called Einstein "one of the greatest scientists of all time, a peer of Galileo, Newton, and Darwin, and certainly the leading physicist of the twentieth century." Yet Weinberg noted that "Tragically, Einstein spent almost all of the last 30 years of his life pursuing [a theory that gave a unified account of gravitation and electromagnetism], not only without success, but without leaving any significant impact on the work of other physicists."[89]

Werner Heisenberg, a Nobel laureate whose uncertainty principle was a foundation of quantum mechanics, offered an analysis of Einstein's late attitude:

> Most scientists are willing to accept new empirical data and to recognize new results, provided they fit into their philosophical framework. But in the course of scientific progress it can happen that a new range of empirical data can be completely understood only when the enormous effort is made to enlarge this framework and to change the very structure of the thought processes. In the case of quantum mechanics, Einstein was apparently no longer willing to take this step, or perhaps no longer able to do so.[90]

In 1926, Einstein wrote to Max Born that "Quantum mechanics is certainly imposing. But an inner voice tells me that it is not yet the real thing." Born was exasperated not only by Einstein's verdict on quantum mechanics, but by the unsatisfactory basis for that verdict: "he rejected it not for any definite reason, but rather by referring to an 'inner voice.'"[91] Born lamented that in his late work Einstein "tried to do without any empirical facts, by pure thinking. He believed in the power of reason to guess the laws according to which God has built the world."[92]

Many scholars have pondered why Einstein would not accept the new paradigm. A friend and biographer of Einstein, the physicist Abraham Pais, linked Einstein's late, unsuccessful stubbornness to his earlier, successful stubbornness. Noting Einstein's early solitary pursuit of general relativity in the face of the overwhelming doubt of his peers, Pais wrote that a portrait of Einstein in 1913 was "altogether remarkable":

> He has no compelling results to show for his efforts. He sees the limitations of what he has done so far. He is supremely confident of his vision. And he stands all alone. It seems to me that Einstein's intellectual strength, courage, and tenacity to continue under such circumstances and then to be supremely vindicated a few years later do much to explain how during his later years he would fearlessly occupy once again a similar position, in his solitary quest for an interpretation of quantum mechanics which was totally at variance with commonly held views.

Pais also attributed Einstein's late intransigence to a change in his mind that was the product of his early discoveries: "As a personal opinion, it seems to me that making great discoveries can be accompanied by trauma, and that the purity of Einstein's relativity theories had a blinding effect on him. He almost said so himself: 'To the discoverer... the constructions of his imagination appear so necessary and so natural that he is apt to treat them not as the creations of his thoughts but as given realities.'"[93] Steven Weinberg pointed to a related aspect of Einstein's intellectual development that may have contributed to his later behavior. Weinberg noted that "In developing the general theory of relativity from 1905 to 1915, Einstein had been guided by an existing mathematical formalism, the Riemann theory of curved space, and perhaps he had acquired too great a respect for the power of pure mathematics to inspire physical theory. The oracle of mathematics that had served Einstein so well when he was young betrayed him in his later years."[94]

When Einstein's general theory of relativity was given dramatic empirical support by the astronomer Sir Arthur Eddington's observation of a solar eclipse in 1919, *The Times* of London headlined its account, "Revolution in Science/New Theory of the Universe/Newtonian Ideas Overthrown," and Einstein almost instantly became famous.[95] Paul Dirac later reflected that "It has never happened before or since in the history of science that a scientific idea has been so much caught up by the public and has produced so much enthusiasm and excitement."[96] In time, Einstein gained a degree of celebrity that was equally unprecedented for a scientist. He appeared on the cover of *Time* magazine no fewer than five times, and in December 1999 *Time* named Einstein the person of the century.[97]

He was the guest of Charlie Chaplin at the Hollywood premiere of *City Lights* in 1931, and the pairing was appropriate, for Einstein's public persona as the disheveled, wild-haired genius had become nearly as widely known as Chaplin's little tramp. And Einstein's fierce individualism and strong moral convictions led him to become a powerful and prominent spokesman against political oppression, racism, and anti-Semitism; the philosopher Yehuda Elkana reflected that Einstein "fought tirelessly on behalf of the underdog."[98]

Albert Einstein was an iconoclastic rebel, who once declared, "Long live impudence!"[99] He had complete confidence in his instincts: "I soon learned to scent out that which was able to lead to fundamentals and to turn aside from everything else, from the multitude of things which clutter up the mind and divert it from the essential."[100] Even at the beginning of his career, he was unafraid of standing virtually alone against an entire scientific discipline, serene in his confidence in his own scholarship.[101] He was an archetypal conceptual innovator, who "made imaginative leaps and discerned great principles through thought experiments rather than by methodical inductions based on experimental data."[102] The foundations of his theories were not measurements made in a laboratory, but "fundamental concepts and postulates" of a "purely fictitious character," by which he unraveled basic secrets of nature.[103] He once explained to an interviewer why imagination was more important than knowledge: "Knowledge is limited. Imagination encircles the world."[104] His prodigious ability to solve scientific problems through deductive reasoning made him a symbol of modern scientific genius. His conclusions depended heavily on his own intuition: he once said that "When I am judging a theory, I ask myself whether, if I were God, I would have arranged the world in such a way."[105]

Yet Einstein's faith in his own intuition prevented him from accepting the discoveries of a younger generation of physicists, and caused him to spend his final decades in growing intellectual isolation from the discipline he had once dominated. In 1949 his friend Max Born plaintively wrote that "Many of us regard this as a tragedy—for him, as he gropes his way in loneliness, and for us who miss our leader and standard-bearer."[106] Yet this was an instance of a general phenomenon Einstein understood, for at 38, just two years after his greatest achievement, he remarked to a friend that "Anything truly novel is invented only during one's youth. Later one becomes more experienced, more famous—and more *blockheaded*."[107]

Muhammad Yunus (1940–)

> I hoped that if I studied poverty at close range, I would understand it more keenly.
>
> Muhammad Yunus[108]

Muhammad Yunus was the son of a prosperous jeweler in Chittagong, the largest port in East Pakistan. He was the fifth of fourteen children, five of whom died young. He was a good student, and he attended Chittagong College and Dhaka University. After he received an MA in 1961, he accepted a job as a lecturer in economics at Chittagong University.[109]

As an undergraduate, Yunus had founded a literary magazine. He was surprised to learn that it had to be produced in West Pakistan, because East Pakistan had no companies that did commercial printing and packaging. While teaching at Chittagong, Yunus started a company that made boxes and other packaging materials. Within two years, the company had one hundred employees.[110] In spite of his success in business, Yunus realized that he wanted to be a teacher. To advance his career, he applied for a Fulbright scholarship to study development economics in the United States. His application was successful, and in 1965 he enrolled in the economics department at Vanderbilt University, in Nashville.

Yunus found his program at Vanderbilt of little interest until he took a class from a Romanian economic theorist, Nicholas Georgescu-Roegen, who became his adviser:

> Through him I realized there was little need for memorizing economic formulas. Far more important was to understand the underlying concepts that drive them to work. He also taught me that things are never as complicated as they seem. It is only our arrogance that prompts us to find unnecessarily complicated answers to simple problems.[111]

Yunus wrote a theoretical dissertation, "Intertemporal Allocation of Resources: A Dynamic Programming Model," received his PhD, and in 1969 became an assistant professor at Middle Tennessee State University in Murfreesboro, 50 miles south of Nashville.[112] In the spring of 1971, he was excited by the news that Bangladesh had declared its independence from Pakistan. He traveled to Washington, DC, and organized efforts to gain diplomatic recognition for the new nation. When Bangladesh won its war for independence, Yunus "knew that I had to return home and participate in the work of nation building."[113]

Upon his return Yunus was appointed to the government's Planning Commission, but he was given little to do, and he soon became bored. He resigned, and returned to Chittagong to become head of the university's economics department. As before, he enjoyed teaching, and he looked forward to a long academic career. In 1974, however, events again disrupted his plans—this time a devastating famine that killed hundreds of thousands of Bangladeshis. Hungry people were all around:

> The starving people did not chant any slogans. They did not demand anything from us well-fed city folk. They simply lay down on our doorsteps and waited to die.[114]

Yunus felt guilty for living in a privileged fantasy world:

> I used to feel a thrill at teaching my students the elegant economic theories that could supposedly cure societal problems of all types. But in 1974, I started to dread my own lectures. What good were all my complex theories when people were dying of starvation on the sidewalks and porches across from my lecture hall? My lessons were like American movies where the good guys always win. But when I emerged from the comfort of the classroom, I was faced with the reality of the city streets.[115]

He was no longer satisfied with the abstractions of economic theory:

> Nothing in the economic theories I taught reflected the life around me. How could I go on telling my students make-believe stories in the name of economics? ... I needed to run away from these theories and from my textbooks and discover the real-life economics of a poor person's existence.[116]

In desperation, Yunus began a new intellectual life, in a poor village near his university:

> I decided I would become a student all over again, and the people of Jobra would be my professors. I vowed to learn as much as possible about the village.[117]

Instead of teaching the theories of others, Yunus now became an innovator. And his innovations would be experimental, with concepts that grew directly from empirical observation, and practices constructed by trial and error:

> My repeated trips to the villages around the Chittagong University campus led me to discoveries that were essential to establishing the Grameen Bank. The poor taught me an entirely new economics. I learned about the problems that they face from their own perspective. I tried a great number of things. Some worked. Others did not.[118]

Yunus' most stunning discovery came from a conversation with a young mother of three children, who spent her days making stools from bamboo. Each day she borrowed bamboo stalks worth 22 cents from a supplier, which she used to make a stool. At the end of the day, she gave the stool to the supplier to repay the loan. Because the supplier charged her interest as high as 10 percent a day, she was left with a profit of just 2 cents. In spite of her hard work, the woman could never escape from poverty. Yunus was shocked: "I never heard of anyone suffering for the lack of *twenty-two cents*. It seemed impossible to me, preposterous."[119] But in fact he discovered that this situation was prevalent. Within a week, he and an assistant collected a list of forty-two people in Jobra who depended on usurious loans. In total, these forty-two people needed loans of just $27. Yunus now perceived a key cause of rural poverty:

> People like Sufiya were poor not because they were stupid or lazy. They worked all day long, doing complex physical tasks. They were poor because the financial institutions in the country did not help them widen their financial base. No formal financial structure was available to cater to the credit needs of the poor. This credit market, by default of the formal institutions, had been taken over by the local moneylenders.[120]

Yunus personally gave $27 to the forty-two villagers, to free them from the clutches of the moneylenders, but he realized his response was inadequate: "What was required was an institution that would lend to those who had nothing."[121] Yet when he appealed to the local branch of a large government bank, the manager laughed at him. The loans the villagers needed were too small to justify the necessary documents, and the illiterate poor were in any case unable to fill out forms. Nor would the bank lend to borrowers who had no collateral. After several discussions with bank officials, Yunus became a guarantor: he personally took out a loan from the bank and gave it to the poor of Jobra. This initiated the experimental process by which Yunus became a banker:

> I never intended to become a moneylender. . . . All I really wanted was to solve an immediate problem. Out of sheer frustration, I had questioned the most basic banking premise of collateral. I did not know if I was right. I had no idea of what I was getting myself into. I was walking blind and learning as I went along.[122]

Over time, Yunus and his colleagues devised an effective set of lending practices. Central to these was the use of groups. Loans were made only to villagers who organized themselves into groups of five, each of whom was responsible for the loans of all the group members. Peer pressure was thus used to assure repayment. There were no legal documents for loans: the bank was "built on human trust, not on meaningless paper contracts."[123]

Yunus' first pilot lending program began in August 1976.[124] The next year, he named the project *Grameen*, meaning "rural," or "of the village." In 1979, he took a two-year leave from Chittagong University to manage Grameen full-time. In fact, he would never return to teaching. Yunus' initial goal was to demonstrate the economic feasibility of microlending, then to transfer the program to an existing bank. But in spite of the fact that Grameen consistently realized repayment rates over 95 percent on its loans, conventional banks refused to take it over, insisting—contrary to the evidence Yunus produced—that lending without collateral could not succeed. In October 1983, when Yunus was 43 years old, he launched Grameen Bank as an independent company.[125] He founded Grameen on the experimental principle that experience is the best guide. All the bank's employees are encouraged to suggest changes at any time in even the bank's most basic rules if they see better procedures for dealing with the problems they encounter in their daily work.

Grameen's success as an independent institution was dramatic. It rapidly gained new borrowers and branches, and diversified into loans for housing and irrigation. In 2006, Yunus could report that Grameen was making loans to a total of nearly seven million people, 97 percent of whom were women, in 73,000 villages throughout Bangladesh. Since its inception, the bank had made loans totaling $6 billion, with a repayment rate of 99 percent. The bank's success was such that Yunus reported these figures in his acceptance speech for the 2006 Nobel Peace Prize, awarded jointly to him and the bank, in recognition of the development of microcredit into a powerful tool in the struggle against poverty.[126]

Within Bangladesh, Grameen has expanded into an industrial empire, comprising more than two dozen separate nonprofit companies, ranging from the largest telecommunications company in Bangladesh, through fabric manufacturing and fish and livestock breeding, to health care services for the poor.[127] And beyond Bangladesh, independent of Grameen, microcredit has spread throughout the world. Sharing a common set of characteristics—an explicit social mission, a requirement that borrowers use their loans for microbusiness, group lending, frequent group meetings to make loan payments, and an emphasis on women's economic empowerment—today more than one thousand separate microcredit institutions operate on six continents, serving more than 150 million borrowers.[128] Scholars who have studied microcredit have generally found it to have a major impact on poverty reduction in poor countries.[129]

Grameen Bank's microlending violated a fundamental tenet of banking—one that was supported by such powerful intuitive appeal that it had never been seriously tested. Muhammad Yunus' successful challenge to that assumption, which produced a fundamentally new form of banking, was based wholly on empirical observation. He later reflected that "I began with a small problem in a small village. I was shocked by the harshness of the problem of moneylending, but I was excited by the simplicity of the solution."[130] His ability to find this solution was a product of his rejection of the conceptual approach to economics he had learned in school: instead of beginning with the theoretical assumption that collateral was necessary for lending, he approached banking without preconceptions, by speaking to villagers about their problems, and used the knowledge he gained from them to build up an institution that met their needs. And his experience led him to a new belief in the potential for economic growth in poor countries. He argues that "if you go out into the real world, you cannot miss seeing that the poor are poor not because they are untrained or illiterate but because they cannot retain the returns of their labor." The conclusion follows: "it is the ability to control capital that gives people the power to rise out of poverty." Yunus contends that traditional economic theory fails to recognize this crucial fact because of its erroneous theoretical dichotomy between entrepreneurs and laborers, which "disregards the creativity and ingenuity of each human being and considers widespread self-employment in Third World countries as a symptom of underdevelopment."[131]

In 1974, when he became a witness to an economic catastrophe, Muhammad Yunus decided that it was not enough to *imagine* the world, but that he had to *see* it.[132] His desperate decision to learn about rural poverty directly from those who suffered from it eventually led him to become a banker and entrepreneur, and a major figure in the fight against world poverty. And he did this by becoming an experimental innovator, using his own observations to create powerful new institutional forms that violated the theoretical assumptions of traditional economic theory.

Steve Jobs (1955–2011)

> I understand the appeal of a slow burn, but personally I'm a big-bang guy.
>
> Steve Jobs[133]

Steve Jobs grew up during the 1960s in California's Santa Clara Valley, which would soon become known as Silicon Valley. His early interests were not unusual for those coming of age in that time and place: vegetarianism, Zen Buddhism, recreational drugs, rock music, and electronics. All of these had a lasting impact on his career, and life.

Stubborn and rebellious, Steve devoted little effort to school, and dropped out of college before finishing his freshman year. But a key event occurred earlier, in 1969, when Jobs met Steve Wozniak. Although Wozniak was five years older than the 14-year-old Jobs, the two shared a love of transgressive pranks and electronics, and immediately became friends. They soon began selling Blue Boxes, illegal devices Wozniak engineered that made free long-distance telephone calls. They gave up this business when a customer pulled a gun on them. Wozniak later reflected that it was "probably a bad idea selling them, but it gave us a taste of what we could do with my engineering skills and his vision."[134]

Wozniak was a genius at electronics. In 1975, he developed a computer that became the Apple I: in his words, with it he experienced "the first time in history anyone had typed a character on a keyboard and seen it show up on a screen right in front of them."[135] Wozniak intended to give away his invention for free, but Jobs insisted they sell it, and Wozniak saw the pattern: "Every time I'd design something great, Steve would find a way to make money for us."[136] What the pair sold as Apple I was merely a circuit board with no power supply, monitor, or keyboard, that could only be used as a component by computer hobbyists.[137] But Jobs' success in selling fifty of them to a local computer store convinced Wozniak to produce a new integrated version for a larger market. In 1976, Wozniak made a prototype of his masterpiece, the Apple II, that he described as the "first low-cost computer which, out of the box, you didn't have to be a geek to use."[138] Jobs wanted it to look as elegant as a Cuisinart food processor, and hired a designer to produce a sleek plastic case. The Apple II, which eventually sold nearly six million units, initiated the personal computer industry, and led to the establishment of the Apple Computer Corporation in 1977. The company's success was almost immediate: Jobs would later comment that he was worth more than $1 million at 23, more than $10 million at 24, and over $100 million at 25.[139]

Wozniak did not want to become an executive, and his collaboration with Jobs effectively ended with the incorporation of Apple. Remarkably, by the age of 25, working alone Wozniak had built the first practical home computer, had given it a color display, had written its programming language, and had brought mass memory to general computer users. The journalist Michael Malone marveled: "Hardware, software, display and storage: Woz pulled off an engineering hat trick that has not been matched." And perhaps equally remarkably, the conceptual Wozniak would never again make a major contribution to advanced technology.[140] In contrast, Jobs would become the person most responsible for Apple's rise to the most valuable company in the world in 2011, the year he died.

When illness forced Steve Jobs to retire from Apple, in August 2011, Ken Auletta of *The New Yorker* called him "the twentieth century's Thomas Edison," and concluded that "Like Edison, he's been an inventor and a man who has changed our lives."[141] The characterization of Jobs as an inventor prompted a flurry of protests. But challenges to this description began much earlier, at the very start of Jobs' career. In 1976, when Jobs and Steve Wozniak were first starting a company, Wozniak's father, who was an engineer, vehemently objected to the partnership agreement that gave Jobs and his son equal shares. Jobs' biographer, Walter Isaacson, described a scene that occurred when Jobs visited the Wozniaks' house:

> "You don't deserve shit," [Jerry Wozniak] told Jobs. "You haven't produced anything." Jobs began to cry.... He told Steve Wozniak that he was willing

to call off the partnership. "If we're not fifty–fifty," he said to his friend, "you can have the whole thing."[142]

Steve Wozniak ignored his father's objection and accepted the equal partnership, because he understood the value of their division of labor. He explained that Jobs "was the one who thought we could make money. I was the one who designed the computer . . . and I had written the software, but Steve is the one who had the idea that we could sell the schematics." He added: "Steve was the hustler, the entrepreneur type."[143] The roles of the partners were not concealed. A 1983 profile of Jobs by *Time* magazine declared that it was he, "more than anyone, who kicked open the door and let the personal computer move in." But the same story quoted Wozniak saying that "Steve didn't do one circuit, design or piece of code."[144]

Many observers have offered descriptions of Jobs' career. Geoffrey Moore, a Silicon Valley venture capitalist, called him the "product picker," the "key person in a company who decides which products to develop."[145] Michael Malone considered Jobs "a natural 'finder and minder,' the guy who could identify and land the big products and then seduce, cajole, and threaten his partners (and later subordinates) to not only get the job done but accomplish far greater things than they could imagine."[146] To the writer Michael Moritz, Jobs was an inspired salesman: "Steve, more than any one person, has turned modern electronics into objects of desire."[147] Andrew Pollack of the *New York Times* agreed, calling Jobs "the Andrew Lloyd Webber of product introductions."[148] John Sculley, who was hired by Jobs to be president of Apple, later forced Jobs out of the company, and still later was forced out by Jobs, observed that Jobs "didn't create anything really, but he created everything. . . . Steve lacked the engineering ability to create a product, but he instinctively knew what needed to be created to succeed."[149] Walter Isaacson considered Jobs "the greatest business executive of our era, the one most certain to be remembered a century from now."[150]

Jobs once listed his own skills as "that 'vision thing,' public speaking, motivating teams, and helping to create really amazing products."[151] His greatest pleasure was developing new products: "I enjoy, and I'm best working with, a small team of talented people."[152] He ran Apple as a dictatorship, in which he made not only all major decisions, but also most minor ones, from lunch menus to the color of the signs for restrooms in Apple stores. Larry Ellison of Oracle, an Apple board member, commented that

Jobs "was obsessed by every detail of the aesthetic and the service experience"; Mickey Drexler of J. Crew, another Apple board member, added that Jobs wanted "complete control of the entire experience of his product, from how it was designed and made to how it was sold."[153]

Jobs' approach was highly conceptual. His understanding of creativity did not involve protracted effort or research but rather momentary inspiration: "Creativity is just connecting things. When you ask creative people how they did something, they feel a little guilty, because they didn't really *do* it, they just *saw* something. It seemed obvious to them after a while." Creativity flourished in the absence of expertise: "There's a phrase in Buddhism, 'beginner's mind.' It's wonderful to have a beginner's mind."[154] He had a scientific explanation for why experience was the enemy: "Our minds are sort of electrochemical computers. Your thoughts construct patterns like scaffolding in your mind. You are really etching chemical patterns. In most cases, people get stuck in these patterns, just like grooves in a record, and they never get out of them."[155]

Jobs' enormous early success fostered his confidence in his own intuition. Jeffrey Young and William Simon contended that "Too young and definitely too inexperienced to know what he couldn't achieve, and ruled by the passion of ideas, he had no sense of why something was impossible. This made him willing to try things that wiser people would have said couldn't be done."[156] Mike Murray, an Apple marketing director, agreed: "Steve just doesn't have the limits that the rest of us do. Because of his background and his early success, he doesn't have any boundaries. He doesn't know that anything is impossible because ... he's always been able to do anything he wanted."[157] One consequence was Jobs' disdain for market research in conceiving and selling new products: Murray said "Steve did his market research by looking into the mirror every morning."[158] Jobs maintained that customers couldn't know they wanted revolutionary products: "Our job is to figure out what they're going to want before they do. I think Henry Ford once said, 'If I'd asked customers what they wanted, they would have told me, 'A faster horse!'"[159] He liked to quote the great hockey player Wayne Gretzky: "Skate where the puck's going, not where it's been."[160]

Jobs considered Bob Dylan "one of my all-time heroes."[161] Steve Wozniak first turned him on to Dylan, and one of their earliest joint activities was searching out bootleg tapes of Dylan's concerts, then spending hours interpreting the lyrics: Wozniak explained that "Dylan's words struck chords of creative thinking." Jobs boasted that he had more than one hundred hours of Dylan tapes, including every concert on his 1965 and 1966 tours.[162] Jobs' admiration for Dylan only grew over time: he opened the public unveiling of the Macintosh by quoting a verse of "The Times They Are a-Changin'," and played "Like a Rolling Stone" at the launches of both the iPhone and the iPad.[163] Apple was the first advertiser ever to use a genuine Dylan recording in a commercial.[164] Jobs considered Dylan a role model:

> As I grew up, I learned the lyrics to all his songs and watched him never stand still. If you look at the artists, if they get really good, it always occurs to them at some point that they can do this one thing for the rest of their lives, and they can be really successful to the outside world but not really successful to themselves. That's the moment that an artist really decides who he or she is. If they keep on risking failure, they're still artists. Dylan and Picasso were always risking failure.[165]

When Jobs turned 30, he told an interviewer that he feared getting stuck: "It's rare that you see an artist in his 30s or 40s able to contribute something amazing."[166] His reference above not only to Dylan, but also to Picasso, suggests that he had thought carefully about how to avoid losing his creativity, and recognized that two great conceptual innovators had done this by repeatedly making radical changes in their art. As he turned 30, Jobs reflected that "If you want to live life in a creative way, as an artist, you have to not look back too much. You have to be willing to take whatever you've done and whoever you were and throw them away."[167] Jobs acted on this analysis, for what set him apart most clearly from other great entrepreneurs of his time may be the large number of different markets he affected within a brief span of time—not only computers, but also movies, music, and telephones— and for the ways his products connected functions that had previously been performed only by separate products.

Jobs judged all products—those made by other companies as well as his own—by a consistent set of principles. Above all, these were simplicity, ease of operation, and beauty. And all of these were subsumed under what he called *design*: "In most people's vocabularies, 'design' means veneer. . . . But to me, nothing could be further from the meaning of design. Design is the fundamental soul of a man-made creation."[168] Great design required deep understanding: "To design something really well, you have to get it. You have to really grok what it's all about."[169] Apple's design mantra, stated in its first brochure, was taken from Leonardo da Vinci: "Simplicity is the ultimate sophistication."[170] Apple did not make the first digital music player, or the first tablet computer, but it brought beauty and elegance to these products. And this was a persistent source of Apple's success, for Isaacson noted that "the distinctiveness of its designs—of the iMac, the iPod, the iPhone, and the iPad—would set Apple apart and lead to its triumphs."[171] Tim Cook, who succeeded Jobs as CEO of Apple, noted that a consistent characteristic of the company's products stemmed from Jobs' belief that thin was beautiful: "We have the thinnest notebook, the thinnest smartphone, and we have made the iPad thin and then even thinner."[172] Jobs summarized his overall goal at Apple as "to bring really great design and simple capability to something that doesn't cost much."[173]

Steve Jobs never personally wired a circuit or drew a design for a product. But as an Apple executive—from its creation in 1977 until 1985, then again from 1997 until 2011—he was involved in virtually every decision, small and large, concerning the function, design, and marketing of a series of innovative products. He was responsible for creating Apple as a company, and later for transforming it from making computers to making a range of consumer products. He had a talent for targeting markets that were dominated by inferior products, for hiring excellent engineers and designers, and, through a mixture of charm and intimidation, inspiring them to create excellent products. He had a flair for stirring up excitement around these products, and for convincing a broad public that they needed them. He became a symbol of innovation, who stood out even among the technology titans of Silicon Valley, because he was a conceptual innovator who made not one but a series of bold innovations, that served a wide variety of purposes and spanned markets that were not previously connected. He attributed his success to the fact that "I'm one of the few people who understands how producing technology requires intuition and creativity and how producing something artistic requires real discipline."[174] His longtime rival Bill Gates agreed that Jobs had a rare combination of skills: "I'd see Steve make the decision based on a sense of people and product that, you know, is hard for me to explain. The way he does things is just different and I think it's magical."[175]

Language

Charles Darwin's experimental approach to science was manifested in the very language he used. He wrote to a friend in 1863 that "all that I do is to try to get the subject as clear as I can in my own head, and express it in the commonest language that occurs to me." He conceded, however, that achieving this was laborious: "I generally have to think a good deal before the simplest arrangement and words occur to me."[176] The literary scholar Gillian Beer observed that "Darwin's is not an austere Descartian style"; it was not "an elegantly simple, mathematicized description of the natural world." This reflected Darwin's view of nature: "Elegance was not the most striking property of the world as he conceived it." His language followed his goal of describing concrete sensory reality: "Conversation rather than abstraction is the predominant mode, and the emphasis is on things individually seen, heard, smelt, touched, tasted."[177]

Darwin's most important writing was of course in the *Origin of Species*. In offering the book to a publisher, Darwin wrote: "The book should be popular with a large body of scientific and semi-scientific readers.... Only some small portions are at all abstruse." The biographer Paul Johnson judged that "No scientific innovator has ever taken more trouble to smooth the way for lay readers without descending into vulgarity. What is almost miraculous about the book is Darwin's generosity in sharing his thought process, his lack of condescension."[178]

Darwin realized that his use of vernacular language would result in ambiguity. Beer contended this use of the vernacular was "no mere stylistic quirk but part of his desire that his theory should be equivalent to the evidence of the natural world in all its diversity." She argued that Darwin's prose embodied the concepts of his theory:

> The multivocality of Darwin's language reaches its fullest extent in the first edition of the *Origin*. His language is expressive rather than rigorous. He accepts the variability within words, their tendency to dilate and contract across related senses, or to oscillate between significations. He is interested less in singleness than in mobility. In his use of words he is more preoccupied with relations and transformations than with limits. Thus his language practice and his scientific theory coincide.[179]

The philosopher Jacques Roger agreed that Darwin's prose not only stated, but mirrored his view of nature: "Darwin's way of writing ... [corresponds] to a peculiar view of nature, according to which diversity, polymorphic interrelations, and evolving equilibria are of higher value and significance than clear-cut distinctions, well-defined entities and static one-to-one relationships." Roger contended that it called attention to the means of the theory's construction: "It also witnesses an infant-stage of a theory struggling for existence, that is, trying to pass from the state of a powerful and blurred vision of nature into a consistent and articulate scientific theory." Thus Darwin was displaying the process of transforming empirical observations into generalizations that would pass muster with the logical standards of academic science. Roger noted that Darwin began this, and others continued it, but that in the process much of the complexity of Darwin's original metaphors was lost: "I am not at all sure, for example, that our modern translation in terms of population genetics of the Darwinian phrase 'struggle for existence' really conveys the full meaning of Darwin's consciously and carefully chosen metaphor. What has been lost in that particular case is a sense of reality, a perception of the concrete environmental conditions under which living things, and not genotypes only, have to struggle to survive and reproduce."[180]

Darwin's language grew directly from his observation of nature. A conceptual scholar, concerned with the formulation of precisely abstracted models of reality, would have chosen the precise and unambiguous language of formal science; Darwin preferred ambiguous but evocative language that paralleled the reality of nature. James Secord observed that "Darwin's texts are complicated, rich and ambiguous. They do not give simple doctrines." For Secord, the importance of Darwin's works lies in their uncertainty: "They open up questions and opportunities for debate, discussion and conversation.... They are important because of—not in spite of—seeming contradictions and ambiguities."[181] The form of Darwin's writing thus underscores the fundamentally inductive nature of Darwin's enterprise.

Darwin's language consistently underscored the importance he placed on actual observation. The literary scholar George Levine wrote that

> It is no accident that the very first sentence of the first chapter of *The Origin of Species* begins with the phrase "When we look." In one sense, the whole of the *Origin* is an education in looking, determined by the refusal to take any visible phenomenon for granted, requiring that all things visible be questioned and accounted for, and requiring as well the capacity to observe minutely, detect aberrations, and recognize similarities. Darwin often talks about being "struck" by some object of vision, but he is "struck" because of his uncanny sensitivity to the visual. When he set out on the *Beagle* he did not have a theory on which to base his work, only that remarkable,

probably instinctive capacity to "see," to "look," and to be "struck by" natural phenomena.[182]

Darwin's language contributed to the enormous impact of his work outside scientific circles. Reading the *Origin of Species* less than a month after its publication, the novelist George Eliot wrote to a friend that "it makes an epoch." Yet she believed that the book was too poorly written and too abstract to become popular, complaining that it was "ill written and sadly wanting in illustrative facts."[183] Her first judgment proved more accurate than the second. Nearly three decades later, the novelist Margaret Oliphant observed that Darwin's books had been read "according to a very unusual formula ... like novels." She noted that his books had been "discussed in every drawing-room ... because of the lucidity and interest of the style and the manner of putting these wonderful new doctrines—from their character as literature, in short."[184] Darwin's ideas permeated the culture of the late nineteenth and early twentieth centuries to a remarkable degree. References to Darwin and his doctrines appeared in the novels of—among others—Dickens, Zola, Dostoevsky, Tolstoy, Eliot, Forster, Woolf, Joyce, and Fitzgerald, in the poems of Dickinson, Robert Browning, Hardy, Frost, and Pound, and in the plays of Chekhov and O'Neill.[185] Even Sherlock Holmes quoted Darwin, in *A Study in Scarlet*.[186] Robert Frost admired Darwin for his ability to generalize from careful, detailed observation of nature, and *The Voyage of the Beagle* was one of his favorite books; he considered it one of the best books of prose written in the nineteenth century, and wherever he taught he would ask his students to buy it.[187] The accessibility of Darwin's prose clearly had a great deal to do with this literary acceptance: the Bloomsbury Group writer Lytton Strachey, for example, considered him "one of the great stylists."[188]

The physicist Abraham Pais described Albert Einstein's papers as "translucent"; he commented that "The early Einstein papers are brief, their content is simple, their language sparse."[189] In a 1941 lecture, Einstein specifically asked, "What distinguishes the language of science from language as we ordinarily understand the word?" His answer was the goal of precision: "What science strives for is an utmost acuteness and clarity of concepts as regards their mutual relation and their correspondence to sensory data."[190]

Earlier, Einstein had spoken of how the theoretical physicist's picture of the world differed from those of other disciplines. He stressed the centrality of mathematics: "It demands the highest possible standard of rigorous precision in the description of relations, such as only the use of mathematical language can give." He conceded that this rigor severely limited the physicist's range of subject matter: "he must content himself with describing the most simple events.... Supreme purity, clarity, and certainty at the cost of completeness."[191] On another occasion, Einstein drew an implication of this position in defining physics as the group of natural sciences that based its concepts on measurement: "Its realm is accordingly defined as that part of the sum total of our knowledge which is capable of being expressed in mathematical terms."[192]

Einstein had little interest in what he disdained as "everyday life with its painful crudity and hopeless dreariness"; he preferred to live in a highly conceptual world "of objective perception and thought."[193] Late in his life, he confessed that "every true theorist is a kind of tamed metaphysicist," who believed that "the totality of all sensory experience can be comprehended on the basis of a conceptual system built on premises of great simplicity." And mathematics was the natural language of this conceptual world, for Einstein believed that "nature is the realization of the simplest conceivable mathematical ideas."[194]

Language has been central to the experimental innovation of Muhammad Yunus. Microlending was created to help poor villagers, so its effectiveness depended critically on overcoming their distrust of outsiders and gaining their voluntary participation. Early on, Grameen instituted the rule that borrowers could apply only in groups of five. To secure recognition for the group, all the members had to undergo at least seven days of training in Grameen's policies, then "demonstrate their understanding of those policies in an oral examination administered by a senior bank official."[195] The exam was oral in order to eliminate illiteracy as a barrier to credit. And the language of the examination was that of the villagers rather than the formal rhetoric of legal documents. As Yunus explained, "There are no legal instruments between the lenders and the borrowers. We were convinced that the bank should be built on human trust.... Grameen would succeed or fail depending on the strength of personal relationships."[196] Gaining the trust of villagers could be done only by using their own language. Just as Grameen's practices were built up experimentally from conversations with villagers, the bank could achieve success only by carrying out these practices in the language of those conversations.

Steve Jobs routinely used the melodramatic and hyperbolic language of a salesman or a motivational speaker: Walter Isaacson noted that Jobs' favorite words were "revolutionary" and "incredible."[197] He became notorious for what one of his software designers, Bud Tribble, dubbed his "reality distortion field"—a term Tribble took from a *Star Trek* episode in which aliens created a new world through sheer mental force. Tribble explained that in Jobs' presence, "reality is malleable. He can convince anyone of practically anything."[198] Another Apple engineer, Andy Hertzfeld, observed that "The reality distortion field was a confounding mélange of charismatic rhetorical style, indomitable will, and eagerness to bend any fact to fit the purpose at hand."[199] Yet another engineer, Debi Coleman, unwittingly revealed the devaluation of language within Apple even as she stressed the effectiveness of Jobs' distortions: "You did the impossible, because you didn't realize it was impossible."[200] Bill Atkinson, an Apple programmer, believed that Jobs actually deceived himself: "It allowed him to con people into believing his vision, because he has personally embraced and internalized it."[201] But Jobs' technique went beyond mere suasion to a willingness to fabricate. Isaacson noted that Jobs "would assert something—be it a fact about world history or a recounting of who suggested an idea at a meeting—without even considering the truth," and that he could do this freely because of his conviction that normal rules of behavior didn't apply to him; Andy Hertzfeld confirmed that Jobs "thinks there are a few people who are special—people like Einstein and Gandhi and the gurus he met in India—and he's one of them."[202]

One of Jobs' consistent motivational themes was the enormous importance of the work Apple was doing. Early in his career, he repeatedly told the team developing the Macintosh computer that they were creating an "insanely great" product.[203] In one meeting, he told the members of the group that what they were doing "is going to send a giant ripple through the universe."[204] He also used this theme in recruiting employees. When he first hired Bill Atkinson, Jobs concluded a three-hour pitch by saying, "We are inventing the future.... Come down here and make a dent in the universe."[205] The importance of Apple's mission of course overshadowed that of other companies. Hiring an engineer away from Xerox, Jobs told him, "Everything you've ever done in your life is shit, so why don't you come work for me?"[206] And when Jobs was wooing John Sculley away from his job as president of Pepsi Cola to do the same job at Apple, Jobs famously asked him, "Do you want to spend the rest of your life selling sugared water, or do you want a chance to change the world?"[207] Jobs called his employees "the most talented people on the planet."[208] Even Apple's new headquarters would be "the best office building in the world."[209]

Jobs' hyperbolic rhetoric was not restricted to private statements. When he announced his resignation from Apple in 1984, he told the press that "computers are the most incredible invention that man has ever invented."[210] And when Jobs returned to the company in 1996, Christopher Escher, the company's public relations director, had no trouble drafting Jobs' statement: "Steve likes big, dramatic, advertising-copy kind of shit. Dramatic bullshit about 'returning to the journey.' Self-dramatizing. Self-glorifying."[211]

Jobs' mental world was a simplistic one, in which people and things were placed in binary categories: Walter Isaacson wrote that "People were either 'enlightened' or 'an asshole.' Their work was either 'the best' or 'totally shitty.'" Nor was this merely a matter of verbal expression: "He did not like to wrestle with complexity, or make accommodations. This was true in products, design, and furnishings for the house. It was also true when it came to personal commitments."[212] Jobs' exaggerated and intemperate language thus reflected his conceptual creed, in which he admitted to his private world only the people and things he approved, and banished those he did not.

11
Generality

The scholar Adam Bradley titled his study of a great American novelist *Ralph Ellison in Progress*. In the Introduction, he characterized Ellison as a writer:

> [E]xperimental artists work incrementally, letting their goals evolve over time to fit the shape of their changing conceptions. Ellison was an experimentalist par excellence.... He was a perfectionist driven by high standards of craft and aesthetic purpose. He doggedly pursued a single objective in his fiction. He engaged in seemingly endless repetition over decades, rewriting the same small set of scenes time and again, often with only subtle variations. Paradoxically, he seems both to have reveled in this process and to have grown increasingly frustrated by his inability to publish a second novel.[1]

Ellison published his only novel, *Invisible Man*, in 1952, at the age of 39. It won the National Book Award for fiction, and is now considered one of the most important novels of the twentieth century. Ellison died in 1994, after spending four decades working on a second novel that he never finished, although he left more than two thousand pages of a manuscript. Numerous explanations have been offered for Ellison's inability to complete a second book, but Bradley contends that the answer lay in the unattainability of his aspiration: "Ellison took on the seemingly impossible task of rendering in fiction the American experience in the second half of the twentieth century." In a 1974 interview, Ellison explained that "At its best, fiction allows for a summing up.... [I]t is that aura of summing up, that pause for contemplation of the moral significance of the history we've been through, that I have been reaching for in my work on this new book." In terms reminiscent of Cézanne's quest for his elusive goal of realization, Bradley argues that Ellison's decades-long struggle was occasioned by "the search for a form that could encompass the audacious aim expressed in the 'aura of summing up,' a way of imaginatively projecting a nation on the page."[2]

Bradley's study of Ellison is one example of how recent scholarship has contributed to demonstrating the generality of the analysis of experimental and conceptual creativity. This chapter surveys some of this research, which serves to increase the diversity of the innovators considered by this book—by time, gender, race, nationality, and discipline.

Old Masters

The differences in goals and practices that separate experimental and conceptual innovators are not unique to the modern era. This section illustrates the presence of the distinction much earlier by providing analyses of four great visual artists—three from the Italian Renaissance, and one from Holland's Golden Age.

Leonardo da Vinci (1452–1519)

Leonardo took an experimental approach to all his varied activities, for he believed that "those sciences are vain and full of error which are not born of experience."[3] The scholar Martin Kemp called Leonardo's visual approach to drawing revolutionary: "Never before had any artist worked out his compositions in such a welter of alternate lines.... Such flexibility of preparatory sketching became the norm for later centuries; it was introduced almost single-handedly by Leonardo." Leonardo thus did make preliminary sketches, but they functioned as a point of departure rather than a final image: Kemp observed that "the painting's format never settled in his mind into a fixed pattern which could be systematically realized in a series of orderly steps.... The flow of his thought cascaded onwards in a rough and tumble of ideas, sometimes splashing off in unexpected directions—unexpected, we may suspect, even to Leonardo himself."[4] Leonardo believed that painters should always be prepared to change their paintings in progress, warning other artists: "do not articulate the individual parts of those pictures with determinate outlines ... for it frequently happens that the creature represented fails to move its limbs in accordance with the movements of the mind; and once such a painter has given a beautiful and graceful finish to the articulated limbs he will think it damaging to shift these limbs higher or lower or forward or backward."[5] Pietro Marani, an art historian who studied

Leonardo's *Adoration of the Magi* (1481), observed that although the artist made preparatory studies for the painting, "Absolutely none of the studies is duplicated precisely in the painted version, where everything resembles but also differs from the drawings." Marani considered the final painting "a work in progress, a visible rendering of a continuous accumulation of ideas and refinements."[6]

Leonardo painted his work most frequently illustrated in art history surveys, *The Last Supper*, when he was 46.[7] He tried to make careful plans for the great mural of more than 400 square feet, but technical examination has revealed that he made numerous changes in the composition as he worked on it. Martin Kemp noted that one conspicuous deviation from the plans involved the placement of the figure of Christ, observing that the painting's central point of interest is not located in its center: "The focus of the perspective and the center of the grid are slightly but unquestionably out of conjunction." Kemp suggested that Leonardo moved the figure for visual reasons, one of a number of "intuitive adjustments . . . even if these adjustments were incompatible with the rules of scientific naturalism."[8]

Leonardo began painting his most popular work, the *Mona Lisa*, when he was 41, and may not have completed it until he had passed the age of 60. Kemp attributes the famously enigmatic expression of *Mona Lisa* to Leonardo's unwillingness late in his career to create definite contours, as he devised "the equivalent of a mobile face, in which the physiognomic signs do not constitute a single, fixed, definitive image." He achieved this with a succession of superimposed glazes, creating "a series of tonal transitions which denote changes of contours" without delineating discrete boundaries.[9]

The richness of Leonardo's late work, the ambiguous and elusive quality of his images, and his evident reluctance to finish his paintings are all consistent with the practice of an experimental innovator. Robert Jensen agreed: "Leonardo's invention was an experimental activity, grounded in constant revision and a lively, ever-changing response to the craft of drawing or painting." Jensen observed that one of Leonardo's major contributions to the history of Western art was his "revolutionary discovery of working methods that allowed maximum freedom to the artist to evolve and refine his ideas as he worked."[10]

The development of Leonardo's art reflects the path of his intellectual development in general, as his early belief in mathematical certainty was gradually but inexorably replaced by a belief in the uncertainty of direct observation. The latter in turn stemmed from his growing conviction that all of nature was in a state of continual change.[11] In painting, this led him away from clarity of color and line, and toward the subtle gradations of light and shadow that came to be called *sfumato*. Leonardo wrote that "between light and dark there is infinite variation, because their quantity is continuous."[12] The attempt to represent infinite variation did not lead to definitive endings, and Leonardo once wrote that he regretted that he had never finished a single painting.[13] Alexander Nagel explained that Leonardo's "notorious inability to finish paintings was the consequence of an artistic process that strove to make the work of painting embody the infinitely subtle workings by which nature makes itself manifest to the senses. In other words, his technique embodied the principle of infinity to such an extent as to make it impossible to establish when a painting could be called finished." Nagel called Leonardo the prototype of Balzac's Frenhofer—the fictional master who pursued the experimental impossible dream of creating an image so perfect that the materiality of the painting would disappear, and the subject of the work would come to life.[14]

Leonardo's novel approach to the convincing portrayal of depth had a profound impact on Western art. Kenneth Clark observed that "In his use of light and shade, Leonardo was the precursor of all subsequent European painting." His exploration of the effects of light equally made him a forerunner of later experimental painters, as Clark wrote that "Leonardo anticipated the impressionistic doctrine that everything is more or less reflected in everything else."[15]

Michelangelo Buonarroti (1475–1564)

In 1508, Pope Julius II summoned 33-year-old Michelangelo to Rome to decorate the vast ceiling of the Vatican's Sistine Chapel. Michelangelo resisted, pleading that painting was not his art, but the pope insisted, and during the next four years Michelangelo produced the fresco that many consider the single greatest work in the history of Western art.[16]

Michelangelo soon discarded his initial intention as "a poor thing," and expanded the project into a complex work that portrayed the Hebrew prophets and pagan sibyls who foresaw the coming of a Messiah, and nine scenes from Genesis, making it, in the words of the scholar Howard Hibbard, "the most grandiose pictorial ensemble in all of Western art."[17] Michelangelo made preparatory drawings for individual figures and groups, but made no plans for the work as a whole; Robert Jensen described the ceiling as "a brilliantly improvisational ensemble rather than the realization of a carefully preconceived program."[18] Michelangelo's style as a painter was still developing during the years he worked on the ceiling, and the absence of any overall plan resulted in significant differences between early and late portions, as Hibbard observed that the "scenes over the altar area of the Chapel, which Michelangelo painted last, are more powerful, majestic, and awesome than the early scenes and figures near the entrance."[19]

Michelangelo considered himself a sculptor, but a perennial puzzle concerns why so many of his sculptures were never finished.[20] It has been estimated that nearly three-fifths of all his sculptures remain unfinished, and that more than a third were abandoned—never delivered to their intended projects or patrons. In the last thirty years of his life, he completed only three sculptures.[21] His friend and admirer Giorgio Vasari explained that "he was never content with anything he did," and that over time he grew ever more exacting, so that "there are few finished statues to be seen of all that he made in the prime of his manhood, and . . . those he did finish completely were executed when he was young."[22]

Vasari recounted that "Michelangelo used to say that if he had had to be satisfied with what he did, then he would have sent out very few statues, or rather none at all. This was because he had so developed his art and judgment that when on revealing one of his figures he saw the slightest error he would abandon it and run to start working on another block."[23] But dissatisfaction did not always cause Michelangelo to abandon a sculpture. William Wallace observed that he changed his sculptures as he worked—"made adjustments, altered the disposition of limbs, and constantly refined his conceptions as he carved." Vasari wrote that Michelangelo actually anticipated the need to make changes, as he taught sculptors "how to carve figures . . . so that they may always be carefully improved by carving away some of the marble while leaving enough for redesigning or altering the piece as is sometimes necessary."[24]

Wallace described Michelangelo's approach to sculpture as provisional: "His was a visual and manual intelligence in which the creative process involved discovery, revision, and continuous evolution." Wallace stated that his understanding of Michelangelo's process was "consistent with the recent hypothesis . . . that the artist exhibits an 'experimentalist approach to art' which is characterized by constant revision and a 'lack of clear vision of the final form of the image—which is only discovered in the working process.'" Wallace concluded that for Michelangelo, "Mastery was hard earned and never easy, less a theory than the product of experience and a lifetime dedicated to manual work."[25] Michelangelo may have regarded his own career in just this way, for he wrote in a poem that "No one has mastery until he is at the end of his art and his life."[26]

Michelangelo made one of his most celebrated contributions at the very end of his long life. In 1547, Pope Paul III appointed him the supreme architect of the new St. Peter's Basilica. The foundation stone had been laid in 1506, but construction had stagnated for what was intended to be the grandest building in Christendom. Michelangelo resisted the appointment, protesting that architecture was not his profession, but he ultimately yielded, and at the age of 72 took the job of creating the centerpiece of Vatican City. He remained in this position for seventeen years, until his death in 1564, even though this meant he could never realize his wish to return to his beloved Florence. Michelangelo immersed himself in all aspects of the building's design and construction, and although the basilica would not be completed until 1626, he achieved his goal of working "until I had brought the fabric of St. Peter's to a stage at which my design could not be spoilt or altered." He fixed the building's plan, space, and proportions, so that Vasari could declare that Michelangelo "established the form of the building." William Wallace observed that Michelangelo devoted more time to this than any other project of his career, and that "in just seventeen years he corrected what had gone before and largely shaped what came afterward." His innovative design for St. Peter's great dome has made it a prominent feature of Rome's skyline even to the present, and inspired later monuments including Christopher Wren's design for St. Paul's Cathedral in London.[27]

Raffaelo Santi (1483–1520)

Robert Jensen called Raphael "an early paradigmatic example of the young genius and conceptual artist."[28] Both his process and products came to represent order and rationality in art. The scholar Francis Ames-Lewis explained that Raphael did not originate the use of drawing to explore and invent pictorial ideas, but he raised it to a higher level: "from the very start of Raphael's career he seems to have brought the activity of drawing to bear on the pictorial problems at hand in a much more concentrated way than had any earlier painter. Raphael seems to have perceived more clearly than earlier artists the benefit to a final design of a logical and increasingly elaborate preparatory drawing procedure." He worked purposefully, so "throughout the preparatory process he kept fully in mind the character and purpose of the final work."[29] An interesting consequence of Raphael's skillful planning of his work led to a contrast between his practice and those of both Leonardo and Michelangelo, for not only did he rarely leave works unfinished during his lifetime, but his meticulous preparatory studies enabled assistants to finish the paintings Raphael left incomplete upon his premature death.[30]

In 1774, the painter Sir Joshua Reynolds wrote of Raphael that "It is from his having taken so many models that he himself became a model for all succeeding painters; always imitating and always original."[31] Two centuries later, John Pope-Hennessy agreed that imitation of earlier artists was central to Raphael's style: for him, "painting was not confined to the rendering of what his mind conceived or what lay before his eyes, but involved as well the imbibing of a whole series of precedents, in the work of his contemporaries as well as in antiquity."[32] Ames-Lewis marveled that Raphael's "receptivity was astonishing: the speed with which he took up a design procedure pioneered by Leonardo da Vinci, or a novel technique for representing form learned from Michelangelo's drawings... is an indicator of the fertile vigor of his responsiveness to the challenge of new artistic problems."[33] Raphael's practice of synthesizing devices taken from other artists is characteristic of conceptual innovators, but it sometimes caused resentment. So for example the experimental Michelangelo considered Raphael a plagiarist, writing in 1542 that "what he knew of art he learned from me."[34] But it also made Raphael a key figure in the Renaissance exploitation of classical art. Pope-Hennessy contended that "the greatest single influence on Raphael's imaginative process was the antique," and observed that "it was Raphael who first worked out a means whereby the antique could be assimilated, integrally and without distortion, into the fabric of the art of his own day."[35]

Raphael completed his work most often illustrated in art history surveys, *The School of Athens* in the Vatican's Stanza della Segnatura, when he was 28. This enormous fresco portrayed Plato and Aristotle surrounded by fifty other ancient Greek philosophers and scientists. To deal with the challenge of organizing so many figures, Raphael made a great full-scale cartoon that included fifty-one of the fifty-two figures in the final work.[36] Ames-Lewis judged that it was his imaginative solution to the problem of composition posed by this complex work that "set Raphael head and shoulders above his contemporaries in this field."[37] Sydney Freedberg agreed, noting that in *The School of Athens* Raphael benefited from having seen Michelangelo's treatment of figures in the Sistine Chapel, but then surpassed Michelangelo in the arrangement of his figures: "Where Michelangelo almost always sees his figures singly, as if they might be forms of sculpture isolated in a neutral space, Raphael conceives figures in relationships, of form and of communication, which take place in an including unity of space."[38]

The economist Federico Etro noted that the brilliant young Raphael "quickly became one of the highest-paid painters of the Renaissance," and the great demand for his work prompted him to devise an innovative means of increasing his output.[39] Pope-Hennessy remarked that after 1515 "Raphael over a large part of his work became an ideator instead of an executant," as he created preparatory works that would then be painted by assistants.[40] Raphael's was not the first workshop, but it was the largest that had ever been assembled, as Vasari reported that Raphael "was never seen at court without some fifty painters."[41] Raphael devised a novel system of organization in which trained section leaders each supervised a separate group of assistants. The large size and efficient operation of his studio allowed Raphael not only to undertake more painting commissions, but also to expand "into a very broad area of production, including architecture, printmaking, and archeological recuperation and publication. All of these creative efforts were generated from the master artist's ideas... and were produced by the ability of carefully chosen collaborators and assistants to pool their own skills in the service of Raphael's goals."[42] The diversity of the activities he supervised effectively made Raphael a forerunner of such modern entrepreneurial conceptual innovators as Andy Warhol and Damien Hirst.[43]

Rembrandt van Rijn (1606–1669)

The poet Paul Valéry reflected that in his late works Rembrandt had risen "to the sublime level, to the point where art itself grows imperceptible," while the art historian Seymour Slive declared that in the late work he had "opened a new field in the history of painting... the world which lies behind visible appearances."[44] Many scholars have studied Rembrandt's techniques, in an attempt to understand how he achieved effects that seem to transcend the limits of his art.

Rembrandt was a prolific draftsman, but few of his hundreds of surviving drawings were made in preparation for paintings. Svetlana Alpers concluded that his "habit was not to work out his inventions in advance through drawings, but rather to invent paintings in the course of their execution."[45] Ernst van de Wetering agreed, observing that "perhaps more than those of any other seventeenth-century painter, Rembrandt's paintings have to be understood as a process."[46]

X-rays of Rembrandt's paintings show that he often made changes in the composition of his works in progress, and that the frequency of these increased over the course of his career.[47] Seymour Slive considered *Sampling Officials of the Amsterdam Drapers' Guild* of 1662 to have been Rembrandt's greatest group portrait for its "ideal solution of the principal problem of painting a portrait group." Slive noted that x-rays of the painting reveal that "Rembrandt struggled to attain the impression of equilibrium." Thus he shifted all the painting's figures while he worked, most frequently the servant: "He tried placing him in two different positions on the extreme right, he also posed him between the two officials on the right, and finally gave him his place, after taking some liberties with the laws of perspective, above the two seated officials in the center of the group."[48] Rembrandt's process of revision could be lengthy, and he sometimes kept unfinished commissions in his studio for years before completing them: Alpers noted that his "characteristic working and reworking of the paint meant that ... the achievement of completion [was] impossible to judge."[49]

An inventory of Rembrandt's possessions included books of prints made after the paintings of Michelangelo, Raphael, Titian, and others. Yet he rarely based paintings on canonical images: Alpers wrote that "it was the model in the studio, not the art of the past, that Rembrandt wanted before his eyes." And one of the models he studied was himself. Rembrandt was the first artist to paint himself more than a few times: his self-portraits numbered fifty paintings, twenty etchings, and ten drawings, made over a period of forty years.[50] These are among his most celebrated works: Slive considered that "the late self-portraits are on the level of the greatest achievements of self-characterization in literature. They rank with the *Confessions* of Augustine and Jean-Jacques Rousseau's *Confessions*."[51]

More than fifty younger artists are known to have worked in Rembrandt's studio at various times. Yet scholars have puzzled over the fact that Rembrandt did not collaborate with assistants but that, in Alpers' words, "Rembrandt's idiosyncrasy was that he ... treated the painting of a picture as a definitively individual enterprise."[52] Interestingly, however, during the 1970s and 1980s the Rembrandt Research Project concluded that a large number of paintings previously believed to be from Rembrandt's hand were in fact made by others in his studio.[53] This suggests that Rembrandt's practice may not have been idiosyncratic, but rather a consequence of his experimental approach. Assistants to such conceptual painters as Raphael and Rubens routinely executed paintings from preparatory drawings supplied by their masters. But lacking preparatory drawings, Rembrandt's pupils could not make paintings planned by the master, so they instead made paintings that resembled his. And the same explanation would apply to the practice of two other experimental masters, Leonardo and Michelangelo, whom Alpers also identified as unable to work with assistants.[54]

Seymour Slive reflected that "During the last years no basic change occurs in Rembrandt's style. His expressive power, however, grows until the very end.... Very few artists—one thinks of Michelangelo, Titian, Goya—offer the same spectacle of an ever-increasing power of expression which culminated at the end of their lives."[55] A central element was Rembrandt's evolution from the smooth surfaces of his early paintings to the rough style of his late years, with uneven surfaces and coarse brushstrokes. The raised areas of paint work together with the dramatic chiaroscuro lighting of the late paintings to intensify the visual force of the focal points of these works. His paradoxical ability to display the materiality of the paint while simultaneously achieving a heightened realism has made Rembrandt an inspiration for experimental painters even into the modern era, as for example the British painter Francis Bacon marveled at the power of a late self-portrait in which "the mystery of fact is conveyed by an image being made out of non-rational marks."[56] In awe of Rembrandt's achievement, van de Wetering contended that it was the product of "skill [that] can only be built up through endless practice from an early age on."[57]

Women Artists

Cindy Sherman is the first female visual artist whose critical status in the art world has surpassed that of her male peers during her lifetime.[58] But she was preceded by other important women artists. This section analyzes the creative life cycles of three of these.

Georgia O'Keeffe (1887–1986)

When Georgia O'Keeffe was asked to write a description of one of her paintings, she protested that "It is easier for me to paint it than write about it and I would so much rather people would look at it than read about it. I see no reason for painting anything that can be put into any other form as well." But the brief account she then provided constituted a succinct experimental credo: "Color is one of the great things in the world that makes life worth living to me and as I have come to think of painting it is my effort to create an equivalent with paint color for the world—life as I see it."[59]

A friend, the painter Marsden Hartley, wrote that O'Keeffe "is satisfied that appearance tells everything and that the eye is a better vehicle of truth for picture purposes than the mind can ever be."[60] O'Keeffe painted without preliminary sketches: a 1929 *New Yorker* profile reported that "she does no under-painting on her canvases; she rarely even blocks out her design in advance."[61] She often painted in series, and explained that "I have a single-track mind. I work on an idea for a long time. It's like getting acquainted with a person, and I don't get acquainted easily." Some of the series were extended. In one case, between 1946 and 1960 she made more than twenty paintings of the door of her adobe house near Santa Fe. She told a friend that she had bought the house because of that door: "I'm always trying to paint that door—I never quite get it. It's a curse—the way I feel I must continually go on with that door." She couldn't explain why the door interested her: "I wish I knew. It fascinates me."[62] Even her abstract paintings grew out of observation: "Sometimes I start in very realistic fashion, and as I go from one painting to another of the same thing, it becomes simplified till it can be nothing but abstract."[63]

O'Keeffe believed that art required persistence. When she was 41, she told an interviewer that "The notion that you can make an artist overnight, that there is nothing but genius and a dash of temperament in artistic success is a fallacy. Great artists don't just happen, any more than writers, or singers, or other creators. They have to be trained, and in the hard school of experience."[64] When O'Keeffe was 73, the curator Daniel Catton Rich observed that her art had developed gradually: "Her work shows a complete organic growth. There have been no sudden reversals, no abrupt shifts in style."[65]

The single year from which O'Keeffe's paintings are most often illustrated in published surveys of art history is 1926, when she was 39.[66] O'Keeffe had moved to New York in 1918, but it was not until 1926 that she began to paint the city, with images of skyscrapers dramatically illuminated by rays of sunlight or neon signs. At the same time, she continued a series of large paintings of individual flowers. These were influenced by the hectic pace of life in the city, as O'Keeffe recalled that "I said to myself—I'll paint what I see—what the flower is to me but I'll paint it big and they will be surprised into taking time to look at it—I will make even busy New Yorkers take time to see the flowers."[67]

Frida Kahlo (1907–1954)

Frida Kahlo's art was dominated by images of herself. More than a third of all her paintings, and all of her most celebrated works, were self-portraits.[68] She used her own image to explore not only her life, but a wide range of religious and political issues. To do this, she created a complex symbolic language that drew on the history of European art, Mexican folklore, Aztec culture, and Eastern spirituality.

When the poet and founder of Surrealism, André Breton, visited Mexico and saw Kahlo's art in 1938, he declared that she belonged to that movement, even though she had been unaware of it.[69] Kahlo welcomed the attention, but she never fully accepted the identification. The biographer Hayden Herrera contended that her contact with Surrealism reinforced Kahlo's inclination toward fantasy and made her paintings more complex, and she painted her single most celebrated work, *The Two Fridas*, at the age of 32, within a year after meeting Breton.[70] Yet Kahlo's distinctive contribution was to make Surrealism personal. Unlike the European Surrealists, who sought to create visual metaphors for the experience of dreams and the subconscious, Kahlo's art expressed her own thoughts and emotions. In 1953, she emphasized the difference: "They thought I was a Surrealist, but I wasn't. I never painted dreams. I painted my own reality."[71]

Kahlo became a model for many later women artists, including Kiki Smith, Ana Mendieta, and Tracey Emin, who wanted to use their art to express their feelings about their own lives and societies. So for example a Kahlo self-portrait that showed her growing from the earth like a plant was a direct inspiration for the earth/body sculptures Mendieta made during the 1970s.[72] Kahlo created a personal conceptual art that synthesized a number of elements that became central to advanced art: the critic Peter Wollen noted that "Whether we look at Kahlo from the vantage-point of women's art, Third World art or surrealism; whether we are interested in the appropriation of vernacular forms or the crossover between outsider and fine art, we will find Kahlo's paintings staring us right in the face."[73]

Louise Bourgeois (1911–2010)

Louise Bourgeois described herself as a long-distance runner: "It takes me years and years and years to produce what I do."[74] She spent her career working experimentally to create a visual art that would explore the unconscious. This did not arrive in the form of a preconceived vision, but as a result of exploration, as in 1954 she remarked that "The finished work is often a stranger to, and sometimes very much at odds with what the artist felt or wished to express when he began." Fifteen years later she declared that "for a lifetime I have wanted to say the same thing. Inner consistency is the test of the artist." Yet another twenty years later, she was still not satisfied: "That's why I keep going. The resolution never appears; it's like a mirage." In 1993, the 82-year-old sculptor explained that having her work exhibited at the prestigious Venice Biennale was not what was important to her: "The progression in the work is important. The self-knowledge that I get ... the self-knowledge is its own reward." She believed in the value of experience: "You know, artists improve.... Otherwise, what's the use of working?"[75]

As a late bloomer, Bourgeois is extraordinary even among great experimental artists, for the five-year period in her career most heavily represented in art history surveys did not begin until the age of 80.[76] In 1988, she continued to insist that art should not be made primarily from the art of the past, as in the practice of prominent younger conceptual artists, but should grow out of perception and experience: "Art is not about art. Art is about life, and that sums it up." The greatest art came with age, for with time "you become better in every way, morally, intellectually.... You become better, which is really the Chinese philosophy—the wisdom of the elders."[77]

Jazz Musicians

The saxophonist Sam Newsome pointed out a contrast between conceptual and experimental musicians:

> Many conceptual thinkers write for a large array of instrumentations and have a vast group of players to call on to help them realize their musical visions. This makes it easier to form numerous groups. Experimental thinkers tend to have a core group of players for whom they write and with whom they play. Think about the seventy recordings John Coltrane made.

He probably didn't use more than thirty core musicians—typical of experimental thinkers.

Newsome cited Louis Armstrong, Art Tatum, Charlie Parker, Ornette Coleman, and Anthony Braxton as natural geniuses who seemed to arrive fully formed. Parker, for example, had fully developed the radical new language of bebop by the time he was in his early 20s: "It took him countless hours of practicing and playing to really bring it to fruition, but the initial idea was a true epiphany." And although Parker cited Lester Young as an influence, Newsome notes that in recordings at age 20 "he already sounds like the Charlie Parker we know and love," and that his approach to the saxophone did not develop significantly thereafter. Parker's dramatic career also illustrates Newsome's observation that "conceptual innovators typically receive most of the ink in jazz history books." Newsome explained: "Sorry, but conceptual thinkers, quite frankly, are just more interesting subjects to interview and read about. They're more likely to discuss new ideas and offer fresh perspectives."[78]

Miles Davis (1926–1991)

In 1945, not yet 20 years old, Miles Davis dropped out of Juilliard, joined Charlie Parker's quintet, and played with Parker, Dizzy Gillespie, and Max Roach on a recording session that became a landmark of bebop jazz.[79] Davis' career as a sideman was brief. In 1947 he formed the first of a long series of Davis-led groups that would change the history of jazz. Or perhaps more accurately, would become the history of jazz: the biographer Ian Carr contended that Davis' influence was so great "that an account of his career from 1945 to 1975 amounts to a history of the main events which have taken place in jazz during that period."[80]

Duke Ellington called Davis the Picasso of jazz, and John Szwed explained why the epithet resonated: "in terms of these two men's frequent changes of style, the volume, range, and impact of their artistic output, their involvement with numerous women, it was a fair comparison."[81] Sam Newsome agreed:

Conceptual innovators... "often consider they have accomplished exactly what they wanted to do, and can, therefore, go on to work on a very different problem"—a perfect description of Miles Davis.... Unlike experimental innovators who work on the same idea for years, Davis was in and out of different styles once he felt he had made his point.... Within twenty-five years, he was at the forefront of five different movements in jazz. He had multiple musical epiphanies and quickly brought his concepts to fruition.[82]

Davis was often asked to play music from his past, and his standard response was, "Why do you want me to do that again? Didn't I do it good the first time?"[83] In his autobiography, he reflected that from early in his childhood he had always been excited by the prospect of going forward into the unknown, and that he considered this his personal philosophy. His celebrated stylistic transformations were a consequence: "If anybody wants to keep creating they have to be about change." He always wanted to stay on what he called the cutting edge: "to be and stay a great musician you've got to always be open to what's new." Radical change required fresh viewpoints: "The way to stay young is to forget, to have a bad memory." And he understood that conceptual innovators were sprinters, not marathoners: "Me, I'm basically a quarter horse."[84]

In 1959, at 33, Davis recorded *Kind of Blue* with his sextet, that included John Coltrane and the pianist Bill Evans. This is widely regarded as a high point not only of Davis' career, but of jazz in general. So for example the critic Stephen Erlewine wrote that *Kind of Blue* is "generally considered as the definitive jazz album. To be reductive, it's the *Citizen Kane* of jazz—an accepted work of greatness that's innovative and entertaining"—qualities that have made it the best-selling jazz album in history.[85]

John Coltrane (1926–1967)

The earliest known recordings of John Coltrane are a set of privately pressed 78s of an informal jam session in 1946, when he was in the Navy. The scholar Lewis Porter observed that these recordings of the 20-year-old saxophonist "reshape our view of his development. He was not, as one might have thought, a great talent who took a long time to get recognized. He was, rather, someone who did not begin with obvious exceptional talent, and that makes his case all the more interesting—one can become one of the great musicians of all time and not start off as some kind of prodigy."[86]

The musicologist Carl Woideck called Coltrane

one of relatively few musicians in jazz history who embraced the ideal of continuous artistic evolution. The search was an integral part of his musical journey ... Coltrane seemed to celebrate musical style as a process, not as an arrival point. If the ideal of steady change was one of the positive hallmarks of his style, it was also a potential liability. Coltrane could be obsessive in his need for change and in his perpetual dissatisfaction with what he had found in his search.[87]

One product of Coltrane's need to experiment was his long solos. The drummer Jimmy Cobb recalled that in 1960, when he and Coltrane were in Miles Davis' quintet, "Miles had to make him stop, because he would play an hour solo himself, and we were only supposed to be on the stand for forty minutes.... On one occasion when Coltrane said he didn't know how to stop, Miles said: 'Try taking the saxophone out of your mouth!'"[88] Coltrane needed to play variations of a tune over and over in a process that had no fixed goal or end: "I don't know what I'm looking for. Something that hasn't been played before.... I'll just keep searching." He played instinctively: "I just have to feel it. If I don't, then I keep trying."[89] He wanted to lose his way, "because what would interest me greatly is to discover paths that I'm perhaps not aware of."[90]

Coltrane was an archetypal experimental innovator in his perennial uncertainty and dissatisfaction. In 1965, *A Love Supreme* was named album of the year by *DownBeat* magazine, Coltrane was voted best tenor saxophonist and Jazzman of the Year, and he was elected to the magazine's Hall of Fame. No artist had ever received so many awards from *DownBeat* in one year. But Coltrane was not reassured, telling an interviewer, "I don't know if you can ever be a complete musician. I'm not. But I don't think I'll know what's missing from my playing until I find it."[91] Sam Newsome commented that Coltrane continued to produce innovative and exploratory music until the end of his life; *A Love Supreme*, generally considered his masterpiece, was released just two years before his premature death.[92]

Entrepreneurs

Experimental entrepreneurship is often overlooked: experimentalists are less flamboyant than their conceptual peers, and the gradual development of their innovations makes their stories less dramatic than the sudden discoveries of conceptual innovators. But many important entrepreneurs have gained greater knowledge and judgment over long periods, and have arrived at their greatest achievements later in their lives. Three prominent entrepreneurs illustrate this pattern.

Sam Walton (1918–1992)

When he left the Army in 1945, Sam Walton planned to open a department store in St. Louis. But his wife objected: she had grown up in a small town, and refused to live in a big city. Helen Walton's ultimatum would have a profound effect on American retailing.[93]

Walton's plan B was to buy a franchise from a variety store chain, for a shop in Newport, Arkansas (population 7,000). He had a lot to learn about running a store, but he was a hard worker. And he soon began experimenting: "that's just the way I am and always have been." He discovered that he could save money by buying directly from manufacturers, and increase his profits by charging lower prices. He also enjoyed promotions: he put a popcorn machine on the sidewalk, and soon thereafter borrowed "the astronomical sum of $1,800" to put an ice cream machine next to it. He was relieved when the experiment was a success: "I really didn't want to be remembered as the guy who lost his shirt on some crazy ice cream machine."[94]

The Newport store did well, but Walton was never satisfied: "I could never leave well enough alone, and I think my constant fiddling and meddling with the status quo may have been one of my biggest contributions to the later success of Wal-Mart." The store did so well that his landlord took it over after five years, exploiting the novice businessman's failure to include a clause in the lease allowing him to renew. Walton considered this the low point of his business life: he had built the best variety store in the region, and was being kicked out of town. He and his wife hated to leave Newport, but they began looking for a new town.[95]

Walton found a store in Bentonville, Arkansas (population 3,000), that even Helen considered a "sad-looking country town." When Walton opened in Bentonville in 1950, his was only the third self-service variety store in the country—a new concept he had read about and had gone to see at two stores in Minnesota—with checkout registers only at the front, another innovation that he would continue throughout his career.[96] Walton later remembered those days "mostly as a time of always looking around for ideas and items that would make our stores stand out." The plural was a result of the profitability of Bentonville, prompting Walton to open more stores. As he expanded, however, he became aware that the volume of his stores was too small to make large profits. He wanted to combine discounting with larger stores, but couldn't find a wholesaler willing to back him. So he decided to go ahead on his own.[97]

In 1962, Walton opened Wal-Mart No. 1 in Rogers, Arkansas—at 18,000 square feet, more than triple Newport's 5,000. The early Wal-Mart stores were unattractive—David Glass, later the CEO of Wal-Mart, called the third store in Harrison, Arkansas, "the worst retail store I had ever seen"—but prices were 20 percent below the competition: "We were trying to find out if customers in a town of 6,000 people would come to our kind of barn and buy the same merchandise strictly because of price. The answer was yes." More, and larger, Wal-Marts followed, initially all in small towns: "the first big lesson we learned that there was much, much more business out there in small-town America than anybody, including me, had ever dreamed of."[98] Wal-Mart would eventually become the largest retail company in the world.

Sam Walton acknowledged that the early Wal-Mart stores were "really poorly done" in many respects, but he never stopped experimenting to improve them. He was always willing to make changes: his son Jim laughed at writers who portrayed Sam as "a grand strategist who intuitively developed complex plans and implemented them with precision. Dad thrived on change, and no decision was ever sacred." Walton himself stressed that Wal-Mart was built on experience:

> Somehow over the years, folks have gotten the impression that Wal-Mart was something I dreamed up out of the blue as a middle-aged man, and that it was just this great idea that turned into an overnight success. It's true that I was forty-four when we opened our first Wal-Mart in 1962, but the store was totally an outgrowth of everything we'd been doing since Newport—another case of me being unable to leave well enough alone, another experiment. And like most other overnight successes, it was about twenty years in the making.[99]

Warren Buffett (1930–)

As a boy in Omaha, Warren Buffett loved numbers. He also loved systems and rules. And he loved making money.[100] Loving numbers, rules, and money, it is not surprising that when Warren discovered the work of the famous investor Benjamin Graham he had found his idol. Graham had developed the first systematic approach to investing. His practice was to buy the stock of companies that had assets considerably greater than their liabilities, calculated from publicly available information.[101] Buffett was a star student in Graham's course at Columbia Business School, and worked at Graham's investment firm during 1954–1956, leaving only when Graham retired. Buffett would subsequently run his own investment firm, and his career would witness the evolution of his investment philosophy away from the strict mathematical rules of Graham.

Buffett's evolution was closely connected to his friendship with Charlie Munger, whom he met in 1959. Munger disagreed with Graham's narrow concentration on statistical bargains, and instead believed in investing in "wonderful businesses"—companies that would be consistently profitable because of such qualitative factors as managerial excellence or brand loyalty. Buffett underwent what he called "this Charlie Munger–influenced type transition," which he compared to the Protestant Reformation: "I would listen to Martin Luther one day and the Pope the next. Ben Graham, of course, being the Pope."[102]

Gradually, Buffett developed a distinctive philosophy, that he called "a less compulsive approach to superior investment results than when I was younger." Above all, "we look for first-class businesses accompanied by first-class management." Buffett would invest only in technologies and products he could understand, and in companies whose managers he liked and admired.[103]

An example of Buffett's mature philosophy was a large investment in Coca-Cola in the 1980s. The true value of the company lay not in its modest physical capital, but in the intangible asset that Buffett described as "the accumulated memory of all those ballgames and good experiences as children which Coke was a part of." A biographer contended that for Buffett, "Valuing companies such as Coca-Cola took wisdom forged by years of experience." In his annual letter to Berkshire Hathaway shareholders in 1983, Buffett wrote facetiously that "It must be noted that your Chairman, always a quick study, required only 20 years to recognize how important it was to buy good businesses."[104]

Early in his career, Warren Buffett enthusiastically embraced Benjamin Graham's systematic approach to investing, based on mathematical calculation. Over time, however, he developed a more flexible approach that used calculation as an element, but added other factors not subject to precise measurement: he observed that "the really sensational ideas I have had over the years have been heavily weighted toward the qualitative side."[105] Buffett's status as the Oracle of Omaha stemmed from his ability to develop the wisdom and judgment that transformed him from a good conceptual investor into an exceptional experimental one.

James Dyson (1947–)

Early in his career, James Dyson worked for an inventor and entrepreneur named Jeremy Fry. He was struck by the simplicity of Fry's approach: "he did not, when an idea came to him, sit down and process it through pages of calculations, he didn't argue it through with anyone; he just went out and built it." For Dyson, Fry's approach was "mind-blowing.... No research, no 'workings,' no preliminary sketches. If it didn't work one way, he would just try it another way, until it did." Dyson understood the key to Fry's method: "The trick is to recognize when you have gone wrong and correct the damage."[106]

Dyson's most celebrated innovation originated in 1978, when he became frustrated with his Hoover vacuum. When he took it apart, he discovered that its suction was greatly reduced because the bag that collected the dirt quickly became clogged. In pondering how to eliminate the bag, he thought of a 30-foot-high cone he had seen at a sawmill, that used centrifugal force to pull wood shavings from the air. Reasoning that this should work in miniature, he made a prototype with cardboard, and soon he was "the only man in the world with a bagless vacuum."[107]

Lacking a theoretical solution, Dyson followed the empirical approach he had learned from Fry: "test, and test, and test until it works best." Dyson claims eventually to have made 5,127 prototypes: "Slow, slow, slow. These things cannot be hurried." And finally success: "On 2 May 1992, I found myself looking at the first, fully operational, visually perfect, Dyson Dual Cyclone." Dyson was 31 years old when he tore the bag off his Hoover; May 2, 1992, was his forty-fifth birthday.[108]

Dyson contends that the greatest barrier to innovation is impatience: "We always want to create something new out of nothing, and without research, and without long hours of effort. But there is no such thing as a quantum leap." Entrepreneurs should have a thorough knowledge of their product: "If you have the intimate knowledge of a product that comes with dreaming it up and then designing it ... you will be better able to sell it and then, reciprocally, to go back and improve it."[109] In his memoir, Dyson reflected on his career: "To use a Hollywood cliché, it is said that to be an overnight success takes years of effort. So it has proved with me." His advice to entrepreneurs is simple: "Patience, patience, patience."[110]

Scientists

The physicists Dashun Wang and Albert-László Barabási have done extensive quantitative research on the careers of scientists. One of their conclusions is that scientists can be divided into conceptual and experimental innovators. Their example of the former is Werner Heisenberg, a founder of quantum mechanics, who made his greatest discovery at 24:

> Heisenberg earned his PhD in Munich with Arnold Sommerfeld in 1923 and moved on to work with Max Born in Gottingen, where he developed matrix mechanics in 1925. The following year he became Niels Bohr's assistant in Copenhagen, where, at the age of 25, he proposed the uncertainty principle. In the past century, historians have repeatedly documented his "extraordinary abilities: complete command of the mathematical apparatus and daring physical insight"—to borrow from Sommerfeld, his PhD advisor.[111]

Wang and Barabási note that "Conceptual innovators tend to do their most important work earlier in their careers than their experimental colleagues," both because "conceptual innovators like Heisenberg do not need to accumulate large amounts of experience in order to make their contributions," and because "some of the most important conceptual work involves radical departures from existing paradigms, and it may be easier to disrupt a paradigm shortly after initial exposure to it, before an individual has produced a large body of work that rests upon the prevailing wisdom."[112] Their example of an experimental scientist is Charles Darwin, whose career was considered earlier in this book.

Wang and Barabási report a quantitative analysis of the career histories of 2,856 physicists. The most important publication of each was identified, measured by total citations. Distributing these greatest hits by the age at which they were published revealed that most physicists published their best paper within twenty years after the date of their first publication, suggesting that "once scientists pass their mid-career, the possibility of creating breakthrough work becomes depressingly unlikely."[113]

But the story proved to be more complicated, for Wang and Barabási also found that the shape of the distribution described above was the same as that of the distribution obtained by randomizing the order in which each scientist's papers were published. This implies that across all the scientists in the study, maximum creativity was equally likely to occur at any point within the sequence of a scientist's published papers. Wang and Barabási called this the random impact rule, and observed that it changes our understanding of scientists' creative life cycles:

> [D]ecades of research have documented that major discoveries often come early in a scientist's career. This has led to the view that creativity equals youth, a myth deeply ingrained in popular culture. The random impact rule helps us decouple age and creativity. It tells us that the chance of a breakthrough is completely random within the sequence of works produced in a career. To be precise, every project we do has the same chance of becoming our personal best.[114]

The probability of a breakthrough thus declines with age not because of a loss of creativity, but because scientists tend to publish less as they grow older. But those who persist, and whose output does not decline with age, have as great a chance of a breakthrough late in their lives as early. Moreover, Wang and Barabási found that the random impact rule also appears in analyses of the careers of thousands of painters and film directors.[115]

Experimental creativity has often been overlooked. One reason for this, seen throughout this book, is that the gradual, incremental innovations of experimentalists are often less conspicuous than the sudden, dramatic breakthroughs of conceptualists. But another contributing factor has been the widespread popular belief, reinforced by the research of a series of academic psychologists, that creativity is primarily, even exclusively, the domain of the young. In recent years, studies of many important individual experimental innovators have shown that the psychologists' contention that age is the enemy of creativity is far from a universal rule. And now Wang and Barabási have produced powerful quantitative evidence that the psychologists' belief that creativity is the prerogative of youth is false for large groups of physicists, painters, and movie directors.

What emerges is a new and improved understanding of the life cycle of creativity in general. Age tends to be harmful to the creativity of *conceptual* artists and scholars, because the accumulation of knowledge and establishment of habits of thought inhibit the radical simplifications that underlie important conceptual breakthroughs. But the same is not true for *experimental* innovators. Experimentalists in all domains accumulate stores of knowledge, and construct new techniques for making this knowledge the basis for ever more powerful generalizations. And so we can now see clearly the two faces of creativity: old age and experience may be lethal for the creativity of conceptual young geniuses, but they are the lifeblood of the innovations of experimental old masters.

Identification

This chapter has considered a number of innovators whose careers further illustrate the applicability of this book's analysis across time, gender, race, and disciplines. The generality of the analysis is also demonstrated by cases in which innovators have recognized themselves. The saxophonist Sam Newsome sees himself as conceptual, noting that "there's a certain finality to each project/album. I don't feel a need to flesh out the documented work further after it's been recorded. In fact, after the release of each recording, I immediately move on to the next idea."[116] The composer Kyle Gann was heartened: "reading such a mass of personal process reports by all these other experimental types, I began to relax about my own composing process.... You read a biography of a single artist and it doesn't really sink in, but seeing so many reinforcing comments in one book is therapeutic."[117]

The novelist William Landay wrote that reading about the two types of creativity helped him understand his own creative method:

> I am very much an "experimental" writer. No lightning bolts, no visionary insights, no "Eureka!" Only gradual, uncertain, incremental iterations of idea after idea, draft after draft. I plane my sentences over and over, like a carpenter, yet they never feel finished. No book ever feels completed, only abandoned. And always flawed.

Yet he was encouraged:

> The good news? Experimental writers tend to reach their peak later and hold it longer. That feels right to me, also. I am convinced that my peak is still ahead of me and that ten years hence I will be writing much better books than I am now. But then, that attitude is probably the mark of an "experimentalist" personality too—the actual, completed books feel hopelessly botched, but the faith remains that someday, by rigorous trial and error, I will chisel out a "perfect" book.[118]

For one innovator, the analysis solved a longstanding puzzle. William Siemering, who authored the original statement of Mission and Purpose for National Public Radio, wrote that reading about the difference between experimental and conceptual approaches "solved a mystery that I've been trying to understand since December 10, 1971, when I was dismissed from my job as director of programming at NPR." Just months before *All Things Considered*, the daily evening news program Siemering had developed, won NPR's first Peabody Award for excellence in broadcasting, he was surprised to be fired as the network's first programming director. Years later, he understood that "the way I work, as an experimentalist, was at variance to the expectations of my colleagues." The directors of NPR wanted it "to sound like the big guys, a *real* network." They didn't share Siemering's "high tolerance for ambiguity," and rejected his flexible approach—"a conversational style, outside of the studio when possible, that capitalized on the unique strengths of radio as a sound, storytelling, personal medium that would 'speak with many voices and many dialects.'" Reading about this analysis made him realize that it was "the way I worked that made others uncomfortable," and helped him understand "that my experimental approach is okay. It's the way I work."[119]

Siemering went on to manage public radio stations in Minnesota and Philadelphia, and founded the nonprofit Developing Radio Partners, to help independent radio stations in Africa and Asia. He never lost his belief in the power of the radio as a source of information and imagination, or his experimental conviction that "Every experience prepares you for the next one."[120] He likes to quote Ralph Waldo Emerson: "All life is an experiment. The more experiments you make the better."[121]

12

Innovators Alone and Together

Enemies

Experimental and conceptual innovators are natural enemies. Fundamental differences between them in both methods and goals have defined fault lines that run through the foundations of the modern arts, and scholarly disciplines.

Some of the most celebrated artistic arguments and feuds of the modern era can be understood as the direct results of clashes between experimental and conceptual values. One elevated disagreement of this sort occurred in 1922, when Virginia Woolf and T. S. Eliot differed about the merits of James Joyce's new novel, *Ulysses*. Woolf recorded in her diary that when she began reading, she was "amused, stimulated, charmed, interested," but that after a few chapters she became "puzzled, bored, irritated and disillusioned by a queasy undergraduate scratching his pimples." She was surprised by Eliot's high opinion of it: "Tom, great Tom, thinks this on a par with *War and Peace*!" When she finished *Ulysses* a few weeks later, she judged it "a mis-fire. Genius it has, I think; but of the inferior water." She found the book superficial, and questioned Joyce's maturity: "A first rate writer, I mean, respects writing too much to be tricky; startling; doing stunts. I'm reminded all the time of some callow board school boy ... and one hopes he'll grow out of it; but as Joyce is 40 this scarcely seems likely." The book was too diffuse to have real power: "I feel that myriads of tiny bullets pepper one and spatter one; but one does not get one deadly wound straight in the face—as from Tolstoy, for instance; but it is entirely absurd to compare him with Tolstoy." Another few weeks later, Woolf discussed *Ulysses* with Eliot, who had recently completed *The Waste Land*, his own conceptual masterpiece. She reported that Eliot praised Joyce as "a purely literary writer," and predicted that *Ulysses* would be "a landmark, because it destroyed the whole of the nineteenth century," and "showed up the futility of all the English styles." But Woolf could not consider *Ulysses* important because—as Eliot conceded—it gave no "new insight into human nature—said nothing new like Tolstoy."[1]

In a separate essay, Woolf made it clear that her belief in Tolstoy's superiority lay in his experimental qualities: he was "the greatest of all novelists" because he "sees what we see," and made his vision into a recognizably real world, "in which the postman's knock is heard at eight o'clock, and people go to bed between ten and eleven." Tolstoy saw every detail, "so that we know his people, not only by the way they love and their views on politics and the immortality of the soul, but also by the way they sneeze and choke." Woolf's praise took the form of a visual, perceptual metaphor: readers of Tolstoy felt they "had a telescope put into our hands. Everything is astonishingly clear and absolutely sharp."[2]

Woolf and Eliot could not come to an agreement on the importance of *Ulysses* because of their fundamentally different values for literature. The conceptual Eliot correctly predicted that *Ulysses* would revolutionize the novel, because of its formal literary innovations. He could acknowledge that there was no "great conception" in *Ulysses* without this lowering his opinion of the book's importance, because he understood "that was not Joyce's intention," and believed that Joyce had accomplished "completely what he meant to do." For the experimental Woolf, however, these concessions were devastating for *Ulysses*, because a great novel had to have a great conception, in which real people carried out real lives; a novel could not be great merely because it changed the way novels were written, but had to give "new insight into human nature."[3]

The persistent and bitter animosity between Robert Frost and T. S. Eliot has sometimes been attributed simply to a clash of personalities, but in fact its basis appears to lie in their radically differing aesthetics. Although the two did not meet until 1928, their enmity dated back at least to 1922, when Eliot wrote dismissively in an English literary journal that Frost specialized in "New England torpor; his verse, it is regretfully said, is uninteresting, and what is uninteresting is unreadable, and what is unreadable is not read. There, that is done." Stung, Frost responded privately with criticisms of Eliot, calling him "the best of the whole gang of obscure poets," and contending that Eliot's obscurity was a product of his inability to express genuine emotions. Frost declared that "the need of being versed in country things was far greater, and often harder to achieve, than the need of being versed in pseudo-intellectual myths and symbols."[4] In a letter to his daughter, Frost charged that Eliot and his friend Ezra Pound had "striven for distinction by a show of learning, Pound in old French [and] Eliot in forty languages. They quote and you try to see if you can place the quotation."[5]

Eliot's criticism of Frost can be understood as a conceptual response to an experimental art that emphasized sensory perception over intellectual abstraction: Eliot considered Frost unintelligent and unsophisticated. In return, Frost's attack on Eliot as a snob and a fake—"the worst things you could be in Frost's way of thinking"—was a straightforward experimental reaction to a conceptual art based on complex and often obscure allusions rather than direct expression and observation.[6]

A stark and hostile confrontation between experimental and conceptual approaches to painting occurred in the early 1960s, when the sudden rise of the highly conceptual Pop art challenged the dominance of the experimental Abstract Expressionism in New York's art world. In one dramatic episode, when the dealer Sidney Janis presented an exhibition of the new art, four Abstract Expressionists, including Mark Rothko and Robert Motherwell, angrily quit Janis' gallery in protest. The critic Calvin Tomkins explained that the common denominator of the younger artists appeared to be "mockery and rejection of all serious art, especially Abstract Expressionism."[7] Later in the decade, a drunken Willem de Kooning turned on Andy Warhol at a party and told him, "You're a killer of art, you're a killer of beauty, and you're even a killer of laughter. I can't bear your work!," and Motherwell declared that Pop could not be fine art: "their detachment from aesthetic problems is incomprehensible to me. It fills me with a sort of horror."[8] When the conceptual prodigy Frank Stella exhibited large canvases filled entirely with parallel black lines, Motherwell commented "it's not painting," and a prominent critic who had championed Abstract Expressionism declared that Stella "isn't an artist, he's a juvenile delinquent."[9]

The Abstract Expressionists were separated from the Pop artists not just by differences in style, but by fundamental differences in their conception of art. Experimental painters who had spent decades working slowly and painstakingly toward imprecise and elusive artistic goals could not accept the validity of a new conceptual art made by brash and callow young artists who not only mocked their goals, but rejected aesthetic criteria altogether. The masters of Abstract Expressionism believed that they had created the art of the future: for them gestural abstraction was not merely a new form of art, but a new paradigm, comparable to that of the Renaissance, that would affect the attitudes of painters toward their art for centuries to come. They were shocked when their hegemony was challenged, barely a decade after it had been won, by cynical young practitioners who had no interest in their belief in art as a moral act of self-discovery. The suddenness of the success of the younger artists further infuriated the older experimentalists whose success had been gained so much more slowly and painfully, and so much later in their lives. The conceptual revolution initiated by Pop art produced such a vast change in values that the very survival of painting as a fine art seemed in doubt to the Abstract Expressionists, and it is not surprising that many of them expressed their outrage and hostility to the younger artists.

The above are a few among many clashes between experimental and conceptual artists, and demonstrate many of the recurrent elements of these disagreements. Not all of these elements will appear in any given episode, but the most common charges can be listed briefly.

Experimental artists often consider their conceptual peers pretentious and inauthentic. Experimental artists value sincere and direct expression of the artist's own perceptions, presented in the artist's own vocabulary. The accusation that conceptual artists' many allusions to earlier art constitute plagiarism is an example of this criticism. Robert Frost objected not only to T. S. Eliot's constant use of quotation in *The Waste Land*, but also to Eliot's attachment of footnotes to the poem: Frost declared that he would never use footnotes, because they "robbed the heart of the chance to see for itself what a poem is all about," and "would be a condescension to the people that can't keep up with me."[10] The experimental poet William Carlos Williams considered Eliot's formal language a means of hiding: "We can admire Eliot's distinguished use of sentences and words and the tenor of his mind, but as for substance—he is for us a cipher."[11] Even Eliot's dandyish attire on a visit to Paris was an affront to Williams: "appearing at the Dôme and other bars in a top hat, cutaway, and striped trousers. It was intended as a gesture of contempt." Williams' personal distaste for Eliot made the latter's conceptual revolution based on technique all the more painful: "being an accomplished craftsman, better skilled in some ways than I could ever hope to be, I had to watch him carry my world off with him, the fool, to the enemy."[12]

Virginia Woolf's criticism of *Ulysses*, like Alberto Moravia's declaration that Ernest Hemingway had never progressed beyond an "infantile and precocious state of arrested development," represented a common experimental criticism of the art of conceptual innovators as perennially immature. In this vein, the poet Louise Glück recalled her early infatuation with T. S. Eliot's poetry: "I read this poetry for the first time as an adolescent. And understood it immediately, by which I mean I felt a connection to it. I heard the tone." But later in her life, she saw that what had appealed to her as an adolescent was an adolescent quality of Eliot's poetry: "If there is a criticism to make, it may [be] ... that in the intensity and unchangingness of its emotion it is adolescent."[13] The poet Adam Kirsch made the same point: "I loved Eliot so much as an adolescent because he is, in some ways, an essentially adolescent writer." Noting that *The Waste Land* now seems to him "a kind of young person's performance," Kirsch observed that he now reads Eliot less often, and concluded that "there may be different kinds of greatness, suited for different phases of our growth."[14] A precocious artist may in fact be one who never matures. Joyce Carol Oates said just this of another great conceptual poet: "[Sylvia] Plath's meticulously documented example suggests how precocity is not maturity, and may in fact impede maturity."[15] And Zoë Heller recently looked back with surprise on her own early enthusiasm for Plath's art: "while it's impossible not to admire the technical virtuosity of the poems, I'm frankly amazed that I ever affected to 'relate to' or be consoled by their cruelty, their masochism, their terrifying 'ice-eye.' "[16]

In William Faulkner's long-running feud with Ernest Hemingway, the experimental Faulkner consistently cited the conceptual Hemingway's failure to grow beyond his early successes as his reason for ranking Hemingway below Thomas Wolfe, John Dos Passos, and Faulkner himself among American novelists of their generation—"because of Hemingway having taught himself a pattern, a method which he could use and he stuck to that without splashing around to try to experiment."[17] In language clearly intended to provoke the macho Hemingway—that succeeded in this aim—Faulkner declared that Hemingway "has no courage, he has never climbed out on a limb," but remained tied to his early simplistic style: "He has never used a word where the reader has to check his usage by a dictionary."[18] The scholar Philip Young acknowledged that Hemingway's work left him vulnerable to the accusation: "Nowhere in this writer can you find the mature, brooding intelligence, the sense of the past, the grown-up relationships of adult people, and many of the other things we normally ask of a first-rate novelist. Only battles, or their preludes and aftermaths, and Hemingway hypnotized by the one note he sounds."[19] Decades earlier, in a review of a volume of Hemingway's short stories, Virginia Woolf had made a similar criticism, complaining that Hemingway's characters were not developed into convincing, three-dimensional people. And Woolf went further, turning one of Hemingway's own aspersions against him. Seizing on a charge that Hemingway had made against a bullfighter who created a "faked look of danger" by leaning against a bull after the horns had safely passed, Woolf contended that Hemingway had similarly used his technical virtuosity to give the appearance of realism without the substance:

> For in truth story-writing has much in common with bullfighting. One may twist one's self like a corkscrew and go through every sort of contortion so that the public thinks one is running every risk and displaying superb gallantry. But the true writer stands close up to the bull and lets the horns—call them truth, reality, whatever you like—pass him close each time.[20]

Andy Warhol and Joseph Beuys, like such later artists as Jeff Koons and Damien Hirst, were conceptual innovators who appear to have deliberately—and disingenuously—provoked the criticism that they were ignorant and disrespectful of earlier work in their discipline. In a strategy pioneered by Marcel Duchamp, these brash and transgressive young conceptual innovators made ambiguity a powerful tool to publicize their work, as they benefited from heated and extended public debate over whether their radical innovations were serious or in jest. Warhol and Beuys, among other artistic tricksters who followed Duchamp, also created elaborate personas that made their eccentric and unconventional behavior inseparable from their art, as they made it necessary for viewers or listeners to consider the intentions of the artist in interpreting their work. This was anathema for those with experimental values, who believe that art should be considered on its own merits, independent of its creator, and long lists of angry denunciations of Duchamp and his prominent conceptual heirs can be culled from the writings of experimental artists and writers.[21]

T. S. Eliot's condescending criticisms of Robert Frost's poetry were typical of the most common criticism of experimental artists by their conceptual peers, that their work is unintelligent and unsophisticated. Hemingway's counterattack on Faulkner is another example of this, as he criticized the experimental novelist's open endings as a technical flaw, declaring that Faulkner "is a good writer when he is good and could be better than anyone if he knew how to finish a book."[22] More generally, the conceptual Marcel Duchamp expressed his contempt for the visual experimental art of the Impressionists: "All through the last half of the nineteenth century in France there was an expression, *'bête comme un peintre'* [stupid as a painter]. And it is true; that kind of painter who just puts down what he sees *is* stupid."[23]

The basic difference in artistic values between experimental and conceptual practitioners makes them natural enemies. Specific feuds have often been ascribed entirely to idiosyncratic differences in taste or personality, but in many cases the terms of debate can be recognized as symptomatic of underlying differences in artists' conceptions of the purposes of their disciplines. Louise Glück succinctly explained this in discussing why the experimental poet William Carlos Williams considered T. S. Eliot his enemy: "That Williams didn't like Eliot is hardly surprising. . . . He had a moral commitment to the actual, which meant the visual, whereas it was Eliot's compulsion to question the world."[24]

Collaboration

In the history of Western culture, there have been few advocates for individual creativity more steadfast than Albert Einstein. In 1934, he declared that "It can easily be seen that all the valuable achievements, material, spiritual, and moral, which we receive from society have been brought about in the course of countless generations by creative individuals."[25] A decade later he denounced organized collaborative research, asserting that "Only a free individual can make a discovery," and asking rhetorically "Can you imagine an organization of scientists making the discoveries of Charles Darwin?"[26] Yet in 1912, when Einstein was searching for a mathematical approach to general relativity, he appealed to a friend, the mathematician Marcel Grossmann, for help. Grossmann showed him that the appropriate tool was Riemannian geometry, and a year later the two published a coauthored paper that used this to make progress toward the general theory. Riemannian geometry became the mathematical language of general relativity, and the biographer Abraham Pais observed that Einstein's introduction to it changed his outlook on physics for the rest of his life.[27] That even the zealously individualistic Einstein would resort to collaboration makes a forceful statement for its value, while the nature of his collaboration and its enormous impact on him illustrate a key virtue of the practice.

Collaboration in intellectual activities is a broad phenomenon that takes many different forms. Some of these occur in the course of training. Important innovators usually work closely with at least one teacher who has a strong influence on them, and almost without exception develop their skills at an early stage of their careers in the company of talented peers in their own discipline. Collaboration also occurs in production. Most important innovators collaborate informally, during part or all of their careers, with colleagues. Some also collaborate formally, by coauthoring work. Many innovators participate in all of these forms of collaboration, but virtually none fail to participate in any. This ubiquity of collaboration in intellectual creativity might appear to call into question the value of the analysis presented in this book, which has been presented and developed with reference to individual creativity. There is in fact no significant problem, however, for two central reasons. One is that many instances of joint effort nonetheless lead to the distinctive creativity of an individual. The other is that even in cases of genuinely joint creativity, the positive association of experimental with other experimental innovators, and of conceptual with other conceptuals, means that the analysis can nearly always be applied successfully to the joint creative efforts. These two propositions can be considered in turn.

The distinctiveness of individual innovations in spite of the important influence of teachers, fellow students, and colleagues can readily be illustrated in the modern history of painting. Cézanne never forgot the great debt he owed to "the humble and colossal" Pissarro for the instruction he received in the early 1870s, when the two worked closely together: he freely acknowledged Pissarro's influence on his art—he told a visitor to his studio in 1902 that Pissarro had been "like a father to me. You could always ask him questions"—and in two exhibition catalogues late in his life he had himself identified as "Pupil of Pissarro."[28] In 1895, Pissarro was irritated when a critic failed to recognize his impact on Cézanne, complaining that "He simply doesn't know that Cézanne was influenced like all the rest of us.... Cézanne was first influenced by Delacroix, Courbet, Manet and even Legros, like all of us; he was influenced by me at Pontoise, and I by him.... Naturally, we were always together!" But Pissarro equally recognized that the fact that Cézanne had been influenced "detracts nothing from his qualities." Critics naively believed "that artists are the sole inventors of their styles and that to resemble someone else is to be unoriginal," but in spite of the similarity between Cézanne's paintings and his own, their contributions were clearly distinct: "what cannot be denied is that each of us kept the only thing that counts, the unique 'sensation'! This could easily be shown."[29] Pissarro had earlier worked closely with Monet, as part of the core group—with Renoir and Sisley—that created Impressionism. Yet again, the specific contributions of these colleagues were clearly recognized not only by later artists, but by the collaborators themselves. Thus Pissarro reported in 1895 that both he and Cézanne had seen a new exhibition of Monet's work, and were in complete agreement that Monet's paintings displayed "the intangible nuances of effects that are realized by no other painter."[30]

Another important example of informal collaboration from a more recent period of visual art was that between Jasper Johns and Robert Rauschenberg. The two worked closely together during the late 1950s, when both were developing what became their most important contributions. Rauschenberg recalled that "Jasper and I literally traded ideas. He would say, 'I've got a terrific idea for you,' and then I'd have to find one for him."[31] Johns reflected that "I learned more about painting from Bob than I learned from any other artist or teacher, and working as closely as we did and more or less in isolation, we developed a strong feeling of kinship."[32] At a time when the two were hardly recognized by the art world, Rauschenberg explained that the encouragement they gave each other provided "permission to do what we wanted."[33] Their understanding of each other's work was so deep that Johns believes that he coined the name "combine" for the new genre that became Rauschenberg's signal innovation.[34] But those combines, that used found objects to extend painting into three dimensions, are radically different from the paintings of two-dimensional motifs with which Johns startled the art world. These early innovations of both Johns and Rauschenberg played a central role in launching the revolution in which the experimental art of Abstract Expressionism was displaced by Pop, Minimalism, and a series of other conceptual movements, but their forms were so different that no significant work by either artist could be mistaken for a product of the other: as Rauschenberg explained, "Ours were two very different sensibilities, and being so close to each other's work kept any incident of similarity from occurring."[35]

Formal collaboration in the production of intellectual innovations is common, and becoming increasingly prevalent, in our society. In scholarship, coauthorship has become the norm in the physical and social sciences, and is increasing in the humanities.[36] In the arts, collaboration has long been common in some activities, and is currently growing in importance in others. And collaboration within business firms is pervasive. An important fact for understanding the nature of these formal collaborations is that in all these activities, it appears that in the vast majority of instances the creative process can clearly be categorized as either experimental or conceptual, because there is a powerful effect tending to make collaborative pairs or teams homogeneous in this respect. This effect is a direct consequence of the logic of successful collaboration.

Important innovations often combine ideas that were previously considered unrelated: the more unrelated the ideas, potentially the more radical the synthesis. A primary value of collaboration is that it increases access to knowledge, and more potential syntheses, because groups of people can collectively have a greater amount of expertise than individuals. This is particularly true if the group is diverse, in the sense of having members with a range of non-overlapping expertise. Yet there is a critical condition that limits the diversity of collaborative groups. Specifically, collaborators must be able to communicate effectively, and to resolve disagreements that arise in the course of their work. The scientist Michael Nielsen has called the elements necessary to satisfy this condition—a common body of knowledge and agreement on techniques—a *shared praxis*. Nielsen observed that "for collective intelligence to be successful, participants must be committed to a shared body of methods for reasoning, so disagreements between participants can be resolved, and do not cause permanent rifts." If collaborators do not share a body of methods for reasoning, disagreements will arise that cannot be resolved, and the collaboration will break down.[37]

The need for a shared praxis explains why creative collaboration generally does not follow the standard economic model of the gains from trade, in which each party specializes in a distinct aspect of production. Intel makes computer chips and Apple makes computers. Apple accepts Intel's work at the point of exchange. There may be collaboration in the specification of the item to be exchanged, but not in its actual production. How Intel produces its chips, or Apple its computers, is irrelevant to the success of their trade. Creative collaboration typically differs from this in that collaborators work together in producing their innovations, so that they not only check each other's work when it is completed, but follow it at every stage of its progress. The collaborators must therefore agree not only on the value of the final product, but also on the process by which it is produced. Creative collaboration consequently substitutes shared praxis for diversity. Most formal coauthorship in scholarship involves individuals who share the same specialization within a discipline. One consequence of the necessity for shared praxis is that conceptual innovators generally collaborate with other conceptualists, and experimentalists with other experimentalists.[38]

Collaborative research has become more common in the modern era, both in scholarship and in the arts. The American painter Barnett Newman contended that "Modern painting begins with the Impressionists precisely because for the first time in history, a group of artists . . . decided to devote themselves exclusively to solving a technical problem in painting."[39] The Impressionists all shared an experimental commitment to creating a new kind of visual art, as later did Newman and his fellow Abstract Expressionists. In contrast, the members of such groups as the Fauves and Cubists were exclusively conceptual.[40] Fauvism followed from Henri Matisse's realization "that one could work with expressive colors that are not necessarily descriptive colors."[41] It developed from a brief but intense collaboration between Matisse and the younger painter André Derain, who later explained that "We painted with theories, ideas."[42] The two artists deliberately violated the conventions of painting—Matisse declared that "I spoiled everything on principle"—in their excitement at making a radical new departure: in Derain's words, "Colors became sticks of dynamite. They were primed to discharge light."[43] Picasso recalled that he and Braque worked so closely together in the early development of Cubism that they met in their studios almost every evening: "Each of us *had* to see what the other had done during the day. We criticized each other's work. A canvas wasn't finished until both of us felt it was." He described their work as "a kind of laboratory research from which every pretension or individual vanity was excluded."[44] The effectiveness of all of these groups resulted from the agreement of the artists involved on the goals of the research project in question and on the appropriate methods to use in their pursuit.

Collaborative production can be either hierarchical or between peers. In scholarship, hierarchical production is typically a professor with research assistants, whereas joint production by peers is done through coauthorship. Hierarchical collaboration has a long history in painting, as many Old Masters had workshops in which paintings were jointly produced. Interestingly, however, most if not all cases in which this occurred involved conceptual masters who made detailed plans, in the form of preparatory drawings, for paintings that were then executed by assistants. Raphael and Rubens are known to have worked in this way. The experimental artists Leonardo, Michelangelo, and Rembrandt did not use this division of labor, presumably because of their inability to delegate the execution of their works to assistants because the masters could not anticipate the final appearance of their paintings.[45]

Andy Warhol became a prototype for many contemporary artists, in having his paintings executed by assistants. Warhol had earlier had assistants for his commercial art, and in 1963 he hired Gerard Malanga as the first of a series of assistants who helped with—or made—his silk-screened canvases (Malanga later explained that "When the screens were very large, we worked together; otherwise, I was pretty much left to my devices").[46] Jeff Koons, Damien Hirst, and Takashi Murakami are among those who have more recently extended Warhol's practice, by employing ever larger numbers of artists to produce their paintings—in each case, as many as a hundred assistants.[47] Each of these artists plans the work, often with the aid of a computer, and assistants execute it, sometimes under the artist's direct supervision, sometimes in another location. Koons once explained that this practice actually made him a better artist, because it allowed him to "continue to grow as much as possible as an artist, instead of being tied down in the execution of the work"; Hirst has noted that the practice improves the technical quality of his art, as for example in making his famous spot paintings: "I only ever made five spot paintings . . . and any spots I painted are shite. . . . The best spot painting you can have by me is one painted by Rachel [Howard]."[48] Warhol, Koons, Hirst, and Murakami are all conceptual innovators, who believe that the value of their art derives primarily from the conception rather than the execution. It is unlikely that an experimental artist could ever have his works executed in this manner by assistants, because of the fundamental experimental belief that the essence of creativity lies in the process of making the work.

Collaboration between peers has been less common in painting. Only occasional instances can be found prior to the modern era. Peter Paul Rubens and Jan Brueghel the Elder, the two most important painters in Antwerp in the early seventeenth century, jointly executed about two dozen canvases. Each contributed his specialty, as Brueghel painted the background landscapes, and Rubens the figures. The paintings contain few pentimenti (changes during the process of execution), suggesting they were planned carefully in advance; that both Brueghel and Rubens were conceptual artists, accustomed to painting from detailed preparatory drawings, must have facilitated the process of making these joint works.[49]

Formal coauthorship has become more common in visual art in recent decades. A new practice has emerged in which pairs of artists have worked together from the beginnings of their careers, making all of their art jointly. Perhaps the most influential of these teams is Gilbert and George (Gilbert Proesch and George Passmore), who met when they were students of sculpture at St. Martin's School of Art in London in the late 1960s. Both were dissatisfied with the program's emphasis on form over content, and decided to join together to make a new type of art that would privilege ideas. Declaring themselves "living sculptures," their first work—and still their most frequently illustrated in textbooks of art history—was a performance in London's Charing Cross in which they painted their faces bronze, wore matching tweed suits, and sang an old music hall song, "Underneath the Arches," continuously for eight hours. They subsequently began producing large drawings, but when viewers attempted to separate their contributions, they abandoned drawing for photography, "to make one art that doesn't distinguish between us." They are committed to the proposition that "Two people make one artist. We think we are an artist." When asked how they resolve disagreements about their work, they deny they have any: "we never argue." Their photographs nearly always feature themselves, usually in identical tweed suits, but occasionally in the nude, with texts that refer to religion, homosexuality, AIDS, and other topics of social significance. The images and language are often shocking, but the messages are generally unclear.[50]

Gilbert and George have been successful at reaching a wide audience—their motto is "Art for All"—and at creating controversy. Their complete and consistent joint production of their art has effectively created a successful model for coauthorship of advanced art, that has successfully overcome the art world's traditional conception of the artist as an autonomous agent. The language of the official introduction to their 2007 retrospective exhibition at London's most important museum of modern art simultaneously demonstrated the English art world's view of their importance and the acceptance of the pair as a unit, noting that "it is fitting that *Gilbert & George: Major Exhibition* is the largest of any artist to be held at Tate Modern." That their success has been greater in England than elsewhere may account for the greater prominence there of artistic teams of the next generation.[51]

The need for a shared praxis among collaborators implies that the analysis presented in this book can be applied not only to teams of scholars or artists, but also to researchers within corporations. Just as scholars and artists choose to work with others who share their approach to their discipline, so entrepreneurs will generally hire employees who share their approach. Examples of this are afforded by two entrepreneurs considered in this book, Steve Jobs and Muhammad Yunus.

Apple functioned as a conceptual innovator, due to the leadership of Steve Jobs. Jobs would imagine a new product that didn't yet exist: "I can see the product as if it's sitting right there in the center of the table. It's like what I've got to do is materialize it and bring it to life." Lacking the technical skills to create these products himself, Jobs hired engineers who would translate his vision into a real product. He supervised their work closely, typically meeting daily with a technical team. When an engineer complained that a feature or process Jobs described was not practical, Jobs' response was simple: "If you can't do it, I'll find someone else who can."[52] As a result, teams of workers at Apple collectively took on the approach of a conceptual innovator.

Whereas Jef Raskin, a manager at Apple, described Jobs as a dictator who "would have made an excellent king of France," the experimental Muhammad Yunus was a democratic leader who encouraged discussion and debate among Grameen's employees, because he believed that "innovation can only sprout in an atmosphere of tolerance, diversity, and curiosity."[53] Managers of new Grameen branches were given minimal formal training before being sent out to begin working, because Yunus found "that the villages of Bangladesh teach young people more about life than the pages of any book ever could."[54] Grameen's policies are made jointly by meetings of department heads, and all branch managers are encouraged to try out their own ideas, and to pass on successful practices for testing and replication elsewhere.[55]

Even in today's wired and connected world of constant communication, many of the most important innovations continue to come from the sudden insights and inspirations of individual conceptual innovators, and the extended and painstaking research of individual experimental innovators. And even in cases in which this is not true, and major innovations emerge from the collaboration of pairs or larger groups of innovators, the analysis presented in this book remains relevant for understanding the processes and products involved. The primary reason for this is that successful collaboration in any intellectual activity requires a shared praxis, and a central element of this is that effective collaboration can generally occur only when the collaborators are either all experimental or all conceptual in orientation. Conceptual innovators may be inspired by experimental work, as for example both Matisse and Picasso were by the art of Cézanne, but they will invariably choose to work with other conceptual practitioners, as Matisse did with André Derain in inventing Fauvism, and Picasso did with Braque in creating Cubism.

Two Paths to Creativity

Why do you think I date everything I make? Because it's not enough to know an artist's works. One must also know when he made them, why, how, under what circumstances. No doubt there will some day be a science, called "the science of man," perhaps, which will seek above all to get a deeper understanding of man via man-the-creator. I often think of that science, and I want the documentation I leave to posterity to be as complete as possible. That's why I date everything I make.[56]

So declared Pablo Picasso to a friend, the photographer Brassaï, in 1943. His concern with precise dating stemmed from his belief that artistic discoveries occurred suddenly: "in art there is no ascendant progress, but . . . certain ups and downs that might occur at any time."[57] When Picasso made these statements, he had already blatantly violated three basic principles that had governed painting since the Renaissance, by creating images that no longer imitated the appearance of real objects, placing materials other than paint on the surfaces of his canvases, and refusing to adhere to a single trademark style. He had made each of these revolutionary innovations, deliberately and decisively, before the age of 35.

Robert Frost's attitude toward time was very different. Achievement came gradually: "one of the things about art is that you have to find a refuge, while you're starting it, from hasty judgments. And farming was one for me. And teaching was another. And newspaper work was another. The years of hasty judgment I got by that way." Past the age of 80, Frost reflected that he had "never got called [poet] till I was forty. And I was embarrassed when I was first called it, though I'd been writing for twenty years." He had not been in a hurry: he did not publish his first book of poems until he was 39, and did not write his greatest poem for another decade after that. Looking back, he considered "it's all been kind of haphazard and accidental."[58]

The differing attitudes of Picasso and Frost toward time reflected the differing nature of their creativity. For the conceptual Picasso, an innovation was the product of a new thought: "If an artist varies his mode of expression this only means he has changed his manner of thinking." This could occur at any moment: "the ideas of people change and with them their mode of expression."[59] For the experimental Frost, the most important discoveries were not clear ideas that arrived in a moment of insight, but rather feelings that dawned gradually, that developed from vague impressions "I was unaware of and so made no note of at the time."[60] He did not think of his discoveries as imposing his ideas on his subjects, but as bringing out the qualities inherent in the people and places he observed, the way a skilled craftsman made an axe:

> the lines of a good helve
> Were native to the grain before the knife

>   Expressed them, and its curves were no false curves
>   Put on it from without.[61]

Following nature's lines made for stronger poetry, just as it made for a stronger axe.

There are no absolute and invariant rules of behavior for individuals, and innovators are often idiosyncratic. As a result, no general statement of specific attitudes and practices can be assumed to apply to all experimental or all conceptual innovators. Yet there are powerful tendencies that separate members of the two groups, so although individuals may not exhibit all the traits considered here, most innovators embody many of these, and can clearly be categorized as experimental or conceptual.

For conceptual innovators, creativity consists of new ideas, that can arrive suddenly and completely. These ideas are surprising combinations of elements that had previously been unrelated, and the innovator's connection of these may appear to be almost effortless—hence Steve Jobs' contention that innovators often don't *do* anything, but merely *see* something. The most radical conceptual innovations combine elements that had previously existed in different domains, and the ability to connect these requires imagination and intellectual freedom. This freedom involves recognizing a novel approach to an old problem, and is greatest for those who are least committed to existing approaches. This is why radical conceptual innovation is nearly always the prerogative of recent entrants into a discipline, who have not had time to become constrained in their thinking by becoming accustomed to following the discipline's existing conventions and practices. The aging Orson Welles looked back wistfully to the creative freedom of his youth: "I'd never set foot on a set before filming *Citizen Kane*. No doubt I was touched by the grace of total ignorance."[62] Because most new entrants to intellectual disciplines are young, important conceptual innovations are usually made at early ages.

Uncertainty about their goals often leaves experimental innovators unable to complete their works. After the dealer Ambroise Vollard had spent more than one hundred sessions sitting for his portrait, Paul Cézanne put the painting aside, complaining of the elusiveness of his intentions: "the contour keeps slipping away from me." Cézanne promised to return to the painting on a future visit to Paris, but he never did, and the portrait was left unfinished. Vollard explained that Cézanne was not troubled by this, since for him "to paint from nature was not a question of copying the subject, but solely of realizing his sensations," and Cézanne was resigned to falling short of "this unheard-of conscientiousness."[63] In contrast, the clarity of conceptual innovators' goals leaves them in no doubt that a work is complete. Brassaï wrote of an incident in 1943, when a collector came to Picasso's studio with an unsigned painting, which the artist immediately recognized as a work he had done in the summer of 1922. When the owner asked him to sign it, Picasso replied that was unnecessary: "If you don't see my signature and the date, madam, it's because the frame is hiding it."[64] He could be sure of this, because he knew he always signed and dated his paintings; unlike Cézanne, he never left works unsigned in the hope of improving them, for he considered each the product of a particular time. Thus he told Françoise Gilot that his paintings were like the pages of a journal: "The future will choose the pages it prefers. It's not up to me to make the choice."[65]

Picasso was a prototypical example of a conceptual innovator whose ability to produce definitive statements of his ideas freed him to change his work radically from one period to the next—satisfied that he had achieved one goal, he could embark upon another that was completely different. Another member of this group was Picasso's conceptual rival Marcel Duchamp, who explicitly vowed to avoid repetition, and once declared, "I've had thirty-three ideas; I've made thirty-three paintings."[66] The inability of experimental innovators to achieve the full expression they seek can in contrast tie them to a single problem or theme for long spells. Mark Rothko defended his use of his trademark image of stacked rectangles for hundreds of paintings over more than two decades by explaining that "If a thing is worth doing once, it is worth doing over and over again—exploring it, probing it."[67] William Faulkner explained why he continued writing: "I believe as long as I live I will still try to write the good book which up to now I have never quite done."[68] These artists are often committed to incremental change so gradual that it may be imperceptible to others: "Even so, it's another step," Piet Mondrian once said to a friend who was looking at a new painting of his, "or don't you think so? Don't you find that it represents even a little step forward?"[69] The experimental novelist Ross Macdonald explained that his repeated use of similar themes and characters was not mere duplication: "Every time you do it, you dig deeper."[70]

Robert Frost gave countless public readings of his poems to earn a living, but when audience members asked what a poem meant, he declined: "I tell 'em that if I wanted them to know what I was saying I would have told them."[71] Frost worked assiduously to find the particular sounds and rhythms that would allow his poems to express his perceptions, and he wanted others to experience them directly and firsthand, without commentary that might distract from the poem itself. When Alfred Stieglitz was asked about the meaning of his photographs, he replied that "if the artist could explain in words what he has made, he would not have had to create it."[72] Experimental innovators generally believe that the most important elements in their work are not subject to analysis or articulation. Thus after describing how he conceived his designs, Frank Lloyd Wright reflected that "Of course what is most vitally important in all that I have tried to say and explain cannot be explained at all." Thinking of working in his studio surrounded by assistants, he mused that "in this searching process may be seen the architect's mind at work, as boys in the studio would crowd around and participate in it.... Certain hints coming through between the lines that may help someone who needs help in comprehending what planning a building really means."[73] Experimental creativity could be witnessed, but not verbalized. When five leading Abstract Expressionist painters founded an art school in New York in the late 1940s, they offered no formal courses because, as Robert Motherwell explained, "in a basic sense art cannot be taught." They believed that "The way to learn to paint ... is to hang around artists," and this was the opportunity their school would provide.[74] Frost, Stieglitz, Wright, and Motherwell all had the experimental conviction that works of art make their statements in a particular form that cannot be adequately communicated in any other way—hence Frost's celebrated definition of poetry as "that which is lost out of both prose and verse in translation."[75]

Conceptual artists more often believe that the messages of their works can be translated. Jean-Luc Godard, for example, considers film the best way to express his ideas, but not the only way: "Were the cinema to disappear, I would simply accept the inevitable and turn to television; were television to disappear, I would revert to pencil and paper."[76] Conceptual artists are also more inclined to use written texts to accompany their works in other genres. In 1883, Vincent van Gogh wrote to his brother,

> One of these days I will write you a letter; I shall write it carefully and try to make it short, but say everything I think necessary. You might keep that letter then, so that in case you should meet somebody who might be induced to buy some of my studies, you could tell that man my own thoughts and intentions exactly. My thought in this being especially: one of my drawings, taken separately will never give satisfaction in the long run, but

a number of studies, however different in detail they may be, will nevertheless complement each other.[77]

Van Gogh was a prototype of a kind of artist who would become more common later in the modern era, a conceptual innovator who created a personal symbolic language that held specific meanings for him, that would not be apparent to other observers unless they studied many of his works.

Van Gogh's suggestion that he would write a text explaining his art to potential buyers presaged a significant development in the art of the next century. Published statements by painters on behalf of their art became so numerous in the first half of the twentieth century that the critic Arthur Danto named this the Age of Manifestos.[78] Hundreds of these manifestos were produced by conceptual artists, who used them to publicize their work, to explain their innovations to collectors, and to claim their superiority to earlier movements.[79] The key to the effectiveness of many of these manifestos was the highly theoretical goals and practices of the artists involved: theory often preceded practice, and often overshadowed it. Marjorie Perloff observed of one example that "the real point is that the theory *is* the practice.... To talk about art became equivalent to making it."[80] And to read about art became equivalent to seeing it, so that conceptual innovations could diffuse much more rapidly and widely than previously.[81] The nearly complete absence of experimental innovators from this outpouring of texts is not surprising, for perceptions are less easily verbalized than ideas, and artistic seekers are acutely aware of this. When the bookish Robert Motherwell looked back on the failure of Abstract Expressionism to produce a manifesto, he reflected that "the very nature of a manifesto is to affirm forcefully and unambiguously, and not to express the existential doubt and the anxiety that we all felt. Certain kinds of paintings are easier to describe and to evoke (and perhaps to make) than others."[82]

Conceptual innovations often arrive suddenly, complete and fully realized. Their clear and radical departures from existing practices often make their arrival dramatic and conspicuous, and their clarity and simplicity often make their diffusion rapid. In contrast, experimental innovations usually arrive gradually, and their subtle contributions are often initially overlooked. In a typical observation about experimental creativity, Timothy Steele wrote of Robert Frost that "His art conceals art. It is easy to overlook his dexterities because he appears to achieve them effortlessly."[83] The appearance of ease was deliberate, because experimental innovators typically want their technique to disappear: Auguste Rodin declared that "There is no good style except that which makes itself forgotten in order to concentrate all the attention of the viewer on the subject."[84] Admirers of great experimental artists often compare their works to those of nature: the composer Harold Arlen said of Irving Berlin that "His songs sound as though they were born that way—not written."[85]

A central concern of this book has been the difference in the creative life cycles of experimental and conceptual innovators. For experimentalists, long spans of hard work are often necessary to hone the skill that produces new forms, and to develop the novel technique that expresses them. At 71, Robert Frost told Octavio Paz that he had had to create his own language, and "I had to wait a long time before I found my words."[86] It also took time to learn what made art genuinely powerful: "Young would-be poets would watch a sunset, and instead of describing it they would express how they felt about it.... A good poet would so master his technique that he could describe the sunset in a way that made his readers see and feel it."[87] Experimentalists are committed to craftsmanship, and expect mastery to require a long apprenticeship. Thus at 72 Mark Twain reflected that "in all arts it is training that brings the act to perfection," and at 74 the British painter Francis Bacon declared simply that "Painting is an old man's business."[88]

In contrast, experience is the enemy of conceptual creativity. Conceptual innovations require radical departures from existing approaches, and the ability to perceive these is greatest upon first exposure to a new problem or discipline. T. S. Eliot believed that poetic inspiration almost necessarily diminished with age: the conceptual Eliot assumed that significant experiences and intense passions occurred only early in life, so that poets who practiced their art into middle age became repetitive and uninspired.[89] Orson Welles contended that he had been most creative at the beginning of his career because he had made innovations that an experienced director never would have attempted, in the belief they were impossible. He dismissed the possibility that growing expertise might compensate for this loss of early naiveté, recalling that while making *Citizen Kane* his cameraman Gregg Toland, "like all great men, I think, who are masters of a craft, told me right at the outset that there was nothing about the camera work that I couldn't learn in half a day, that any intelligent person couldn't learn in half a day. And he was right." Welles had no doubt that experience was overrated. "You know, the great mystery that requires 20 years doesn't exist in any field."[90]

The creative life cycles of conceptual and experimental innovators thus differ not by chance, or by choice, but because the two types of innovators think and work differently, and produce very different kinds of products. Conceptual innovators inhabit mental worlds of clarity and certainty. They simplify problems by isolating specific elements of reality, and creating an abstraction that they embody in a model. This idealized representation then becomes the basis for their finished product: once the model has been formulated, their creative process no longer refers to the complexity of reality, but rather to the simplification of their scheme. They are willing to sacrifice many dimensions of reality in order to capture with precision those they select.

Experimental innovators want their products to emerge from sustained direct observation of reality. Although they are aware that their work can never embody the full complexity of reality, they strive to avoid simplification, and are typically dissatisfied with the inevitable incompleteness of their works. This continuing frustration with their inability to grasp the whole complexity of reality is the cause of their reluctance ever to consider a particular work complete or finished, and of their eagerness to move on to the next work, to try to do better.

Conceptual innovators make their greatest contributions early in their careers because this is when they can see problems most simply, and are least constrained in taking radical new approaches. In contrast, the late innovations of experimental innovators are their most powerful because they are based on greater accumulated knowledge, and formulated with greater technical skills developed over long periods of study. Conceptual innovators often leap abruptly to a sharp peak of precocious innovation, which is often followed by an equally abrupt decline in their creativity. Experimentalists develop more gradually, working incrementally toward what is often an extended plateau of creativity.

Seekers and Finders

This book has demonstrated that there are two fundamentally different types of creativity. They are products of very different approaches, taken by innovators with very different goals. This difference in approach generally causes these innovators to follow very different patterns of creativity over the life cycle.

The case studies presented here demonstrate how recognition of the two types of creativity increases our understanding of innovators and their contributions. For conceptual innovators, youth is freedom. The early stages of their careers are usually their most creative, for this is when their imagination is least constrained by the accumulation of knowledge and entrenched habits of thought. Conceptual innovators need relatively little knowledge about a discipline or problem—enough to feel dissatisfaction with existing products or practices, but not enough to have assimilated these practices and to have had them constrain their ability to perceive radically different approaches. Conceptual innovators are iconoclastic and often transgressive; they change their disciplines by breaking accepted rules and customs, and often redefine their disciplines' boundaries. They leap to dramatic and shocking innovations that often create immediate revolutions.

In contrast, for experimental innovators experience—and consequently age—is power. Experience in a discipline allows them to develop better technical methods of analysis and expression, based on the knowledge they have gained from years of study. Their understanding of how they learn yields wisdom, in the form of better judgment, both in separating successful from failed experiments and in drawing general conclusions from the evidence they have accumulated. Their innovations typically arrive incrementally, often almost imperceptibly, over extended periods, late in their careers.

Conceptual innovators are society's brash young geniuses, and experimental innovators its wise old masters. Recognizing the differences between the two types gives us a deeper understanding of the products of each and of the nature of human creativity in general. It also has many implications for future investigation.

The analysis has significant implications for helping innovative individuals maximize their creativity. Conceptual innovators face the danger of becoming captives of an early achievement, and of repeating the same analysis or product, while adding little of value. The advantage of conceptual innovators is in the ability to change their approach quickly, to take on new problems. The more radical the changes they make, the greater the potential for completely new approaches, and thus for important new contributions.

Conversely, experimental innovators face the danger of the pressure to compete with conceptual practitioners of their disciplines, by changing problems frequently. They must resist this temptation, and select new problems similar in structure to those they have already tackled, to take advantage of the methods and knowledge they have already acquired. The reward for their patience will be growing mastery.

The analysis also has implications for maintaining the health of intellectual disciplines. Disciplines dominated or monopolized by either approach will tend to deteriorate. As noted earlier in this chapter, experimental and conceptual innovators are natural enemies, and the tension between them can serve as a challenge to both. And although the individuals of the two types will rarely work together, their work can often be complementary. Conceptual innovations can build on experimental innovations, as theorists can formalize and systematize the discoveries of empiricists, while experimental innovators can test—and potentially overthrow—the generalizations of conceptualists. The greatest progress will generally occur when the two approaches are actively competing within a discipline.

Notes

Introduction
1. Jonathan Cott, ed., *Bob Dylan* (New York: Wenner Books, 2006), 427.
2. David Sheff, "Playboy Interview: Steven Jobs," *Playboy*, February 1, 1985.
3. Howard Gardner, *Creating Minds* (New York: Basic Books, 1993), 376.
4. Mihaly Csikszentmihalyi, *Creativity* (New York: Harper Collins, 1996), 39; Felicia Lee, "Going Early into That Good Night," *New York Times*, April 24, 2004, A15.
5. Frank Kermode, ed., *Selected Prose of T. S. Eliot* (New York: Farrar, Straus and Giroux, 1975), 117.
6. Joyce Carol Oates, *Uncensored* (New York: Harper Collins, 2005), 6.
7. Richard Nelson, "Some Features of Research by Economists on Technological Change Foreshadowed by 'The Rate and Direction of Inventive Activity,'" in *The Rate and Direction of Inventive Activity Revisited*, ed. Josh Lerner and Scott Stern (Chicago: University of Chicago Press, 2012), 38.
8. Josh Lerner and Scott Stern, "Introduction," in Lerner and Stern, *The Rate and Direction of Inventive Activity Revisited*, 1.
9. Lerner and Stern, "Introduction", 1; Richard Nelson, "Introduction," in *The Rate and Direction of Inventive Activity*, ed. Richard Nelson (Princeton, NJ: Princeton University Press, 1962), 7.
10. Kenneth Arrow, "Economic Welfare and the Allocation of Resources for Invention," in Nelson, *The Rate and Direction of Inventive Activity*, 624.
11. Simon Kuznets, "Inventive Activity: Problems of Definition and Measurement," in Nelson, *The Rate and Direction of Inventive Activity*, 32.
12. Alan Bowness, *The Conditions of Success: How the Modern Artist Rises to Fame* (New York: Thames and Hudson, 1990), 7, 9, 11, 16.
13. Walter Sickert, *The Complete Writings on Art* (Oxford: Oxford University Press, 2000), 253.

Chapter 1
1. Robert Jensen, "Measuring Canons," in *Partisan Canons*, ed. A. Brzyski (Durham, NC: Duke University Press, 2007), 32.
2. Helen Vendler, *Coming of Age as a Poet* (Cambridge, MA: Harvard University Press, 2003), 117.
3. James Dickey, *Babel to Byzantium* (New York: Farrar, Straus and Giroux, 1960), 5.

Chapter 2
1. Roger Fry, *Last Lectures* (Cambridge: Cambridge University Press, 1939), 3, 14–15. On the selection of artists for this chapter, see David Galenson, "Quantifying Artistic Success," *Historical Methods*, 35, no. 1 (2002): 5–20; Galenson, "Was Jackson Pollock the Greatest Modern American Painter?," *Historical Methods*, 35, no. 3 (2002): 117–28; Galenson, "Do the Most Important Artists Make the Most Expensive Paintings?" (Becker Friedman Institute Working Paper No. 2018-73, University of Chicago, Chicago, IL).
2. On Titian and Rembrandt as experimental innovators, see Robert Jensen, "Anticipating Artistic Behavior," *Historical Methods*, 37, no. 3 (2004): 137–53.
3. Alan Bowness, *Modern European Art* (London: Thames and Hudson, 1972), 73.
4. Richard Shiff, *Cézanne and the End of Impressionism* (Chicago: University of Chicago Press, 1984), 222.
5. David Galenson, *Artistic Capital* (New York: Routledge, 2006), 6.
6. Paul Cézanne, *Letters* (New York: Da Capo Press, 1995), 329–30.
7. Roger Fry, *Cézanne: A Study of His Development* (Chicago: University of Chicago Press, 1989), 33.
8. Michael Doran, ed., *Conversations with Cézanne* (Berkeley: University of California Press, 2001), 22; David Galenson, *Conceptual Revolutions in Twentieth-Century Art* (Cambridge: Cambridge University Press, 2009), 283.

9. Jon Kear, *Paul Cézanne* (London: Reaktion Books, 2016), 108, 155.
10. Cézanne, *Letters*, 303.
11. Fry, *Cézanne*, 35.
12. Doran, *Conversations with Cézanne*, 169.
13. Cézanne, *Letters*, 231.
14. Cézanne, *Letters*, 293–94.
15. John Rewald, *Paul Cézanne* (London: Spring Books, 1965), 152.
16. Doran, *Conversations with Cézanne*, 59.
17. John Rewald, *The Paintings of Paul Cézanne* (New York: Harry N. Abrams, 1996), 1:146.
18. Cézanne, *Letters*, 303.
19. Ambroise Vollard, *Cézanne* (New York: Dover Publications, 1984), 86.
20. Fry, *Cézanne*, 52.
21. Rewald, *Paintings of Paul Cézanne*. My count from Rewald's catalogue raisonné of Cézanne's paintings is that sixty-four of the total of 954 works, or 7 percent, are signed.
22. Cézanne, *Letters*, 302.
23. Cézanne, *Letters*, 333.
24. Fry, *Cézanne*, 3.
25. Cézanne, *Letters*, 327.
26. Cézanne, *Letters*, 310.
27. David Galenson, *Old Masters and Young Geniuses* (Princeton, NJ: Princeton University Press, 2006), 26.
28. Cézanne, *Letters*, 337.
29. Clive Bell, "The Debt to Cézanne," in *Modern Art and Modernism*, ed. Francis Frascina and Charles Harrison (New York: Harper and Row, 1982), 75; Clement Greenberg, *The Collected Essays and Criticism* (Chicago: University of Chicago Press, 1993), 3:83.
30. Hilarie Sheets, "Not Off the Grid, but Often in Flight," *New York Times*, November 25, 2012; Michael Kimmelman, *Portraits* (New York: Modern Library, 1999), 198.
31. Hilary Spurling, *The Unknown Matisse* (New York: Alfred A. Knopf, 1998), 181–82.
32. Cézanne, *Letters*, 317.
33. Jack Flam, ed., *Matisse on Art*, rev. ed. (Berkeley: University of California Press, 1995), 80, 124, 255.
34. Erle Loran, *Cézanne's Composition* (Berkeley: University of California Press, 1963), 76.
35. Will Gompertz, *What Are You Looking At?* (New York: Dutton, 2012), 78.
36. Brassaï, *Conversations with Picasso* (Chicago: University of Chicago Press, 1999), 107.
37. John Richardson, *A Life of Picasso* (New York: Random House, 1996), 2:97; Jack Flam, *Matisse and Picasso* (New York: Westview Press, 2003), 236.
38. Jack Tworkov, *The Extreme of the Middle* (New Haven, CT: Yale University Press, 2009), 179–80; John Rewald, *The History of Impressionism*, rev. ed. (New York: Museum of Modern Art, 1961), 578.
39. Joachim Gasquet, *Joachim Gasquet's Cézanne* (New York: Thames and Hudson, 1991), 148.
40. Meyer Schapiro, *Paul Cézanne* (New York: Harry Abrams, 1988), 18–19.
41. Gasquet, *Joachim Gasquet's Cézanne*, 150.
42. Doran, *Conversations with Cézanne*, 125.
43. Doran, *Conversations with Cézanne*, 62.
44. Cézanne, *Letters*, 337.
45. Cézanne, *Letters*, 313.
46. Cézanne, *Letters*, 324.
47. Françoise Gilot and Carlton Lake, *Life with Picasso* (New York: Anchor Books, 1964), 199.
48. Galenson, *Artistic Capital*, 6.
49. Alfred Barr, *Picasso: Fifty Years of His Art* (New York: Museum of Modern Art, 1946), 270.
50. John Golding, *Cubism*, rev. ed. (Boston: Boston Book and Art Shop, 1968), 15.
51. David Galenson, "Analyzing Artistic Innovation: The Greatest Breakthroughs of the Twentieth Century," *Historical Methods*, 41, no. 3 (2008), table 4, 116.
52. John Richardson, *A Life of Picasso* (New York: Random House, 1991), 1:411–19.
53. William Rubin, Hélène Seckel, and Judith Cousins, *Les Demoiselles d'Avignon* (New York: Museum of Modern Art, 1994), 14, 119.
54. Galenson, *Artistic Capital*, 7.
55. Galenson, *Conceptual Revolutions*, 82.
56. George Heard Hamilton, *Painting and Sculpture in Europe, 1880–1940* (Harmondsworth, UK: Penguin Books, 1967), 235.

57. Golding, *Cubism*, 51.
58. Richardson, *Life of Picasso*, 2:45, 83.
59. Douglas Cooper, *The Cubist Epoch* (London: Phaidon Press, 1994), 42.
60. Golding, *Cubism*, 60.
61. John Berger, *The Success and Failure of Picasso* (New York: Vintage International, 1993), 56-57.
62. John Berger, *Selected Essays* (New York: Vintage Books, 2001), 84.
63. Marilyn McCully, ed., *A Picasso Anthology* (Princeton, NJ: Princeton University Press, 1981), 57.
64. Barr, *Picasso*, 270.
65. Kirk Varnedoe and Adam Gopnik, *High and Low* (New York: Museum of Modern Art, 1990), 39.
66. Galenson, *Conceptual Revolutions*, chap. 6.
67. Galenson, *Conceptual Revolutions*, 355.
68. Christopher Reed, ed., *A Roger Fry Reader* (Chicago: University of Chicago Press, 1996), 115.
69. Barr, *Picasso*, 271.
70. Berger, *Success and Failure of Picasso*, 35.
71. Michel Sanouillet and Elmer Peterson, eds., *The Writings of Marcel Duchamp* (New York: Da Capo Press, 1989), 157.
72. Gerhard Richter, *The Daily Practice of Painting* (Cambridge, MA: MIT Press, 1995), 115, 92-93.
73. Daniel-Henry Kahnweiler, *My Galleries and Painters* (New York: Viking Press, 1971), 46.
74. Galenson, *Artistic Capital*, 7.
75. Cooper, *Cubist Epoch*, 12.
76. For example, see Marjorie Perloff, *The Futurist Moment* (Chicago: University of Chicago Press, 1986).
77. Galenson, *Old Masters and Young Geniuses*, 26.
78. John Richardson, "Picasso: A Retrospective View," in McCully, *Picasso Anthology*, 284.
79. Selden Rodman, *Conversations with Artists* (New York: Capricorn Books, 1961), 82.
80. Steven Naifeh and Gregory Smith, *Jackson Pollock* (New York: Clarkson N. Potter, 1989), 119, 145.
81. Kirk Varnedoe, *Jackson Pollock* (New York: Museum of Modern Art, 1998), 22.
82. Naifeh and Smith, *Jackson Pollock*, 184.
83. B. H. Friedman, *Jackson Pollock* (New York: Da Capo Press, 1995), 45.
84. Varnedoe, *Jackson Pollock*, 31.
85. Sylvia Pollock, ed., *American Letters, 1927-1947* (Cambridge: Polity Press, 2011), 178-79.
86. Galenson, *Artistic Capital*, 57.
87. Pepe Karmel, ed., *Jackson Pollock: Interviews, Articles, and Reviews* (New York: Museum of Modern Art, 1999), 51.
88. Karmel, *Jackson Pollock*, 52.
89. Karmel, *Jackson Pollock*, 15, 17.
90. Karmel, *Jackson Pollock*, 75.
91. Karmel, *Jackson Pollock*, 18.
92. Karmel, *Jackson Pollock*, 22.
93. Harold Rosenberg, *The Tradition of the New* (New York: Da Capo Press, 1994), 23-39.
94. Stephanie Terenzio, ed., *The Collected Writings of Robert Motherwell* (New York: Oxford University Press, 1992), 161-66.
95. Karmel, *Jackson Pollock*, 36.
96. Kirk Varnedoe and Pepe Karmel, eds., *Jackson Pollock* (New York: Museum of Modern Art, 1999), 241.
97. Karmel, *Jackson Pollock*, 15.
98. Karmel, *Jackson Pollock*, 19.
99. Allan Kaprow, *Essays on the Blurring of Art and Life*, exp. ed. (Berkeley: University of California Press, 2003), 6-9; Carter Ratcliff, *The Fate of a Gesture* (New York: Farrar, Straus Giroux, 1996), 175-76.
100. Galenson, *Conceptual Revolutions*, 124.
101. Michael Kimmelman, *Portraits* (New York: Modern Library, 1998), 52-54, 58, 64.
102. Galenson, *Artistic Capital*, 57.
103. E. A. Carmean, "Jackson Pollock: Classic Paintings of 1950," in *American Art at Mid-Century*, ed. E. A. Carmean and Eliza Rathbone (Washington, DC: National Gallery of Art, 1978), 127-31; Karmel, *Jackson Pollock*, 170; Varnedoe and Karmel, *Jackson Pollock*, 106-107; Galenson, *Artistic Capital*, 50.

338 NOTES

104. Karmel, *Jackson Pollock*, 22.
105. Friedman, *Jackson Pollock*, 157–60.
106. Carmean, "Jackson Pollock," 133–39.
107. Friedman, *Jackson Pollock*, 183.
108. Galenson, *Artistic Capital*, 48.
109. Galenson, *Artistic Capital*, chap. 4; Friedman, *Jackson Pollock*, 145–48.
110. Dore Ashton, *The New York School* (Berkeley: University of California Press, 1992), 152; Mark Stevens and Annalyn Swan, *de Kooning* (New York: Alfred A. Knopf, 2004), 209; Rudi Blesh, *Modern Art USA* (New York: Alfred A. Knopf, 1956), 253–54.
111. Carmean, *Jackson Pollock*, 151.
112. Karmel, *Jackson Pollock*, 63–64.
113. Friedman, *Jackson Pollock*, 211–13.
114. Naifeh and Smith, *Jackson Pollock*, 557, 683.
115. Sam Hunter, *Jackson Pollock* (New York: Museum of Modern Art, 1956); Francis O'Connor, *Jackson Pollock* (New York: Museum of Modern Art, 1967), 73.
116. Kenneth Goldsmith, ed., *I'll Be Your Mirror: The Selected Andy Warhol Interviews* (New York: Carroll and Graf, 2004), 18.
117. Victor Bockris, *Warhol* (New York: Da Capo Press, 1997), 82–83.
118. Bockris, *Warhol*, 11.
119. Rainer Crone, "Form and Ideology: Warhol's Techniques from Blotted Line to Film," in *The Work of Andy Warhol*, ed. Gary Garrels (Seattle: Bay Press, 1989), 86–88.
120. Galenson, *Artistic Capital*, 50.
121. Bockris, *Warhol*, 145–50.
122. Steven Madoff, ed., *Pop Art* (Berkeley: University of California Press, 1997), 106.
123. Galenson, *Conceptual Revolutions*, 82.
124. John Coplans, *Andy Warhol* (New York: New York Graphic Society, 1970), 49.
125. Bockris, *Warhol*, 153, 164, 170.
126. Galenson, *Conceptual Revolutions*, chap. 8.
127. Goldsmith, *I'll Be Your Mirror*, 90–91.
128. Harold Rosenberg, *Art and Other Serious Matters* (Chicago: University of Chicago Press, 1985), 137.
129. Roger Kimball, *Art's Prospect* (Chicago: Ivan Dee, 2003), 215; Annette Michelson, ed., *Andy Warhol* (Cambridge, MA: MIT Press, 2001), 69; Arthur Danto, *Philosophizing Art* (Berkeley: University of California Press, 1999), 9; Kelly Cresap, *Pop Trickster Fool* (Urbana: University of Illinois Press, 2004), 110–14.
130. Heiner Bastian, ed., *Andy Warhol* (London: Tate Publishing, 2001), 45.
131. Andy Warhol, *THE Philosophy of Andy Warhol* (San Diego: Harcourt Brace, 1975), 178.
132. David Galenson, *Painting outside the Lines* (Cambridge, MA: Harvard University Press, 2001), 138.
133. Goldsmith, *I'll Be Your Mirror*, 17.
134. Bockris, *Warhol*, 145.
135. Warhol, *THE Philosophy of Andy Warhol*, 149.
136. Andy Warhol and Pat Hackett, *POPism: The Warhol Sixties* (Orlando, FL: Harcourt, 1980), 3.
137. Goldsmith, *I'll Be Your Mirror*, 17.
138. Goldsmith, *I'll Be Your Mirror*, 387.
139. Goldsmith, *I'll Be Your Mirror*, 90.
140. Bockris, *Warhol*, 458.
141. Warhol and Hackett, *POPism*, 22.
142. Warhol, *THE Philosophy of Andy Warhol*, 135.
143. Bockris, *Warhol*, 281, 378–79, 414; Bob Colacello, *Holy Terror* (New York: Vintage Books, 2014), 120, 376.
144. Warhol, *THE Philosophy of Andy Warhol*, 13, 100–101.
145. Goldsmith, *I'll Be Your Mirror*, 99.
146. Madoff, *Pop Art*, 106.
147. John Russell and Suzi Gablik, eds., *Pop Art Redefined* (New York: Frederick A. Praeger, 1969), 115.
148. Anthony Haden-Guest, *True Colors* (New York: Atlantic Monthly Press, 1996), 151.
149. Virginia Button, *The Turner Prize* (London: Tate Publishing, 2003), 116.
150. David Sylvester, *About Modern Art* (New York: Henry Holt, 1997), 384–85.

NOTES 339

151. Galenson, "Analyzing Artistic Innovation," tables 2, 4.
152. Warhol and Hackett, *POPism*, 142–45.
153. David Bourdon, *Warhol* (New York: Harry N. Abrams, 1989), 10, 301, 378.
154. Michael Archer, *Art since 1960*, new ed. (London: Thames and Hudson, 2002), 183.
155. Warhol and Hackett, *POPism*, 50.
156. Jordana Saggese, ed., *The Jean-Michel Basquiat Reader* (Berkeley: University of California Press, 2021), 47.
157. Phoebe Hoban, *Basquiat* (New York: Penguin, 2004), chaps. 2–3.
158. Hoban, *Basquiat*, chaps. 3–4.
159. Saggese, *Jean-Michel Basquiat Reader*, 106, 120.
160. Saggese, *Jean-Michel Basquiat Reader*, 111.
161. Hoban, *Basquiat*, 108–10.
162. Hoban, *Basquiat*, 160–67.
163. Jordana Saggese, *Reading Basquiat* (Berkeley: University of California Press, 2014), 17.
164. Saggese, *Reading Basquiat*, 93; Hoban, *Basquiat*, 340–41.
165. Hoban, *Basquiat*, 201–204.
166. Rudy Chiappini, ed., *Jean-Michel Basquiat* (Milan: Skira, 2005), 70.
167. Nathalie Heinich, "Les vieux maitres et les jeunes genies," *Temporalités*, 14 (2011).
168. Saggese, *Jean-Michel Basquiat Reader*, 42.
169. Galenson, *Conceptual Revolutions*, chap. 11.
170. Saggese, *Jean-Michel Basquiat Reader*, 208–209.
171. For example, Saggese, *Reading Basquiat*.
172. Saggese, *Reading Basquiat*, 7.
173. Galenson, *Conceptual Revolutions*, 113–14, 357–58.
174. Saggese, *Jean-Michel Basquiat Reader*, 159.
175. Chiappini, *Jean-Michel Basquiat*, 56.
176. Saggese, *Jean-Michel Basquiat Reader*, 232.
177. Saggese, *Jean-Michel Basquiat Reader*, 118.
178. Hoban, *Basquiat*, 246.
179. Hoban, *Basquiat*, 294.
180. Saggese, *Jean-Michel Basquiat Reader*, 142.
181. Saggese, *Jean-Michel Basquiat Reader*, 160.
182. Saggese, *Jean-Michel Basquiat Reader*, 61, 126.
183. Saggese, *Jean-Michel Basquiat Reader*, 138.
184. Blake Gopnik, *Warhol* (New York: Harper Collins, 2020), 863.
185. Hoban, *Basquiat*, 283–85.
186. Saggese, *Jean-Michel Basquiat Reader*, 220.
187. Hoban, *Basquiat*, 311; Saggese, *Jean-Michel Basquiat Reader*, 210.
188. Chiappini, *Jean-Michel Basquiat*, 40.
189. Saggese, *Jean-Michel Basquiat Reader*, 188.
190. Hoban, *Basquiat*, 348.
191. Peter Schjeldahl, *Let's See* (New York: Thames and Hudson, 2008), 215.
192. David Galenson and Simone Lenzu, "Two Old Masters and a Young Genius: The Creativity of Francis Bacon, Lucian Freud, and Jean-Michel Basquiat," *Journal of Cultural Economics*, 47 (2023): 489–511.
193. Cézanne, *Letters*, 309.
194. Cézanne, *Letters*, 315.
195. Doran, *Conversations with Cézanne*, 163, 59.
196. Cézanne, *Letters*, 317.
197. Meyer Schapiro, *Paul Cézanne* (New York: Harry N. Abrams, 1988), 19.
198. Barr, *Picasso*, 270.
199. Barr, *Picasso*, 271.
200. Flam, *Matisse and Picasso*, 125–26.
201. Kevin Dettmar, *The Illicit Joyce of Postmodernism* (Madison: University of Wisconsin Press, 1996), 211.
202. Barr, *Picasso*, 270.
203. Ashton, *New York School*, chap. 12; Barnett Newman, *Selected Writings and Interviews* (Berkeley: University of California Press, 1992), 251; Terenzio, *Collected Writings of Robert Motherwell*, 45–46.

204. Karmel, *Jackson Pollock*, 17–18.
205. Karmel, *Jackson Pollock*, 20–23.
206. Karmel, *Jackson Pollock*, 45.
207. Goldsmith, *I'll Be Your Mirror*, 17.
208. Bourdon, *Warhol*, 138.
209. Goldsmith, *I'll Be Your Mirror*, 196.
210. Gunnar Kvaran, Hanna Veland, and Grete Arbu, eds., *Andy Warhol by Andy Warhol* (Turin: Skira, 2008), 149.
211. Goldsmith, *I'll Be Your Mirror*, 96.
212. Henry Geldzahler, *Making It New* (San Diego: Harcourt Brace, 1994), 250–51.
213. Goldsmith, *I'll Be Your Mirror*, 88.
214. Gopnik, *Warhol*, 327.
215. Saggese, *Jean-Michel Basquiat Reader*, 45.
216. Saggese, *Jean-Michel Basquiat Reader*, 42.
217. Saggese, *Jean-Michel Basquiat Reader*, 44.

Chapter 3

1. Stephen Spender, *The Making of a Poem* (London: Hamish Hamilton, 1955), 48. On the selection of poets for this chapter, see David Galenson, "Literary Life Cycles," *Historical Methods*, 38, no. 2 (2005): 45–60.
2. Robert Lowell, *Collected Prose* (New York: Farrar, Straus and Giroux, 1987), 244–45.
3. Sidney Cox, *A Swinger of Birches* (New York: New York University Press, 1957), 112.
4. Mark Richardson, ed., *The Collected Prose of Robert Frost* (Cambridge, MA: Harvard University Press, 2007), 165.
5. Lawrance Thompson, *Robert Frost: The Years of Triumph, 1915–1938* (New York: Holt, Rinehart and Winston, 1970), 322.
6. Robert Frost, *A Boy's Will* (New York: Henry Holt, 1915), 59.
7. Jeffrey Cramer, *Robert Frost among His Poems* (Jefferson, NC: McFarland and Company, 1996), 26; Lawrance Thompson, *Fire and Ice* (New York: Russell and Russell, 1961), 95.
8. Elaine Barry, *Robert Frost on Writing* (New Brunswick, NJ: Rutgers University Press, 1973), 35.
9. Lawrance Thompson, ed., *Selected Letters of Robert Frost* (New York: Holt, Rinehart and Winston, 1964), 88.
10. Thompson, *Selected Letters of Robert Frost*, 102, 111, 79.
11. Thompson, *Selected Letters of Robert Frost*, 80.
12. Elaine Barry, *Robert Frost* (New York: Frederick Ungar, 1973), 12.
13. Thompson, *Selected Letters of Robert Frost*, 111, 98.
14. Richardson, *Collected Prose of Robert Frost*, 128, 196.
15. Thompson, *Selected Letters of Robert Frost*, 102.
16. Joseph Brodsky, Seamus Heaney, and Derek Walcott, *Homage to Robert Frost* (New York: Farrar, Straus and Giroux, 1998), 103–104.
17. Lowell, *Collected Prose*, 9.
18. Thompson, *Selected Letters of Robert Frost*, 103.
19. Jay Parini, *Robert Frost* (New York: Henry Holt, 1999), 417.
20. Thompson, *Selected Letters of Robert Frost*, 426.
21. Thompson, *Selected Letters of Robert Frost*, 84.
22. Thompson, *Selected Letters of Robert Frost*, 141.
23. Louis Untermeyer, ed., *The Letters of Robert Frost to Louis Untermeyer* (New York: Holt, Rinehart and Winston, 1963), 92.
24. Donald Greiner, *Robert Frost* (Chicago: American Library Association, 1974), 121, 131; Philip Gerber, ed., *Critical Essays on Robert Frost* (Boston: G. K. Hall and Co., 1982), 103, 212–13.
25. Richardson, *Collected Prose of Robert Frost*, 104.
26. Parini, *Robert Frost*, 153–55; William Pritchard, *Frost* (New York: Oxford University Press, 1984), 27.
27. Cramer, *Robert Frost among His Poems*, 77.
28. Untermeyer, *Letters of Robert Frost*, 163; David Galenson, *Artistic Capital* (London: Routledge, 2006), 149.
29. Edward Lathem, ed., *The Poetry of Robert Frost* (New York: Holt, Rinehart and Winston, 1969), 224–25.

30. Richard Poirier, *The Work of Knowing* (Stanford, CA: Stanford University Press, 1990), 181; Morris Dickstein, ed., *Robert Frost* (Pasadena, CA: Salem Press, 2010), 196.
31. Vladimir Nabokov, *Pale Fire* (New York: G. P. Putnam's Sons, 1962), 203–204.
32. Edward Lathem, ed., *Interviews with Robert Frost* (New York: Holt, Rinehart and Winston, 1966), 188.
33. Josephine Jacobsen, *The Instant of Knowing* (Ann Arbor: University of Michigan Press, 2002), 182.
34. Thompson, *Selected Letters of Robert Frost*, 344.
35. Richardson, *Collected Prose of Robert Frost*, 131.
36. Barry, *Robert Frost on Writing*, 10.
37. Richardson, *Collected Prose of Robert Frost*, 132.
38. Lathem, *Interviews with Robert Frost*, 58, 117, 174.
39. Brodsky, Heaney, and Walcott, *Homage to Robert Frost*, 62–63.
40. James Cox, "Robert Frost and the Edge of the Clearing," in Gerber, *Critical Essays on Robert Frost*, 151.
41. Richardson, *Collected Prose of Robert Frost*, 132–33.
42. Edward Lathem and Lawrance Thompson, eds., *The Robert Frost Reader* (New York: Russell and Russell, 1961), 382.
43. Barry, *Robert Frost on Writing*, 160.
44. Richardson, *Collected Prose of Robert Frost*, 145.
45. Parini, *Robert Frost*, 344; Thompson, *Fire and Ice*, 33.
46. Lathem, *Poetry of Robert Frost*, 307.
47. Peter Stanlis, *Conversations with Robert Frost* (New Brunswick, NJ: Transaction Publishers, 2010), 110.
48. Stanlis, *Conversations with Robert Frost*, 40.
49. Jeffrey Meyers, *Robert Frost* (Boston: Houghton Mifflin, 1996), 324.
50. Randall Jarrell, *No Other Book* (New York: HarperCollins, 2000), 233.
51. Lowell, *Collected Prose*, 10.
52. Meyers, *Robert Frost*, 351–52.
53. Edwin Cady and Louis Budd, *On Frost* (Durham, NC: Duke University Press, 1991), 133–46.
54. Robert Faggen, ed., *The Cambridge Companion to Robert Frost* (Cambridge: Cambridge University Press, 2001), 75.
55. Galenson, *Artistic Capital*, 152–56.
56. Untermeyer, *Letters of Robert Frost*, 22.
57. Lathem and Thompson, *Robert Frost Reader*, 419.
58. Frank Kermode, ed., *Selected Prose of T. S. Eliot* (New York: Farrar, Straus and Giroux, 1975), 65.
59. Lyndall Gordon, *T. S. Eliot* (New York: W. W. Norton, 1998), 14–26; A. David Moody, ed., *The Cambridge Companion to T. S. Eliot* (Cambridge: Cambridge University Press, 1994), 16–17.
60. T. S. Eliot, *To Criticize the Critic and Other Writings* (New York: Farrar, Straus and Giroux, 1965), 126.
61. Eliot, *To Criticize the Critic*, 126; Gordon, *T. S. Eliot*, 42; Christopher Ricks, ed., *Inventions of the March Hare* (London: Faber and Faber, 1996), 399–400.
62. Gordon, *T. S. Eliot*, 98; Moody, *Cambridge Companion to T. S. Eliot*, 49.
63. Galenson, *Artistic Capital*, 149; Alan Shucard, Fred Moramarco, and William Sullivan, *Modern American Poetry* (Boston: Twayne, 1989), 99.
64. W. B. Yeats, *Essays and Introductions* (London: Macmillan, 1961), 499.
65. James Atlas, *Delmore Schwartz* (New York: Farrar, Straus and Giroux, 1977), 26–27.
66. Leonard Unger, ed., *T. S. Eliot* (New York: Russell and Russell, 1966), 50.
67. Unger, *T. S. Eliot*, 30.
68. Kermode, *Selected Prose of T. S. Eliot*, 38, 40–41, 43, 65.
69. Edmund Wilson, *Axel's Castle* (New York: Farrar, Straus and Giroux, 2004), 89.
70. Conrad Aiken, *A Reviewer's ABC* (New York: Meridian Books, 1958), 177.
71. Louis Menand, "Practical Cat," *The New Yorker*, September 19, 2011, 81.
72. Rita Dove, ed., *The Best American Poetry 2000* (New York: Scribner, 2000), 269–85.
73. C. B. Cox and Arnold Hinchliffe, eds., *T. S. Eliot: "The Waste Land"* (London: Macmillan, 1986), 58, 62.
74. This discussion is indebted to the analysis in David Perkins, *A History of Modern Poetry: From the 1890s to the High Modernist Mode* (Cambridge, MA: Harvard University Press, 1976), 498–513.

75. Moody, *Cambridge Companion to T. S. Eliot*, 183.
76. Stephen Spender, *T. S. Eliot* (New York: Viking Press, 1976), 78; Marjorie Perloff, *The Futurist Moment* (Chicago: University of Chicago Press, 1976), 72.
77. Kermode, *Selected Prose of T. S. Eliot*, 153.
78. Spender, *T. S. Eliot*, 108.
79. Spender, *T. S. Eliot*, 119–20.
80. A. Walton Litz, ed., *Eliot in His Time* (Princeton, NJ: Princeton University Press, 1973), 4.
81. Evelyn Waugh, *Brideshead Revisited* (Boston: Little, Brown, 1946), 33; Steve Ellis, *T. S. Eliot* (London: Continuum, 2009), 52–53.
82. John Unterecker, *Voyager: A Life of Hart Crane* (New York: Farrar, Straus and Giroux, 1969), 242, 272.
83. William Carlos Williams, *The Autobiography of William Carlos Williams* (New York: Random House, 1951), 174.
84. Valerie Eliot, ed., *The Letters of T. S. Eliot* (San Diego: Harcourt Brace Jovanovich, 1988), 1:280.
85. Gordon, *T. S. Eliot*, 142.
86. Unger, *T. S. Eliot*, 36–37; Spender, *T. S. Eliot*, 136.
87. Gordon, *T. S. Eliot*, 223.
88. Gordon, *T. S. Eliot*, 519.
89. Gordon, *T. S. Eliot*, 520.
90. Kermode, *Selected Prose of T. S. Eliot*, 249–53.
91. Spender, *T. S. Eliot*, 3.
92. George Monteiro, ed., *Conversations with Elizabeth Bishop* (Jackson: University Press of Mississippi, 1996), 99.
93. Jeffrey Meyers, ed., *Robert Lowell* (Ann Arbor: University of Michigan Press, 1988), 160.
94. Brett Millier, *Elizabeth Bishop* (Berkeley: University of California Press, 1993), 187.
95. Thomas Travisano and Saskia Hamilton, eds., *Words in Air: The Complete Correspondence between Elizabeth Bishop and Robert Lowell* (New York: Farrar, Straus and Giroux, 2008), 809–10.
96. Monteiro, *Conversations with Elizabeth Bishop*, 126.
97. Richard Gray, *A History of American Literature* (Oxford: Blackwell, 2004), 231; Paul Mariani, *Lost Puritan* (New York: W. W. Norton, 1994), 28.
98. The description of Bishop is that of the poet Dana Gioia, a student of Bishop's at Harvard; Monteiro, *Conversations with Elizabeth Bishop*, 139. The description of Lowell is that of the critic Alfred Kazin; Meyers, *Robert Lowell*, 251.
99. Jonathan Price, ed., *Critics on Robert Lowell* (Coral Gables, FL: University of Miami Press, 1972), 37.
100. Robert Lowell, *Collected Poems* (New York: Farrar, Straus and Giroux, 2003), 15; Stephen Yenser, *Circle to Circle* (Berkeley: University of California Press, 1975), 62.
101. Lloyd Schwartz and Sybil Estess, eds., *Elizabeth Bishop and Her Art* (Ann Arbor: University of Michigan Press, 1983), 181; Lowell, *Collected Prose*, 76.
102. Elizabeth Bishop, *Poems, Prose, and Letters* (New York: Library of America, 2008), 33–34.
103. Monteiro, *Conversations with Elizabeth Bishop*, 24.
104. Elizabeth Bishop, *One Art* (New York: Farrar, Straus and Giroux, 1994), 621.
105. Schwartz and Estess, *Elizabeth Bishop and Her Art*, 281.
106. Monteiro, *Conversations with Elizabeth Bishop*, 99.
107. Monteiro, *Conversations with Elizabeth Bishop*, 99–103.
108. Monteiro, *Conversations with Elizabeth Bishop*, 43.
109. Anne Stevenson, *Elizabeth Bishop* (New York: Twayne Publishers, 1966), 66.
110. William Brown and Andrew Fabian, eds., *Darwin* (Cambridge: Cambridge University Press, 2010), 75.
111. Meyers, *Robert Lowell*, 169.
112. Lowell, *Collected Prose*, 227.
113. Stanley Kunitz, *A Kind of Order, a Kind of Folly* (Boston: Little, Brown, 1975), 154; Lowell, *Collected Poems*, 992.
114. Ian Hamilton, *Robert Lowell* (New York: Random House, 1982), 232.
115. Lowell, *Collected Prose*, 227; David Kalstone, *Becoming a Poet* (New York: Farrar, Straus and Giroux, 1989), 174.
116. Kalstone, *Becoming a Poet*, 174.

NOTES 343

117. Thomas Travisano, *Elizabeth Bishop* (Charlottesville: University Press of Virginia, 1988), 154.
118. Kalstone, *Becoming a Poet*, 174; Lowell, *Collected Prose*, 226.
119. Lowell, *Collected Prose*, 227.
120. Lowell, *Collected Prose*, 284.
121. Terri Witek, *Robert Lowell and Life Studies* (Columbia: University of Missouri Press, 1993), 13.
122. Bishop, *One Art*, 348–52.
123. Price, *Critics on Robert Lowell*, 80.
124. Neil Roberts, ed., *A Companion to Twentieth-Century Poetry* (Oxford: Blackwell Publishers, 2001), 489.
125. Kermode, *Selected Prose of T. S. Eliot*, 43.
126. Robert Phillips, *The Confessional Poets* (Carbondale: Southern Illinois University Press, 1973), xi, 1–7.
127. Galenson, *Artistic Capital*, 149; Phillips, *Confessional Poets*, 24.
128. Lowell, *Collected Poems*, 51; David Kalstone, *Five Temperaments* (New York: Oxford University Press, 1977), 51.
129. Donald Hall, *The Weather for Poetry* (Ann Arbor: University of Michigan Press, 1982), 195.
130. Travisano and Hamilton, *Words in Air*, 708.
131. Kalstone, *Becoming a Poet*, 193.
132. Bishop, *Poems, Prose, and Letters*, 167.
133. Galenson, *Artistic Capital*, 149.
134. Seamus Heaney, *Finders Keepers* (New York: Farrar, Straus and Giroux, 2002), 375.
135. Travisano, *Elizabeth Bishop*, 154–205.
136. Bishop, *One Art*, 621.
137. Elizabeth Bishop, *Edgar Allan Poe & the Juke-Box* (New York: Farrar, Straus and Giroux, 2006), 207.
138. Schwartz and Estess, *Elizabeth Bishop and Her Art*, 200.
139. Schwartz and Estess, *Elizabeth Bishop and Her Art*, 213.
140. Heaney, *Finders Keepers*, 374.
141. Colm Toibin, *On Elizabeth Bishop* (Princeton, NJ: Princeton University Press, 2015), 47.
142. Elizabeth Bishop, *The Collected Prose* (New York: Farrar, Straus and Giroux, 1984), 58.
143. Monteiro, *Conversations with Elizabeth Bishop*, 42; Bishop, *One Art*, 408.
144. Lowell, *Collected Prose*, 246–47.
145. Monteiro, *Conversations with Elizabeth Bishop*, 51.
146. Heaney, *Finders Keepers*, 220.
147. Kunitz, *Kind of Order*, 156.
148. Lowell, *Collected Poems*, 737.
149. Monteiro, *Conversations with Elizabeth Bishop*, 104.
150. George Plimpton, ed., *Writers at Work: The "Paris Review" Interviews*, 2nd series (New York: Viking Press, 1965), 346–47.
151. Lowell, *Collected Poems*, 991, 993.
152. Bishop, *One Art*, 350.
153. Karen Kukil, ed., *The Journals of Sylvia Plath, 1950–1962* (London: Faber and Faber, 2000), 438.
154. Peter Orr, ed., *The Poet Speaks* (London: Routledge and Kegan Paul, 1966), 167; Paul Alexander, *Rough Magic* (New York: Viking Penguin, 1991), 36.
155. Sylvia Plath, *Letters Home* (New York: Harper and Row, 1975), 289.
156. Alexander, *Rough Magic*, 60–62.
157. Alexander, *Rough Magic*, 157; Anne Stevenson, *Bitter Fame* (Boston: Houghton Mifflin, 1989), 39.
158. Alexander, *Rough Magic*, 106–15.
159. Stevenson, *Bitter Fame*, 46–47.
160. Kukil, *Journals of Sylvia Plath*, 395.
161. Kukil, *Journals of Sylvia Plath*, 395, 618–21.
162. Edward Butscher, ed., *Sylvia Plath* (New York: Dodd, Mead and Company, 1977), 62.
163. Kukil, *Journals of Sylvia Plath*, 492.
164. Orr, *Poet Speaks*, 172.
165. Kukil, *Journals of Sylvia Plath*, 212.
166. Plath, *Letters Home*, 233.
167. Charles Newman, ed., *The Art of Sylvia Plath* (Bloomington: Indiana University Press, 1970), 58.

168. Ted Hughes, *Winter Pollen* (London: Faber and Faber, 1994), 162.
169. Newman, *Art of Sylvia Plath*, 188, 193.
170. Hughes, *Winter Pollen*, 161.
171. Galenson, *Artistic Capital*, 149.
172. Plath, *Letters Home*, 467.
173. Plath, *Letters Home*, 466.
174. Ted Hughes, ed., *The Collected Poems of Sylvia Plath* (New York: Harper and Row, 1992), 270.
175. Linda Wagner, ed., *Sylvia Plath* (London: Routledge, 1988), 60.
176. Orr, *Poet Speaks*, 167–70.
177. A. Alvarez, *The Savage God* (New York: Random House, 1972), 26.
178. Lowell, *Collected Prose*, 122.
179. Elizabeth Hardwick, *Seduction and Betrayal* (New York: New York Review of Books, 2001), 110.
180. Hughes, *Collected Poems of Sylvia Plath*, 224.
181. Helen Vendler, *Coming of Age as a Poet* (Cambridge, MA: Harvard University Press, 2003), 117; Alvarez, *Savage God*, 21.
182. Plath, *Letters Home*, 466; Stevenson, *Bitter Fame*, 265.
183. Hughes, *Collected Poems of Sylvia Plath*, 245.
184. Alvarez, *Savage God*, 16–17.
185. Edna Longley, ed., *The Bloodaxe Book of 20th Century Poetry* (Tarset, UK: Bloodaxe Books, 2000), 20–21; Paul Bentley, *The Poetry of Ted Hughes* (London: Longman, 1998), 27–30; Earl Ingersoll, ed., *Conversations with Rita Dove* (Jackson: University Press of Mississippi, 2003), 117.
186. Jo Gill, ed., *The Cambridge Companion to Sylvia Plath* (Cambridge: Cambridge University Press, 2006), 52.
187. Wagner, *Sylvia Plath*, 204.
188. Gill, *Cambridge Companion to Sylvia Plath*, 129.
189. Kukil, *Journals of Sylvia Plath*, 210.
190. Plath, *Letters Home*, 468.
191. Richardson, *Collected Prose of Robert Frost*, 133.
192. Lathem, *Interviews with Robert Frost*, 174.
193. Lathem, *Interviews with Robert Frost*, 133.
194. Richardson, *Collected Prose of Robert Frost*, 133.
195. Meyers, *Robert Frost*, 82–83.
196. Lawrance Thompson, *Robert Frost: The Early Years, 1874–1915* (New York: Holt, Rinehart and Winston, 1996), 595–97.
197. Thompson, *Robert Frost: Years of Triumph*, 596–98.
198. Cox and Hinchliffe, *T. S. Eliot*, 73.
199. Lyndall Gordon, *Eliot's New Life* (New York: Farrar, Straus and Giroux, 1988), 231; Litz, *Eliot in His Time*, 87.
200. Spender, *T. S. Eliot*, 92–93, 107.
201. Litz, *Eliot in His Time*, 92.
202. Gordon, *T. S. Eliot*, 539–44.
203. Richard Badenhausen, *T. S. Eliot and the Art of Collaboration* (Cambridge: Cambridge University Press, 2004), 13.
204. Kermode, *Selected Prose of T. S. Eliot*, 38.
205. Kermode, *Selected Prose of T. S. Eliot*, 40; T. S. Eliot, *Selected Essays* (London: Faber and Faber, 1961), 322; Badenhausen, *T. S. Eliot and the Art of Collaboration*, 13, 44.
206. Cox and Hinchliffe, *T.S. Eliot*, 73.
207. Plimpton, *Writers at Work*, 96.
208. Litz, *Eliot in His Time*, 76.
209. Hannah Sullivan, *The Work of Revision* (Cambridge, MA: Harvard University Press, 2013), 110.
210. Plimpton, *Writers at Work*, 15.
211. Thompson, *Robert Frost: The Early Years*, 590.
212. Lathem, *Interviews with Robert Frost*, 75–76.
213. Plimpton, *Writers at Work*, 350.
214. Meyers, *Robert Lowell*, 27.
215. Hamilton, *Robert Lowell*, 384–422.

216. Lowell, *Collected Poems*, vii.
217. Meyers, *Robert Lowell*, 58–59.
218. Kunitz, *Kind of Order*, 159.
219. Travisano and Hamilton, *Words in Air*, 776.
220. Lowell, *Collected Poems*, xii.
221. Lowell, *Collected Poems*, xiii.
222. Bishop, *Poems, Prose, and Letters*, 178.
223. Kalstone, *Becoming a Poet*, 261; Millier, *Elizabeth Bishop*, 533.
224. Meyers, *Robert Lowell*, 27.
225. Monteiro, *Conversation with Elizabeth Bishop*, 7, 27.
226. Bishop, *Collected Prose*, 137.
227. Millier, *Elizabeth Bishop*, 466.
228. Bishop, *One Art*, 334, 568.
229. Millier, *Elizabeth Bishop*, 466.
230. Lowell, *Collected Poems*, 595. For an earlier version of this poem, see Robert Lowell, *Notebook* (New York: Farrar, Straus and Giroux, 1970), 235–36.
231. Linda Anderson and Jo Shapcott, eds., *Elizabeth Bishop* (Tarset, UK: Bloodaxe Books, 2002), 15.
232. Millier, *Elizabeth Bishop*, 506–507.
233. Millier, *Elizabeth Bishop*, 508–13; Bishop, *Edgar Allan Poe*, 223–40.
234. Richard Tillinghast, *Poetry and What Is Real* (Ann Arbor: University of Michigan Press, 2004), 112.
235. Monteiro, *Conversations with Elizabeth Bishop*, 76.
236. Lowell, *Collected Poems*, 595.
237. For example, see Newman, *Art of Sylvia Plath*, 273–79.
238. Susan Van Dyne, *Revising Life* (Chapel Hill: University of North Carolina, 1993), 56–60.

Chapter 4

1. Alan Bowness, *Modern European Art* (New York: Thames and Hudson, 1995), 176. On the selection of sculptors for this chapter, see David Galenson, *Old Masters and Young Geniuses* (Princeton, NJ: Princeton University Press, 2006), 111–12.
2. Auguste Rodin, *Rodin on Art and Artists* (New York: Dover, 1983), 11.
3. Albert Elsen, ed., *Auguste Rodin* (Englewood Cliffs, NJ: Prentice-Hall, 1965), 145.
4. George Heard Hamilton, *Painting and Sculpture in Europe, 1880–1940* (Harmondsworth, UK: Penguin, 1972), 62; Galenson, *Old Masters and Young Geniuses*, 122.
5. Albert Elsen, ed., *Rodin Rediscovered* (Washington, DC: National Gallery of Art, 1987), 157.
6. Elsen, *Auguste Rodin*, 110, 114–15, 151.
7. Judith Cladel, *Rodin: The Man and His Art* (New York: Century Co., 1917), 107.
8. Albert Elsen, *Rodin* (New York: Museum of Modern Art, 1963), 141.
9. Elsen, *Auguste Rodin*, 164.
10. Catherine Lampert, *Rodin* (London: Arts Council of Great Britain, 1986), 61, 135.
11. Elsen, *Rodin*, 141.
12. Elsen, *Rodin*, 145.
13. Leo Steinberg, *Other Criteria* (London: Oxford University Press, 1972), 395–98.
14. Rosalind Krauss, *Passages in Modern Sculpture* (Cambridge, MA: MIT Press, 1981), 30.
15. Elsen, *Auguste Rodin*, 155.
16. Elsen, *Auguste Rodin*, 31.
17. Elsen, *Rodin Rediscovered*, 161, 166.
18. Elsen, *Rodin*, 39.
19. Camille Mauclair, *Auguste Rodin* (London: Duckworth and Co., 1909), 24–25.
20. Elsen, *Rodin Rediscovered*, 69–73.
21. Albert Elsen, *Rodin's "Thinker" and the Dilemmas of Modern Public Sculpture* (New Haven, CT: Yale University Press, 1985).
22. Albert Elsen, *"The Gates of Hell" by Auguste Rodin* (Stanford, CA: Stanford University Press, 1985), 146.
23. Raphael Masson and Veronique Mattiussi, *Rodin* (Paris: Flammarion, 2015), 33.
24. Elsen, *"The Gates of Hell,"* 243.
25. Mauclair, *Auguste Rodin*, 24–25.

26. Elsen, "The Gates of Hell," 158.
27. Galenson, *Old Masters and Young Geniuses*, 113.
28. Elsen, *Rodin*, 93.
29. Frederic Grunfeld, *Rodin* (New York: Henry Holt, 1987), 316.
30. Elsen, *Rodin*, 102.
31. Albert Elsen, *Origins of Modern Sculpture* (New York: George Braziller, 1974), 29.
32. Elsen, *Origins of Modern Sculpture*, 28.
33. Elsen, *Rodin*, 103.
34. Elsen, *Rodin*, 89.
35. Rudolf Wittkower, *Sculpture: Processes and Principles* (New York: Harper and Row, 1977), 239.
36. Elsen, *Rodin*, 102.
37. Hamilton, *Painting and Sculpture in Europe*, 68.
38. Helene Marraud, *Balzac* (Paris: Rodin Museum, 2014), 143.
39. Marraud, *Balzac*, 156–57.
40. Edward Steichen, *A Life in Photography* (New York: Harmony Books, 1985), chaps. 2, 4.
41. Elsen, *Origins of Modern Sculpture*, 74.
42. Wittkower, *Sculpture*, 253–55.
43. Grunfeld, *Rodin*, 394; Ruth Butler, *Rodin* (New Haven, CT: Yale University Press, 1993), 340.
44. Ester Coen, *Umberto Boccioni* (New York: Metropolitan Museum of Art, 1988), xviii.
45. Coen, *Umberto Boccioni*, xix.
46. John Golding, *Boccioni "Unique Forms of Continuity in Space"* (London: Tate Gallery, 1985), 6.
47. Umbro Apollonio, ed., *Futurist Manifestos* (New York: Viking Press, 1973), 19–24.
48. Apollonio, *Futurist Manifestos*, 24–31; Golding, *Boccioni*, 9.
49. Apollonio, *Futurist Manifestos*, 27.
50. Apollonio, *Futurist Manifestos*, 28.
51. Golding, *Boccioni*, 13–14.
52. Joshua Taylor, *Futurism* (New York: Museum of Modern Art, 1961), 127–28.
53. Coen, *Umberto Boccioni*, 94.
54. Coen, *Umberto Boccioni*, xxiii.
55. Coen, *Umberto Boccioni*, 234.
56. Gino Severini, *The Life of a Painter* (Princeton, NJ: Princeton University Press, 1995), 110.
57. Taylor, *Futurism*, 134.
58. Severini, *Life of a Painter*, 110–11; Apollonio, *Futurist Manifestos*, 51.
59. Coen, *Umberto Boccioni*, 242.
60. Golding, *Boccioni*, 16.
61. Severini, *Life of a Painter*, 125.
62. Coen, *Umberto Boccioni*, 255.
63. Coen, *Umberto Boccioni*, 216; David Galenson, *Conceptual Revolutions in Twentieth-Century Art* (Cambridge: Cambridge University Press and NBER, 2009), table 3.2, 64.
64. Coen, *Umberto Boccioni*, xxix.
65. Caroline Tisdall and Angelo Bozzola, *Futurism* (New York: Oxford University Press, 1978), 81; Elsen, *Origins of Modern Sculpture*, 34; Coen, *Umberto Boccioni*, 218.
66. Guillaume Apollinaire, *Apollinaire on Art* (Boston: MFA Publications, 2001), 320–21.
67. Coen, *Umberto Boccioni*, 204.
68. Golding, *Boccioni*, 27.
69. Véronique Wiesinger, ed., *The Studio of Alberto Giacometti* (Paris: Centre Pompidou, 2007), 79.
70. Ángel González, *Alberto Giacometti* (Barcelona: Ediciones Polígrafa, 2006), 139.
71. González, *Alberto Giacometti*, 147.
72. Galenson, *Old Masters and Young Geniuses*, 26–27, 56.
73. Galenson, *Old Masters and Young Geniuses*, 112.
74. Laurie Wilson, *Alberto Giacometti* (New Haven, CT: Yale University Press, 2003), 110.
75. Reinhold Hohl, ed., *Giacometti* (Ostfildern-Ruit, Germany: Verlag Gerd Hatje, 1998), 63.
76. González, *Alberto Giacometti*, 131.
77. Rosalind Krauss, *Passages in Modern Sculpture* (New York: Viking Press, 1977), 111–13.
78. William Rubin, *Dada, Surrealism, and Their Heritage* (New York: Museum of Modern Art, 1968), 116–17; Wilson, *Alberto Giacometti*, 120–25, 133–38.
79. González, *Alberto Giacometti*, 131; David Sylvester, *Looking at Giacometti* (New York: Henry Holt, 1996), 142.

80. González, *Alberto Giacometti*, 139–40.
81. Hohl, *Giacometti*, 83.
82. Sylvester, *Looking at Giacometti*, 92.
83. Felix Baumann and Poul Erik Tojner, *Cézanne & Giacometti* (Ostifildern, Germany: Hatje Cantz Verlag, 2008), 96.
84. Sylvester, *Looking at Giacometti*, 125.
85. Baumann and Tojner, *Cézanne & Giacometti*, 159, 284, 286.
86. González, *Alberto Giacometti*, 150–51.
87. James Lord, *A Giacometti Portrait* (New York: Museum of Modern Art, 1965), 44–46, 56–57.
88. Wiesinger, *Studio of Alberto Giacometti*, 27.
89. Alberto Giacometti, *Exhibition of Sculptures, Paintings, Drawings* (New York: Pierre Matisse Gallery, 1948), 4, 6, 16.
90. Galenson, *Old Masters and Young Geniuses*, 113.
91. Michael Kimmelman, *Portraits* (New York: Modern Library, 1998), 61; Sylvester, *Looking at Giacometti*, 61.
92. González, *Alberto Giacometti*, 151.
93. Sylvester, *Looking at Giacometti*, 12.
94. González, *Alberto Giacometti*, 151.
95. Jack Flam, ed., *Robert Smithson: The Collected Writings* (Berkeley: University of California Press, 1996), 192.
96. Flam, *Robert Smithson*, 279, 285; Robert Hobbs, ed., *Robert Smithson: Sculpture* (Ithaca, NY: Cornell University Press, 1981), 231.
97. Flam, *Robert Smithson*, 272; Hobbs, *Robert Smithson*, 232.
98. Alan Brilliant to David Galenson, email, December 1, 2004.
99. Flam, *Robert Smithson*, 175.
100. Flam, *Robert Smithson*, 283–84.
101. Flam, *Robert Smithson*, 52–60, 284.
102. For example, see Lucy Lippard, *Six Years: The Dematerialization of the Art Object from 1966 to 1972* (Berkeley: University of California Press, 1997), xiii–xvii; Adachiara Zevi, *Sol Lewitt: Critical Texts* (Rome: Editrice Inonia, 1995), 84.
103. Flam, *Robert Smithson*, 100.
104. Flam, *Robert Smithson*, 212.
105. Flam, *Robert Smithson*, 178.
106. Amy Dempsey, *Art in the Modern Era* (New York: Harry N. Abrams, 2002), 260–62; Lippard, *Six Years*, 57.
107. Marjorie Perloff, *The Futurist Moment* (Chicago: University of Chicago Press, 1986), 215–34.
108. Hobbs, *Robert Smithson*, 185–86; Ron Graziani, *Robert Smithson and the American Landscape* (Cambridge: Cambridge University Press, 2004), 107–11.
109. Flam, *Robert Smithson*, 146; Hobbs, *Robert Smithson*, 191.
110. David Galenson, *Artistic Capital* (London: Routledge, 2006), chap. 8.
111. Hobbs, *Robert Smithson*, 192–95.
112. Flam, *Robert Smithson*, 143–53.
113. Galenson, *Conceptual Revolutions*, chap. 16.
114. Arthur Danto, "The American Sublime," *The Nation*, September 1, 2005.
115. Peter Boswell, ed., *Maya Lin* (Milan: Electa, 1998), 60.
116. Corinne Robins, *The Pluralist Era* (New York: Harper and Row, 1984), 85.
117. Kirk Varnedoe, *Pictures of Nothing* (Princeton, NJ: Princeton University Press, 2006), 168.
118. Grunfeld, *Rodin*, 289.
119. Grunfeld, *Rodin*, 508.
120. Grunfeld, *Rodin*, 510.
121. Cladel, *Rodin*, 224.
122. Coen, *Umberto Boccioni*, 241.
123. Tisdall and Bozzola, *Futurism*, 81.
124. Coen, *Umberto Boccioni*, 241.
125. Sylvester, *Looking at Giacometti*, 17.
126. Sylvester, *Looking at Giacometti*, 111.
127. Flam, *Robert Smithson*, 3–4.
128. Grunfeld, *Rodin*, 399.
129. Hohl, *Giacometti*, 196.

Chapter 5

1. Robert Jelliffe, ed. *Faulkner at Nagano* (Tokyo: Kenkyusha, 1956), 109. On the selection of novelists for this chapter, see David Galenson, "A Portrait of the Author as a Young or Old Innovator," *Historical Methods*, 39, no. 2 (2006): 51–72.
2. Frederick Gwynn and Joseph Blotner, eds., *Faulkner in the University* (Charlottesville: University Press of Virginia, 1995), 103.
3. Matthew Bruccoli, ed., *F. Scott Fitzgerald: A Life in Letters* (New York: Charles Scribner's Sons, 1994), 455.
4. David Galenson, *Artistic Capital* (New York: Routledge, 2006), 188–91, 196–99.
5. Bruccoli, *F. Scott Fitzgerald*, 80.
6. Bruccoli, *F. Scott Fitzgerald*, 169.
7. Herman Melville, *Moby-Dick; Or, The Whale* (Berkeley: University of California Press, 1983), 135.
8. Herman Melville, *Tales, Poems, and Other Writings* (New York: Modern Library, 2002), 41.
9. Andrew Delbanco, *Melville* (New York: Alfred A. Knopf, 2005), 106–108.
10. James Barbour, "'All My Books Are Botches': Melville's Struggle with *The Whale*," in James Barbour and Tom Quirk, eds., *Writing the American Classics* (Chapel Hill: University of North Carolina Press, 1990), 27.
11. Melville, *Tales, Poems, and Other Writings*, 59.
12. Melville, *Tales, Poems, and Other Writings*, 52, 55.
13. Barbour, "'All My Books Are Botches,'" 27.
14. Melville, *Moby-Dick*, 466.
15. David Kirby, *Herman Melville* (New York: Continuum, 1993), 75.
16. Melville, *Moby-Dick*, 379; Nathaniel Philbrick, *Why Read Moby-Dick?* (New York: Viking, 2011), 1.
17. Howard Vincent, *The Trying-Out of Moby-Dick* (Carbondale: Southern Illinois University Press, 1949), 47–48; Newton Arvin, *Herman Melville* (New York: William Sloane Associates, 1950), 49, 144–48; Leon Howard, *Herman Melville* (Berkeley: University of California Press, 1951), 115–16, 162–65.
18. Philbrick, *Why Read Moby-Dick?*, 19.
19. Melville, *Moby-Dick*, 389; Barbour, "'All My Books Are Botches,'" 32.
20. Melville, *Moby-Dick*, 78; Barbour, "'All My Books Are Botches,'" 34–35.
21. Melville, *Moby-Dick*, 52.
22. Melville, *Moby-Dick*, 168.
23. Delbanco, *Melville*, 178.
24. John Bryant, "Moby-Dick as Revolution," in Robert Levine, ed., *The Cambridge Companion to Herman Melville* (Cambridge: Cambridge University Press, 1998), 70; Delbanco, *Melville*, 11.
25. D. H. Lawrence, *Selected Literary Criticism* (New York: Viking, 1956), 390.
26. Delbanco, *Melville*, 12; C. L. R. James, *Mariners, Renegades and Castaways* (Detroit: Bewick, 1978), 71.
27. Watson Branch, ed., *Melville: The Critical Heritage* (London: Routledge and Kegan Paul, 1974), 415–16.
28. Melville, *Tales, Poems, and Other Writings*, 39–41.
29. Delbanco, *Melville*, 225.
30. Galenson, *Artistic Capital*, 196.
31. Arvin, *Herman Melville*, 210–11; F. O. Matthiessen, *American Renaissance* (London: Oxford University Press, 1941), 491–92; Lewis Mumford, *Herman Melville* (New York: Harcourt, Brace and Company, 1929), 224–55.
32. Delbanco, *Melville*, 252.
33. Victor Doyno, *Writing "Huck Finn"* (Philadelphia: University of Pennsylvania Press, 1991), 105.
34. Gregg Canfield, ed., *The Oxford Companion to Mark Twain* (Oxford: Oxford University Press, 2003), 354–55.
35. Shelley Fishkin, ed., *The Mark Twain Anthology* (New York: Library of America, 2010), 217.
36. Mark Dawidziak, *Mark My Words* (New York: St. Martin's Press, 1996), 13, 47, 49, 53, 55.
37. Doyno, *Writing "Huck Finn,"* 94, 102; Henry Nash Smith, *Mark Twain* (Cambridge, MA: Harvard University Press, 1962), 113–14; Bernard DeVoto, *Mark Twain at Work* (Cambridge, MA: Harvard University Press, 1942), 52; Tom Quirk, *Coming to Grips with "Huckleberry Finn"* (Columbia: University of Missouri Press, 1993), 25.
38. Doyno, *Writing "Huck Finn,"* 105.

39. W. D. Howells, *My Mark Twain* (Brooklyn: Haskell House Publishers, 1977), 166-67.
40. Franklin Rogers, ed., *Mark Twain's Satires and Burlesques* (Berkeley: University of California Press, 1968), 5-6.
41. Smith, *Mark Twain*, 113.
42. Samuel Clemens, "My Methods of Writing," *Mark Twain Quarterly*, 8, no. 3 (1949): 1.
43. Barbour and Quirk, *Writing American Classics*, 101.
44. Mark Twain, *Adventures of Huckleberry Finn* (Berkeley: University of California Press, 1985), xxxi.
45. Clemens, "My Methods of Writing," 1.
46. Twain, *Adventures of Huckleberry Finn*, 148, 171.
47. Doyno, *Writing "Huck Finn,"* 95.
48. T. S. Eliot, "Introduction to *The Adventures of Huckleberry Finn*," in *Mark Twain*, ed. Harold Bloom, updated ed. (New York: Chelsea House, 2006), 34-35.
49. Ernest Hemingway, *Green Hills of Africa* (New York: Charles Scribner's Sons, 1963), 22.
50. Twain, *Adventures of Huckleberry Finn*, 178-79.
51. Mark Twain, *The Adventures of Tom Sawyer* (New York: Oxford University Press, 1996), 121.
52. Ron Powers, *Mark Twain* (New York: Free Press, 2006), 460.
53. Ralph Ellison, *Going to the Territory* (New York: Random House, 1986), 316.
54. Twain, *Adventures of Huckleberry Finn* (1985), 306-308.
55. Walter Blair, *Mark Twain and Huck Finn* (Berkeley: University of California Press, 1962), 143.
56. Lionel Trilling, *The Liberal Imagination* (New York: Viking Press, 1950), 105-16.
57. Doyno, *Writing "Huck Finn,"* 19.
58. Doyno, *Writing "Huck Finn,"* 19-23; Quirk, *Coming to Grips*, 13-16; Blair, *Mark Twain and Huck Finn*.
59. Powers, *Mark Twain*, 477.
60. Eliot, "Introduction," 36.
61. Henry Nash Smith, "Introduction," in *Adventures of Huckleberry Finn*, by Mark Twain (Cambridge, MA: Riverside Press, 1958), 22.
62. Twain, *Adventures of Huckleberry Finn*, 317.
63. Victor Doyno, "Afterword," in *Adventures of Huckleberry Finn*, by Mark Twain (New York: Oxford University Press, 1996), 13-14.
64. For example, see Bloom, *Mark Twain*, 33; Philip Young, *Ernest Hemingway* (University Park: Pennsylvania State University Press, 1966), 212; Mark Twain, *The Adventures of Huckleberry Finn* (New York: Harper and Brothers Publishers, 1931); Mark Twain, *Adventures of Huckleberry Finn* (Berkeley: University of California Press, 2001), 378.
65. Twain, *Adventures of Huckleberry Finn* (1985), 413.
66. Everett Emerson, *Mark Twain* (Philadelphia: University of Pennsylvania Press, 2000), 161-62.
67. Jeffrey Steinbrink, "Who Wrote Huckleberry Finn? Mark Twain's Control of the Early Manuscript," in *One Hundred Years of "Huckleberry Finn,"* ed. Robert Sattelmeyer and J. D. Crowley (Columbia: University of Missouri Press, 1985), 92-93.
68. Smith, *Mark Twain*, 119-21.
69. For example, see the essays in Laurie Champion, ed., *The Critical Response to Mark Twain's "Huckleberry Finn"* (New York: Greenwood Press, 1991).
70. Fishkin, *Mark Twain Anthology*, 221-22.
71. Fishkin, *Mark Twain Anthology*, 1.
72. DeVoto, *Mark Twain at Work*, 100.
73. Virginia Woolf, *Collected Essays* (New York: Harcourt, Brace, and World, 1967), 2:99.
74. Lyndall Gordon, *Virginia Woolf* (New York: W. W. Norton, 1984), chaps. 1, 2, 6.
75. John Mepham, *Virginia Woolf* (London: Macmillan, 1991), chaps. 2, 3.
76. Virginia Woolf, *A Writer's Diary* (San Diego: Harcourt, Brace and Company, 1982), 85.
77. Woolf, *Writer's Diary*, 134.
78. Woolf, *Collected Essays*, 2:109.
79. Mepham, *Virginia Woolf*, xvi.
80. Woolf, *Collected Essays*, 2:106-107.
81. Roger Fry, *Vision and Design* (London: Chatto and Windus, 1929), 11; Richard Kendall, ed., *Monet by Himself* (New York: Knickerbocker Press, 1999), 172.
82. Woolf, *Collected Essays*, 2:107.
83. Virginia Woolf, *Moments of Being* (New York: Harcourt Brace Jovanovich, 1976), 70-72.
84. Roger Fry, *Cézanne* (Chicago: University of Chicago Press, 1989), 36.

85. Woolf, *Moments of Being*, 73.
86. Mepham, *Virginia Woolf*, xiii.
87. Woolf, *Moments of Being*, 36.
88. Woolf, *Moments of Being*, 87.
89. Woolf, *Writer's Diary*, 46, 52.
90. Woolf, *Writer's Diary*, 56.
91. Woolf, *Writer's Diary*, 71.
92. Woolf, *Writer's Diary*, 101; Virginia Woolf, *The Diary of Virginia Woolf* (New York: Harcourt Brace Jovanovich, 1980), 3:152.
93. Galenson, *Artistic Capital*, 194–95.
94. Gordon, *Virginia Woolf*, 39.
95. Gordon, *Virginia Woolf*, 29.
96. Woolf, *Moments of Being*, 85.
97. Virginia Woolf, *To the Lighthouse* (Orlando, FL: Harcourt, 1981), 18, 48, 53, 157.
98. Woolf, *To the Lighthouse*, 19.
99. Woolf, *To the Lighthouse*, 171.
100. Joan Bennett, *Virginia Woolf*, 2nd ed. (Cambridge: Cambridge University Press, 1964), 27, 91, 98, 142, 148.
101. Sue Roe and Susan Sellers, eds., *The Cambridge Companion to Virginia Woolf* (Cambridge: Cambridge University Press, 2000), 19.
102. Panthea Reid, *Art and Affection* (New York: Oxford University Press, 1996), 306.
103. Woolf, *Writer's Diary*, 98; Woolf, *To the Lighthouse*, 209.
104. Steven Gould Axelrod, *Sylvia Plath* (Baltimore: Johns Hopkins University Press, 1990), 114; Sylvia Plath, *The Journals of Sylvia Plath, 1950–1962* (London: Faber and Faber, 2000), 289.
105. Plath, *Journals of Sylvia Plath*, 342.
106. Plath, *Journals of Sylvia Plath*, 269.
107. Ruth Saxton and Jean Tobin, eds., *Woolf and Lessing* (New York: St. Martin's Press, 1994), 150–53, 163.
108. Matthew Bruccoli, ed., *Conversations with Ernest Hemingway* (Jackson: University Press of Mississippi, 1986), 129.
109. Ernest Hemingway, *The Sun Also Rises* (New York: Charles Scribner's Sons, 1929), prologue.
110. Ernest Hemingway, *Death in the Afternoon* (New York: Charles Scribner's Sons, 1932), 2.
111. Harry Levin, "Observations on the Style of Ernest Hemingway," in *Hemingway and His Critics*, ed. Carlos Baker (New York: Hill and Wang, 1961), 93–115; Philip Young, *Ernest Hemingway* (University Park: Pennsylvania State University Press, 1966), chap. 5.
112. Jeffrey Meyers, ed., *Hemingway: The Critical Heritage* (London: Routledge and Kegan Paul, 1982), 91.
113. Young, *Ernest Hemingway*, 205.
114. Ernest Hemingway, ed., *Men at War* (New York: Crown Publishers, 1942), xv.
115. Michael Reynolds, *Hemingway's First War* (Princeton, NJ: Princeton University Press, 1976), 10.
116. Bruccoli, *Conversations with Ernest Hemingway*, 146.
117. Ernest Hemingway, *The Nick Adams Stories* (New York: Charles Scribner's Sons, 1972), 237.
118. Ernest Hemingway, *A Farewell to Arms* (New York: Charles Scribner's Sons, 1929), 184–85.
119. Hemingway, *Death in the Afternoon*, 4.
120. Hemingway, *Farewell to Arms*, 249.
121. Jeffrey Meyers, *Hemingway* (New York: Da Capo Press, 1999), 25, 98.
122. Young, *Ernest Hemingway*, 208.
123. Galenson, *Artistic Capital*, 196; Reynolds, *Hemingway's First War*, 238.
124. Young, *Ernest Hemingway*, 92.
125. Young, *Ernest Hemingway*, 93.
126. Meyers, *Hemingway*, 240.
127. Bruccoli, *Conversations with Ernest Hemingway*, 124.
128. Jeffrey Meyers, ed., *Hemingway* (London: Routledge and Kegan Paul, 1982), 297–313.
129. Galenson, *Artistic Capital*, 196.
130. For example, see Robert Penn Warren, "Ernest Hemingway," in *Ernest Hemingway*, ed. Harold Bloom (Philadelphia: Chelsea House, 2005), 25–54; obituaries by Irving Howe and Alberto Moravia in Meyers, ed., *Hemingway*, 430–33, 437–42; Young, *Ernest Hemingway*, 245–46.
131. Hemingway, *Death in the Afternoon*, 2.

132. Gwynn and Blotner, *Faulkner in the University*, 206.
133. Meyers, ed., *Hemingway*, 438–41.
134. Hemingway, *Sun Also Rises*, 153.
135. Ernest Hemingway, *Across the River and into the Trees* (New York: Charles Scribner's Sons, 1950), 6–7.
136. Hugh Kenner, *A Homemade World* (Baltimore: Johns Hopkins University Press, 1989), 124–26.
137. Levin, "Observations on the Style," 108–109; Kenner, *Homemade World*, 126.
138. Kenner, *Homemade World*, 126.
139. Bruccoli, *Conversations with Ernest Hemingway*, 128.
140. Meyers, ed., *Hemingway*, 430–31.
141. Joan Didion, *Let Me Tell You What I Mean* (New York: Alfred A. Knopf, 2021), 103.
142. Norman Mailer, *The Spooky Art* (New York: Random House, 2003), 261.
143. Norman Mailer, *Advertisements for Myself* (Cambridge. MA: Harvard University Press, 1992), 21.
144. Mailer, *Spooky Art*, 261.
145. Brian Higgins and Hershel Parker, eds., *Critical Essays on Herman Melville's "Moby-Dick"* (New York: G. K. Hall and Co., 1992), 398.
146. Hershel Parker, ed., *The Recognition of Herman Melville* (Ann Arbor: University of Michigan Press, 1967), 175.
147. Higgins and Parker, *Critical Essays*, 170.
148. Smith, *Mark Twain*, 129; DeVoto, *Mark Twain at Work*, 92.
149. Hemingway, *Green Hills of Africa*, 22.
150. Smith, *Mark Twain*, 133–34.
151. Eliot, "Introduction," 34–40.
152. Doyno, *Writing "Huck Finn,"* 102.
153. Barbour and Quirk, *Writing the American Classics*, 100.
154. Woolf, *Writer's Diary*, 114.
155. Woolf, *Writer's Diary*, 53.
156. Virginia Woolf, *Mrs. Dalloway* (New York: Modern Library, 1928), vii–viii.
157. Woolf, *Writer's Diary*, 68.
158. Woolf, *To the Lighthouse*, 53.
159. Allen McLaurin, *Virginia Woolf* (Cambridge: Cambridge University Press, 1973), 192.
160. Woolf, *To the Lighthouse*, 161.
161. Woolf, *To the Lighthouse*, 208.
162. Bruccoli, *Conversations with Ernest Hemingway*, 113.
163. Bernard Oldsey, *Hemingway's Hidden Craft* (University Park: Pennsylvania State University Press, 1979), 72, 80.
164. Bruccoli, *Conversations with Ernest Hemingway*, 113.
165. Hemingway, *Farewell to Arms*, 126.
166. Young, *Ernest Hemingway*, 93.

Chapter 6

1. Sigfried Giedion, *Space, Time and Architecture* (Cambridge, MA: Harvard University Press, 2008), 414. On the selection of architects for this chapter, see David Galenson, "The Greatest Architects of the Twentieth Century" (NBER Working Paper No. 14182, National Bureau of Economic Research, Cambridge, MA 2008); Galenson, "The Reappearing Masterpiece," *Historical Methods*, 38, no. 4 (2005): 178–88.
2. Frederick Gutheim, ed., *Frank Lloyd Wright on Architecture* (New York: Duell, Sloan and Pearce, 1941), 19.
3. Gutheim, *Frank Lloyd Wright on Architecture*, 16, 19.
4. Gutheim, *Frank Lloyd Wright on Architecture*, 257.
5. Frank Lloyd Wright, *An Autobiography* (New York: Duell, Sloan and Pearce, 1943), 11.
6. Meryle Secrest, *Frank Lloyd Wright* (Chicago: University of Chicago Press, 1998), 58.
7. Gutheim, *Frank Lloyd Wright on Architecture*, 178.
8. Secrest, *Frank Lloyd Wright*, 58; Robert McCarter, *Frank Lloyd Wright* (London: Reaktion Books, 2006), 16–17.
9. Gutheim, *Frank Lloyd Wright on Architecture*, 33–34.

10. Giedion, *Space, Time and Architecture*, 414.
11. Grant Manson, *Frank Lloyd Wright to 1910* (New York: Van Nostrand Reinhold, 1958).
12. McCarter, *Frank Lloyd Wright*, 64–65.
13. Giedion, *Space, Time and Architecture*, 426–27, 496; Vincent Scully, *Modern Architecture and Other Essays* (Princeton, NJ: Princeton University Press, 2002), 56–60; Vincent Scully, *Frank Lloyd Wright* (New York: George Braziller, 1960), 23–24.
14. Joseph Connors, *The Robie House* (Chicago: University of Chicago Press, 1984), 26.
15. Gutheim, *Frank Lloyd Wright on Architecture*, 108, 139.
16. Brendan Gill, *Many Masks* (New York: G. P. Putnam's Sons, 1987), 359–70.
17. Bruce Pfeiffer, ed., *Frank Lloyd Wright Collected Writings* (New York: Rizzoli, 1992), 1:126–37.
18. Gutheim, *Frank Lloyd Wright on Architecture*, 136.
19. Gill, *Many Masks*, 347.
20. Gutheim, *Frank Lloyd Wright on Architecture*, 232.
21. Neil Levine, "Frank Lloyd Wright's Diagonal Planning Revisited," in *On and by Frank Lloyd Wright*, ed. Robert McCarter (London: Phaidon Press, 2005), 232–63.
22. Donald Hoffmann, *Frank Lloyd Wright's Fallingwater*, 2nd ed. (New York: Dover Publications, 1993), 25.
23. Franklin Toker, *Fallingwater Rising* (New York: Alfred A. Knopf, 2003), 207.
24. Toker, *Fallingwater Rising*, chap. 8.
25. Goran Schildt, *Alvar Aalto: The Decisive Years* (New York: Rizzoli, 1986), 154; Giedion, *Space, Time and Architecture*, 645–48.
26. Galenson, "Greatest Architects of the Twentieth Century," tables 1 and 2.
27. Galenson, "Greatest Architects of the Twentieth Century," table 2.
28. Terence Riley, ed., *Frank Lloyd Wright* (New York: Museum of Modern Art, 1994), 270–74.
29. Frank Lloyd Wright, *The Guggenheim Correspondence* (Carbondale: Southern Illinois University Press, 1986), 284, 301–302.
30. Jonathan Lipman, "Consecrated Space: Wright's Public Buildings," in McCarter, *On and by Frank Lloyd Wright*, 264–85.
31. John Sergeant, *Frank Lloyd Wright's Usonian Houses* (New York: Whitney Library of Design, 1976).
32. Patrick Meehan, ed., *Frank Lloyd Wright Remembered* (Washington, DC: Preservation Press, 1991), 133.
33. Colin St. John Wilson, *The Other Tradition of Modern Architecture* (London: Black Dog Publishing, 2007), 111.
34. Donald Hoffman, *Understanding Frank Lloyd Wright's Architecture* (New York: Dover Publications, 1995), 7.
35. Gutheim, *Frank Lloyd Wright on Architecture*, 38; Wright, *Autobiography*, 158.
36. Gutheim, *Frank Lloyd Wright on Architecture*, 58.
37. Gutheim, *Frank Lloyd Wright on Architecture*, 158; Robert McCarter, ed., *Frank Lloyd Wright* (New York: Princeton Architectural Press, 1991), 247.
38. Gutheim, *Frank Lloyd Wright on Architecture*, 174.
39. Le Corbusier, *Creation Is a Patient Search* (New York: Frederick A. Praeger, 1960).
40. Nicholas Weber, *Le Corbusier* (New York: Alfred A. Knopf, 2008), 93; Le Corbusier, *Creation Is a Patient Search*, 21.
41. Weber, *Le Corbusier*, 93.
42. Galenson, "Greatest Architects of the Twentieth Century," table 1.
43. Le Corbusier, *Creation Is a Patient Search*, 21.
44. Le Corbusier, *Towards a New Architecture* (New York: Dover Publications, 1986), 4, 6, 29, 164.
45. Peter Blake, *Le Corbusier* (Baltimore: Penguin, 1960), 34; also Scully, *Modern Architecture and Other Essays*, 238, 243.
46. Le Corbusier, *Towards a New Architecture*, 7.
47. Galenson, "Greatest Architects of the Twentieth Century," table 2. The Villa Savoye totaled thirty-seven illustrations in the twenty-two textbooks consulted, compared to Fallingwater's thirty-five illustrations.
48. Charles Jencks, *Le Corbusier and the Continual Revolution in Architecture* (New York: Monacelli Press, 2000), 173.
49. Le Corbusier, *Journey to the East* (Cambridge, MA: MIT Press, 1987), 230.
50. Giedion, *Space, Time and Architecture*, 524–28.
51. Le Corbusier, *New World of Space* (New York: Reynal and Hitchcock, 1948), 23.
52. Giedion, *Space, Time and Architecture*, 547.

53. Jencks, *Le Corbusier and the Continual Revolution*, 254.
54. Jencks, *Le Corbusier and the Continual Revolution*, 258.
55. Blake, *Le Corbusier*, 124.
56. Galenson, "Greatest Architects of the Twentieth Century," table 2.
57. Danièle Pauly, *Le Corbusier: La Chapelle de Ronchamp* (Paris: Fondation Le Corbusier, 1997), 59–60.
58. Jacques Guiton, ed., *The Ideas of Le Corbusier on Architecture and Urban Planning* (New York: George Braziller, 1981), 46.
59. Le Corbusier, *Creation Is a Patient Search*, 166.
60. Weber, *Le Corbusier*, 658–59.
61. Weber, *Le Corbusier*, 690.
62. Scully, *Modern Architecture and Other Essays*, 247; Jencks, *Le Corbusier and the Continual Revolution*, 10, 267, 309.
63. Jencks, *Le Corbusier and the Continual Revolution*, 267.
64. Giedion, *Space, Time and Architecture*, 567–69.
65. Weber, *Le Corbusier*, 13.
66. Weber, *Le Corbusier*, 690.
67. Susan Gray, ed., *Architects on Architects* (New York: McGraw-Hill, 2002), 13.
68. Barbara Isenberg, *Conversations with Frank Gehry* (New York: Alfred A. Knopf, 2009), 268–69.
69. Louis Kahn, *Writings, Lectures, Interviews* (New York: Rizzoli, 1991), 307.
70. Le Corbusier, *The Final Testament of Père Corbu* (New Haven, CT: Yale University Press, 1997), 85, 89.
71. Guiton, *Ideas of Le Corbusier*, 50.
72. Guiton, *Ideas of Le Corbusier*, 72.
73. Martin Filler, *Makers of Modern Architecture* (New York: New York Review of Books, 2007), 74, 90.
74. Scully, *Modern Architecture and Other Essays*, 236–49.
75. Scully, *Modern Architecture and Other Essays*, 243.
76. Mildred Friedman, ed., *Gehry Talks* (New York: Universe Publishing, 2002), 195.
77. Filler, *Makers of Modern Architecture*, 170.
78. Galenson, "Greatest Architects of the Twentieth Century," table 1.
79. Christina Bechtler, ed., *Frank O. Gehry/Kurt W. Forster* (Ostfildern-Ruit, Germany: Cantz Verlag, 1999), 53–55, 87–88.
80. J. Fiona Ragheb, ed., *Frank Gehry, Architect* (New York: Solomon R. Guggenheim Foundation, 2001), 289.
81. Filler, *Makers of Modern Architecture*, 185.
82. Ragheb, *Frank Gehry, Architect*, 308.
83. Ragheb, *Frank Gehry, Architect*, 311.
84. Friedman, *Gehry Talks*, 47.
85. Charles Jencks, ed., *Frank O. Gehry* (London: Academy Editions, 1995), 42; Galenson, "Greatest Architects of the Twentieth Century."
86. Friedman, *Gehry Talks*, 42.
87. Jencks, *Frank O. Gehry*, 41.
88. Brooke Hodge, ed., *FOG: Flowing in All Directions* (Los Angeles: Museum of Contemporary Art, 2003), preface.
89. Ragheb, *Frank Gehry, Architect*, 290.
90. Friedman, *Gehry Talks*, 18.
91. Friedman, *Gehry Talks*, 53.
92. Roger Fry, *Cézanne: A Study of His Development* (Chicago: University of Chicago Press, 1989), 3.
93. Paul Goldberger, *Building Art* (New York: Alfred A. Knopf, 2015), 292.
94. Isenberg, *Conversations with Frank Gehry*, 62.
95. Goldberger, *Building Art*, 192.
96. Isenberg, *Conversations with Frank Gehry*, 155.
97. Bechtler, *Frank O. Gehry/Kurt W. Forster*, 32–33.
98. Ragheb, *Frank Gehry, Architect*, 304.
99. Marvin Trachtenberg and Isabelle Hyman, *Architecture*, 2nd ed. (New York: Harry N. Abrams, 2002), 567.
100. Friedman, *Gehry Talks*, 54.
101. Ragheb, *Frank Gehry, Architect*, 309.

354 NOTES

102. Charles Jencks, *The Iconic Building* (London: Frances Lincoln, 2005), 12.
103. Jencks, *Iconic Building*, 12.
104. Jencks, *Iconic Building*, 164.
105. Galenson, "Greatest Architects of the Twentieth Century," table 2.
106. Friedman, *Gehry Talks*, 47.
107. Hans Ulrich Obrist, *Lives of the Artists, Lives of the Architects* (London: Allen Lane, 2015), 141.
108. Friedman, *Gehry Talks*, 17.
109. Coosje van Bruggen, *Frank O. Gehry* (New York: Solomon R. Guggenheim Foundation, 1999), 138.
110. Friedman, *Gehry Talks*, 50.
111. Filler, *Makers of Modern Architecture*, 170.
112. Filler, *Makers of Modern Architecture*, 187.
113. Friedman, *Gehry Talks*, 226.
114. Isenberg, *Conversations with Frank Gehry*, 163.
115. Maya Lin, *Boundaries* (New York: Simon and Schuster, 2000), 3:09.
116. Lin, *Boundaries*, 4:45, 5:04–05.
117. Lin, *Boundaries*, 4:08–10, 4:45.
118. Lin, *Boundaries*, 4:11.
119. Lin, *Boundaries*, 4:11.
120. Lin, *Boundaries*, 4:09–12.
121. James Reston, *A Rift in the Earth* (New York: Arcade Publishing, 2017), 48–50.
122. Anne Wagner, *A House Divided* (Berkeley: University of California Press, 2012), 67; Reston, *Rift in the Earth*, 44.
123. Jan Scruggs and Joel Swerdlow, *To Heal a Nation* (New York: Harper and Row, 1985), 120–21.
124. Lin, *Boundaries*, 4:16.
125. Lin, *Boundaries*, 2:05.
126. Lin, *Boundaries*, 3:05–11; Peter Boswell, ed., *Maya Lin* (Milan: Electa, 1998), 10, 18.
127. Boswell, *Maya Lin*, 32.
128. Scruggs and Swerdlow, *To Heal a Nation*, 76; Boswell, *Maya Lin*, 60.
129. Albert Elsen, *Origins of Modern Sculpture* (New York: George Braziller, 1974), 26.
130. Galenson, *Artistic Capital*, 129.
131. Eleanor Munro, *Originals*, new ed. (New York: Da Capo Press, 2000), 485–86.
132. Galenson, *Artistic Capital*, 128.
133. Lin, *Boundaries*, 11:03.
134. Wright, *Autobiography*, 35.
135. Le Corbusier, *Final Testament of Père Corbu*, 105.
136. Wright, *Autobiography*, 156.
137. Le Corbusier, *Creation Is a Patient Search*, 37.
138. Frank Gehry, *On Line* (New Haven, CT: Yale University Press, 2008), 22.
139. van Bruggen, *Frank O. Gehry*, 103.
140. Gehry, *On Line*, 26.
141. André Wogenscky, *Le Corbusier's Hands* (Cambridge, MA: MIT Press, 2006), 31, 35.
142. Boswell, *Maya Lin*, 18.
143. Boswell, *Maya Lin*, 22.
144. Wright, *Autobiography*, 138.
145. Guiton, *Ideas of Le Corbusier*, 50.
146. Ragheb, *Frank Gehry, Architect*, 309.
147. van Bruggen, *Frank O. Gehry*, 130.
148. Lin, *Boundaries*, 12:03.

Chapter 7

1. Siegfried Kracauer, *The Theory of Film* (New York: Oxford University Press, 1960), 8–19. On the selection of photographers for this chapter, see David Galenson, "The Greatest Photographers of the Twentieth Century" (NBER Working Paper No. 15278, National Bureau of Economic Research, Cambridge, MA, 2009).
2. Brooks Johnson, ed., *Photography Speaks* (New York: Aperture Foundation, 2004), 86.
3. The biographical information given here is taken from John Szarkowski and Maria Hambourg, *The Work of Atget*, 2 (New York: Museum of Modern Art, 1982).

NOTES   355

4. Szarkowski and Hambourg, *Work of Atget*, 2:14–15.
5. Julien Levy, *Memoir of an Art Gallery* (New York: G. P. Putnam's Sons, 1977), 92.
6. Szarkowski and Hambourg, *Work of Atget*, 2:16.
7. Johnson, *Photography Speaks*, 86.
8. Szarkowski and Hambourg, *Work of Atget*, 2:30; James Borcoman, *Eugène Atget* (Ottawa: National Gallery of Canada, 1984), 69.
9. Szarkowski and Hambourg, *Work of Atget*, 2:25–27.
10. Susan Laxton, *Paris as Gameboard* (New York: Wallach Art Gallery, 2002), 1.
11. Paul Hill and Thomas Cooper, eds., *Dialogue with Photography* (Manchester, UK: Cornerhouse Publications, 1979), 23; David Featherstone, ed., *Observations* (Carmel, CA: Friends of Photography, 1984), 25–26.
12. Molly Nesbit, *Atget's Seven Albums* (New Haven, CT: Yale University Press, 1992), 1; Hill and Cooper, *Dialogue with Photography*, 23–24.
13. Berenice Abbott, *The World of Atget* (New York: Paragon Books, 1979), viii.
14. Hank O'Neal, *Berenice Abbott, American Photographer* (New York: McGraw-Hill, 1982), 11–12.
15. O'Neal, *Berenice Abbott*, 12.
16. Peter Barberie, *Looking at Atget* (New Haven, CT: Yale University Press, 2005), 87.
17. Beaumont Newhall, ed., *Photography* (New York: Museum of Modern Art, 1980), 235.
18. Barberie, *Looking at Atget*, 69.
19. Nancy Newhall, ed., *The Daybooks of Edward Weston* (New York: Aperture Foundation, 1990), 2:202.
20. Ansel Adams, *Ansel Adams, An Autobiography* (Boston: Little, Brown, 1985), 264; John Szarkowski and Maria Hambourg, *The Work of Atget* (New York: Museum of Modern Art, 1985), 4:18.
21. Szarkowski and Hambourg, *Work of Atget*, 4:17.
22. John Hill, *Walker Evans: Lyric Documentary* (Gottingen, Germany: Steidl Publishers, 2006), 12–23.
23. Peter Bunnell, *Inside the Photograph* (New York: Aperture Foundation, 2006), 144.
24. Szarkowski and Hambourg, *Work of Atget*, 4:18.
25. John Szarkowski, *Atget* (New York: Museum of Modern Art, 2000), 17.
26. Galenson, "Greatest Photographers of the Twentieth Century."
27. John Szarkowski and Maria Hambourg, *The Work of Atget* (New York: Museum of Modern Art, 1981), 1:23.
28. Borcoman, *Eugène Atget*, 69; Maria Morris, "Eugène Atget, 1857–1927" (PhD diss., Columbia University, 1980), 337; Geoff Dyer, *The Ongoing Moment* (New York: Vintage Books, 2005), 225–26.
29. Szarkowski and Hambourg, *Work of Atget*, 1:20.
30. Abbott, *World of Atget*, x.
31. Alfred Stieglitz, *Stieglitz on Photography* (New York: Aperture, 2000), 226.
32. Richard Whelan, *Alfred Stieglitz* (Boston: Little, Brown, 1995), 79.
33. Katherine Hoffman, *Stieglitz* (New Haven, CT: Yale University Press, 2004), 51.
34. Dorothy Norman, *Alfred Stieglitz* (New York: Random House, 1973), 27.
35. Norman, *Alfred Stieglitz*, 30–31.
36. Whelan, *Alfred Stieglitz*, 76.
37. Whelan, *Alfred Stieglitz*, 108; Sarah Greenough and Juan Hamilton, *Alfred Stieglitz* (Washington, DC: National Gallery of Art, 1983), 206.
38. Stieglitz, *Stieglitz on Photography*, 210.
39. Robin Kelsey, *Photography and the Art of Chance* (Cambridge, MA: Harvard University Press, 2015), 156, 168–69.
40. Greenough and Hamilton, *Alfred Stieglitz*, 18.
41. William Innes Homer, *Alfred Stieglitz and the American Avant-Garde* (Boston: New York Graphic Society, 1977), 58–62.
42. Greenough and Hamilton, *Alfred Stieglitz*, 195.
43. Greenough and Hamilton, *Alfred Stieglitz*, 26.
44. Norman, *Alfred Stieglitz*, 10.
45. Stieglitz, *Stieglitz on Photography*, x, 103, 210.
46. Stieglitz, *Stieglitz on Photography*, 226.
47. Phyllis Rove, *Alfred Stieglitz* (New Haven, CT: Yale University Press, 2019), 43–44.
48. Galenson, "Greatest Photographers of the Twentieth Century."

49. Stieglitz, *Stieglitz on Photography*, 194–97.
50. Carolyn Burke, *Foursome* (New York: Alfred A. Knopf, 2019), 316.
51. Edward Steichen, *A Life in Photography* (New York: Harmony Books, 1985), chap. 10.
52. Alfred Stieglitz, *Georgia O'Keeffe, A Portrait* (New York: Metropolitan Museum of Art, 1978), n.p.
53. Laurie Lisle, *Portrait of an Artist: A Biography of Georgia O'Keeffe* (New York: Seaview Books, 1980), 108.
54. Greenough and Hamilton, *Alfred Stieglitz*, 205; Sarah Whitaker Peters, *Becoming O'Keeffe* (New York: Abbeville Press, 1991), 129.
55. Barbara Buhler Lynes, *O'Keeffe, Stieglitz, and the Critics, 1916–1929* (Chicago: University of Chicago Press, 1989), 180.
56. Lisle, *Portrait of an Artist*, 104.
57. Stieglitz, *Georgia O'Keeffe*, n.p.
58. Peters, *Becoming O'Keeffe*, 275.
59. Whelan, *Alfred Stieglitz*, 264.
60. Norman, *Alfred Stieglitz*, 203.
61. Stieglitz, *Georgia O'Keeffe*, n.p.
62. Whelan, *Alfred Stieglitz*, 284.
63. Peters, *Becoming O'Keeffe*, 219.
64. Louis Kronenberger, ed., *Quality* (New York: Balance House, 1969), 170, 206.
65. Galenson, "Greatest Photographers of the Twentieth Century," table 1.
66. Kronenberger, *Quality*, 170.
67. Greenough and Hamilton, *Alfred Stieglitz*, 205.
68. Arturo Schwarz, *Man Ray* (New York: Rizzoli, 1977), 228.
69. Mason Klein, ed., *Alias Man Ray* (New Haven, CT: Yale University Press, 2009), 129, 162–63.
70. Man Ray, *Self Portrait* (Boston: Little, Brown, 1963), 4.
71. Hill and Cooper, *Dialogue with Photography*, 20.
72. Man Ray, *Self Portrait*, 5–6.
73. Man Ray, *Self Portrait*, 20.
74. Neil Baldwin, *Man Ray* (New York: Clarkson N. Potter, 1988), 16.
75. Man Ray, *Self Portrait*, 59.
76. On Duchamp as conceptual innovator, see David Galenson, *Conceptual Revolutions in Twentieth-Century Art* (Cambridge: Cambridge University Press, 2009), 39–41, 161–66.
77. Arturo Schwarz, *New York Dada* (Munich: Prestel-Verlag, 1973), 86.
78. Schwarz, *Man Ray*, 228.
79. Hill and Cooper, *Dialogue with Photography*, 17.
80. Man Ray, *Self Portrait*, 20; Hill and Cooper, *Dialogue with Photography*, 20.
81. Jennifer Mundy, ed., *Duchamp, Man Ray, Picabia* (London: Tate Publishing, 2008), 103.
82. Man Ray, *Self Portrait*, 227.
83. Merry Foresta, et al., *Perpetual Motif* (New York: Abbeville Press, 1988), 44.
84. Man Ray, *Self Portrait*, 145.
85. Man Ray, *Self Portrait*, 73.
86. Schwarz, *Man Ray*, 39.
87. Schwarz, *New York Dada*, 91.
88. Man Ray, *Self Portrait*, 17.
89. Jed Rasula, *Destruction Was My Beatrice* (New York: Basic Books, 2015), 182.
90. Baldwin, *Man Ray*, 100–103; Foresta et al., *Perpetual Motif*, 154.
91. Man Ray, *Self Portrait*, 118; Sylvia Beach, *Shakespeare and Company* (New York: Harcourt, Brace, 1959), 111–12.
92. Schwarz, *Man Ray*, 284–85.
93. Baldwin, *Man Ray*, 117.
94. John Szarkowski, *Looking at Photographs* (New York: Museum of Modern Art, 1973), 82.
95. Mundy, *Duchamp, Man Ray, Picabia*, 99.
96. Baldwin, *Man Ray*, 99.
97. Man Ray, *Self Portrait*, 128.
98. Galenson, "Greatest Photographers of the Twentieth Century."
99. Roland Penrose, *Man Ray* (Boston: New York Graphic Society, 1975), 92.
100. Galenson, "Greatest Photographers of the Twentieth Century," table 2.

101. André Breton, *Surrealism and Painting* (Boston: MFA Publications, 2002), 33.
102. Michel Sanouillet and Elmer Peterson, eds., *The Writings of Marcel Duchamp* (New York: Da Capo Press, 1989), 152.
103. Schwarz, *Man Ray*, 309.
104. Baldwin, *Man Ray*, 266, 335, 352.
105. Coosje van Bruggen, *Bruce Nauman* (New York: Rizzoli, 1988), 14.
106. Schwarz, *Man Ray*, 309.
107. Laurie Simmons, *Cindy Sherman* (Tokyo: Parco Co., 1987), 42.
108. Calvin Tomkins, *Lives of the Artists* (New York: Henry Holt, 2008), 26; Joanne Kesten, ed., *The Portraits Speak* (New York: A.R.T. Press, 1997), 343.
109. Cindy Sherman, *The Complete "Untitled Film Stills"* (New York: Museum of Modern Art, 2003), 11.
110. Sherman, *Complete "Untitled Film Stills,"* 4.
111. Tomkins, *Lives of the Artists*, 27.
112. Michael Kimmelman, *Portraits* (New York: Modern Library, 1999), 146.
113. David Brittain, ed., *Creative Camera* (Manchester, UK: Manchester University Press, 1999), 188.
114. Tomkins, *Lives of the Artists*, 27.
115. Brittain, *Creative Camera*, 192.
116. Brittain, *Creative Camera*, 187–88.
117. Galenson, *Conceptual Revolutions*, 352, 363.
118. Sherman, *Complete "Untitled Film Stills,"* 8.
119. Tomkins, *Lives of the Artists*, 30, 35.
120. Sandy Nairne, *State of the Art* (London: Chatto and Windus, 1987), 132.
121. Sherman, *Complete "Untitled Film Stills,"* 9.
122. Kesten, *Portraits Speak*, 337.
123. Kristine Stiles and Peter Selz, eds., *Theories and Documents of Contemporary Art* (Berkeley: University of California Press, 1996), 792.
124. Kimmelman, *Portraits*, 144.
125. Stiles and Selz, *Theories and Documents of Contemporary Art*, 791.
126. Wendy Slatkin, *The Voices of Women Artists* (Englewood Cliffs, NJ: Prentice Hall, 1993), 317.
127. Galenson, *Conceptual Revolutions*, 352.
128. Peter Schjeldahl and Lisa Phillips, *Cindy Sherman* (New York: Whitney Museum of American Art, 1987), 13.
129. Richard Polsky, *Art Market Guide, 1995–96 Season* (New York: D.A.P., 1995), 129.
130. Peter Meyer, ed., *Brushes with History* (New York: Nation Books, 2001), 445.
131. Brittain, *Creative Camera*, 189.
132. Tomkins, *Lives of the Artists*, 34–35.
133. Tomkins, *Lives of the Artists*, 25.
134. Schjeldahl and Phillips, *Cindy Sherman*, 13.
135. Tomkins, *Lives of the Artists*, 31.
136. Slatkin, *Voices of Women Artists*, 317.
137. Kimmelman, *Portraits*, 147.
138. Kimmelman, *Portraits*, 148.
139. Szarkowski and Hambourg, *Work of Atget*, 4:29.
140. Szarkowski and Hambourg, *Work of Atget*, 4:20.
141. Newhall, *Daybooks of Edward Weston*, 2:201.
142. Abbott, *World of Atget*, xxv, xxxi.
143. Lisle, *Portrait of an Artist*, 106.
144. Hoffman, *Stieglitz*, xvi.
145. Stieglitz, *Stieglitz on Photography*, x.
146. Man Ray, *Self Portrait*, 54.
147. Schwarz, *Man Ray*, 228.
148. Baldwin, *Man Ray*, 96.
149. Slatkin, *Voices of Women Artists*, 310–11.
150. Kesten, *Portraits Speak*, 344.
151. Sherman, *Complete "Untitled Film Stills,"* 9.

Chapter 8

1. André Bazin, *What Is Cinema?* (Berkeley: University of California Press, 1967), 1:24–28. On the selection of filmmakers for this chapter, see David Galenson and Joshua Kotin, "Filming Images or Filming Reality: The Life Cycles of Important Movie Directors from D. W. Griffith to Federico Fellini," *Historical Methods*, 40, no. 3 (2007): 117–34; Galenson and Kotin, "From the New Wave to the New Hollywood: The Life Cycles of Important Movie Directors from Godard and Truffaut to Spielberg and Eastwood," *Historical Methods*, 43, no. 1 (2010): 29–44.
2. Roy Armes, *French Film* (London: Studio Vista Limited, 1970), 11–14.
3. Gerald Mast and Bruce Kawin, *A Short History of the Movies*, 6th ed. (Boston: Allyn and Bacon, 1996), 34.
4. Maurice Bessy, *Orson Welles* (New York: Crown Publishers, 1971), 112; Galenson and Kotin, "Filming Images or Filming Reality," 120, 124.
5. John Ford, *Interviews* (Jackson: University Press of Mississippi, 2001), 64.
6. Ford, *Interviews*, 58; Scott Eyman, *Print the Legend* (New York: Simon and Schuster, 1999), 30; Joseph McBride, *Searching for John Ford* (New York: St. Martin's Press, 1999), 21.
7. Ford, *Interviews*, 62–63.
8. Peter Bogdanovich, *John Ford* (Berkeley: University of California Press, 1978), 107.
9. Ford, *Interviews*, 47.
10. McBride, *Searching for John Ford*, 288.
11. Glenn Frankel, *The Searchers* (New York: Bloomsbury, 2013), 309.
12. Ford, *Interviews*, 71; Joseph McBride and Michael Wilmington, *John Ford* (New York: Da Capo Press, 1975), 47.
13. Gaylyn Studlar and Matthew Bernstein, eds., *John Ford Made Westerns* (Bloomington: Indiana University Press, 2001), 291.
14. George Stevens, *Conversations at the American Film Institute with the Great Moviemakers: The Next Generation* (New York: Vintage Books, 2012), 212.
15. Ford, *Interviews*, 16.
16. Ford, *Interviews*, 39.
17. Bogdanovich, *John Ford*, 31.
18. Ford, *Interviews*, 4; Orson Welles, *Interviews* (Jackson: University Press of Mississippi, 2002), 135.
19. Eyman, *Print the Legend*, 214–16; Bogdanovich, *John Ford*, 76.
20. George Custen, *Twentieth Century's Fox* (New York: Basic Books, 1997), 229–31; John Steinbeck, *Steinbeck: A Life in Letters* (New York: Viking Press, 1975), 195.
21. McBride and Wilmington, *John Ford*, 18; Ford, *Interviews*, 47.
22. "The Sight and Sound Top Ten Poll 2002," accessed April 1, 2010, www.bfi.org.uk/sightandsound/topten/.
23. McBride, *Searching for John Ford*, 103, 632–33; Brian Spittles, *John Ford* (Essex, UK: Pearson Education, 2002); Sidney Pearson, ed., *Print the Legend* (Lanham, MD: Lexington Books, 2009).
24. Ford, *Interviews*, 51.
25. Eyman, *Print the Legend*, 492.
26. Bogdanovich, *John Ford*, 86.
27. Bogdanovich, *John Ford*, 100.
28. McBride, *Searching for John Ford*, 570.
29. Donald Richie, *The Films of Akira Kurosawa* (Berkeley: University of California Press, 1965), 196; Joan Mellen, *Voices from the Japanese Cinema* (New York: Liveright, 1975), 41; McBride, *Searching for John Ford*, 300.
30. McBride, *Searching for John Ford*, 300.
31. Welles, *Interviews*, 76.
32. Leighton Grist, *The Films of Martin Scorsese, 1963–77* (New York: St. Martin's Press, 2000), 144–45; McBride, *Searching for John Ford*, 571.
33. Galenson and Kotin, "From the New Wave to the New Hollywood," 38; Ian Christie and David Thompson, eds., *Scorsese on Scorsese*, rev. ed. (London: Faber and Faber, 2003), 146.
34. Bogdanovich, *John Ford*, 108.
35. Ford, *Interviews*, 158.
36. François Truffaut, *Interviews* (Jackson: University Press of Mississippi, 2008), 59.
37. Sidney Gottlieb, ed., *Hitchcock on Hitchcock* (Berkeley: University of California Press, 1997), 48.
38. Gottlieb, *Hitchcock on Hitchcock*, 143.
39. Gottlieb, *Hitchcock on Hitchcock*, 109.

40. Robin Wood, *Hitchcock's Films Revisited*, rev. ed. (New York: Columbia University Press, 2002), 123–24.
41. François Truffaut, *Hitchcock*, rev. ed. (New York: Simon and Schuster, 1984), 20.
42. Alfred Hitchcock, *Interviews* (Jackson: University Press of Mississippi, 2003), 130.
43. Gottlieb, *Hitchcock on Hitchcock*, 60.
44. Gottlieb, *Hitchcock on Hitchcock*, 113.
45. Gottlieb, *Hitchcock on Hitchcock*, 109, 209.
46. Hitchcock, *Interviews*, 9.
47. Hitchcock, *Interviews*, 79, 90.
48. Hitchcock, *Interviews*, 120.
49. Gottlieb, *Hitchcock on Hitchcock*, 255–56, 299.
50. Gottlieb, *Hitchcock on Hitchcock*, 298.
51. Gottlieb, *Hitchcock on Hitchcock*, 48.
52. Hitchcock, *Interviews*, 121.
53. Hitchcock, *Interviews*, 182.
54. Gottlieb, *Hitchcock on Hitchcock*, 247.
55. Gottlieb, *Hitchcock on Hitchcock*, 208.
56. Gottlieb, *Hitchcock on Hitchcock*, 291.
57. Gottlieb, *Hitchcock on Hitchcock*, 259.
58. Truffaut, *Hitchcock*, 48.
59. Gottlieb, *Hitchcock on Hitchcock*, 114, 314.
60. Robert Kolker, *The Extraordinary Image* (New Brunswick, NJ: Rutgers University Press, 2017), 122–24.
61. Truffaut, *Hitchcock*, 73.
62. Albert LaValley, ed., *Focus on Hitchcock* (Englewood Cliffs, NJ: Prentice Hall, 1972), 24, 145–73; Dan Auiler, *Vertigo* (New York: St. Martin's Griffin, 2000), 156–59; Stephen Rebello, *Alfred Hitchcock and the Making of "Psycho"* (New York: Dembner Books, 1990), 100–118.
63. LaValley, *Focus on Hitchcock*, 24.
64. Gottlieb, *Hitchcock on Hitchcock*, 288.
65. Truffaut, *Hitchcock*, 246.
66. Auiler, *Vertigo*, 159.
67. Edward White, *The Twelve Lives of Alfred Hitchcock* (New York: W. W. Norton, 2021), 3.
68. Steven DeRosa, *Writing with Hitchcock* (New York: Faber and Faber, 2001), 84.
69. Patrick McGilligan, *Alfred Hitchcock* (New York: HarperCollins, 2003), 476–79, 522–23, 653; Charlotte Chandler, *It's Only a Movie* (New York: Simon and Schuster, 2005), 19–20.
70. LaValley, *Focus on Hitchcock*, 58.
71. François Truffaut, *The Films in My Life* (New York: Da Capo Press, 1994), 77–89.
72. Eric Rohmer and Claude Chabrol, *Hitchcock* (New York: Frederick Ungar Publishing, 1979), 152.
73. Richard Brody, *Everything Is Cinema* (New York: Henry Holt, 2008), 580.
74. Truffaut, *Hitchcock*, 14.
75. Stevens, *Conversations at the American Film Institute*, 690.
76. Joseph McBride, *Steven Spielberg* (New York: Simon and Schuster, 1997), 120–21.
77. Auiler, *Vertigo*, xi–xiii; White, *Twelve Lives of Alfred Hitchcock*, 277.
78. J. M. Wood, "Under the Influence," accessed April 1, 2010, http://www.moviemaker.com/issues/47/index.html. The ranking placed D. W. Griffith second, Orson Welles third, Jean-Luc Godard fourth, and John Ford fifth.
79. Jay Carr, ed., *The A List: The National Society of Film Critics' 100 Essential Films* (New York: Da Capo Press, 2002), 229, 310.
80. Bill Crohn, *Hitchcock at Work* (London: Phaidon Press, 2000), 114.
81. Truffaut, *Hitchcock*, 314.
82. Truffaut, *Hitchcock*, 94.
83. Gottlieb, *Hitchcock on Hitchcock*, 115, 216.
84. Gottlieb, *Hitchcock on Hitchcock*, 62.
85. Robert Kapsis, *Hitchcock* (Chicago: University of Chicago Press, 1992), 72; Peter Bogdanovich, *Who the Devil Made It* (New York: Alfred Knopf, 1997), 554.
86. Kapsis, *Hitchcock*, 73.
87. Truffaut, *Hitchcock*, 11–12.
88. Gottlieb, *Hitchcock on Hitchcock*, 292.

89. Welles, *Interviews*, 102.
90. Barbara Leaming, *Orson Welles* (New York: Viking, 1985), 10.
91. Joseph McBride, *What Ever Happened to Orson Welles?* (Lexington: University Press of Kentucky, 2006), x.
92. Welles, *Interviews*, 179.
93. Mícheál MacLiammóir, *All for Hecuba* (Boston: Branden Press, 1967), 127, 129.
94. Leaming, *Orson Welles*, 46.
95. Leaming, *Orson Welles*, 44–45.
96. Orson Welles and Peter Bogdanovich, *This Is Orson Welles* (New York: HarperCollins, 1992), 10–11.
97. Simon Callow, *Orson Welles: The Road to Xanadu* (New York: Penguin, 1995), 320–21.
98. Richard France, *The Theatre of Orson Welles* (Lewisburg, PA: Bucknell University Press, 1977), 55; James Naremore, *Orson Welles's "Citizen Kane"* (Oxford: Oxford University Press, 2004), 263.
99. Patrick McGilligan, *Young Orson* (New York: Harper, 2015), 453–54.
100. Hadley Cantril, *The Invasion from Mars* (Princeton, NJ: Princeton University Press, 1940), vii.
101. Leaming, *Orson Welles*, 161–63; Cantril, *Invasion from Mars*.
102. Welles, *Interviews*, 18; Harlan Lebo, *Citizen Kane* (New York: St. Martin's Press, 2016), 18.
103. Truffaut, *Films in My Life*, 281.
104. F. Scott Fitzgerald, *The Pat Hobby Stories* (New York: Charles Scribner's Sons, 1962), 47.
105. André Bazin, *Orson Welles* (New York: Harper and Row, 1978), 3.
106. Ronald Gottesman, ed., *Focus on "Citizen Kane"* (Englewood Cliffs, NJ: Prentice-Hall, 1971), 69–77.
107. Russell Ash, *Top 10 of Film* (New York: DK Publishing, 2003), 194–95. In the 2012 *Sight and Sound* poll of critics, *Citizen Kane* fell to second place, behind Hitchcock's *Vertigo*.
108. Claude-Jean Philippe, *100 Films pour une cinémathèque idéale* (Paris: Cahiers du cinema, 2008), 16.
109. Welles, *Interviews*, 124.
110. Welles, *Interviews*, 19.
111. Welles, *Interviews*, 81.
112. Welles and Bogdanovich, *This Is Orson Welles*, 60.
113. Gottesman, *Focus on "Citizen Kane,"* 74.
114. Gottesman, *Focus on "Citizen Kane,"* 71.
115. Bazin, *Orson Welles*, 11.
116. Welles and Bogdanovich, *This Is Orson Welles*, 91.
117. Gottesman, *Focus on "Citizen Kane,"* 127.
118. Ronald Gottesman, ed., *Perspectives on "Citizen Kane"* (New York: G. K. Hall, 1996), 59.
119. Leaming, *Orson Welles*, 200.
120. Truffaut, *Films in My Life*, 279–81, 284.
121. Ronald Gottesman, ed., *Focus on Orson Welles* (Englewood Cliffs, NJ: Prentice-Hall, 1976), 104.
122. Bazin, *Orson Welles*, 2.
123. Welles, *Interviews*, 37.
124. Peter Cowie, *A Ribbon of Dreams* (South Brunswick, NJ: A. S. Barnes, 1973), 13.
125. Cowie, *Ribbon of Dreams*, 3.
126. Welles, *Interviews*, 31.
127. Welles, *Interviews*, 88.
128. Welles, *Interviews*, 46.
129. Welles, *Interviews*, 102.
130. Welles, *Interviews*, 99.
131. Andrew Sarris, *The American Cinema* (New York: E. P. Dutton, 1968), 78.
132. Leaming, *Orson Welles*, 381.
133. Welles, *Interviews*, 209.
134. So for example in the 2002 *Sight and Sound* poll, Welles' *Touch of Evil* (1958) appeared on eleven critics' lists of the ten best films ever made—far less than *Kane*'s forty-five, but more than any single film by such important directors as Ingmar Bergman, Charlie Chaplin, or Howard Hawks; Galenson and Kotin, "Filming Images or Filming Reality," table 2, 129.
135. For example, Robert Garis, *The Films of Orson Welles* (Cambridge: Cambridge University Press, 2004), 1; Paolo Mereghetti, *Orson Welles* (Paris: Cahiers du cinema Sarl, 2011), 76.

NOTES   361

136. Welles, *Interviews*, 80.
137. Welles and Bogdanovich, *This Is Orson Welles*, 511; Frank Brady, *Citizen Welles* (New York: Charles Scribner's Sons, 1989), 591.
138. Leaming, *Orson Welles*, 481.
139. Jean Narboni and Tom Milne, eds., *Godard on Godard* (New York: Da Capo Press, 1972), 204.
140. Jean-Luc Godard, *Interviews* (Jackson: University Press of Mississippi, 1998), 35.
141. Colin MacCabe, *Godard* (New York: Farrar, Straus and Giroux, 2003), 390.
142. Narboni and Milne, eds., *Godard on Godard*, 19.
143. Jean Collet, *Jean-Luc Godard* (New York: Crown Publishers, 1970), 6.
144. Narboni and Milne, *Godard on Godard*, 147.
145. Truffaut, *Films in My Life*, 19.
146. Narboni and Milne, *Godard on Godard*, 171.
147. Jean-Luc Godard, *The Future(s) of Film* (Berne: Verlag Gachnang and Springer, 2002), 15.
148. MacCabe, *Godard*, 123.
149. Susan Sontag, *Styles of Radical Will* (New York: Farrar, Straus and Giroux, 1969), 150; Narboni and Milne, *Godard on Godard*, 173.
150. Peter Cowie, *Revolution!* (New York: Faber and Faber, 2004), 133.
151. Peter Graham, ed., *The French New Wave* (London: Palgrave Macmillan, 2009), 231.
152. "Sight and Sound Top Ten Poll 2002," accessed April 1, 2010, www.bfi.org.uk/sightandsound/topten/.
153. Philippe, *100 Films*.
154. Brody, *Everything Is Cinema*, 67–68.
155. Brody, *Everything Is Cinema*, 68.
156. Narboni and Milne, *Godard on Godard*, 181.
157. Godard, *Interviews*, 13.
158. Collet, *Jean-Luc Godard*, 32; Godard, *Interviews*, 29.
159. Narboni and Milne, *Godard on Godard*, 238.
160. Narboni and Milne, *Godard on Godard*, 239.
161. Narboni and Milne, *Godard on Godard*, 113.
162. Brody, *Everything Is Cinema*, 139.
163. Narboni and Milne, *Godard on Godard*, 21.
164. Richard Roud, *Jean-Luc Godard*, 2nd rev. ed. (Bloomington: Indiana University Press, 1970), 49.
165. Godard, *Interviews*, 30.
166. Jean-Luc Godard and Youssef Ishaghpour, *Cinema* (Oxford: Berg, 2005), 131–32.
167. Godard, *Interviews*, 4.
168. Narboni and Milne, *Godard on Godard*, 175; Godard, *Interviews*, 5.
169. Peter Wollen, *Paris Hollywood* (London: Verso, 2002), 76; MacCabe, *Godard*, 123.
170. Godard, *Interviews*, 23.
171. MacCabe, *Godard*, 146.
172. Godard, *Interviews*, 102.
173. Royal Brown, ed., *Focus on Godard* (Englewood Cliffs, NJ: Prentice Hall, 1972), 143.
174. Brody, *Everything Is Cinema*, 177–78.
175. For example Brody, *Everything Is Cinema*, 61.
176. For example see Hans Richter, *Dada* (London: Thames and Hudson, 1966), 48.
177. Godard, *Interviews*, 135.
178. Manny Farber, *Negative Space*, exp. ed. (New York: Da Capo Press, 1998), 259.
179. Wollen, *Paris Hollywood*, 80–81.
180. Brody, *Everything Is Cinema*, xiii.
181. For example Brody, *Everything Is Cinema*, 301–11, 557–60.
182. Brody, *Everything Is Cinema*, xv.
183. Stephanie Zacharek, "A Girl and a Gun," *New York Times Book Review* (July 13, 2008), 12.
184. Cowie, *Revolution!*, 241.
185. Cowie, *Revolution!*, 146.
186. Quentin Tarantino, *Interviews* (Jackson: University Press of Mississippi, 1998), 12, 109.
187. Wollen, *Paris Hollywood*, 77.
188. Brody, *Everything Is Cinema*, 72.
189. Graham, *The French New Wave*, 31–33.
190. Brody, *Everything Is Cinema*, 73.

191. Douglas Morrey, *Jean-Luc Godard* (Manchester, UK: Manchester University Press, 2005), 242.
192. Ford, *Interviews*, 48.
193. Ford, *Interviews*, 25.
194. Ford, *Interviews*, 71.
195. Ford, *Interviews*, 71.
196. Gottlieb, *Hitchcock on Hitchcock*, 180.
197. Hitchcock, *Interviews*, 58, 113.
198. Hitchcock, *Interviews*, 37.
199. Hitchcock, *Interviews*, 119.
200. Hitchcock, *Interviews*, 57.
201. Hitchcock, *Interviews*, 119.
202. David Thomson, *Rosebud* (New York: Vintage Books, 1996), 165.
203. Leaming, *Orson Welles*, 388; Cowie, *Ribbon of Dreams*, 224–26.
204. Welles, *Interviews*, 112.
205. McBride, *What Ever Happened to Orson Welles?*, 255.
206. Welles, *Interviews*, introduction, chronology.
207. McBride, *What Ever Happened to Orson Welles?*, 290.
208. Brown, *Focus on Godard*, 33–34.
209. Godard, *Interviews*, 5.
210. Godard, *Interviews*, 15.
211. Godard, *Interviews*, 48–49.
212. Michael Temple and James Williams, eds., *The Cinema Alone* (Amsterdam: Amsterdam University Press, 2000), 19.
213. Galenson and Kotin, "From the New Wave to the New Hollywood," 38–40.
214. Gottlieb, *Hitchcock on Hitchcock*, 63.

Chapter 9

1. "An Old-Fashioned Tune Is Always New"; Robert Kimball and Linda Emmet, eds., *The Complete Lyrics of Irving Berlin* (New York: Alfred A. Knopf, 2001), 334. On the selection of songwriters for this chapter, see David Galenson, "From 'White Christmas' to *Sgt. Pepper*," *Historical Methods*, 42, no. 1 (2009): 17–34.
2. Alexander Woollcott, *The Story of Irving Berlin* (New York: G. P. Putnam's Sons, 1925), 9.
3. Woollcott, *Story of Irving Berlin*, chaps. 2–5.
4. Charles Hamm, *Irving Berlin* (New York: Oxford University Press, 1997), 3.
5. Woollcott, *Story of Irving Berlin*, 214; William McBrien, *Cole Porter* (New York: Alfred A. Knopf, 1998), 200; Mary Ellin Barrett, *Irving Berlin* (New York: Simon and Schuster, 1994), 239.
6. Philip Furia, *Irving Berlin* (New York: Schirmer Books, 1998), 47; Laurence Bergreen, *As Thousands Cheer* (New York: Viking, 1990), 67–68.
7. Bergreen, *As Thousands Cheer*, 68.
8. Edward Jablonski, *Irving Berlin* (New York: Henry Holt, 1999), 286–87.
9. Robert Wyatt and John Johnson, eds., *The George Gershwin Reader* (Oxford: Oxford University Press, 2004), 116–17.
10. Bergreen, *As Thousands Cheer*, 372.
11. Benjamin Sears, ed., *The Irving Berlin Reader* (Oxford: Oxford University Press, 2012), 176.
12. Bergreen, *As Thousands Cheer*, 66.
13. Sheryl Kaskowitz, *God Bless America* (Oxford: Oxford University Press, 2013), 16.
14. Sears, *Irving Berlin Reader*, 175.
15. Jablonski, *Irving Berlin*, 313.
16. Jody Rosen, *White Christmas* (New York: Scribner, 2002), 22.
17. Bergreen, *As Thousands Cheer*, 77.
18. Wilfred Sheed, *The House That George Built* (New York: Random House, 2007), 14.
19. Jablonski, *Irving Berlin*, 290.
20. Bergreen, *As Thousands Cheer*, 46.
21. Kimball and Emmet, *Complete Lyrics of Irving Berlin*, 4.
22. Kimball and Emmet, *Complete Lyrics of Irving Berlin*, 31.
23. Kimball and Emmet, *Complete Lyrics of Irving Berlin*, 231–32.

24. Kimball and Emmet, *Complete Lyrics of Irving Berlin*, 295; James Kaplan, *Irving Berlin* (New Haven, CT: Yale University Press, 2019), 144.
25. Rosen, *White Christmas*, 35.
26. Rosen, *White Christmas*, 13.
27. Woollcott, *Story of Irving Berlin*, 215.
28. Kimball and Emmet, *Complete Lyrics of Irving Berlin*, 322–23.
29. Kaskowitz, *God Bless America*, 93.
30. Rosen, *White Christmas*, 5–8.
31. He had probably written the song two years earlier; Rosen, *White Christmas*, 17–18.
32. Rosen, *White Christmas*, 4.
33. Furia, *Irving Berlin*, 204.
34. Sears, *Irving Berlin Reader*, 83, 149.
35. "I Sleep Easier Now"; Robert Kimball, ed., *The Complete Lyrics of Cole Porter* (New York: Alfred A. Knopf, 1983), 291.
36. George Eells, *The Life That Late He Led* (New York: G. P. Putnam's Sons, 1967), 11–18.
37. Eells, *Life That Late He Led*, 19.
38. McBrien, *Cole Porter*, chap. 2.
39. Kimball, *Complete Lyrics of Cole Porter*, 39.
40. McBrien, *Cole Porter*, 54–55.
41. McBrien, *Cole Porter*, 75.
42. Richard Rodgers, *Musical Stages* (New York: Random House, 1975), 88.
43. Stephen Citron, *Noel and Cole* (New York: Oxford University Press, 1993), 79.
44. Kimball, *Complete Lyrics of Cole Porter*, 72–73.
45. Kimball, *Complete Lyrics of Cole Porter*, 120.
46. McBrien, *Cole Porter*, 171.
47. Kimball, *Complete Lyrics of Cole Porter*, 118.
48. Galenson, "From 'White Christmas' to *Sgt. Pepper*," table A1, 30.
49. Kimball, *Complete Lyrics of Cole Porter*, 108.
50. Kimball, *Complete Lyrics of Cole Porter*, 133.
51. Eells, *Life That Late He Led*, 51.
52. McBrien, *Cole Porter*, 364.
53. Gerald Mast, *Can't Help Singin'* (Woodstock, NY: Overlook Press, 1987), 196–98; Alec Wilder, *American Popular Song* (New York: Oxford University Press, 1972), 249–50.
54. Eells, *Life That Late He Led*, 222; Wilder, *American Popular Song*, 251.
55. "Mr. Tambourine Man"; Bob Dylan, *Lyrics, 1962–1985* (New York: Alfred A. Knopf, 1992), 172.
56. Bob Spitz, *Dylan* (New York: McGraw-Hill, 1989), 25–27.
57. Robert Shelton, *No Direction Home* (New York: William Morrow, 1986), 39.
58. Spitz, *Dylan*, 67–68.
59. Jonathan Cott, ed., *Bob Dylan: The Essential Interviews* (New York: Wenner Books, 2006), 401.
60. Spitz, *Dylan*, 70–98; Cott, *Bob Dylan*, 401.
61. Bob Dylan, *Chronicles: Volume One* (New York: Simon and Schuster, 2004), 55.
62. Benjamin Hedin, ed., *Studio A* (New York: W. W. Norton, 2004), 12–13.
63. Shelton, *No Direction Home*, 113.
64. Dylan, *Lyrics*, 53.
65. Elijah Wald, *Dylan Goes Electric!* (New York: HarperCollins, 2015), 126.
66. Howard Sounes, *Down the Highway* (New York: Grove Press, 2001), 135–36.
67. Shelton, *No Direction Home*, 191.
68. Devin McKinney, *Magic Circles* (Cambridge, MA: Harvard University Press, 2003), 107; Cott, *Bob Dylan*, 9.
69. Cott, *Bob Dylan*, 17.
70. Shelton, *No Direction Home*, 56, 193–98.
71. Cott, *Bob Dylan*, 16.
72. Dylan, *Lyrics*, 56, 59.
73. Spitz, *Dylan*, 199.
74. Shelton, *No Direction Home*, 170, 179; Spitz, *Dylan*, 225–26.
75. Cott, *Bob Dylan*, 16, 26.
76. Bob Dylan, *Younger Than That Now: The Collected Interviews with Bob Dylan* (New York: Thunder's Mouth Press, 2004), 50.
77. Clinton Heylin, *Bob Dylan* (New York: HarperCollins, 2011), 138, 151.

78. Cott, *Bob Dylan*, 63.
79. Shelton, *No Direction Home*, 343-44.
80. Greil Marcus, *Like a Rolling Stone* (London: Faber and Faber, 2006), 70.
81. Marcus, *Like a Rolling Stone*, 121-23; Sounes, *Down the Highway*, 178.
82. Dylan, *Lyrics*, 191.
83. Cott, *Bob Dylan*, 97.
84. Dylan, *Lyrics*, 211.
85. Rolling Stone, "500 Greatest Songs of All Time (2004)," December 11, 2003.
86. Jacob Hoye, ed., *VH1's Greatest Albums* (New York: Barnes and Noble Books, 2003); Joe Levy, ed. *Rolling Stone: The 500 Greatest Albums of All Time* (New York: Wenner Books, 2005), 17.
87. Hedin, *Studio A*, 203.
88. Cott, *Bob Dylan*, 335; Hoye, *VH1's 100 Greatest Albums*, 27.
89. Greil Marcus, *Bob Dylan* (New York: Public Affairs, 2010), 23.
90. Shelton, *No Direction Home*, 424; Cott, *Bob Dylan*, 259-60.
91. Dylan, *Chronicles*, 195, 218-19.
92. Sounes, *Down the Highway*, 122.
93. Cott, *Bob Dylan*, 317.
94. Cott, *Bob Dylan*, 432.
95. Kevin Dettmar, ed., *The Cambridge Companion to Bob Dylan* (Cambridge: Cambridge University Press, 2009), 43.
96. Cott, *Bob Dylan*, 396.
97. Christopher Ricks, *Dylan's Visions of Sin* (New York: HarperCollins, 2003), 8.
98. Hedin, *Studio A*, 203.
99. "Strawberry Fields Forever"; *The Beatles Lyrics* (Milwaukee: Hal Leonard Corporation, 1996), 129.
100. Jonathan Gould, *Can't Buy Me Love* (New York: Harmony Books, 2007), 59-66.
101. W. Fraser Sandercombe, *The Beatles* (Burlington, Canada: Collector's Guide Publishing, 2007), 9.
102. Harry Castleman and Walter Podrazik, *All Together Now* (Ann Arbor, MI: Pierian Press, 1976), 12.
103. Gould, *Can't Buy Me Love*, 108.
104. June Sawyers, ed., *Read the Beatles* (New York: Penguin, 2006), 245.
105. Walter Everett, *The Beatles as Musicians: The Quarry Men through "Rubber Soul"* (Oxford: Oxford University Press, 2001), 31.
106. David Sheff, *All We Are Saying: The Last Major Interview with John Lennon and Yoko Ono* (New York: St. Martin's Press, 2000), 136-37.
107. Sheff, *All We Are Saying*, 137.
108. George Martin, *All You Need Is Ears* (New York: St. Martin's Press, 1979), 131-32.
109. Jann Wenner, *Lennon Remembers* (San Francisco: Straight Arrow Books, 1971), 70.
110. Sheff, *All We Are Saying*, 138.
111. Colin Campbell and Allan Murphy, *Things We Said Today* (Ann Arbor, MI: Pierian Press, 1980), 36.
112. Ian Inglis, ed., *The Beatles, Popular Music and Society* (New York: St. Martin's Press, 2000), 99. The concentration could be considerably greater in particular songs. So, for example, in "P.S. I Love You," recorded in 1962, the three words *I, love,* and *you* account for more than 40 percent of the total; Campbell and Murphy, *Things We Said Today*, 43.
113. Campbell and Murphy, *Things We Said Today*, xxv.
114. Kenneth Womack, *Long and Winding Roads* (New York: Continuum, 2007), 59.
115. Sheff, *All We Are Saying*, 152; *The Oxford English Dictionary*, 2nd ed. (Oxford: Clarendon Press, 1991), 2:35.
116. Ray Coleman, *Lennon* (New York: McGraw-Hill, 1984), 290.
117. Wenner, *Lennon Remembers*, 126.
118. Sheff, *All We Are Saying*, 178-79.
119. Campbell and Murphy, *Things We Said Today*, 32.
120. Steven Stark, *Meet the Beatles* (New York: HarperCollins, 2005), 182.
121. Sheff, *All We Are Saying*, 157.
122. Mark Hertsgaard, *A Day in the Life* (New York: Delacorte Press, 1995), 204.
123. Michael Frontani, *The Beatles* (Jackson: University Press of Mississippi, 2007), 132.

124. Walter Everett, *The Beatles as Musicians: "Revolver" through the "Anthology"* (Oxford: Oxford University Press, 1999), 32.
125. Sheff, *All We Are Saying*, 184–85.
126. Everett, *Beatles as Musicians: "Revolver" through the "Anthology,"* 33.
127. Philip Lambert, *Inside the Music of Brian Wilson* (New York: Continuum, 2007) 224.
128. Ian MacDonald, *Revolution in the Head*, 2nd rev. ed. (London: Pimlico, 2005), 215; Geoff Emerick, *Here, There and Everywhere* (New York: Gotham Books, 2007), 142.
129. Mikal Gilmore, *Stories Done* (New York: Free Press, 2008), 154.
130. Sheff, *All We Are Saying*, 142–43.
131. Inglis, *Beatles, Popular Music, and Society*, 99.
132. Hoye, *VH1's Greatest Albums*; Levy, *Rolling Stone*.
133. Emerick, *Here, There and Everywhere*, 189–91.
134. Gilmore, *Stories Done*, 150.
135. Olivier Julien, ed., *Sgt. Pepper and the Beatles* (Aldershot, UK: Ashgate Publishing, 2007), 5; Kenneth Womack, ed., *The Cambridge Companion to the Beatles* (Cambridge: Cambridge University Press, 2009), 50.
136. Martin, *All You Need Is Ears*, 210–12.
137. Julien, *Sgt. Pepper and the Beatles*, 46.
138. Derek Taylor, *It Was Twenty Years Ago Today* (New York: Simon and Schuster, 1987), 32–38.
139. Clinton Heylin, *The Act You've Known for All These Years* (Edinburgh: Canongate Books, 2007), 116.
140. Sheff, *All We Are Saying*, 197.
141. Frontani, *Beatles*, 139.
142. Richard Poirier, *The Performing Self* (New York: Oxford University Press, 1971), 137; Sawyers, *Read the Beatles*, 127.
143. Taylor, *It Was Twenty Years Ago Today*, 49.
144. Gould, *Can't Buy Me Love*, 58–59.
145. Martin, *All You Need Is Ears*, 137–39.
146. Sawyers, *Read the Beatles*, 247.
147. Sheff, *All We Are Saying*, 152–53.
148. Sheff, *All We Are Saying*, 192–93.
149. Womack, *Long and Winding Roads*, 112.
150. Sheff, *All We Are Saying*, 5, 141.
151. Womack, *Long and Winding Roads*, 304; Gould, *Can't Buy Me Love*, 588.
152. Sawyers, *Read the Beatles*, 249–50.
153. David Sterritt, ed., *Jean-Luc Godard Interviews* (Jackson: University Press of Mississippi, 1998), 15.
154. James Miller, *Flowers in the Dustbin* (New York: Simon and Schuster, 2000), 227–28.
155. Elijah Wald, *How the Beatles Destroyed Rock'n'Roll* (Oxford: Oxford University Press, 2009), 242.
156. Frontani, *Beatles*, 156.
157. Robert Hilburn, *Paul Simon* (New York: Simon and Schuster, 2018), 358.
158. Hilburn, *Paul Simon*, 23–24.
159. Hilburn, *Paul Simon*, 94.
160. Stacey Luftig, ed., *The Paul Simon Companion* (London: Omnibus Press, 1997), 12–13.
161. Hilburn, *Paul Simon*, 111–12.
162. Hilburn, *Paul Simon*, 127–28.
163. Hilburn, *Paul Simon*, 99, 208.
164. Hilburn, *Paul Simon*, 131.
165. Dan Martin, "Paul Simon," *The Guardian*, May 12, 2011.
166. Hilburn, *Paul Simon*, 122, 161.
167. Luftig, *Paul Simon Companion*, 7.
168. Hilburn, *Paul Simon*, 112.
169. Hilburn, *Paul Simon*, 59.
170. Luftig, *Paul Simon Companion*, 208.
171. Paul Rollo, "Paul Simon on Songwriting," *American Songwriter*, September 1, 2011.
172. Tom Moon, "Interview: Paul Simon Discusses *Songwriter* and Songwriting," *American Songwriter*, October 7, 2011.
173. Hilburn, *Paul Simon*, 115, 126, 136.

174. Hilburn, *Paul Simon*, 368.
175. Hilburn, *Paul Simon*, 163–65, 250–52, 257, 385.
176. *Rolling Stone*, "The 500 Greatest Albums of All Time," rollingstone.com, Sept. 22, 2020.
177. Malcom Gladwell, *Miracle and Wonder* (New York: Pushkin Industries, 2021), chap. 3.
178. Luftig, *Paul Simon Companion*, 72–73.
179. Hilburn, *Paul Simon*, 276.
180. Gladwell, *Miracle and Wonder*, chap. 3.
181. McBrien, *Cole Porter*, 45.
182. McBrien, *Cole Porter*, 146; Mast, *Can't Help Singin'*, 42, 194.
183. McBrien, *Cole Porter*, 146, 149–50.
184. Furia, *Irving Berlin*, 165, 174–75.
185. Kaplan, *Irving Berlin*, 201.
186. Cott, *Bob Dylan*, 224.
187. Cott, *Bob Dylan*, 381.
188. Cott, *Bob Dylan*, 430.
189. Wenner, *Lennon Remembers*, 162.
190. Dylan, *Chronicles*, 61–73; Eugen Banach, ed., *Refractions of Bob Dylan* (Manchester, UK: Manchester University Press, 2015), 72–75.
191. Woollcott, *Story of Irving Berlin*, 215.
192. McBrien, *Cole Porter*, 200.
193. Cott, *Bob Dylan*, 41.
194. Shelton, *No Direction Home*, 293.
195. Wenner, *Lennon Remembers*, 29.
196. Sheff, *All We Are Saying*, 158, 197.
197. Bergreen, *As Thousands Cheer*, 142.
198. Dylan, *Chronicles*, 288.
199. David Hajdu, *Positively 4th Street* (New York: North Point Press, 2001), 233–34; Dylan, *Younger Than That Now*, 266.
200. Sawyers, *Read the Beatles*, 248.
201. Hajdu, *Positively 4th Street*, 234; Miller, *Flowers in the Dustbin*, 19.
202. Rosen, *White Christmas*, 182.
203. Cott, *Bob Dylan*, 336.
204. Cott, *Bob Dylan*, 336, 384; Dylan, *Chronicles*, 227.
205. Wenner, *Lennon Remembers*, 115.
206. Luftig, *Paul Simon Companion*, 22, 200.
207. Gladwell, *Miracle and Wonder*, chap. 4.
208. Luftig, *Paul Simon Companion*, 192.

Chapter 10

1. Charles Darwin, *The Autobiography of Charles Darwin, 1809–1882* (New York: W. W. Norton, 2005), 114–15.
2. Ernst Mayr, *One Long Argument* (Cambridge, MA: Harvard University Press, 1991), 3.
3. Gavin de Beer, *Charles Darwin* (New York: Anchor Books, 1965), 23.
4. Darwin, *Autobiography of Charles Darwin*, 27.
5. Adrian Desmond and James Moore, *Darwin* (New York: Warner Books, 1992), 189.
6. Darwin, *Autobiography of Charles Darwin*, 64.
7. William Brown and Andrew Fabian, eds., *Darwin* (Cambridge: Cambridge University Press, 2010), 9.
8. Brown and Fabian, *Darwin*, 5–6.
9. Darwin, *Autobiography of Charles Darwin*, 67.
10. Edward Wilson, ed., *From So Simple a Beginning* (New York: W. W. Norton, 2006), 17; Janet Browne, *Charles Darwin: Voyaging* (New York: Alfred A. Knopf, 1995), 417–22.
11. Mayr, *One Long Argument*, 5.
12. Browne, *Charles Darwin: Voyaging*, 361.
13. For example, see Ralph Colp, *To Be an Invalid* (Chicago: University of Chicago Press, 1977).
14. Darwin, *Autobiography of Charles Darwin*, 98–99.
15. Mayr, *One Long Argument*, 70.
16. David Kohn, ed., *The Darwinian Heritage* (Princeton, NJ: Princeton University Press, 1985), 186.

NOTES   367

17. Browne, *Charles Darwin: Voyaging*, 446–47; Darwin, *Autobiography of Charles Darwin*, 99.
18. Desmond and Moore, *Darwin*, 314.
19. Stephen Jay Gould, *Ever Since Darwin* (New York: W. W. Norton, 1977), 23.
20. James Watson, ed., *Darwin* (Philadelphia: Running Press, 2005), xiii, 340.
21. Brown and Fabian, *Darwin*, 43.
22. Darwin, *Autobiography of Charles Darwin*, 102.
23. Rebecca Stott, *Darwin and the Barnacle* (New York: W. W. Norton, 2003), 82–84; Browne, *Charles Darwin: Voyaging*, 472.
24. De Beer, *Charles Darwin*, 136; Adrian Desmond, James Moore, and Janet Browne, *Charles Darwin* (Oxford: Oxford University Press, 2007), 55.
25. Browne, *Charles Darwin: Voyaging*, 477–80, 512.
26. Browne, *Charles Darwin: Voyaging*, 514.
27. Michael Ruse and Robert Richards, eds., *The Cambridge Companion to the "Origin of Species"* (Cambridge: Cambridge University Press, 2009), 87.
28. Browne, *Charles Darwin: Voyaging*, 511–12.
29. Kohn, *Darwinian Heritage*, 937.
30. Darwin, *Autobiography of Charles Darwin*, 99–100.
31. Desmond, Moore, and Browne, *Charles Darwin*, 64–65.
32. Ruse and Richards, *Cambridge Companion*, xv.
33. Ruse and Richards, *Cambridge Companion*, 333–35, 342–44; Darwin, *Autobiography of Charles Darwin*, 100–101.
34. Thomas Huxley, *Darwiniana* (New York: AMS Press, 1970), 121; also see Kohn, *Darwinian Heritage*, 655.
35. Ruse and Richards, *Cambridge Companion*, xvii.
36. Janet Browne, *Charles Darwin: The Power of Place* (New York: Alfred A. Knopf, 2002), 312.
37. Mayr, *One Long Argument*, 35–36, 69.
38. Janet Browne, *Darwin's "Origin of Species"* (New York: Atlantic Monthly Press, 2007), 57.
39. Kohn, *Darwinian Heritage*, 925.
40. Browne, *Charles Darwin: Power of Place*, 17.
41. Browne, *Charles Darwin: Power of Place*, 10.
42. Steve Jones, *The Darwin Archipelago* (New Haven, CT: Yale University Press, 2011), 178.
43. Browne, *Charles Darwin: Power of Place*, 9–13.
44. John van Wyhe, "Mind the Gap: Did Darwin Avoid Publishing His Theory for Many Years?," *Notes and Records of the Royal Society*, 61 (2007): 194.
45. Watson, *Darwin*, 600.
46. Howard Gruber, *Darwin on Man*, 2nd ed. (Chicago: University of Chicago Press, 1981), 24–33.
47. Darwin, *Autobiography of Charles Darwin*, 114–15, 118, 130.
48. Darwin, *Autobiography of Charles Darwin*, 114–15.
49. Darwin, *Autobiography of Charles Darwin*, 115; Mayr, *One Long Argument*, 10.
50. Kohn, *Darwinian Heritage*, 924.
51. Jones, *Darwin Archipelago*, xi.
52. Darwin, *Autobiography of Charles Darwin*, 113.
53. Watson, *Darwin*, vii.
54. Wilson, *From so Simple a Beginning*, 11.
55. Frederick Burckhardt, ed., *Charles Darwin's Letters* (Cambridge: Cambridge University Press, 1996), x.
56. Browne, *Charles Darwin: Power of Place*, 449–50.
57. L. Robert Stevens, *Charles Darwin* (Boston: Twayne Publishers, 1978), 137.
58. Browne, *Charles Darwin: Power of Place*, 496–97.
59. George Viereck, *Glimpses of the Great* (New York: Macauley, 1930), 447.
60. Paul Schilpp, ed., *Albert Einstein* (Evanston, IL: Library of Living Philosophers, 1949), 9.
61. Walter Isaacson, *Einstein* (New York: Simon and Schuster, 2007), 13–14.
62. Isaacson, *Einstein*, 17–18; Abraham Pais, "*Subtle Is the Lord*" (Oxford: Oxford University Press, 2005), 38.
63. Isaacson, *Einstein*, 47–49, 54–63, 67–72, 77–79, 92–93; John Rigden, *Einstein 1905* (Cambridge, MA: Harvard University Press, 2005); John Stachel, ed., *Einstein's Miraculous Year* (Princeton, NJ: Princeton University Press, 1998).
64. Pais, "*Subtle Is the Lord*", 522.
65. Gerald Holton, *Thematic Origins of Scientific Thought*, rev. ed. (Cambridge, MA: Harvard University Press, 1988), 193–94.

66. Pais, "*Subtle Is the Lord*", 417.
67. Gerald Holton and Yehuda Elkana, eds., *About Einstein* (Princeton, NJ: Princeton University Press, 1982), 28.
68. Rigden, *Einstein 1905*, 95.
69. Kip Thorne, *Black Holes and Time Warps* (New York: W. W. Norton, 1994), 79.
70. Holton, *Thematic Origins of Scientific Thought*, 251.
71. Holton, *Thematic Origins of Scientific Thought*, 250–54.
72. Isaacson, *Einstein*, 352.
73. Albert Einstein, *Ideas and Opinions* (New York: Crown Publishers, 1954), 273–74.
74. Einstein, *Ideas and Opinions*, 307.
75. Schilpp, *Albert Einstein*, 53.
76. Schilpp, *Albert Einstein*, 15–17, 89.
77. Holton and Elkana, *Albert Einstein*, 83.
78. David W. Galenson and Clayne L. Pope, "Experimental and Conceptual Innovators in the Sciences: The Cases of Darwin and Einstein," *Historical Methods*, 46, no. 2 (2013): 109–10; Isaacson, *Einstein*, 26.
79. Isaacson, *Einstein*, 145.
80. Schilpp, *Albert Einstein*, 110.
81. John Brockman, ed., *My Einstein* (New York: Pantheon Books, 2006), 21–22.
82. Isaacson, *Einstein*, 193.
83. Pais, "*Subtle Is the Lord*", 150, 239.
84. Pais, "*Subtle Is the Lord*", 256.
85. Isaacson, *Einstein*, 223–24.
86. Isaacson, *Einstein*, 223–24.
87. Pais, "*Subtle Is the Lord*", 440–57.
88. Max Born, *The Born–Einstein Letters*, new ed. (Houndmills, UK: Macmillan, 2005), 146.
89. Andrew Robinson, ed., *Einstein* (New York: Harry N. Abrams, 2005), 102.
90. Born, *Born–Einstein Letters*, xxxvii.
91. Born, *Born–Einstein Letters*, 88–89.
92. Hans Ohanian, *Einstein's Mistakes* (New York: W. W. Norton, 2008), 300.
93. Pais, "*Subtle Is the Lord*", 236, 463–64.
94. Robinson, *Einstein*, 108.
95. Isaacson, *Einstein*, 264.
96. Holton and Elkana, *Albert Einstein*, 82.
97. Isaacson, *Einstein*, 342, 633.
98. Albert Einstein, *Out of My Later Years* (New York: Philosophical Library, 1950); Holton and Elkana, *Albert Einstein*, 234.
99. Isaacson, *Einstein*, 7.
100. Schilpp, *Albert Einstein*, 17.
101. Rutherford Aris, H. Ted Davis, and Roger Stuewer, eds., *Springs of Scientific Creativity* (Minneapolis: University of Minnesota Press, 1983), 240.
102. Isaacson, *Einstein*, 5.
103. Einstein, *Ideas and Opinions*, 272; Holton, *Thematic Origins of Scientific Thought*, 251.
104. Viereck, *Glimpses of the Great*, 447.
105. Isaacson, *Einstein*, 551.
106. Schilpp, *Albert Einstein*, 163–64.
107. Isaacson, *Einstein*, 316.
108. Muhammad Yunus, *Banker to the Poor* (New York: Public Affairs, 2003), ix.
109. Alex Counts, *Give Us Credit* (New York: Times Books, 1996), 9.
110. Yunus, *Banker to the Poor*, 16; Counts, *Give Us Credit*, 9–10.
111. Yunus, *Banker to the Poor*, 19.
112. Counts, *Give Us Credit*, 11–12.
113. Yunus, *Banker to the Poor*, 29.
114. Yunus, *Banker to the Poor*, vii.
115. Yunus, *Banker to the Poor*, viii.
116. Yunus, *Banker to the Poor*, viii.
117. Yunus, *Banker to the Poor*, ix.
118. Yunus, *Banker to the Poor*, ix.
119. Yunus, *Banker to the Poor*, 48.

120. Yunus, *Banker to the Poor*, 50.
121. Yunus, *Banker to the Poor*, 51.
122. Yunus, *Banker to the Poor*, 57.
123. Yunus, *Banker to the Poor*, 70.
124. Abu Wahid, ed., *The Grameen Bank* (Boulder, CO: Westview Press, 1993), xi.
125. Yunus, *Banker to the Poor*, 120.
126. Muhammad Yunus, *Creating a World without Poverty* (New York: Public Affairs, 2007), 237–48.
127. Yunus, *Creating a World without Poverty*, 78–79.
128. Dean Karlan and Jacob Appel, *More Than Good Intentions* (New York: Dutton, 2011), 61, 66.
129. For example, Karlan and Appel, *More Than Good Intentions*, 140; Abhijit Banerjee and Esther Duflo, *Poor Economics* (New York: Public Affairs, 2011), 168–72; Jeffrey Sachs, *The End of Poverty* (New York: Penguin Books, 2005), 13–14.
130. Yunus, *Creating a World without Poverty*, 103.
131. Yunus, *Banker to the Poor*, 141, 150.
132. David Bornstein, *The Price of a Dream* (Chicago: University of Chicago Press, 1997), 33.
133. George Beahm, ed., *I, Steve* (Chicago: B2 Books, 2011), 66.
134. Walter Isaacson, *Steve Jobs* (New York: Simon and Schuster, 2011), 21–30.
135. Steven Wozniak and Gina Smith, *iWoz* (New York: W. W. Norton, 2006), 166.
136. Isaacson, *Steve Jobs*, 62.
137. Isaacson, *Steve Jobs*, 68.
138. Wozniak and Smith, *iWoz*, 188.
139. Isaacson, *Steve Jobs*, 84; Beahm, *I, Steve*, 69.
140. Michael Malone, *Infinite Loop* (New York: Doubleday, 1988), 152.
141. Ken Auletta, "The Wizard of Apple," *New Yorker*, August 24, 2011.
142. Isaacson, *Steve Jobs*, 73.
143. Malone, *Infinite Loop*, 68.
144. Isaacson, *Steve Jobs*, 139; Jeffrey Young and William Simon, *iCon* (Hoboken, NJ: John Wiley and Sons, 2005), 89.
145. Leander Kahney, *Inside Steve's Brain* (New York: Portfolio, 2008), 120–22.
146. Malone, *Infinite Loop*, 48.
147. Michael Moritz, *Return to the Little Kingdom* (New York: Overlook Press, 2009), 13.
148. Isaacson, *Steve Jobs*, 233.
149. John Sculley, *Odyssey* (New York: Harper and Row, 1987), 160–62.
150. Isaacson, *Steve Jobs*, 566.
151. Beahm, *I, Steve*, 61.
152. Young and Simon, *iCon*, 120.
153. Isaacson, *Steve Jobs*, 372.
154. Gary Wolf, "Steve Jobs," *Wired*, February 1, 1996.
155. David Sheff, "Playboy Interview: Steven Jobs," *Playboy*, February 1, 1985.
156. Young and Simon, *iCon*, 33.
157. Young and Simon, *iCon*, 85.
158. Young and Simon, *iCon*, 102.
159. Isaacson, *Steve Jobs*, 567.
160. Isaacson, *Steve Jobs*, 349.
161. Isaacson, *Steve Jobs*, 416.
162. Isaacson, *Steve Jobs*, 26.
163. Isaacson, *Steve Jobs*, 168, 494.
164. Ken Segall, *Insanely Simple* (New York: Penguin, 2012), 137.
165. Brent Schlender, "The Three Faces of Steve," *Fortune*, November 9, 1998.
166. Sheff, "Playboy Interview."
167. Sheff, "Playboy Interview."
168. Young and Simon, *iCon*, 230.
169. Wolf, "Steve Jobs."
170. Isaacson, *Steve Jobs*, 80.
171. Isaacson, *Steve Jobs*, 345.
172. Isaacson, *Steve Jobs*, 473.
173. Isaacson, *Steve Jobs*, 7.
174. Isaacson, *Steve Jobs*, 397.

175. Isaacson, *Steve Jobs*, 464.
176. Kohn, *Darwinian Heritage*, 561.
177. Kohn, *Darwinian Heritage*, 561, 573; Gillian Beer, *Darwin's Plots* (London: Routledge and Kegan Paul, 1983), 67.
178. Paul Johnson, *Darwin* (New York: Viking, 2012), 80–82.
179. Kohn, *Darwinian Heritage*, 561–62.
180. Kohn, *Darwinian Heritage*, 817.
181. Brown and Fabian, *Darwin*, 55–56.
182. George Levine, *Darwin the Writer* (New York: Oxford University Press, 2011), 53.
183. Thomas Glick, ed., *What about Darwin?* (Baltimore: Johns Hopkins University Press, 2010), 105; Ruse and Richards, *Cambridge Companion*, 239.
184. Glick, *What about Darwin?*, 327.
185. Glick, *What about Darwin?*
186. Glick, *What about Darwin?*, 98.
187. Robert Faggen, *Robert Frost and the Challenge of Darwin* (Ann Arbor: University of Michigan Press, 1997), 6; Mark Richardson, ed., *Robert Frost in Context* (Cambridge: Cambridge University Press, 2014), 123.
188. Glick, *What about Darwin?*, 413.
189. Pais, *"Subtle Is the Lord"*, 417.
190. Einstein, *Ideas and Opinions*, 336.
191. Einstein, *Ideas and Opinions*, 225–26.
192. Einstein, *Ideas and Opinions*, 324.
193. Einstein, *Ideas and Opinions*, 225.
194. Einstein, *Ideas and Opinions*, 274, 342.
195. Yunus, *Banker to the Poor*, 63.
196. Yunus, *Banker to the Poor*, 70.
197. Isaacson, *Steve Jobs*, 150.
198. Isaacson, *Steve Jobs*, 118.
199. Isaacson, *Steve Jobs*, 118.
200. Isaacson, *Steve Jobs*, 119.
201. Isaacson, *Steve Jobs*, 118.
202. Isaacson, *Steve Jobs*, 118–19.
203. Steven Levy, *Insanely Great* (New York: Penguin Books, 1994), 27.
204. Isaacson, *Steve Jobs*, 143.
205. Isaacson, *Steve Jobs*, 94.
206. Isaacson, *Steve Jobs*, 94.
207. Sculley, *Odyssey*, 90.
208. Isaacson, *Steve Jobs*, 367.
209. Brent Schlender and Rick Tetzeli, *Becoming Steve Jobs* (New York: Crown Business, 2015), 401.
210. Young and Simon, *iCon*, 128.
211. Alan Deutschman, *The Second Coming of Steve Jobs* (New York: Broadway Books, 2000), 237–38.
212. Isaacson, *Steve Jobs*, 119, 315.

Chapter 11

1. Adam Bradley, *Ralph Ellison in Progress* (New Haven, CT: Yale University Press, 2010), 6–7.
2. Bradley, *Ralph Ellison in Progress*, 210–12.
3. Hugh Honour and John Fleming, *The Visual Arts*, 5th ed. (New York: Harry N. Abrams, 1999), 475.
4. Martin Kemp, *Leonardo da Vinci* (London: J. M. Dent and Sons, 1981), 54–56, 68.
5. E. H. Gombrich, *Gombrich on the Renaissance* (London: Phaidon Press, 1966), 1:58.
6. Robert Jensen, "Anticipating Artistic Behavior," *Historical Methods*, 37, no. 3 (2004): 147.
7. Jensen, "Anticipating Artistic Behavior," 144.
8. Kemp, *Leonardo da Vinci*, 198–99.
9. Kemp, *Leonardo da Vinci*, 264–70.
10. Jensen, "Anticipating Artistic Behavior," 147.
11. Kenneth Clark, *Leonardo da Vinci*, rev. ed. (London: Penguin, 1993), 38–39.

12. Alexander Nagel, "Leonardo and *Sfumato*," *RES: Anthropology and Aesthetics*, no. 24 (1993): 8–9.
13. Ingrid Rowland and Noah Charney, *The Collector of Lives* (New York: W. W. Norton, 2017), 5.
14. Nagel, "Leonardo and *Sfumato*," 16.
15. Clark, *Leonardo da Vinci*, 129, 167, 212.
16. Jensen, "Anticipating Artistic Behavior," 144.
17. Howard Hibbard, *Michelangelo*, 2nd ed. (Boulder, CO: Westview Press, 1974), 105–108.
18. Jensen, "Anticipating Artistic Behavior," 142.
19. Hibbard, *Michelangelo*, 108.
20. Rudolf Wittkower, *Sculpture* (New York: Harper and Row, 1977), 143–44.
21. William Wallace, "Michelangelo: Separating Theory and Practice," in *Imitation, Representation and Printing in the Italian Renaissance*, edited by R. Eriksen and M. Malmanger (Pisa: Fabrizio Serra Editore, 2009), 105–106.
22. Hibbard, *Michelangelo*, 283.
23. Hibbard, *Michelangelo*, 283.
24. Wallace, "Michelangelo," 106.
25. Wallace, "Michelangelo," 114–17.
26. Wallace, "Michelangelo," 116.
27. William Wallace, *Michelangelo, God's Architect* (Princeton, NJ: Princeton University Press, 2019), 70, 194, 202–203, 209, 222, 239.
28. Jensen, "Anticipating Artistic Behavior," 145.
29. Francis Ames-Lewis, *The Draftsman Raphael* (New Haven, CT: Yale University Press, 1986), 3, 8.
30. Jensen, "Anticipating Artistic Behavior," 145.
31. Marcia Hall, ed., *The Cambridge Companion to Raphael* (Cambridge: Cambridge University Press, 2008), 261.
32. John Pope-Hennessy, *Raphael* (New York: Harper and Row, 1970), 36.
33. Ames-Lewis, *Draftsman Raphael*, 151.
34. Ascanio Condivi, *The Life of Michelangelo*, 2nd ed. (University Park: Pennsylvania State University Press, 1999), 133.
35. Pope-Hennessy, *Raphael*, 36, 128.
36. Pope-Hennessy, *Raphael*, 104.
37. Ames-Lewis, *Draftsman Raphael*, 151.
38. Sydney Freedberg, *Raphael, Michelangelo and Others* (Poughkeepsie, NY: Vassar College Press, 1983), 7–8.
39. Federico Etro, "The Economics of Renaissance Art," *Journal of Economic History*, 78, no. 2 (2018): 526.
40. Pope-Hennessy, *Raphael*, 217.
41. Hall, *Cambridge Companion to Raphael*, 9; Giorgio Vasari, *Vasari's Lives of the Artists* (New York: Simon and Schuster, 1946), 232.
42. Hall, *Cambridge Companion to Raphael*, 185.
43. David Galenson, *Conceptual Revolutions in Twentieth-Century Art* (Cambridge: Cambridge University Press, 2009), chap. 9.
44. Paul Valéry, *Degas, Manet, Morisot* (Princeton, NJ: Princeton University Press, 1960), 81, 113; Seymour Slive, *Dutch Painting 1600–1800* (New Haven, CT: Yale University Press, 1995), 78.
45. Svetlana Alpers, *Rembrandt's Enterprise* (Chicago: University of Chicago Press, 1988), 59–60.
46. Ann Adams, ed., *Rembrandt's "Bathsheba Reading King David's Letter"* (Cambridge: Cambridge University Press, 1998), 36–38.
47. Ernst van de Wetering, *Rembrandt: The Painter at Work* (Berkeley: University of California Press, 2001), 168; Morgan Ainsworth, *Art and Autoradiography* (New York: Metropolitan Museum, 1982), 25–96.
48. Slive, *Dutch Painting*, 87.
49. Alpers, *Rembrandt's Enterprise*, 99.
50. Alpers, *Rembrandt's Enterprise*, 77, 120.
51. Slive, *Dutch Painting*, 85.
52. Alpers, *Rembrandt's Enterprise*, 5.
53. Anna Brzyski, ed., *Partisan Canons* (Durham, NC: Duke University Press, 2007), chap. 10.
54. Alpers, *Rembrandt's Enterprise*, 59–60.
55. Slive, *Dutch Painting*, 85.
56. David Sylvester, *Interviews with Francis Bacon* (New York: Thames and Hudson, 1987), 58.

57. van de Wetering, *Rembrandt*, 274–79.
58. On Sherman and the selection of the artists for this section, see Galenson, *Conceptual Revolutions*, 95–109.
59. Wendy Slatkin, *The Voices of Women Artists* (Englewood Cliffs, NJ: Prentice Hall, 1993), 226.
60. Marsden Hartley, *On Art* (New York: Horizon Press, 1982), 106.
61. Barbara Lynes, *O'Keeffe, Stieglitz and the Critics* (Chicago: University of Chicago Press, 1989), 303.
62. Katharine Kuh, *The Artist's Voice* (New York: Harper and Row, 1962), 190–91.
63. Lloyd Goodrich and Doris Bry, *Georgia O'Keeffe* (New York: Whitney Museum, 1970), 19.
64. Lynes, *O'Keeffe, Stieglitz and the Critics*, 288.
65. Hunter Drohojowska-Philp, *Full Bloom* (New York: W. W. Norton, 2004), 478.
66. Galenson, *Conceptual Revolutions*, 108.
67. Anne Wagner, *Three Artists* (Berkeley: University of California Press, 1996), 70.
68. Galenson, *Conceptual Revolutions*, 98.
69. André Breton, *Surrealism and Painting* (Boston: MFA Publications, 2002), 144.
70. Galenson, *Conceptual Revolutions*, 98; Hayden Herrera, *Frida* (New York: Harper and Row, 1983), 256–57.
71. Herrera, *Frida*, 266.
72. Whitney Chadwick, ed., *Mirror Images* (Cambridge, MA: MIT Press, 1998), 164–67.
73. Peter Wollen, *Paris Manhattan* (London: Verso, 2004), 246.
74. Louise Bourgeois, *Destruction of the Father, Reconstruction of the Father* (Cambridge, MA: MIT Press, 1988), 261.
75. Bourgeois, *Destruction of the Father*, 66, 91, 162, 169, 218, 262, 318.
76. Galenson, *Conceptual Revolutions*, 95.
77. Bourgeois, *Destruction of the Father*, 166, 319.
78. Sam Newsome, *Be Inspired, Stay Focused* (New York: Some New Press, 2021), 44–46, 125–27.
79. John Szwed, *So What* (New York: Simon and Schuster, 2002), 55.
80. Ian Carr, *Miles Davis* (New York: William Morrow, 1982), 232–34.
81. Szwed, *So What*, 404.
82. Newsome, *Be Inspired, Stay Focused*, 46.
83. Eric Nisenson, *The Making of "Kind of Blue"* (New York: St. Martin's Press 2000), 20–21.
84. Miles Davis, *Miles* (New York: Simon and Schuster, 1989), 273, 391, 394; Paul Maher and Michael Dorr, eds., *Miles on Miles* (Chicago: Lawrence Hill Books, 2009), 186; Szwed, *So What*, 207.
85. Stephen Thomas Erlewine, *Kind of Blue* review, https://www.allmusic.com/album/kind-of-blue-mw0000191710.
86. Lewis Porter, *Coltrane* (Ann Arbor: University of Michigan Press, 1999), 44.
87. Carl Woideck, ed., *The John Coltrane Companion* (New York: Schirmer Books, 1998), xiii–xiv.
88. Carr, *Miles Davis*, 120.
89. Chris DeVito, ed., *Coltrane on Coltrane* (Chicago: A Cappella Books, 2010), 142, 145.
90. Ben Ratliff, *Coltrane* (New York: Farrar, Straus and Giroux, 2007), 65.
91. Porter, *Coltrane*, 262.
92. Newsome, *Be Inspired, Stay Focused*, 45; Tony Whyton, *Beyond "A Love Supreme"* (New York: Oxford University Press, 2013), 44–50.
93. Sam Walton, *Made in America* (New York: Bantam Books, 1993), 27.
94. Walton, *Made in America*, 31–34.
95. Walton, *Made in America*, 34–41.
96. Walton, *Made in America*, 41–43.
97. Walton, *Made in America*, 46–55.
98. Walton, *Made in America*, 57–64.
99. Walton, *Made in America*, 45, 90.
100. Alice Schroeder, *The Snowball* (New York: Bantam Books, 2009), chaps. 7–12; Roger Lowenstein, *Buffett* (New York: Random House, 1995), 28.
101. Lowenstein, *Buffett*, 41, 58; Jeremy Miller, *Warren Buffett's Ground Rules* (New York: Harper Collins, 2016), 80.
102. James O'Loughlin, *The Real Warren Buffett* (London: Nicholas Brealey, 2003), 44–45; Schroeder, *Snowball*, 258.
103. Schroeder, *Snowball*, 258, 273, 289; O'Loughlin, *Real Warren Buffett*, 53, 99; Lowenstein, *Buffett*, 100.

104. O'Loughlin, *Real Warren Buffett*, 40; Lowenstein, *Buffett*, 328–32.
105. Lowenstein, *Buffett*, 108.
106. James Dyson, *Against the Odds* (Andover, UK: Cengage Learning, 2001), 55–56.
107. Dyson, *Against the Odds*, 104–107.
108. Dyson, *Against the Odds*, 114, 208.
109. Dyson, *Against the Odds*, 89, 114, 125, 256–57.
110. Dyson, *Against the Odds*, 108, 206.
111. Dashun Wang and Albert-László Barabási, *The Science of Science* (Cambridge: Cambridge University Press, 2021), 6, 46.
112. Wang and Barabási, *Science of Science*, 46–48.
113. Wang and Barabási, *Science of Science*, 53–54.
114. Wang and Barabási, *Science of Science*, 54–56.
115. Wang and Barabási, *Science of Science*, 56.
116. Sam Newsome to David Galenson, email, September 30, 2020.
117. Kyle Gann, "Creativity and Chronology, Rethought," *PostClassic* blog, January 9, 2006, https://www.kylegann.com/PC060109-CreativityChronology.html.
118. William Landay, "Experimental Writers vs. Conceptual Writers," blog, August 30, 2010, March 7, 2013, https://www.williamlanday.com/2010/08/30/experimental-writers-vs-conceptual-writers/.
119. Bill Siemering to David Galenson, letter, November 25, 2007.
120. David Galenson, "'My Experimental Life': An Interview with Bill Siemering," part three, *Huffington Post*, September 27, 2012, https://www.huffpost.com/entry/my-experimental-life-an-i_b_1874897.
121. David Galenson, "'My Experimental Life': An Interview with Bill Siemering," part one, *Huffington Post*, September 11, 2012, https://www.huffpost.com/entry/interview-bill-siemering-1_b_1855894.

Chapter 12

1. Virginia Woolf, *A Writer's Diary* (San Diego: Harcourt Brace and Company, 1982), 46–49.
2. Virginia Woolf, *Collected Essays* (New York: Harcourt, Brace and World, 1967), 1:244–45.
3. Woolf, *Writer's Diary*, 49.
4. Jeffrey Meyers, *Robert Frost* (Boston: Houghton Mifflin, 1996), 199.
5. Arnold Grade, ed., *Family Letters of Robert and Elinor Frost* (Albany: State University of New York Press, 1972), 163.
6. Jay Parini, *Robert Frost* (New York: Henry Holt, 1999), 256.
7. Calvin Tomkins, *Off the Wall* (Harmondsworth, UK: Penguin Books, 1980), 185.
8. Victor Bockris, *Warhol* (New York: Da Capo Press, 1997), 320; Dore Ashton, ed., *The Writings of Robert Motherwell* (Berkeley: University of California Press, 2007), 239.
9. Thierry de Duve, *Kant after Duchamp* (Cambridge, MA: MIT Press, 1996), 216; Caroline Jones, *Machine in the Studio* (Chicago: University of Chicago Press, 1996), 115.
10. Robert Faggen, ed., *The Cambridge Companion to Robert Frost* (Cambridge: Cambridge University Press, 2001), 77.
11. William Carlos Williams, *Selected Essays* (New York: New Directions, 1969), 103.
12. William Carlos Williams, *The Autobiography of William Carlos Williams* (New York: Random House, 1951), 174, 217.
13. Louise Glück, *Proofs and Theories* (Hopewell, NJ: Ecco Press, 1994), 20.
14. Adam Kirsch, "Bookends," *New York Times Book Review*, April 20, 2014, 31.
15. Joyce Carol Oates, *Uncensored* (New York: HarperCollins, 2005), 6.
16. Zoë Heller, "Bookends," *New York Times Book Review*, April 20, 2014, 31.
17. Frederick Gwynn and Joseph Blotner, eds., *Faulkner in the University* (Charlottesville: University Press of Virginia, 1995), 206.
18. Joseph Urgo and Ann Abadie, *Faulkner and His Contemporaries* (Jackson: University Press of Mississippi, 2004), 78.
19. Philip Young, *Ernest Hemingway* (University Park: Pennsylvania State University Press, 1966), 245–46.
20. Virginia Woolf, *Granite and Rainbow* (New York: Harcourt, Brace and World, 1958), 92.
21. David Galenson, *Conceptual Revolutions in Twentieth-Century Art* (New York: Cambridge University Press, 2009), chap. 8.

22. Urgo and Abadie, *Faulkner and His Contemporaries*, 81.
23. Calvin Tomkins, *The Bride and the Bachelors* (New York: Viking Press, 1965), 13.
24. Glück, *Proofs and Theories*, 20.
25. Albert Einstein, *Ideas and Opinions* (New York: Crown Publishers, 1954), 13–14.
26. Thomas Glick, ed., *What about Darwin?* (Baltimore: Johns Hopkins University Press, 2010), 104–105.
27. Abraham Pais, "*Subtle Is the Lord*" (Oxford: Oxford University Press, 2005), chap. 12.
28. Michael Doran, ed., *Conversations with Cézanne* (Berkeley: University of California Press, 2001), 22, 122, 150; John Rewald, *Paul Cézanne* (New York: Simon and Schuster, 1948), 188–89.
29. Camille Pissarro, *Letters to His Son Lucien* (New York: Da Capo Press, 1995), 276.
30. Pissarro, *Letters to His Son Lucien*, 269.
31. Calvin Tomkins, *Off the Wall* (Garden City, NY: Doubleday, 1980), 118.
32. Jasper Johns, *Writings, Sketchbook Notes, Interviews* (New York: Museum of Modern Art, 1996), 280–81.
33. Tomkins, *Off the Wall*, 118.
34. Calvin Tomkins, "Everything in Sight," *New Yorker*, May 23, 2005, 76.
35. Tomkins, *Off the Wall*, 118.
36. For example, see Blaise Cronin, "Collaboration in Art and in Science: Approaches to Attribution, Authorship, and Acknowledgement," *Information & Culture*, 47, no. 1 (2012): 18–37.
37. Michael Nielsen, *Reinventing Discovery* (Princeton, NJ: Princeton University Press, 2012), 31–35, 75–76.
38. David Galenson and Clayne Pope, "Collaboration in Science and Art," *Huffington Post*, July 23, 2012, https://www.huffpost.com/entry/collaboration-in-science_b_1687024; Galenson, *Conceptual Revolutions*, chap. 10.
39. Barnett Newman, *Selected Writings and Interviews* (Berkeley: University of California Press, 1992), 81–82.
40. David Galenson, *Painting Outside the Lines* (Cambridge, MA: Harvard University Press, 2001), 75–146.
41. Jack Flam, *Matisse on Art*, rev. ed. (Berkeley: University of California Press, 1995), 177–78.
42. Galenson, *Painting Outside the Lines*, 102.
43. Hilary Spurling, *The Unknown Matisse* (New York: Alfred A. Knopf, 1998), 323.
44. Françoise Gilot and Carlton Lake, *Life with Picasso* (New York: Anchor Books, 1964), 76–77.
45. Svetlana Alpers, *Rembrandt's Enterprise* (Chicago: University of Chicago Press, 1988), 59, 101; Robert Jensen, "Anticipating Artistic Behavior," *Historical Methods*, 37, no. 3 (2004): 137–53.
46. Victor Bockris, *Andy Warhol* (New York: Da Capo Press, 1997), 164.
47. Cronin, "Collaboration in Art and in Science," 27–29.
48. David Sylvester, *Interviews with American Artists* (New Haven, CT: Yale University Press, 2001), 351; Damien Hirst and Gordon Burn, *On the Way to Work* (New York: Universe Publishing, 2002), 90.
49. Anne Woollett and Ariane von Suchtelen, *Rubens & Brueghel* (Los Angeles: Getty Publications, 2006), 2–36, 215–48.
50. Galenson, *Conceptual Revolutions*, 173–75, 202–205.
51. Galenson, *Conceptual Revolutions*, 173–75, 201–209.
52. John Sculley, *Odyssey* (New York: Harper and Row, 1987), 162–65.
53. Michael Moritz, *Return to the Little Kingdom* (New York: Overlook Press, 2009), 268; Muhammad Yunus, *Banker to the Poor* (New York: Public Affairs, 2003), 102.
54. Yunus, *Banker to the Poor*, 101.
55. Abu Wahid, ed., *The Grameen Bank* (Boulder, CO: Westview Press, 1993), 12.
56. Brassaï, *Conversations with Picasso* (Chicago: University of Chicago Press, 1999), 133.
57. Alfred Barr, *Picasso* (New York: Museum of Modern Art, 1946), 271.
58. Edward Lathem, ed., *Robert Frost Speaking on Campus* (New York: W. W. Norton, 2009), 112, 164.
59. Barr, *Picasso*, 271.
60. Mark Richardson, ed., *The Collected Prose of Robert Frost* (Cambridge, MA: Harvard University Press, 2007), 132.
61. Richard Poirier, *Robert Frost* (Stanford, CA: Stanford University Press, 1977), 279–81.
62. Orson Welles, *Interviews* (Jackson: University Press of Mississippi, 2002), 175.
63. Ambroise Vollard, *Cézanne* (New York: Dover Publications, 1984), 86–87.

64. Brassaï, *Conversations with Picasso*, 92–93.
65. Françoise Gilot and Carlton Lake, *Life with Picasso* (New York: Doubleday, 1989), 123.
66. Thomas McEvilley, *The Triumph of Anti-Art* (Kingston, NY: McPherson and Company, 2005), 28.
67. James Breslin, *Mark Rothko* (Chicago: University of Chicago Press, 1993), 526.
68. Robert Jelliffe, ed., *Faulkner at Nagano* (Tokyo: Kenkyusha, 1956), 90.
69. Michel Seuphor, *Piet Mondrian* (New York: Harry N. Abrams, 1956), 198.
70. Tobias Jones, "A Passion for Mercy," *The Guardian*, July 31, 2009.
71. Edward Lathem, ed., *Interviews with Robert Frost* (New York: Holt, Rinehart and Winston, 1966), 115.
72. Dorothy Norman, *Alfred Stieglitz* (New York: Random House, 1973), 10.
73. Edgar Kauffman, ed., *An American Architecture* (New York: Horizon Press, 1955), 33.
74. Dore Ashton, *The Writings of Robert Motherwell* (Berkeley: University of California Press, 2007), 79.
75. Cleanth Brooks and Robert Penn Warren, *Conversations on the Craft of Poetry* (New York: Holt, Rinehart and Winston, 1961), 7.
76. Tom Milne, ed., *Godard on Godard* (New York: Da Capo Press, 1986), 171.
77. Vincent van Gogh, *The Complete Letters*, 2nd ed. (Greenwich, CT: New York Graphic Society, 1959), 2:119.
78. Arthur Danto, *After the End of Art* (Princeton, NJ: Princeton University Press, 1997), 28–30.
79. For example, see Alex Danchev, ed., *100 Artists' Manifestos* (London: Penguin, 2011).
80. Marjorie Perloff, *The Futurist Moment* (Chicago: University of Chicago Press, 2003), 90.
81. Galenson, *Conceptual Revolutions*, 280–81.
82. Ashton, *Writings of Robert Motherwell*, 334.
83. Robert Faggen, ed., *The Cambridge Companion to Robert Frost* (Cambridge: Cambridge University Press, 2001), 123.
84. Albert Elsen and Kirk Varnedoe, *The Drawings of Rodin* (New York: Praeger, 1971), 120.
85. Benjamin Sears, ed., *The Irving Berlin Reader* (Oxford: Oxford University Press, 2012), ii.
86. Octavio Paz, *On Poets and Others* (New York: Arcade Publishing, 1986), 5.
87. Peter Stanlis, *Conversations with Robert Frost* (New Brunswick, NJ: Transaction Publishers, 2010), 49.
88. Mark Dawidziak, *Mark My Words* (New York: St. Martin's Press, 1996), 56; John Russell, *Francis Bacon*, rev. ed. (New York: Thames and Hudson, 1993), 182.
89. Frank Kermode, ed., *Selected Prose of T. S. Eliot* (New York: Farrar, Straus and Giroux, 1975), 253.
90. Welles, *Interviews*, 81.

Index

Note to print book readers: indexed terms that span two pages (e.g. 64–65) may appear on only one of those pages.

Aalto, Alvar, 150–51, 159
Abbott, Berenice, 173–75, 176–77, 185–86, 191
Adams, Ansel, 174–75
Adams, Henry, 62
Adams, John, 62
Adams, John Quincy, 62
age at time of greatest work: Atget, Jean-Eugène-Auguste, 173, 176; Bishop, Elizabeth, 74; Boccioni, Umberto, 101; Bourgeois, Louise, 299; central question of, vii; Cézanne, Paul, vii, 16, 20; creativity and, 308–9; Dylan, Bob, 234; Einstein, Albert, 262–63, 266; Eliot, T. S., 63–65; Ford, John, 196; Frost, Robert, 62; Gehry, Frank, 161–62; Hemingway, Ernest, 138; Hitchcock, Alfred, 204; Kahlo, Frida, 298; Le Corbusier, 157; Lennon, John and Paul McCartney, 241; Leonardo da Vinci, 289; Melville, Herman, 120–21; O'Keeffe, Georgia, 297–98; Parker, Charlie, 300; Picasso, Pablo, vii; Porter, Cole, 228; Raphael, 293–94; Simon, Paul, 248; Stieglitz, Alfred, 180; Twain, Mark, 124; Warhol, Andy, 43; Welles, Orson, 207–8; Woolf, Virginia, 132, 133; Wright, Frank Lloyd, 150–51. *See also* creative life cycle(s)
Aiken, Conrad, 64–65, 135
Alpers, Svetlana, 295–96
Alvarez, A., 79, 80–81
Ames-Lewis, Francis, 292–94
Anderson, Lindsay, 202–3
Ando, Tadao, 156
Apollinaire, Guillaume, 100–1
Apple Computer Corporation, 275–76, 277–80, 284–86, 323–24
Aragon, Louis, 211–12, 214
architects: conceptual, 164–68; drawing, role of, 168–69; duality of approach among, 146, 169–70; experimental, 146–63; Gehry, Frank, 158–63; Le Corbusier, 153–57; Lin, Maya, 164–68; Wright, Frank Lloyd, 146–53
Arensberg, Walter, 184
Arlen, Harold, 329–30
Armstrong, Louis, 225, 300
Arrow, Kenneth, 2
Astaire, Fred, 249–50
Astruc, Alexandre, 216
Atget, Jean-Eugène-Auguste, 171–77, 191, 192
Atkinson, Bill, 284–85
Auletta, Ken, 276

Bacon, Francis, 296, 330
Baez, Joan, 231–32
Baline, Israel, 220–21. *See also* Berlin, Irving
Balzac, Honoré de, 94, 289–90
Barabási, Albert-László, 307–9
Basquiat, Jean-Michel, 44–49, 53, 189–90
Bazin, André, 193, 211–12
Baziotes, William, 29–30, 32
Beer, Gillian, 280–81
Bell, Clive, 20, 66–67, 129
Bell, Larry, 41–42
Belluschi, Pietro, 165
Bennett, Joan, 133
Benton, Thomas Hart, 29–30
Berger, John, 25–26, 27–28
Bergman, Ingrid, 210–11
Bergmann, Peter, 263–64
Berlin, Irving, 220–26, 227, 228, 229, 246–47, 249–50, 251–53, 329–30
Berlin, Irving, Jr., 250
Bernard, Emile, 15, 18, 19–21, 22–23, 49–50
Berry, Chuck, 237
Berryman, John, 76
Bertolucci, Bernardo, 212–13
Beuys, Joseph, 316
Bidart, Frank, 85–86
Bikel, Theodore, 232
Bishop, Elizabeth, 68–72, 73–76, 85–89
Blake, Eubie, 221–22

378 INDEX

Blake, Peter, 153–54, 241–42, 244–45
Bloom, Harold, 124–25
Boccioni, Umberto, 97–102, 113, 114
Bogdanovich, Peter, 195, 198, 204–5, 208
Boiffard, Jacques-André, 185–86
Boone, Mary, 47, 48
Bordwell, David, 209
Borges, Jorge Luis, 209
Born, Max, 266–67, 269
Bourdon, David, 43
Bourgeois, Louise, 299
Bowness, Sir Alan, 3–4, 15, 90
Bradley, Adam, 287–88
Bradley, Ed, 236
Brancusi, Constantin, 96, 110–11
Brandt, Bill, 185–86
Braque, Georges, 21–22, 24, 25–27, 28, 46, 98, 320–21, 324
Brassaï, 325, 326–27
Braxton, Anthony, 300
Brecht, Bertolt, 214
Breton, André, 103–4, 187, 298
Brueghel the Elder, Jan, 322
Broglie, Louis de, 265
Brooks, Van Wyck, 141
Browne, Janet, 255–56, 258, 260
Buffett, Warren, 304–6
Butler, Christopher, 50–51

Calatrava, Santiago, 163
Cantril, Hadley, 206–7
Carey, Harry, 194–95
Carr, Ian, 300
Cézanne, Paul, vii, 15–23, 24–25, 35–36, 49–50, 51, 52–53, 101–3, 105, 113, 130, 132–33, 159, 160, 179, 200, 287, 318–19, 324, 326–27
Chabrol, Claude, 202–3, 211–12
Chaplin, Charlie, 206–7, 268–69
Clark, Kenneth, 290
Clemens, Samuel, 121. *See also* Twain, Mark
Cobb, Jimmy, 302
Colacello, Bob, 41
Colcord, Lionel, 141
Cole, Nat King, 225, 227
Coleman, Ornette, 300
Coleridge, Samuel Taylor, 118–19
collaboration: conceptual/experimental innovators and, 315–24; Elizabeth Bishop and Robert Lowell, 68–76; Gilbert (Gilbert Proesch) and George (George Passmore), 322–23; John Lennon and Paul McCartney, 237–38 (*see also* Lennon, John

and Paul McCartney); T.S. Eliot and Ezra Pound, 83–84
Coltrane, John, 299–300, 301–2
conceptual innovators: Basquiat, Jean-Michel, 44–49, 53; career pattern of, 8–10; Davis, Miles, 300–1; description of, 5–6; Duchamp, Marcel, 184, 185, 187; Dylan, Bob (*see* Dylan, Bob); Einstein, Albert, 262–69; Eliot, T. S. (Thomas Stearns), 62–67, 83–85, 89; as enemies of experimental innovators, 311–17; Fitzgerald, F. Scott, 115–16; Giacometti, Alberto, 102–4; Godard, Jean-Luc, 210–16; Hemingway, Ernest, 134–40; Jobs, Steve, 275–80; Kahlo, Frida, 298; Lennon, John and Paul McCartney, 237–45; life cycles of, 10–12; Lin, Maya, 164–68; Man Ray, 183–87; Melville, Herman, 116–21; Parker, Charlie, 300; Picasso, Pablo (*see* Picasso, Pablo); Plath, Sylvia, 77–82; Raphael (Raffaelo Santi), 292–94; Sherman, Cindy, 187–91; Smithson, Robert, 107–12; Warhol, Andy, 36–43; Welles, Orson, 205–11; Wozniak, Steve, 275–77
Cook, Tim, 279–80
Cooper, Douglas, 28–29
Copland, Aaron, 244–45
Cortez, Diego, 48
Cowley, Malcolm, 57–58, 63–64
Crane, Hart, 49, 66, 252
creative life cycle(s): of artists, 14–15; of experimental and conceptual innovators, 10–12; innovation and, question of, vii, 1–2; maturation of innovators, 223–24; of old masters of visual art, 288–96; paths to creativity and, 324–33; of poets, 62; of scientists, 307–9; of women artists, 296–99; Wright on the experimental, 152–53. *See also* age at time of greatest work
creativity/innovation: economists and (*see* economics/economists); seekers and finders, 331–33; two paths to, 324–31 (*see also* duality among innovators)
creativity/innovation, loss of: by conceptual filmmakers, 210–11, 215; by conceptual novelists, 120–21, 137–38; by conceptual painters, 28–29, 47; by conceptual photographers, 187; by conceptual poets, 67; by conceptual scientists, 267–69; by conceptual songwriters, 235–36, 243, 244; by experimental novelists, 287
creativity/innovation, process of: for conceptual architects, 166; for conceptual

entrepreneurs, 278, 279–80; for conceptual filmmakers, 209–10, 213–14, 215; for conceptual musicians, 301; for conceptual novelists, 118–19, 134–36; for conceptual p, 64; for conceptual painters, 27–28, 38–39, 46–47, 292–93; for conceptual photographers, 185–86, 187, 190–91; for conceptual poets, 64, 79, 83–84, 88; for conceptual scientists, 263–65; for conceptual sculptors, 98, 108–9; for conceptual songwriters, 236, 240, 243–44; for experimental architects, 148–49, 157, 159–60, 163; for experimental artists, 181; for experimental filmmakers, 198, 201–2, 204; for experimental novelists, 122, 129, 131; for experimental painters, 17, 18, 31–33, 295, 297; for experimental photographers, 176, 179–80, 181–82; for experimental poets, 56, 60 61, 70, 72, 75, 76, 82–83, 86–88; for experimental scientists, 258; for experimental sculptors, 91–92, 95, 103, 105–6, 291–92; for experimental songwriters, 222–23, 229, 247, 248–49
Crosby, Bing, 225
Csikszentmihalyi, Mihaly, 1

Dali, Salvador, 103
Dante Alighieri, 93
Danto, Arthur, 39–40, 111, 190, 329
Darrow, Whitney, 29–30
Darwin, Charles, 70, 117–18, 254–62, 280–83, 307
Davis, Clive, 246–47
Davis, Miles, 300–1, 302
Dean, James, 230, 236–37
de Beer, Gavin, 254
de Kooning, Willem, 35–36, 108, 159, 313
DeNiro, Robert, 197–98
Derain, André, 320–21, 324
DeVoto, Bernard, 121–22, 128, 141
Devries, Gérald, 216
Diaz, Al, 44
Dickey, James, 12–13
Didion, Joan, 140
Dirac, Paul, 264–65, 266, 268–69
Dobzhansky, Theodosius, 261
Dos Passos, John, 315–16
Dove, Arthur, 181–82
Doyno, Victor, 142
Drexler, Mickey, 277–78
duality among innovators: architects, 146, 169–70; collaboration and, 317–24

(*see also* collaboration); conceptual/experimental, 5–8 (*see also* conceptual innovators; experimental innovators); enemies produced by, 311–17; filmmakers, 193–94, 216–19; generality of the analysis of, 288, 309–10; jazz musicians, 299–300; novelists, 115–16, 140–45; old masters of visual art, 288; painters, 14–15; photographers, 171, 191–92; poets, 54–55, 88–89; scientists, 307–9; sculptors, 90, 114; songwriters, 220, 249–53; as two paths to creativity, 324–31
Duchamp, Marcel, 26–28, 39, 184, 185, 187, 316, 327
Dürer, Albrecht, 102
Dylan, Bob, 1, 2, 46, 215–16, 224, 230–37, 239, 240, 241–42, 244–49, 250–52, 278–79
Dyson, James, 306–7

economics/economists: "Bilbao Effect," 161–62; entrepreneurs and, 271–75; individual innovators, failure to study or account for, 2–3; invention and innovation, distinction between, 3; productivity over the life cycle, study of, vii; theoretical abstractions of, inadequacy of, 271, 274–75
Eddington, Sir Arthur, 268–69
Edwards, Hilton, 205–6
Einstein, Albert, 262–69, 283–84, 317
Eisenman, Peter, 161–62
Eisenstein, Sergei, 194, 218–19
Eliot, Abigail Adams, 62
Eliot, Charles William, 62
Eliot, George, 283
Eliot, T. S. (Thomas Stearns), 1, 2, 46, 61, 62–67, 69, 72–73, 83–85, 89, 124, 141–42, 185–86, 311, 312–13, 314–15, 316–17, 330
Elkana, Yehuda, 268–69
Ellington, Duke, 300
Ellison, Larry, 277–78
Ellison, Ralph, 125, 287–88
Elsen, Albert, 91–92, 93, 94–95, 167
Emerick, Geoff, 241–42
Emerson, Ralph Waldo, 310
Emin, Tracey, 298
entrepreneurs, 254, 302–3; Buffett, Warren, 304–6; conceptual, 275–80; Dyson, James, 306–7; experimental, 270–75, 302–7; Jobs, Steve, 275–80, 284–86; language of, 280–86; Walton, Sam, 303–4; Yunus, Muhammad, 270–75, 284
Erlewine, Stephen, 301
Escher, Christopher, 286

Etro, Federico, 294
Evans, Bill, 301
Evans, Walker, 175, 182
experimental innovators: Atget, Jean-Eugène-Auguste, 171–77; Berlin, Irving, 220–26; Bishop, Elizabeth, 68–72, 73–76, 85–89; Boccioni, Umberto, 97–102; Bourgeois, Louise, 299; Buffett, Warren, 304–6; career pattern of, 8–10; Cézanne, Paul (*see* Cézanne, Paul); Coltrane, John, 301–2; Darwin, Charles, 254–62; description of, 5; Dyson, James, 306–7; as enemies of conceptual innovators, 311–17; Faulkner, William, 115–16; Ford, John, 194–98; Frost, Robert, 55–62, 82–83, 85, 88–89; Gehry, Frank, 158–63; Giacometti, Alberto, 102–7; Hitchcock, Alfred, 198–205; Le Corbusier, 153–57; Leonardo da Vinci, 288–90; life cycles of, 10–12; Lowell, Robert (Robert Traill Spence Lowell IV), 68–73, 75–76, 85–87; Michelangelo Buonarroti, 290–92; O'Keeffe, Georgia, 181, 297–98; Porter, Cole, 226–30; Rembrandt van Rijn, 294–96; Rodin, Auguste, 90–97, 167; Simon, Paul, 245–51; Stieglitz, Alfred, 177–82; Twain, Mark, 121–28; Walton, Sam, 303–4; Woolf, Virginia, 128–34; Wright, Frank Lloyd, 146–53; Yunus, Muhammad, 270–75

Fab 5 Freddy, 53
Farber, Manny, 215
Faulkner, William, 115–16, 119–20, 138, 315–16, 327
Feeney, John Martin, 194. *See also* Ford, John
Filler, Martin, 157, 163
filmmakers: conceptual, 205–16; directors and audiences, 216–19; duality of approach among, 193–94, 216–19; experimental, 194–205; Ford, John, 194–98, 216–17, 218–19; Godard, Jean-Luc, 210–16, 218–19; Hitchcock, Alfred, 198–205, 217–19; Welles, Orson, 205–11, 217–19
Fitzgerald, F. Scott, 115–16, 207, 229
Ford, Francis, 194
Ford, Henry, 278
Ford, John, 194–98, 216–17, 218–19
Forster, E. M., 131
Franco, Francisco, 28
Franklin, Aretha, 225
Freedberg, Sydney, 293–94
Friedan, Betty, 81

Friedkin, William, 194–95
Frontani, Michael, 242–43
Frost, Robert, 55–62, 82–83, 85, 88–89, 225–26, 283, 312–13, 314, 316, 325–26, 327–28, 329–30
Fry, Jeremy, 306
Fry, Roger, 14–15, 17, 19, 27–28, 129–33, 160

Gachet, Paul, 18
Gallagher, Ellen, 48
Gallo, Vincent, 53
Gann, Kyle, 309
Gardner, Helen, 83, 84
Gardner, Howard, 1
Garfunkel, Art, 245–46
Gates, Bill, 280
Gehry, Frank, 156, 158–63, 164, 165–66, 168–70
Geldzahler, Henry, 52–53
Georgescu-Roegen, Nicholas, 270
Gershwin, George, 222, 252–53
Giacometti, Alberto, 102–7, 113, 114
Giedion, Sigfried, 146, 147–48
Gilbert (Gilbert Proesch) and George (George Passmore), 322–23
Gillespie, Dizzy, 300
Gilmore, Mikal, 235
Gilot, Françoise, 326–27
Ginsberg, Allen, 233
Gladwell, Malcolm, 248–49
Glass, David, 304
Glück, Louise, 314–15, 316–17
Godard, Jean-Luc, 46, 202–3, 210–16, 218–19, 244–45, 328
Goffin, Gerry, 238
Goldberg, Frank, 158. *See also* Gehry, Frank
Goldberger, Paul, 160
Golding, John, 24, 99–100, 101–2
Goncourt, Edmond de, 112
Gonzalez-Torres, Felix, 48
Gopnik, Blake, 52–53
Gorin, Jean-Pierre, 214
Gould, John, 255–56
Gould, Stephen Jay, 256–57, 261
Goya, Francisco, 296
Graham, Benjamin, 304–6
Grameen Bank, 272, 273–74, 284, 324
Grant, Cary, 201–2
Greenberg, Clement, 20, 31
Gretzky, Wayne, 278
Griffith, D. W., 194
Gropius, Walter, 148, 155
Grossmann, Marcel, 317

INDEX 381

Gruber, Howard, 260
Guggenheim, Peggy, 31
Guthrie, Woody, 230–32

Hall, Donald, 73
Hamilton, George Heard, 24–25, 96
Hamilton, Richard, 244–45
Hannan, Michael, 241–42
Hardwick, Elizabeth, 80
Haring, Keith, 46
Harrison, George, 237–38
Harry, Debbie, 53
Hartley, Marsden, 297
Hawthorne, Nathaniel, 117
Heaney, Seamus, 59–60, 61, 74, 75
Hebdige, Dick, 46–47
Heinich, Nathalie, 46
Heisenberg, Werner, 267, 307
Heller, Zöe, 314–15
Hemingway, Ernest, 81, 115–16, 124–25, 134–40, 141, 144–45, 185–86, 314–16
Hendrix, Jimi, 246
Herbert, Sandra, 258
Herrera, Hayden, 298
Herrmann, Bernard, 207, 208
Hertzfeld, Andy, 284–85
Hesse, Eva, 49
Hibbard, Howard, 290–91
Hilburn, Robert, 248–49
Hirst, Damien, 26–28, 42, 189–90, 294, 316, 321–22
Hitchcock, Alfred, 194–95, 198–205, 211–12, 217–19
Hoban, Phoebe, 45
Hockney, David, 21–22
Hodge, M., 256
Hoffman, Donald, 152–53
Holden, Stephen, 248–49
Holiday, Billie, 224
Holly, Buddy, 197–98, 230, 237
Holton, Gerald, 263, 264–65
Hooker, Joseph, 256–58
Howard, Rachel, 321–22
Howe, Irving, 139–40
Howells, William Dean, 122, 126
Hughes, Robert, 48
Hughes, Ted, 78–79, 80–81
Hull, David, 259
Huxley, T. H., 259

Imhotep, 157
Indiana, Robert, 37–38, 41–42
Ingres, J.A.D., 186–87

innovators: career patterns of, 8–10 (*see also* creative life cycle(s)); collaboration between (*see* collaboration); duality among (*see* duality among innovators); generality of the analysis of, 288, 309–10; important, definition of, 3–4; selection of for study, 12–13; types of, 5–8 (*see also* conceptual innovators; experimental innovators). *see also* creativity/innovation; creativity/innovation, loss of; creativity/innovation, process of
Isaacson, Walter, 276–77, 279–80, 284–85, 286
Ishaghpour, Youssef, 214

Jacobsen, Josephine, 59
James, C. L. R., 119–20
Janis, Sidney, 313
Jarrell, Randall, 61, 68, 69–70
jazz musicians: Coltrane, John, 301–2; Davis, Miles, 300–1; dualities of approach among, 299–300
Jeanneret-Gris, Charles-Edouard. *See* Le Corbusier
Jencks, Charles, 156
Jensen, Robert, 12–13, 289, 290–91, 292–93
Jobs, Steve, 1, 2, 275–80, 284–86, 323–24, 326
Johns, Jasper, 319
Johnson, Paul, 281
Jolson, Al, 224
Jones, Steve, 261
Jong, Erica, 81
Joplin, Janis, 246
Joplin, Scott, 221–22
Joyce, James, 46, 110–11, 119–20, 130, 185–86, 311, 312
Judd, Donald, 113–14
Julius II, 290

Kahlo, Frida, 298
Kahn, Louis, 156
Kahnweiler, Daniel-Henry, 28
Kaprow, Allan, 33–34
Kaufman, James, 1
Kaufmann, E. J., 149–50
Kawin, Bruce, 193–94
Kemp, Martin, 288–89
Kennedy, John F., 61
Kenner, Hugh, 139–40
Kern, Jerome, 221–22, 225–26, 251, 252–53
Kerr, Walter, 210
Kiki of Montparnasse, 186–87

King, Carole, 238
Kirsch, Adam, 314–15
Kohn, Daniel, 256
Koons, Jeff, 42, 189–90, 316, 321–22
Kracauer, Siegfried, 171
Krasner, Lee, 32, 35, 51
Kunitz, Stanley, 76, 85–86
Kurosawa, Akira, 197–98
Kuznets, Simon, 2

Laforgue, Jules, 62–63
Landay, William, 309–10
Lanois, Daniel, 235
Laski, Harold, 66–67
La Vergata, Antonello, 261
Lawrence, D. H., 119–20
Le Corbusier, 148, 153–57, 159, 161–62, 168, 169–70
Leigh, Janet, 201–2
Lennon, John and Paul McCartney, 237–45, 250, 251–52
Leonardo da Vinci, 279–80, 288–90, 292–93, 295–96, 321
Lessing, Doris, 133–34
Levine, George, 282–83
Lewis, C. Day, 65
Liebmann, Lisa, 43, 44–45
life cycles. *See* creative life cycle(s)
Lin, Maya, 112, 164–68, 169, 170
Little Richard, 237
Longo, Robert, 188, 190–91
Loos, Anita, 251–52
Lord, James, 105
Louis, Joe, 53
Lowell, A. Lawrence, 68–69
Lowell, Amy, 68–69
Lowell, James Russell, 68–69
Lowell, Robert (Robert Traill Spence Lowell IV), 54–55, 57, 61, 68–73, 75–76, 78, 80, 85–87
Lucas, George, 219
Lutyens, Sir Edward, 165
Lyell, Charles, 255, 259

Macdonald, Ross, 327
MacLiammóir, Mícheál, 205–6
Madonna, 45, 189–90
Magritte, René, 240
Mailer, Norman, 140
Malanga, Gerard, 38–39, 51–52, 321–22
Malevich, Kazimir, 28–29
Malone, Michael, 276, 277
Malraux, André, 156

Man Ray, 173, 183–87, 192
Mantle, Mickey, 247
Marani, Pietro, 288–89
Marcus, Greilton, 235
Marden, Brice, 20
Marin, John, 181–82
Marinetti, F. T., 97–98, 100–1
Marley, Bob, 225
Marshall, Richard, 46–47
Martin, George, 237–38, 241–42, 243, 244–45
Martin, Linda, 81
Mast, Gerald, 193–94, 249–50
Matisse, Amélie, 20–21
Matisse, Henri, 20–22, 24–25, 179, 320–21, 324
Matta, Roberto, 32
Matterson, Stephen, 72
Mauclair, Camille, 93
Mayr, Ernst, 259
McCartney, Paul. *See* Lennon, John and Paul McCartney
McLaurin, Allen, 143
Méliès, Georges, 194
Melville, Herman, 116–21, 141, 145
Menand, Louis, 64–65
Mendieta, Ana, 49, 298
Mepham, John, 129
Merman, Ethel, 228
Merrill, James, 75
Methfessel, Alice, 73
Michelangelo Buonarroti, 92–93, 95–96, 290–93, 295–96, 321
Miller, Lee, 185–86
Mondrian, Piet, 28–29, 327
Monet, Claude, 16, 17, 129–30, 318–19
Monroe, Marilyn, 37–38, 41–42
Moore, Geoffrey, 277
Moravia, Alberto, 138, 314–15
Moritz, Michael, 277
Morley, Malcolm, 20
Morrey, Douglas, 216
Motherwell, Robert, 29–30, 32, 313, 327–28, 329
Mumford, Lewis, 141
Munger, Charlie, 305
Murakami, Takashi, 48, 321–22
Murray, Mike, 278
musicians: jazz (*see* jazz musicians); songwriters (*see* songwriters)

Nabokov, Vladimir, 59
Nagel, Alexander, 289–90
Nauman, Bruce, 27–28, 187
Nelson, Richard, 2
Nelson, Willie, 225

Newman, Barnett, 108, 320–21
Newsome, Sam, 299–301, 302, 309
Newton, Isaac, 262–63, 264–65
Nichols, Mike, 246
Nielsen, Michael, 320
Norman, Dorothy, 177–78
Norton, Louise, 39
Nosei, Annina, 44–45, 47
novelists: duality of approach among, 115–16, 140–45; Hemingway, Ernest, 134–40 (*see also* Hemingway, Ernest); Melville, Herman, 116–21, 141, 145; plots and endings, 140–45; Twain, Mark, 121–28, 134–35, 141–42, 145; Woolf, Virginia, 66–67, 128–34, 142, 145

Oates, Joyce Carol, 1–2, 314–15
Obama, Barack, 128
O'Keeffe, Georgia, 181–82, 297–98
Oldsey, Bernard, 144–45
Oliphant, Margaret, 283
Ozenfant, Amédée, 153–54

painters: Basquiat, Jean-Michel, 44–49, 53, 189–90; Cézanne, Paul, 15–23 (*see also* Cézanne, Paul); creative life cycles of, vii, 14–15; duality of approach among, 6, 14–15; Kahlo, Frida, 298; Leonardo da Vinci, 288–90; Michelangelo Buonarroti, 290–92; O'Keeffe, Georgia, 181–82, 297–98; Picasso, Pablo, 23–29 (*see also* Picasso, Pablo); Pollock, Jackson, 29–36 (*see also* Pollock, Jackson); Raphael (Raffaelo Santi), 292–94; Rembrandt van Rijn, 294–96; truth and the goal of art for, 49–53; Warhol, Andy, 36–43, (*see also* Warhol, Andy)
Pais, Abraham, 263, 267–68, 283, 317
Palladio, Andrea, 157
Paltrow, Gwyneth, 81
Parker, Charlie, 45, 46–47, 49, 53, 224, 225, 300
Paul III, 292
Paz, Octavio, 75, 330
Perloff, Marjorie, 329
Perret, Auguste, 154
Philbrick, Nathaniel, 118
Phillips, Robert, 72–73
photographers: Atget, Jean-Eugène-Auguste, 171–77; conceptual, 183–91; duality of approach among, 171, 191–92; experimental, 171–77; Man Ray, 183–87; the real world of, 191–92; Sherman, Cindy, 187–91; Stieglitz, Alfred, 177–82

Picabia, Francis, 27–28
Picasso, Pablo, vii, 21–22, 23–29, 35–36, 38, 46, 50–51, 65–66, 96, 98, 101–2, 179, 185–86, 215, 231, 279, 320–21, 324–25, 326–27
Pissarro, Camille, 16–17, 102–3, 318–19
Planck, Max, 266
Plath, Sylvia, 1, 12–13, 49, 73, 77–82, 88, 89, 133–34, 314–15
Plimpton, George, 144–45
Poe, Edgar Allan, 198–99
poets: Bishop, Elizabeth, 68–72, 73–76, 85–89; composing and revising, 82–89; conceptual, 62–67, 77–82, 83–85; duality of approach among, 54–55, 88–89; Eliot, T. S. (Thomas Stearns), 62–67, 83–85, 89; experimental, 55–62, 68–76, 82–83; Frost, Robert, 55–62, 82–83, 85, 88–89; Lowell, Robert (Robert Traill Spence Lowell IV), 68–73, 75–76, 85–87 (*see also* Lowell, Robert (Robert Traill Spence Lowell IV)); Plath, Sylvia, 77–82
Poirier, Richard, 242–43
Polke, Sigmar, 27–28, 42
Pollack, Andrew, 277
Pollock, Charles, 29–30
Pollock, Jackson, 29–36, 51, 52–53, 108, 110–11, 159, 215
Pollock, Sanford, 29–30
Pope-Hennessy, John, 293, 294
Porter, Cole, 221–23, 226–29, 246–47, 249–50, 251–52
Porter, Lewis, 301
Portman, John, 151
Pound, Ezra, 46, 63–64, 66, 83–85, 134–35, 185–86, 312
Presley, Elvis, 225, 230, 237, 245
Prince, Richard, 42
Prol, Rick, 47
Proust, Marcel, 185–86

Quirk, Tom, 123, 142

Radnitzky, Emmanuel, 183. *See also* Man Ray
Raffaelo Santi. *See* Raphael (Raffaelo Santi)
Raphael (Raffaelo Santi), 292–94, 295–96, 321
Raskin, Jef, 324
Rauschenberg, Robert, 27–28, 319
realism: in filmmaking, 195–96, 201; in novels, 122, 128, 136; in photography, 178–79, 191–92; in poetry, 61; in sculpture, 104, 105
Rembrandt van Rijn, 294–96, 321
Renoir, Pierre-Auguste, 318–19

Reynolds, Sir Joshua, 293
Rhodes, Harrison, 229
Ribemont-Dessaignes, Georges, 185
Ricard, Rene, 44, 48
Rich, Daniel Catton, 297
Richardson, John, 28–29
Richter, Gerhard, 27–28, 42, 189–90
Rigden, John, 263–64
Rilke, Rainer Maria, 91, 112
Rimbaud, Arthur, 49, 232–33, 251–52
Rivette, Jacques, 211–12
Roach, Max, 300
Robson, W. W., 57–58
Rodgers, Richard, 221–22, 227
Rodin, Auguste, 90–97, 104, 112–13, 114, 167, 329–30
Roger, Jacques, 281–82
Rogers, Franklin, 122–23
Rohmer, Eric, 202–3, 211–12
Roosevelt, Franklin, 128
Rorem, Ned, 242–43
Rosenberg, Harold, 32, 39–40
Rosenthal, M. L., 80
Roth, Philip, 250
Rothko, Mark, 313, 327
Rubens, Peter Paul, 295–96, 321, 322
Rubin, William, 24
Russell, Ross, 45

Sadoul, Georges, 212–13
Salmon, André, 25–26
Sarris, Andrew, 210
Sartre, Jean-Paul, 106, 209
Schapiro, Meyer, 22–23, 49–50, 70
Schjeldahl, Peter, 48, 190–91
Schlöndorff, Volker, 215–16
Schwabsky, Barry, 47
Schwartz, Delmore, 63–64
scientists, 254; conceptual, 262–69; Darwin, Charles, 254–62, 280–83; dual approaches by and the life cycle of creativity, 307–9; Einstein, Albert, 262–69, 283–84; experimental, 254–62, 280–83; language of, 280–86; Leonardo da Vinci, 288–90
Scorsese, Martin, 197–98, 202, 203–4, 209
Scully, John, 277, 285
Scully, Vincent, 156, 157, 165, 166–67
sculptors: Boccioni, Umberto, 97–102, 113, 114; Bourgeois, Louise, 299; conceptual, 97–102, 107–12; duality of approach among, 90, 114; experimental, 90–97, 102–7; Giacometti, Alberto, 102–7, 113, 114; Michelangelo Buonarroti, 290–92; Rodin, Auguste, 90–97, 112–13, 114; Smithson, Robert, 107–12, 113–14; touch, significance of, 112–14

Secord, James, 256–57, 282
Seeger, Mike, 250–51
Seeger, Pete, 231–32
Segré, Gino, 265
Serra, James, 175
Serra, Richard, 33–34, 168
Seurat, Georges, 49
Severini, Gino, 99, 100
Sexton, Anne, 73
Shakespeare, William, 117, 118–19, 147
Shankar, Ravi, 241–42
Shapiro, Karl, 65
Shaw, George Bernard, 112
Shelton, Robert, 245–46
Sherman, Cindy, 42, 187–91, 192, 296
Sickert, Walter, 4
Siemering, William, 310
Simon, Norton, 160, 161
Simon, Paul, 245–51, 252–53
Simon, William, 278
Sinatra, Frank, 224, 225
Siqueiros, David, 29–30, 32
Sisley, Alfred, 318–19
Skinner, Quinton, 235
Slive, Seymour, 294, 295, 296
Smith, Henry Nash, 123, 141–42
Smith, Kiki, 298
Smithson, Robert, 107–12, 113–14
Snodgrass, W. D., 73
songwriters: Berlin, Irving, 220–26; conceptual, 230–45; craftsmen and artists among, 249–53; duality of approach among, 220, 249–53; Dylan, Bob, 230–37; experimental, 220–30, 245–51; Lennon, John and Paul McCartney, 237–45; Porter, Cole, 226–30; Simon, Paul, 245–51
Sontag, Susan, 212–13
Spender, Stephen, 54, 65–67
Spielberg, Steven, 203–4, 219
Springsteen, Bruce, 234, 236–37
Starr, Ringo, 237
Steele, Timothy, 329–30
Steichen, Edward, 96, 181, 182
Stein, Gertrude, 134–35, 185–86
Steinbeck, John, 195–96
Steinberg, Leo, 91–92
Stella, Frank, 313
Stevens, Wallace, 61
Stewart, Jimmy, 197, 201–2
Stieglitz, Alfred, 96, 177–82, 183, 191–92, 327–28
Sting, 247–48
Stockhausen, Karlheinz, 241–42
Stookey, Noel, 232
Stott, Rebecca, 70

Strachey, Lytton, 283
Streisand, Barbra, 224, 225
Sullivan, Hannah, 84
Sylvester, David, 42, 104, 113
Szarkowski, John, 175, 176–77
Szwed, John, 300

Tarantino, Quentin, 215–16
Tate, Allen, 69
Tatlin, Vladimir, 26–27
Tatum, Art, 300
Taylor, Samuel, 202
Thomas, Linda Lee, 227
Thompson, Lawrance, 60–61
Thomson, David, 217–18
Thomson, Lawrance, 85
Thorne, Kip, 263–64
Tillinghast, Richard, 87–88
Titian (Tiziano Vecello), 296
Toibin, Colm, 75
Toland, Gregg, 207–8, 330
Tolstoy, Leo, 311–12
Tomkins, Calvin, 190, 313
Travisano, Thomas, 74–75
Tribble, Bud, 284–85
Trilling, Lionel, 125
Truffaut, François, 198, 199, 202–5, 207, 208, 209, 211–12
Truman, Harry, 128
Twain, Mark, 121–28, 134–35, 141–42, 145, 330
Tworkov, Jack, 22

Utrillo, Maurice, 172

Valéry, Paul, 294
van der Rohe, Mies, 148, 159
van de Wetering, Ernst, 296
van Gogh, Vincent, 49, 110–11, 328–29
Varnedoe, Kirk, 26–27, 32–33, 39–40, 112
Vasari, Giorgio, 291, 292
Vendler, Helen, 12–13
Vollard, Ambroise, 17–18, 19, 326–27

Walcott, Derek, 57, 252
Wald, Elijah, 244–45
Walker, Kara, 48
Wall, Jeff, 42
Wallace, Alfred Russel, 258, 259
Wallace, William, 291–92
Walton, Helen, 303–4
Walton, Jim, 304
Walton, Sam, 303–4

Wang, Dashun, 307–9
Warhol, Andy, 36–43, 44, 45, 47–49, 51–53, 214, 294, 313, 316, 321–22
Warhola, Andrew, 36–37. *See also* Warhol, Andy
Warner, Charles Dudley, 121–22
Waters, Muddy, 233
Watson, James, 256–57
Waugh, Evelyn, 66
Wayne, John, 196–98
Wedgwood, Josiah, 254
Wedgwood, Emma, 256
Weinberg, Steven, 267, 268
Welles, Orson, 194, 195–96, 197–98, 205–11, 215–16, 217–19, 326, 330
Wells, H. G., 206–7
Wenner, Jann, 246
Weston, Edward, 174–75, 191
Wilder, Alec, 225–26
Williams, Hank, 230
Williams, William Carlos, 66, 314, 316–17
Wilson, Brian, 240–41
Wilson, Edmund, 64–65, 137–38
Wilson, Edward, 255, 259, 261
Winner, Langdon, 242–43
Wogensky, André, 169
Woideck, Carl, 301–2
Wolfe, Thomas, 315–16
Wollen, Peter, 214, 215–16, 298
women artists: Bourgeois, Louise, 299; Kahlo, Frida, 298; O'Keeffe, Georgia, 181–82, 297–98; Sherman, Cindy, 42, 187–91, 192, 296
Wood, Robin, 199
Woolf, Vanessa, 129
Woolf, Virginia, 66–67, 128–34, 142–44, 145, 185–86, 311–12, 314–16
Woollcott, Alexander, 221
Wozniak, Steve, 275–77, 278–79
Wren, Christopher, 292
Wright, Frank Lloyd, 146–53, 154, 159, 161–62, 168, 169–70, 327–28
writers. *See* novelists; poets

Yarrow, Peter, 231–32
Yeats, William Butler, 63–64, 67, 119–20
Young, Jeffrey, 278
Young, Lester, 300
Young, Philip, 135, 137, 144–45, 315–16
Yunus, Muhammad, 270–75, 284, 323, 324

Zanuck, Darryl, 195–96
Zimmerman, Bobby, 230. *See also* Dylan, Bob
Zola, Emile, 94